Buried
Communities

Buried Communities

Wordsworth and the Bonds of Mourning

Kurt Fosso

STATE UNIVERSITY OF NEW YORK PRESS

Cover illustration: from the juvenile chapbook
The Little Maid and The Gentleman; or, We are Seven. 1820.
York: Printed by J. Kendrew, 1840, 15 pp. illus.; p. 8. 9 cm.
Courtesy of the Bodleian Library, University of Oxford.
Reference (shelfmark) Vet. A6 g.45 (17).

Published by
State University of New York Press, Albany

© 2004 State University of New York

For information, address State University of New York Press,
90 State Street, Suite 700, Albany, NY 12207

Production by Christine L. Hamel
Marketing by Anne Valentine

Library of Congress Cataloging-in-Publication Data

Fosso, Kurt, 1958–
    Buried communities : Wordsworth and the bonds of mourning / Kurt Fosso.
    p. cm.
    Includes bibliographical references (p.) and index.
    ISBN 0-7914-5959-4 (alk. paper)
    1. Wordsworth, William, 1770–1850—Criticism and interpretation. 2. Death in literature.
3. Wordsworth, William, 1770–1850—Political and social views. 4. Literature and
society—England—History—19th century. 5. Elegiac poetry, English—History and criticism.
6. Mourning customs in literature. 7. Community in literature. 8. Grief in literature. I.
Title.

PR5892.D35B87 2003
821'.7—dc22
                                                                            2003057291

10   9   8   7   6   5   4   3   2   1

For my father, Harold C. Fosso

CONTENTS

PREFACE

On September 6, 1997, a funeral cortege wound its way down Kensington High Street toward Westminster Abbey, passing on its way an enormous crowd of mourners. Outside the royal palaces, grieving men and women, adults and children, Britons and foreigners, had deposited more than a million bouquets and displays for the deceased Princess of Wales, Diana Spencer. The *New York Times* reported that there seemed "something more Latin than British about the intensity of people's words and actions; a largely Protestant culture that epitomizes restraint and values privacy was galvanized by a need to display its powerful emotions publicly."[1] One mourner told a London *Times* reporter how she had suddenly begun to grieve for this "stranger" and had felt compelled to share her grief with others.[2] Like her, millions of people had been moved to congregate near Buckingham Palace and attend the public rites held on the day of the funeral. "How could one doing such good works die so tragically?" many asked. "How could she be gone?"

Such occasions of massification swiftly transform reporters and others into armchair sociologists delivering up various explanations for whatever group behavior is at issue, in this case that of people crowding before palaces or alongside roadways or in front of television screens. Is the underlying cause the allure of celebrity and glamour? Is it widespread emotional impoverishment? Voyeuristic consumption? A false sense of intimacy fostered by the media? Among the crowds commemorating Princess Diana one could no doubt find testimony to support any of these hypotheses. But for many of the mourners one other, ostensibly simple, fact might best explain their behavior and feelings: when burdened by grief, people wish to assemble with kindred mourners and sufferers—millions of them in the case of Diana Spencer, thousands or hundreds in the cases of others of some renown. Death draws together human beings to mourn, even to mourn the loss of a virtual stranger. They gather to share their burdens of loss and to try, in doing so, to appease or fulfill their need to express their grief and to properly mourn.

Although mourning on the grand scale occasioned by Princess Diana's death is rare, even in these media-driven times, the social phenomenon of shared mourning in response to grief, and the community of mourners it gathers together, is by no means so. One need not look back to the anguished crowd of fans congregated outside the Dakota Apartments in New York City to mourn the death of John Lennon[3] or to the spate of memorial scenes for murdered schoolchildren in American towns like Jonesboro, Arkansas, or Littleton, Colorado. We need not even review the aftermath of grief that followed the disaster of September 11, 2001. The loss of a family member or close friend can as easily spark a desire for the social possibilities afforded by sharing one's grief with others, particularly when that grief is felt to be burdensome or even unbearable. It seems clear from all these social manifestations that for such grief to be shared there must be something *common* to those who gather together, whether what is imparted is grief for the deceased or the unique problems of grief itself. One widower or widow or friend or neighbor seeks out another for comfort and for the particular kind of social cohesion offered by mutual mourning. It was that sense of shared, personal loss that underlay at least some of the national (and global) spectacle associated with Diana's funeral and the memorials that preceded it.

A century and a half earlier a similar experience of loss provoked Britons to parade and exchange their grief, at the occasion of the death of another beloved princess. On Sunday, November 16, 1817, memorial sermons for Princess Charlotte, who had died in childbirth on November 6, were delivered across Britain in Anglican, dissenting, and Catholic churches and in synagogues. That Wednesday her funeral at St. George's Chapel proved an exercise in what Stephen Behrendt, in his study of the mourning and later mythologizing of Charlotte, calls a "grandiose demonstration of Regency ostentation." But it was one that, for all its regal spectacle, "did not have the effect of entirely removing the dead princess from the thoughts—or the view—of those citizens to whom she had meant so much."[4] Such are the powers of the dead and of their survivors' grief. Britain's newspapers and journals brimmed with sensationalized accounts of the funeral, to be followed by countless elegies, funeral songs, and tributes for Charlotte, by the likes of Poet Laureate Robert Southey, Leigh Hunt, Letitia Landon, and, now most famously, Percy Bysshe Shelley. In her study of British mourning in this period, *Bearing the Dead,* Esther Schor describes how, on the day of the lavish funeral, commercial business ground to a halt, "the nation spontaneously channel[ing] its sorrows into a nationwide observance of funeral services for the Princess."[5] Schor and Behrendt are each interested in how the Princess's death and funeral were transformed into myth and spectacle, as one result of the nineteenth-century rise of print culture and its manifestations of national and imperial simultaneity.[6] What Schor and Behrendt demonstrate so well is the extent to which the mourning of Charlotte was mediated and in some manner produced by literary and other fictions. But it is also the case that the dissemination of words concerning Princess Charlotte's death helped to craft a community, even a nation.

Grief's exchange and its socially cohesive effects as shared sympathies and texts can be further understood by considering the mourning-oriented poetry of the titular head of the first generation of so-called British Romantic writers. For Wordsworth's poems helpfully explore, at a literary level, this phenomenon of community prompted by human beings' responses to loss and to grief for the dead. This poet's social vision of mournful community is his particular response to a broad crisis in late eighteenth-century Britain. But his vision also reveals much about the broader dynamics of mourning and community: then, at the turn of the century, and now, in our own times of loss. Wordsworth's poetry repeatedly shows how we the living remain, even despite ourselves, bound together by the dead and by the griefs we share.

This study of mourning and community in Wordsworth found part of its origin and a good deal of guidance in previous scholars' explorations of death and grief, chief among them groundbreaking works by Philippe Ariès, Alan Bewell, Jacques Derrida, David Ferry, Jean-Luc Nancy, and Peter Sacks. Like all books, this one has not been a solitary enterprise. For their early advice and support I am indebted to Hazard Adams, Homer Brown, J. Hillis Miller, Martin Schwab, and the late Albert Wlecke. My deepest thanks go to the manuscript's two principal readers: to William Ulmer, Wordsworthian extraordinaire and friend, who provided thoughtful criticism tempered with encouragement; and to Claudia Nadine, who helped make this book's pages more worthy of print and whose confidence sustained me in my labors. I am grateful as well to my manuscript's readers for State University of New York Press, Stephen Behrendt and Regina Hewitt, and to SUNY Press's James Peltz, Christine Hamel, and Anne Valentine. Thanks also to James Butler, William Galperin, Marilyn Gaull, Susan Harris, and Jack Hart for their kindness and assistance along the way.

I want to thank the editors of the journals in which early portions of this book were first published, and who have granted permission to reproduce revised versions of those pages here. A part of Chapter One's argument originally appeared as "A 'World of Shades': Mourning, Poesis, and Community in William Wordsworth's *The Vale of Esthwaite*" in *The Modern Language Review* 93 (1998): 629–41. A portion of Chapter Three was published as "The Politics of Genre in Wordsworth's *Salisbury Plain*" in *New Literary History* 30 (1999): 159–77. Sections of Chapter Four first appeared as "Community and Mourning in William Wordsworth's *The Ruined Cottage, 1797–1798*" in *Studies in Philology* 92 (1995): 329–45; © 1995 The University of North Carolina Press.

I would like to acknowledge the students, too many to name, whose questions influenced my thinking about Wordsworth and community. I owe a similar debt to my colleagues at several conferences of the North American Society for the Study of Romanticism, where early drafts of parts of this book received helpful responses. For their research assistance, I am obliged to the staff of Lewis & Clark College's Aubrey R. Watzek Library and Information Technology and to the personnel of the William Andrews Clark Memorial Library at the University of California, Los Angeles. I also appreciate the help provided by Jonas Lerman and my two summer-research assistants, Kathryn Riviere and Lynne Nolan. Lewis & Clark generously funded our work and also provided me with a semester-long junior sabbatical, during which I wrote a good share of this study.

For their hospitality and camaraderie during the several journeys that helped to produce this book I am grateful to my friends, family, and colleagues in Washington, Oregon, California, Texas, Alabama, Pennsylvania, and France. A special round of thanks, too, to John Painter and to the band. Finally, I want to express my gratitude to my sons, Jonah and Remy, for their boundless joy and inspiration, and to my mother and my brothers for all their love and confidence. This book is dedicated to the memory of my father.

PORTLAND, OREGON
SEPTEMBER 2002

ABBREVIATIONS
AND EDITIONS

My citations from Wordsworth's poetry are, with a few exceptions, from the reading texts of the Cornell Wordsworth series. The following abbreviations appear in text in parentheses.

2P   *The Prelude, 1798–1799,* ed. Stephen Parrish (Ithaca: Cornell University Press, 1977).

5P   *The Five-Book Prelude,* ed. Duncan Wu (Oxford: Blackwell, 1997).

13P   *The Thirteen-Book "Prelude,"* ed. Mark L. Reed, 2 vols. (Ithaca: Cornell University Press, 1991), vol. 1. 1805 AB-stage reading text.

13P 2   *The Thirteen-Book "Prelude,"* vol. 2.

14P   *The Fourteen-Book "Prelude,"* ed. W. J. B. Owen (Ithaca: Cornell University Press, 1985).

B   *The Borderers,* ed. Robert Osborn (Ithaca: Cornell University Press, 1982).

CLSTC   *The Collected Letters of Samuel Taylor Coleridge,* ed. Earl Leslie Griggs, 6 vols. (Oxford: Clarendon Press, 1956–71).

CWSTC   *The Collected Works of Samuel Taylor Coleridge,* gen. ed. Kathleen Coburn, 16 vols. Bollingen Series 75 (Princeton: Princeton University Press, 1971–2001).

DS   *Descriptive Sketches,* ed. Eric Birdsall (Ithaca: Cornell University Press, 1984).

EPF   *Early Poems and Fragments, 1785–1797,* ed. Carol Landon and Jared Curtis (Ithaca: Cornell University Press, 1997).

EW   *An Evening Walk,* ed. James H. Averill (Ithaca: Cornell University Press, 1984).

Ex   *The Excursion 1814,* introd. Jonathan Wordsworth (Oxford: Woodstock Books, 1991).

EY   *The Letters of William and Dorothy Wordsworth: The Early Years, 1787–1805,* ed. Ernest de Selincourt, rev. Chester L. Shaver (Oxford: Clarendon Press, 1967).

FN   *The Fenwick Notes of William Wordsworth,* ed. Jared Curtis (London: Bristol Classics Press, 1993).

GL   *Guide to the Lakes* (1835), ed. Ernest de Selincourt (London: Oxford University Press, 1977).

HG   *"Home at Grasmere": Part First, Book First, of "The Recluse,"* ed. Beth Darlington (Ithaca: Cornell University Press, 1977, corr. 1989).

HW   Kenneth R. Johnston, *The Hidden Wordsworth: Poet, Lover, Rebel, Spy* (New York: Norton, 1998).

LB   *"Lyrical Ballads," and Other Poems, 1797–1800,* ed. James Butler and Karen Green (Ithaca: Cornell University Press, 1992).

LY   *The Letters of William and Dorothy Wordsworth: The Later Years, 1821–1850,* ed. Ernest de Selincourt, rev. Alan G. Hill, 4 vols. (Oxford: Clarendon Press, 1978–88).

MY   *The Letters of William and Dorothy Wordsworth: The Middle Years, 1806–1820,* ed. Ernest de Selincourt, rev. Mary Moorman and Alan G. Hill, 2 vols. (Oxford: Clarendon Press, 1969–70).

NCP   *The Prelude: 1799, 1805, 1850,* ed. Jonathan Wordsworth, M. H. Abrams, and Stephen Gill (New York: Norton, 1979).

PHS   James H. Averill, *Wordsworth and the Poetry of Human Suffering* (Ithaca: Cornell University Press, 1980).

PrW   *The Prose Works of William Wordsworth,* ed. W. J. B. Owen and Jane Smyser, 3 vols. (Oxford: Clarendon Press, 1974).

PTV   *"Poems, in Two Volumes," and Other Poems, 1800–1807,* ed. Jared Curtis (Ithaca: Cornell University Press, 1983, corr. 1990).

PW   *The Poetical Works of William Wordsworth,* ed. Ernest de Selincourt and Helen Darbishire, 5 vols. (Oxford: Clarendon Press, 1940–49, rev. 1952–59).

RC   *"The Ruined Cottage" and "The Pedlar,"* ed. James Butler (Ithaca: Cornell University Press, 1977).

SE   *The Standard Edition of the Complete Psychological Works of Sigmund Freud,* ed. and trans. James Strachey et al., 24 vols. (London: Hogarth Press, 1953–74).

ShP   *Shorter Poems, 1807–1820,* ed. Carl H. Ketcham (Ithaca: Cornell University Press, 1989).

SPP   *The Salisbury Plain Poems of William Wordsworth,* ed. Stephen Gill (Ithaca: Cornell University Press, 1975, corr. 1991).

TP   *"The Tuft of Primroses," with Other Late Poems for "The Recluse,"* ed. Joseph F. Kishel (Ithaca: Cornell University Press, 1986).

WCh   F. B. Pinion, *A Wordsworth Chronology* (London: Macmillan, 1988).

WE   Alan Bewell, *Wordsworth and the Enlightenment: Nature, Man, and Society in the Experimental Poetry* (New Haven: Yale University Press, 1987).

WL   Stephen Gill, *William Wordsworth: A Life* (New York: Oxford University Press, 1989).

WP   Geoffrey Hartman, *Wordsworth's Poetry, 1787–1814* (Cambridge: Harvard University Press, 1964, rpt. 1987).

WR   Duncan Wu, *Wordsworth's Reading, 1770–1799* (Cambridge: Cambridge University Press, 1993).

WW   Mary Moorman, *William Wordsworth: A Biography,* vol. 1, *The Early Years, 1770–1803* (Oxford: Clarendon Press, 1957, rpt. 1967).

INTRODUCTION

There is a spiritual community binding together the living and
the dead.

—The Convention of Cintra

So burdensome, still paying, still to owe. . . .

—Paradise Lost

A nine-year-old boy, newly arrived to the north England village of Hawkshead, peers out from a small crowd of onlookers as a drowned man's body is
recovered from a lake:

> There came a company, and in their boat
> Sounded with iron hooks and with long poles.
> At length the dead man 'mid that beauteous scene
> Of trees, and hills, and water, bolt upright
> Rose with his ghastly face.
>
> (*2P* 1.275–79)

It is a startling image. Judging from the record, the former owner of that face
was James Jackson, a schoolmaster from the nearby village of Sawrey, reported
to have drowned in Esthwaite Water on June 18, 1779. The young witness, if
one trusts the account quoted above from the two-part *Prelude* (1798–99), was
of course William Wordsworth. Wandering along the lakeshore the preceding
day, he had spotted a neglected pile of clothes,[1] and he now anxiously watched
this distinctly social event unfold.

Commonly referred to as the "Drowned Man" episode, this childhood
anecdote has long been a locus classicus of Wordsworth criticism.[2] It is one of
but a few precious "spots of time," defined as memories, primarily from early
childhood, that possess a mysterious "fructifying virtue" to repair depressed

1

spirits, "[e]specially the imaginative power" (1.288–93). The scene's status and strange character prompt an important but difficult question: Why does this spot of time dwell upon death?[3] Or, put differently, why should the memory of witnessing a corpse's retrieval now rise up singly from the flood of other childhood remembrances? For that matter, what is so "fructifying" about death such that all of *The Prelude*'s spots of time should directly or indirectly concern it? The answer to these queries leads back to earlier, indeed early, poems in Wordsworth's oeuvre and to the foundations of Wordsworthian community.

Concluding his account of the Drowned Man, Wordsworth describes this childhood *spot* as containing for him

> images, to which in following years
> Far other feelings were attached, with forms
> That yet exist with independent life
> And, like their archetypes, know no decay.
>
> (284–87)

What the "other feelings" were in this case he does not tell. Revised versions of the episode refer to the salutary aestheticizing and anesthetizing effects his early reading had upon his perception of the corpse. But at this point in the 1799 text the narrator "advert[s]" from his haunting recollection to mention, as a further possible topic of interest, the extensive record of other such "accidents" and "tragic facts / Of rural history" (279–83). Although this advertence serves much the same function as Wordsworth's later reference to reading (considered below), the diversion here has the added value of suggesting the episode's historical materiality and potential, oddly ritual-like recurrence. Such scenes as this one evidently are not so uncommon in Lake District history. They cannot be, in Wordsworth at least, for these sites are central to his complex vision of the foundations of northern English collectivity—and all collectivity. Although in the 1799 *Prelude,* as in the versions of 1804 and 1805, these images and their feelings attest to the imagination's power to trump death and decay, there are other, more mysterious and more social "powers" at work, pertaining to the dead's fundamental "fructifying virtue." It is this social power that the present study examines in Wordsworth's early and mature poetry, from the date of the poet's first surviving writings (circa 1785) to the culminating publication of *The Excursion* of 1814. In so doing, *Buried Communities* follows in a tradition of scholarship concerned, in various ways, with Wordsworth's longstanding preoccupation with death and mourning.

In "Memorial Verses" Matthew Arnold became the first critic to acknowledge this poet as a second, English "Orpheus" who had revived "spirits that had long been dead." Wordsworth's poems indeed bear repeated witness to their author's professed "aspiration" to compose "verse . . . fitted to the

Orphean lyre" (*5P* 1.228–32): dead-oriented verse that aspires to produce social "brotherhood" (237), as Arnold discerned. Few readers would be surprised by Arnold's special praise of Wordsworth, certainly not after David Ferry's *The Limits of Mortality*.[4] In the forty years since that landmark study, numerous other critical works have explored the topic of death in Wordsworth's writings, notably in terms of its relationship to the author's psychology and biography[5] as well as to genre, language, and British culture.[6]

In recent years, scholarly interest in the more strictly social aspects of death and the dead in Wordsworth has moved to the forefront. Such attention may in part be owed to Philippe Ariès's analysis of western death practices, *The Hour of Our Death,* and to other studies of mourning and of funerary rites.[7] It is also likely owed (certainly owed, in my case) to recent philosophical considerations of death and mourning, including Jean-Luc Nancy's inquiry about the means and limits of social cohesion, *The Inoperative Community,*[8] and to Alan Bewell's seminal literary study, *Wordsworth and the Enlightenment,* which finds Wordsworth implicitly writing a "history of death" (*WE* 144). In the wake of these works, Esther Schor's *Bearing the Dead* and several other, nearly contemporaneous studies have discovered connections between death or mourning and community in Wordsworth.[9] Yet, for all these recent insights, no study has yet fully examined the longstanding, profound connection between mourning and community in the poet's oeuvre. For mourning in fact underlies and makes possible most of the communities Wordsworth envisioned for his turbulent, reform-minded Romantic age, an age that yearned for alternative possibilities of social cohesion.[10] As Geoffrey Hartman said a good many years ago of *The Excursion,* in Wordsworth "man stands in communion not only with the living but also with the dead" (*WP* 321). The following pages will examine the genealogy of such community, with special attention given to how the hidden scheme is developed, revised, revisited, and contested in the work of this "deeply social" poet.[11]

I. WORDSWORTH AND THE DEAD

To return to that spot of time, one discerns the singular detail of the boat's "company" sounding Esthwaite Water for the dead. The term "company," from the Latin word *compania,* for sharing bread, has communal denotations in English as well, designating a group gathered together for social purposes, including martial or even nautical ones as in the case of a boat's crew. The term underlines the social significance of the depicted occasion and of this spot of time, as does one of Wordsworth's revisions of the episode, which adds to the company an "anxious crowd / Of friends & neighbours" watching from the shore.[12] The implication is that the "company" includes not just those searching but also those looking, worrying, and beginning to grieve. These participants collectively form a community congregated in observance of the dead, in a rite analogous to that of breaking bread at Communion. And, as in the latter rite, it is the deceased who gathers together the company.

Those people standing on the shoreline, and certainly those afloat on the lake, are akin to Orpheus in Wordsworth's "Orpheus and Eurydice," translated from Virgil's *Georgics*. There the elegiac hero seeks to reclaim his lost beloved from death's subterranean abode (see Chapter One). In this mournful light, the Drowned Man becomes an allegory of the poetic process, with the crew's "long poles" signifying the poet's pen, and the ghostly corpse the hidden contents revealed in and as elegy. Indeed, lines from the five-book *Prelude* (1804) proclaim that the poet's "favourite aspiration" is to reveal an "awful burden" of truth drawn from "deep / Recesses" via "Orphean" verse (*5P* 1.228–33). Like the company, Wordsworth strives to reclaim the dead, to recover them through an Orphic power of imagination, described by Bewell as being akin to "the discovery of the Underworld" (*WE* 213).[13] As the first of the poet's *Essays upon Epitaphs* (1809) implies, commemoration of the dead lurks near the origins of culture (*PrW* 1: 49–51).

Also illustrating this social and poetic power, the two-part *Prelude*'s succeeding spot of time recalls Wordsworth's earlier memory of "stumbling" upon the "mouldered" stub of a "gibbet mast" set beside a grassy mound shaped "like a grave" (*2P* 1.307–13)—what in the 1805 *Prelude* becomes turf "engraven" with "the Murderer's name" in a "monumental writing" (*13P* 11.294–95). The revision's quasi-grave and nominal epitaph further emphasize death's sociological import, the scant markers having been maintained, we are told, "[b]y superstition of the neighbourhood" (11.297). The Latin term *superstitio* denotes a specifically reverential act, that of *standing over* a grave or tomb, and the English word "superstition" conveys a similar signification in Wordsworth's text, where the boy stands in awe over this strangely epitaphic memorial. In the Drowned Man much the same can be said of the company's actions above the watery coffers of Esthwaite Lake—actions by which the dead man is to be retrieved and, one infers, thereafter examined, sanctified, interred, and mourned by that or another "anxious crowd" of companions. As Michele Turner Sharp observes, writing of the *Essays upon Epitaphs* but in terms that could as easily apply to this text, "the return of the body to its proper place, giving it a proper burial, grounds the constitution of the ideal community." In Wordsworth, granting the recovered dead "a proper burial . . . comes to mark and identify . . . [an ideal] rural community, a community that includes the dead with and within the living."[14]

By the time Wordsworth relates these tales in 1799, they are by no account his only depictions of communities articulated between the living and the dead. Just prior to composing the two-part *Prelude,* in "We are Seven" from *Lyrical*

Ballads (1798), he had posed a simple yet provocative question related implicitly to this social vantage, and, as it turns out, to the Drowned Man episode itself: "A simple child . . . / What should it know of death?" (*LB*, ll. 1, 4). In the ensuing narrative, the speaker recalls his conversation with a rustic child who stubbornly refused to distinguish between the living and dead of her family. In doing so, the young girl aptly dramatizes Wordsworth's dictum that children are unable "to admit the notion of death as a state applicable" to their being (*FN* 61). Yet, according to Bewell, her protestations also serve to challenge the adult interlocutor's Enlightenment understanding of immortality and death (*WE* 195). Rejecting his empiricist idea of physical death as both annihilation and separation ("But they are dead; those two are dead! / Their spirits are in heaven!" [65–66]), she proclaims an alternative notion of human mortality, one that integrates the dead into her natural and social surroundings.

The import of "We are Seven" is that those dead belong to and with the living of this locality as an integral part of their history, affections, and environment. Hence the child is allowed and perhaps even encouraged by her mother to "sit and sing" to her dead siblings—even to take her "porringer" and eat supper among their graves (44, 47–48). Here, to live as a social being is to exist in close physical and psychological relation to the dead: to count them among one's loves, to feel them as a part of one's activities ("My stockings there I often knit, / My 'kerchief there I hem" [41–42]), and to see them as a fundamental part of one's familial and social ties. For Thomas McFarland, the girl's community of the living and the dead indeed is "in Wordsworth's most mature conception . . . indispensable to the idea of meaningful community."[15] Borrowing the words of Gabriel García Márquez's character José Arcadio Buendía, Bewell goes so far as to say that for Wordsworth a person does not even "belong to a place until there is someone dead under the ground" (*WE* 213). Bewell (and Buendía) may be right. For in fact the naïf's repeated remonstrances—that despite the deaths of two of her seven siblings their number is still "seven"—demonstrate a more important Wordsworthian dictum: that, in Bewell's words, "death is not a private but a communal state" (196). The poet's political tract *The Convention of Cintra* (1809) puts it better still: "There is a spiritual community binding together the living and the dead" (*PrW* 1: 339). In similar terms, *The Prelude* proclaims there to be but "One great Society alone on earth, / The noble Living, and the noble Dead" (*13P* 10.968–69), while the *Essays upon Epitaphs* praise the "wholesome influence of th[e] communion" churchyard topographies foster "between [the] living and dead" (*PrW* 2: 66). The churchyard serves as the "visible centre of a community of the living and the dead; a point to which are habitually referred the nearest concerns of both" (56), a wellspring of familial and local attachments (56–57). Wordsworth's prose and poetry frequently depict churchyards, ruins, and other death-imbued topographies as sites of such "spiritual community."

This poet's view of "the living and the dead" is arguably secondary to the *Essays'* concern with the writing and appraisal of churchyard epitaphs and to *Cintra*'s immediate political argument about the English generals' betrayal of Spain. But in their *in situ* contexts, Wordsworth's statements do nonetheless concern social formations and values. In their orientation, the *Essays* are in fact nearly as sociological as they are aesthetical or rhetorical. They treat the origins and aims of burial and epitaph, the civic virtues of epitaphic sentiment, the sociological exemplarity of the churchyard as a register of "homely life," and the inherent communitarian[16] value of the latter site's promoting of a "natural interchange" between the living and dead (*PrW* 2: 66). In *Cintra* Wordsworth advances from his broad political statements about transmortal community to compare society to a spider's web, at the center of whose "concentric circles" rests the individual feeling self. From that self's "tremor[s]" of joy and sorrow, and from those tremors' ties to the dead, proceed the binding, interdependent "links" of social cohesion (1: 340). It is not the individual or his or her personal feelings, then, but the self's cohesive, dead-oriented affections that will make up society's encircled core.

This sort of interdependent, web-like structural model was not untypical of social conceptualization in the late eighteenth century, as can readily be seen from Thomas Paine's Smithian sounding proclamation at the beginning of the second part of *Rights of Man:*

> The mutual dependence and reciprocal interest which man has upon man, and all parts of a civilized community on each other, create that great chain of connection which holds it together. The landholder, the farmer, the manufacturer, the merchant, the tradesman, and every occupation, prospers by the aid which each receives from the other, and from the whole.[17]

Wordsworth probably agreed with Paine in this regard. But in his poetry the fundamental source of social cohesion—of the "bonds that bind all men together"[18]—is not economic interdependence. Nor for that matter is it virtuous feeling or action per se, as in the compassionate communities of sentiment in Thomas Gray and in novels like Fielding's *Joseph Andrews* and Henry Mackenzie's *The Man of Feeling.* The source of such cohesion resides not in pre- or post-revolutionary fraternity, either, or in the late century's developing literary conceptions of regionalism and primitivism, typified by Robert Burns and Ann Yearsley, and later by John Clare—significant and influential as all these formations were for Wordsworth and his contemporaries.[19] Wordsworthian community instead is founded upon human beings' shared mourning of the dead, which is to say upon their shared indebtedness to those dead, a form of indebtedness neither wholly willed nor conscious, neither a product of reason nor entirely a bond of compassion or other feeling. The poet's communities of mourning are tied to place and to specific individuals, but they are not necessarily tied to a specific *kind* of place—not even the exemplary church-yard—or to a defined class or gender, despite the fact that the poems frequently depict communities formed between lower-class men and women in predominantly rural areas.[20] For what is essential to Wordsworth's "spiritual communit[ies]" is the relationship of mourners, of mourners responding to and sharing their particular griefs.

This type of community can be schematized as a process originating in a loss that, as the object of memorialization, forges a bond of grief between mourners and between the living and the dead. Although the terms *grief* and *mourning* are often interchangeable in Wordsworth, and in my analysis as well, the latter word tends to denote the enacting or expressing of grief (*OED*), whereas *grief* and *grieve* usually signify the pain or sorrow the survivor feels for the dead and/or for his or her loss. Yet this line between grief and mourning is a thin one, especially in Wordsworth, where to grieve is often to feel one's overwhelming indebtedness to the dead as well as the impossibility of ending one's grief. Unlike in Freud's dichotomous analysis of mourning and melancholia,[21] in Wordsworth grief and mourning lead not toward an "interiorizing idealization" of the dead (i.e., to mourning's interiorized acts of substitution)[22] but outward to memorializing tributes and to the bonds of mourning. This power of unfinished, insufficient mourning-work (what Freud disparagingly diagnoses as the pathology of melancholia) becomes, in its supplementation, the foundation of Wordsworth's social vision of transmortal community.

Implicit in my argument, then, is that in Wordsworth it is not community that leads to a connection to the dead so much as it is the dead, and more specifically the relationship of the living to them, that leads to community. The relationships produced are in this way more than friendships, for they are forged by a problem of mourning that *binds* the living to one another via the dead. That the communities formed tend to be comprised of few rather than many mourners attests chiefly to this formation's reliance upon conversation as well as to its composition as a symptom of the alienation and isolation which prompt the very desire for modern social cohesion. A degree of pathos, loneliness, and insufficiency attends all of Wordsworth's depicted communities—communities raised in the shadows of social instability, poverty, failed fraternity, and war. These intimate but potentially expandable collectivities stand in sharp contrast to the mass numbers of late eighteenth-century Britain's urbanized society and culture.

In so distinguishing between community and society my thinking is, like Wordsworth's, not far afield from William Godwin's and Tom Paine's Rousseauian distinction between society and government: the result of our needs and "our wickedness," respectively.[23] I draw some of my understanding of social cohesion, certainly of its eighteenth-century formation, from Godwin and Paine, and more than a little from the nineteenth-century sociologist Ferdinand Tönnies's neo-Rousseauian notion of *Gemeinschaft*: a more familial and local than legal and contractual formation (viz. *Gesellschaft*), delimiting "all intimate, private, and exclusive living together."[24] At the same time, I concur with Jean-Luc Nancy that Tönnies tends to present the fiction "of a lost age in which community was woven of tight, harmonious, and infrangible bonds, and in which above all it played back to itself . . . its own immanent unity, intimacy, and autonomy." Hence Nancy declares that "community, far from being what society has crushed or lost, is *what happens to us . . . in the wake of society*."[25] Unlike the universalist visions of community or society constituted by a common essence, as proposed by Spinoza, Rousseau, Edmund Burke, and other late-Enlightenment philosophers,[26] such community is predicated not upon an essence or presence but upon something or someone *missing*, held "*in* common . . . without letting itself be absorbed in a common substance."[27] In mourning the dead, this fundamental commonality is never fully communicated, never fully made present or even felt.

In this way, Wordsworth's implicit social formation of "spiritual community" resists the era's reduction of human beings to their economic functions, nationalities, and sensibilities, evading or challenging what Marc Redfield perceptively describes as the century's dawning nationalist "unification both of the citizen and the community and of the community with universal humanity."[28] Wordsworthian community is no forerunner or ally of emergent British nationalism, at least insomuch as the paradigm's reliance upon mourning's and the mourned dead's unfinished, particular character destabilizes Burkean nationalist or other conceptions of generalizeable loss, unified immanence, and common identity. This conception reveals consolidation, anonymity, subsumption, and the universal (perhaps even the poet's own claim that "we have all of us one human heart") to be forms of violence inflicted upon the dead and the living.

As Ian Buruma and Avishai Margalit have recently observed about our own deadly times, for East and West "the way out of mediocrity, say the sirens of the death cult, is to submerge one's petty ego into a mass movement, whose awesome energies will be unleashed to create greatness in the name of the Führer, the Emperor, God, or Allah."[29] In that self-renunciation rests and has long rested the intoxicating basis for fascism and religious fanaticism. For Nancy, the immanence that characterizes such familiar Christian-derived, Rousseauian communal models is tantamount to a suppression of community, having helped perpetrate the totalitarian "communal fusion" of the putative Aryan community of Nazism. The alternative community he posits can resist such fusion, emerging as it does not out of its members' "fusional assumption in some collective hypostasis" but around the mortal loss of each member's immanence, the singularity of loss and grief.[30] Indeed, this community (which Nancy views as post-romantic) "is revealed in the death of others." It is "what takes place always through others and for others," and so is "not a communion that fuses . . . *egos* into an *Ego* or a higher *We*."[31] One discovers much the same form of community in Wordsworth, a formation that may, albeit indirectly, have influenced Nancy's thinking about modernity.

Communities in Wordsworth are of course not always founded upon mourning the dead, nor for that matter are they always resistant to such fusion or violence. As Chapter Five shows, "The Female Vagrant," excerpted from *Salisbury Plain* (1793–94), and the play *The Borderers* (1796–99) each depicts an outlaw band organized not by grief but by the group's difference from the law and from society. *The Prelude* nostalgically recalls the French Revolution's heyday of universal fraternity, before it devolved into the Terror. And there are also those communities formed at least in part by virtuous, compassionate feeling, as in "The Old Cumberland Beggar" (1797), or by shared appreciation of external nature, as in a few poems from *Lyrical Ballads* and in the "One Life" lines of *The Ruined Cottage* (1797–98). In *Home at Grasmere* (1800–6) and *Guide to the Lakes* (1820–23, 1835), Wordsworth influentially portrays Lake District communities as mini-republics of human habitation in nature.[32] Finally, there are the poet's democratizing poetical deployments of "the real language of men," and his representations, also in the words of the Preface to *Lyrical Ballads,* of "low and rustic life" (*LB* 757, 743). In these and other ways, the poet draws upon and explores the late eighteenth century's incredible variety of social visions and possibilities.

Yet, as the chapters that follow will show, even some of these alternative conceptions of community, most notably the One Life, are implicated in the scheme of mournful community. This underlying social paradigm, which I also refer to as "the Dead," extends, moreover, throughout the poet's early and later, mature writings, and is by far the most central to his developing poetics and sociology. It also seems, for all its eighteenth-century and prior influences, to be the more idiosyncratic and peculiar of all these models. The scheme's indebtedness to the dead may appear to some readers to be akin to, or even to be indebted to, Burke's conservative argument for respecting one's ancestors and their bequest of a constitutional legacy. But Wordsworth's earliest writing on the topic of such indebtedness, *The Vale of Esthwaite* (1787), preceded by a few years Burke's *Reflections on the Revolution* (1790).[33] The poet's social vision is, moreover, to be distinguished from that ultraconservative's vantage in its *un*Burkean sense of the past as imperfect, unfinished, and downright haunting, laden with an enduring, guilty legacy, that of grief. Yet the poet's social conception is not without its likely literary and other influences, including Gray's "Elegy Written in a Country Churchyard" (1742–50), with its mention of epitaphic "tribute," and Adam Smith's description, in *Theory of Moral Sentiments* (1759), of our "tribute" of sympathetic feeling for the deprivations we imagine the dead to endure.[34]

Wordsworth undoubtedly draws upon late eighteenth-century notions of sympathy, mourning, exchange, and tribute, such philosophers as Smith and Condorcet having similarly advocated moral formations of conversational sociability and egalitarian friendship.[35] But his poetry's representation of the mourned dead as a communitarian force is a social formulation largely peculiar to himself. The poet's search for community is nonetheless a part of a broader Romantic sociology born in such times of cultural repression and social decline, when, according to Kenneth Johnston, "culture recoils from politics, and small groups of like-minded people think about gathering together in isolated places . . . to form temporary experimental communities."[36] There were many such social experiments, including the radical-in-hiding John Thelwall's Llyswen ("Liswyn") farm, slyly alluded to in Wordsworth's "Anecdote for Fathers," Southey and Coleridge's envisioned American commune of Pantisocracy, and, later, the Wordsworth family's beloved Grasmere. As a poet of such oppressive yet socially adventurous times, Wordsworth implicitly explores through his writing an alternative form of community based upon the relationship between mourners and the dead they mourn.[37] That vision seems to have been focused by his early poetry's representation of his own inadequate, lingering mourning—a key source for his later, powerful depictions of socially cohesive griefs.

II. A HISTORY OF GRIEF

> The days gone by
> Come back upon me from the dawn almost
> Of life; the hiding-places of my powers
> Seem open; I approach, and then they close.
>
> —*The Prelude*

The events are generally well known but merit recounting. In 1778, before Wordsworth's eighth birthday, his mother died. Mary Moorman speculates the cause was pneumonia (*WW* 18). Ann Wordsworth's untimely death effectively broke up the household: the following year, likely at their "stunned and inconsolable" father's behest (18), the nine-year-old William and his elder brother Richard were sent to attend the grammar school at Hawkshead. There they were to live under the watchful eye of Ann Tyson, in her cottage near Esthwaite Lake. Wordsworth's younger brothers John and Christopher would join them, while his sister, Dorothy, was obliged to live with an aunt at Halifax. In this way, Ann Wordsworth's death proved all the more traumatic for her five children, leaving them, as Wordsworth recalled in *The Prelude*, "destitute, and as we might / Trooping together" (*13P* 5.259–60).[38]

Following the Drowned Man and Hanged Man spots of time, the two-part *Prelude* turns to its final "fructifying" spot, depicting three of the brothers waiting for horses to convey them home to Cockermouth at the start of Christmas vacation, 1783:

> 'twas a day
> Stormy, and rough, and wild, and on the grass
> I sate, half-sheltered by a naked wall;
> Upon my right hand was a single sheep,
> A whistling hawthorn on my left, and there,
> Those two companions at my side, I watched
> With eyes intensely straining as the mist
> Gave intermitting prospects of the wood
> And plain beneath. Ere I to school returned
> That dreary time, ere I had been ten days
> A dweller in my Father's house, he died,
> And I and my two Brothers, orphans then,
> Followed his body to the grave.
>
> (1.341–53)

Thus their mother's loss was compounded by the death of their father, John Wordsworth, just five years later. (He in fact had become "ill as a result of spending the night in the open after losing his way on the journey back from his duties as Coroner of the Millom area" [*WL* 33]).[39] The five orphans, now dependent upon and subject to their ill-natured relations, the Cooksons, became homeless in a further, more deeply felt sense. The four boys were to continue living with Tyson, under stricter financial supervision, but, as Duncan Wu points out, their poor treatment by these newly empowered relations made it all too apparent to them "that they were alone and unprotected in the world."[40] As Dorothy revealed in an early letter,

> Many a time have . . . [my brothers] and myself shed tears together, tears of the bitterest sorrow, we all of us, each day, feel more sensibly the loss we sustained when we were deprived of our parents. . . . [We] always finish our conversations . . . with wishing we had a father and a home. (*EY* 3–5)

For the Wordsworth children, William especially, the effects of their father's loss appear to have been even more keenly felt and long lasting than those that attended their mother's death. According to Stephen Gill,

> What the 13-year-old boy felt at this second bereavement it is impossible to say, but, although father and son can hardly have been close, it was

clearly a profound shock. Memories [of this event] surface in the *Vale of Esthwaite* and inspire some of the finest writing in the *1799 Prelude*. (*WL* 33–34)

His father's death seems to have been registered by William in various ways, not the least of which was as guilt, owed, to judge by his recounting of the trauma in *The Vale of Esthwaite*, to having not mourned enough. Wu argues that Wordsworth's incomplete grieving for his father resulted in a species of "disordered mourning,"[41] a Freudian perspective I take up, and take some issue with, in my reading of the *Vale* in Chapter One. The shadow of that paternal trauma can be detected, Gill contends, in Wordsworth's later sympathy for the homeless and above all in "the strength of his later reverence for the values of rootedness, continuity, and sustained love" (35). It likely also influenced his longstanding fascination with death and mourning, as well as his abiding interest in community.[42]

Perhaps it was this haunting experience of paternal loss and of homelessness that the orphaned and alienated William had in mind when he jotted in his notebook, in early 1788, that:

> Death like a Rock his shade has cast
> Black o'er the chill [sad] vale of my days[.]
> I view his lowering form aghast
> Still as I tread the shadowy maze.

(EPF 579)

Paternal death was the trauma and dilemma out of which much of his poetry, and still more of his poetry's sociology, appears to have sprung. The French Revolution may have been the Romantic era's signal event, as Shelley contended, but for Wordsworth's development the prime event occurred five or more years before the storming of the Bastille and three years after the Gordon Riots, with his father's death in December 1783. For that personal loss cost him and his siblings their last vestiges of home and parental security, and, more importantly for his later sense of community, left him with troubling feelings both about his world and about mourning itself. Salman Rushdie has observed that a "writer's injuries are his strengths, and from his wounds will flow his sweetest, most startling dreams."[43] Wordsworth's "shadowy maze" of traumas similarly reveals traces of the winding, uncertain path by which his "life as we know it found its way into his art."[44]

For the Wordsworth children the aftermath of their father's death was more immediately one of economic dependency accompanied by unending legal actions against John Wordsworth's obstinate, better represented former employer, Sir James Lowther, the Earl of Lonsdale, who refused to pay the

£4,700 he owed the estate. This arduous legal inaction probably served as the young Wordsworths' "first conscious encounter with social evil and injustice."[45] Before the Terror or Britain's repressive domestic policies, these *Bleak House*-like deferrals of justice impressed upon the five children the rueful existence of aristocratic, legal, and governmental inequity—summed up in Dorothy's exasperated decrial of "the cruel Hand of lordly Tyranny" (*EY* 84). Her brother William was made sensitive to the inequalities and inequities of the social system, and came to view government, in the age of Paine, as the nemesis both of family and of his adopted Lake District's relative social-political equality.[46]

Such exasperation was not untypical of a time of outrage at governmental corruption and "tyranny," when the desire for reform was common amid people's looming sense of alienation, dislocation, injustice, and grief—much like what the Wordsworth children had endured, albeit at an acute, microcosmic level. According to R. W. Harris, social change and new revolutionary ideas, when coupled with the rapidly rising English urban population and with famine and other problems, bred "discontent and revolt" among the lower orders, "while among the governing classes there was a mixture of fear, misgivings and social conscience."[47] In addition to the loss of the American colonies and to the disquieting, but for many also appealing, ideas of Paine, Godwin, Richard Price, and other radicals,

> rampant industrial and commercial development threw into lurid contrast the poverty, ignorance and misery of so many common people, at a time when many thoughtful people were accepting a deeper and more corporate view of society than had been usual in the eighteenth century.[48]

That "deeper and more corporate" social view was produced by such crisis, responding to or bubbling up from the era's socioeconomic cauldron of misery, skepticism, urban rioting, and reformism. Paine's previously cited argument for the "mutual dependence" of one sector upon another posits in government's place a "great chain of connection" based, like economic society in Smith's *Wealth of Nations,* upon horizontal linkages of mutual economic self-interest and interdependence. It was one way of "binding together" some sort of society, much as the Plutarchan allegory of the body politic had achieved in antiquity or as the divinely ranked "Great Chain" of hierarchized analogues had done throughout the sixteenth and seventeenth centuries.[49]

Such questions and problems as these occupied the minds of many in the 1780s and 1790s. For the "magnitude of the problem" of class discontent and revolt alone, Harris states,

> was so enormous that it would be fair to say that no contemporary either fully understood it, or had an adequate solution for it, but at least there was

no lack of attempts at both, and there were few writers of the period who were not touched by it, for the seriousness of the problem burnt itself upon the minds of all who thought about it.[50]

Out of this time of discontent arose social and political reforms, culminating in the Reform Act of 1832. In addition to the pacifying, solidifying projects of British reform and nationalism, cultural energies were also directed to the problems of moral and social improvement and of community. Evangelism was one result, experimental society another. The literature of the Revival, which Wordsworth embraced and also imitated, was yet another: a means of responding to a crisis of social upheaval and decline, including decadence and ruin often attributed to the French or to English francophiles.[51] Such ubiquitous turmoil was countered by "reviving" indigenous literary forms and by the related attempts of writers, ranging from James Macpherson to Sir Walter Scott, to rediscover or envision alternative concepts of social order and fraternity. The latter conception had of course been understood and propagated by European literati and other elites well before the Revolution, whereupon it was universalized and in part nationalized.[52]

A. D. Harvey argues that late eighteenth-century writers' and readers' fascination with the past was understandably, and inevitably, linked

> to the growing awareness that society was undergoing a fundamental social and economic transformation. As society more and more moved away from its past, into a new social and economic era, so it was more and more able to see its past as something separate, distinct and rather remarkable. . . . Awareness of the process of change inevitably generated a growing interest in what had been lost. From Dyer's *The Ruins of Rome* (1740) onwards, English writers began more and more to celebrate the irrevocable pastness of the past.[53]

The poignant awareness of "what had been lost" in England's transformation from its agrarian past to its urban present—informed by a cult of sentimentality valorizing benevolence and the releasing of "real human passions from the trammels of 'civilization'"[54]—encouraged numerous writers to lament, condemn, and re-envision. And what authors like James Beattie, Scott, and Macpherson envisioned were alternative, often nostalgic, forms of economy and society. For with the waning of past models of social-political order, and with the "dusk of religious modes of thought," soon "the search was on," Benedict Anderson contends, "for a new way of linking fraternity, power and time meaningfully together."[55]

Britain's landscape was still dotted with remains of that dusk, including the ruins of Tintern Abbey. The great Cistercian abbey had been destroyed, and its charitable brotherhood banished, by Henry VIII's Act of Dissolution in 1536 (see Chapter Five). Such ruins signified both the promise and the loss of community to an age in which order and collectivity were so desired and when energies of the Revival, especially those associated with gothic and romance revivalism, were directed toward exploring the attractions and repulsions of a Catholic past's different sense of order and interconnectedness. According to Stephen Greenblatt, Henry VIII's and his successors' actions in fact had destroyed Englishmen's traditional means of "negotiating with the dead"—with those purgatorial souls who, in their ability to "speak, appeal, and appall," were thus "not completely dead."[56] Prior to the Dissolution, the ghostly borderland between the living and dead had not been "firmly and irrevocably closed," for living mourners could, through their suffrages, maintain a "relationship with one important segment of th[os]e dead" by doing specific things for them, things that engaged, therapeutically and socially, the mourners' own "intimate, private feelings."[57] For Greenblatt, the ghost of *Hamlet* testifies to the endurance of this desire for the kind of negotiating with the dead that the banished doctrine of Purgatory, and the ritual collectivity of Catholicism itself, had once provided.

This religious past offered to Revival artists' imaginations a further draught of communitarian spirit. For those monasteries and other ruins—the stuff of romance, gothic, and ballad—also helped, C. John Sommerville states, to create a new secularizing sense of "the past as irrevocably gone," while at the same time promoting the "concentration on the present age" that characterized the advent of modernity.[58] Such a sense of the pastness of the past was a defining characteristic of the eighteenth-century Revival, which, although often concentrated on imagining a past, also sought to awaken even as it lamented such bygone systems, symbols, and associated literary genres of collectivity. To revisit Spenserian romance or other antiquated forms was to recall a time before the Dissolution, to remember England as a land governed by a more religious, unified culture and, seen through the mist of romantic nostalgia, as a land with a good deal more brotherhood and stability. At a time when the age-old "securities of class and status and theological assumptions" were being shattered,[59] when distrust of the old orthodoxies of order was rampant, and when outright ideological fissures were opening in England's social, political, and economic landscape, a good many Britons understandably desired such alternative revived or new forms of social organization and subjectivity. To take but one example, the essayist and critic William Hazlitt would himself strive, McFarland states, "to establish an analogy between the compact that binds together the community at large," one then threatened if not defunct, "and that which binds together the several families that compose it."[60]

Although only thirteen at the time of his father's death, Wordsworth had surely by then already heard talk of crisis—of rioting, at least—and of desire for reform, even for those more radical changes inspired by events in America. One wonders whether Dorothy, for her part, would have voiced matters in quite the terms she did about "the cruel Hand of lordly *Tyranny*" had there not existed a climate of class tension and of concerns about the social, political, and economic arrangement of things. So, like many of his contemporaries, Wordsworth must have felt vexed by such troubles, poignantly focused for him and his siblings by the Lowther action. As one displaced and victimized, he was particularly attracted to the cultural enterprise of the Revival and the related sociological quest to transform an oppressive, alienating, and by some accounts dysfunctional, modern world, capped by an ailing and mad king.[61] But what could be done? Years before, in 1756, Burke had pessimistically determined that political society must inevitably be based upon injustice of one sort or another. Paine and Godwin each proscribed government itself as being inherently corrupting and constraining.

Yet, between the sensation-loving cult of sentimentality and the Revival's literary project of retrieval and revaluation there was much talk of feeling and sympathy, loosely or directly linked to reform. It had its effect upon Hazlitt, years later, and upon Wordsworth in the early 1780s. For, as mentioned, like his siblings Wordsworth had experienced a good deal of such sensation in his grief, uncertainty, and outrage. By this combination of inadequate grief, of living in a broken family of mutually consoling mourners, of desiring stability in a culture of considerable discontent, Wordsworth consciously or unconsciously gleaned a redemptive force: unfinished mourning-work like his own could be the basis for an indigenous form of community, one well fitted to his era's search for fraternity and equality. A small community, founded upon grief and articulated by the shared mourning of its individual members, would in effect be bound together—be held in common *by* the common—be rooted in the past and present, and be enduring, like little else in Wordsworth's life and world. In this way, his desire for a means to bind or link together "the living and the dead" must, for all its personal and idiosyncratic aspects, be read as a part of this larger cultural quest for revival. In fact, while it is reasonable to assume that the poet's sociology was influenced in some measure by his personal life-and-death experiences, at the same time, for all their personal aspects his sufferings were never far removed from the late century's tribulations and from his fellow Britons' desires for change. At least in its expression, Wordsworth's view of the social virtue of mourning-related suffering was influenced by his reading of a sentimental, melancholy, gloomy Georgian era's fictions of death, grief, and social revision.

III. Books

Wordsworth's intellectual journey toward his sociology of community may have begun on that day in June by Esthwaite Water or several years later in his grief over his father's death.[62] But it was clearly influenced by his early reading of works from a late eighteenth-century English cultural tradition that treasured elegies, epitaphs, graveyard meditations, and scenes of pathos. A boy who had experienced the trauma of death and developed a taste for literary melancholy and death-oriented sensationalism would find in Revival and sentimental works no end of objective correlatives. And he would find them amid a culture in which such texts and their tenets held distinct value. In fact, the power of those works was not lost on *The Prelude*'s poet when he came to review the significance of books in that privileged childhood experience on the shore of Esthwaite Lake.

By 1805 that scene would be placed in "Books," the subtitled fifth book of the thirteen-book *Prelude,* with the corpse's recovery now also exemplifying the powers of reading—what Leslie Brisman calls "the rereading of experience"—in Wordsworth's vision of the dead.[63] Here this most visceral of mortal encounters is recast in terms of literature:

> no vulgar fear . . .
> Possess'd me; for my inner eye had seen
> Such sights before, among the shining streams
> Of Fairy Land, the Forests of Romance:
> Thence came a spirit, hallowing what I saw
> With decoration and ideal grace;
> A dignity, a smoothness, like the works
> Of Grecian Art, and purest Poesy.
>
> (5.473–81)

The scene's retelling in 1804/5 underlines its literary character: the manner in which the boy is spared the "vulgar fear" of the crowd by his prior reading of romances, classical myths and legends (perhaps including those of Medusa or Pygmalion), and eastern tales of death, texts which here exert astonishing force. The previously quoted 1799 account betrays this same literary subtext. In adverting from the corpse to "numerous accidents in flood or field" (*2P* 1.280)—an allusion to Othello's recollection of "moving accidents by flood and field" (*Othello* I.iii.135)—and thence to "disasters" and other "tragic facts" (1.282), the two-part *Prelude* reveals not just a boy's ex post facto transformation of corpse to text or stone. It also reveals the underlying literariness of that corpse's initial, "ghastly" appearance, described in 1805 as "a spectre-shape / Of terror even!" (*13P* 5.472–73). The corpse bursts forth from rural history into the "ghastly" (ghostly, spectral, horrible)[64] hues of the gothic, cast in the literary mold of *Othello, Otranto,* and Mark Akenside's *Pleasures of Imagination,* as a terrifying thing sprung from books.[65] The spot's depiction of arresting and arrested horror is thus timely, marked as being very much of its gothic-loving era—in 1779 as in 1799. The scene participates in the vogue of sensationalism and death: the frisson of gothic, the unsettling contemplations of mortality related in "Graveyard School" poetry, the sublime terror analyzed by Burke, the scenes of suffering and death depicted in sentimental poems and domestic fiction.[66]

Wordsworth's brother Christopher noted that their father fostered in William a love of Milton, Spenser, and Shakespeare, with the result that early on in his life he could "repeat large portions" of their works.[67] But it was at Hawkshead Grammar School that Wordsworth truly entered into the Revival's nostalgic, alternativist, and sensationalistic culture, a culture enthusiastically transmitted by schoolmaster William Taylor and his successor Thomas Bowman. From Bowman, Wordsworth probably borrowed Beattie's gothic-sentimental *Minstrel*[68] along with graveyard works by the Wartons and by Charlotte Smith. Bowman also likely lent him Percy's revivalist anthology, *Reliques of Ancient English Poetry,* which Wordsworth, given his "taste for Gothic horror" (*EPF* 2) and death, doubtless savored. He certainly read Revival ballads of grief like David Mallet's ancient-styled "William and Margaret" (1724) and the traditional minstrel song "Sir John Grehme and Barbara Allan," all the while lapping up sentimentalism and its topoi of melancholy, pathos, and sympathy—so much so that he later professed himself to be of "two natures . . . joy the one / The other melancholy" (*13P* 10.868–69), the emotional diptych of Milton's *L'Allegro* and *Il Penseroso.* The latter text was a principal source for graveyard-style melancholy and was an unmistakable influence upon Wordsworth's early lines "To Melpomene," as *Lycidas* was upon his Hawkshead-era idyll "The Dog."

As his allusion to the Miltonic diptych reveals, Wordsworth's "melancholy" nature was highly literary and decidedly vogue, in line with the flowering cult of sensibility and the related work of William Collins, Helen Maria Williams, Edward Young, and others already mentioned. Such books taught readers *how* to feel: how to grieve, mourn, and be melancholy. Wordsworth's poetry is indebted to this sentimentalism, as it is of course to then-current theories of the picturesque, the sublime, and sympathy. His first published poem, the sensationalist "Sonnet, on seeing Miss Helen Maria Williams weep at a Tale of Distress," was itself an imitative exercise "in the rhetoric of sentiment."[69] To write on literary "distresses and disasters" (*2P* 1.282) was to wade into the main current of eighteenth-century taste and approbation.[70] In addition, as their genres suggest, Wordsworth's Hawkshead writings—his elegies, elegiac idylls, epitaphs, and mournful narratives—also present a clear case for his early interest in death and grief. His translation of Catullus's *Carmina* III ("The Death of the Starling") and his later, Cambridge-era translations of Moschus's "Lament for Bion" and Virgil's "Orpheus and Eurydice" attest to this interest and, moreover, to his particular fascination with the topos of *troubled* mourning: a form of mourning that, for one reason or another, is insufficient for the living or the dead.

Having established Wordsworth's taste for melancholy, for the ghoulish, and for lamentation, to what literary or other sources might one attribute his less traditional focus upon the grieving self's insufficient mourning of the deceased? One might argue that a precocious young poet simply had read between the lines of classical and neoclassical elegies and deduced their elegists' implicit inadequacy as mourners in their transferring of guilt onto others. But that is granting a great deal to the fledgling writer. In casting the net farther, one catches no such similar representations of a mourner's personal insufficiency in Revival ballads or epitaphs, or for that matter even in the graveyard poetry of Collins, James Thomson, Thomas Parnell, and Smith. There is, however, a well-known picture of "fruitless" mourning in Gray's elegiac sonnet for Richard West, later critiqued in fact in the 1800 Preface to *Lyrical Ballads*. But Gray's grief is insufficient mainly for being unheard, which is to say it is insufficient in its communication rather than in terms of the elegist's own feelings. One gets closer to such truly troubled mourning by looking back to the fourth edition of *An Essay Concerning Human Understanding* (1701)[71] and the example, in Locke's discussion of a "wrong connexion of ideas," of a form of enduring personal grief: the strange phenomenon of "incurable sorrow." Locke cites the case of a mother who, mourning her dead child, became unable to distinguish past happy memories from her present sense of loss. She and other afflicted mourners "spend their lives in mourning," he argues, "and carry an incurable sorrow to their graves."[72] As Anselm Haverkamp observes, what Locke calls "incurable sorrow" stems from an inability to disconnect memories,[73] memory being the basis, in Locke as in Freud and Wordsworth, for melancholia's peculiar pathology and power.

One could look from Locke to Goethe's melancholy Werther or, more importantly as a possible model for Wordsworth's sense of mournful insufficiency, to Shakespeare's brooding Hamlet, who incurably suffers the slings and arrows of not being all the grieving son he ought to be. The Prince was in this respect well suited to an age in love with sorrow. In *The Hamlet Vocation of Coleridge and Wordsworth*, Martin Greenberg contends that Shakespeare's Prince, because he "does not know what he should do" or what "part he should play," aptly emblematized the Georgian era's own desperation regarding its inability "to make *up* for itself a story to be in" and related sense of its alienated self-consciousness.[74] It was an age of Hamlet, when the great actor David Garrick dazzled British audiences with his portrayal of the Prince and when Wordsworth himself is said to have proclaimed, "There is more mind in *Hamlet* than in any other play, more knowledge of human nature."[75] In such an age there were many Hamlets to play: Hamlet the rationalist philosopher, Hamlet the aimless wanderer, and Hamlet the soliloquist of mortality. It is with this latter figure that Wordsworth seems particularly to have identified, brooding in *The Vale of Esthwaite,* "I mourn because I mourn'd no more."

In his reading of mourning in Book 5 of the thirteen-book *Prelude,* Lionel Morton interprets its famous apostrophe to the Imagination as "taking the first act of *Hamlet* from the battlements of Elsinore to the Alps," where, as in Shakespeare's play, the ghostly dead, if they choose to come, "threaten to overwhelm the summoner."[76] One likewise discovers this burden of the dead in the Immortality Ode's oft-noted allusion to *Hamlet,* describing "High instincts, before which our mortal Nature / Did tremble *like a guilty Thing* surpriz'd" (*PTV,* ll. 149–50; emphasis added; cf. *Hamlet* I.i.129). Here the attributes of the deceased King are transferred to the "mortal Nature" of his obstinately questioning son. In the play Hamlet appears in mourning garb, burdened by the weight of his filial obligation to the dead; "too much i' th' sun," he quips (I.ii.67). Claudius in turn berates him for his "obstinate con- dolement" and its "unmanly grief" (93–94).[77] Hamlet mourns too much but never enough. Rebellious and resistant, he is troubled by what has been lost in death as well as by what hauntingly, imposingly survives. This melancholy fig- ure is Wordsworth's real Hamlet: guilty and haunted, made introspective by mortality and his own grief. A Hamlet for the late eighteenth century, but a Hamlet of communitarian desire? The play hardly seems to exemplify social cohesion, even in the melancholy Dane's death. And yet, as Greenblatt previ- ously argued, the purgatorial ghost of *Hamlet* ultimately testifies to the endurance of a desire for and fascination with the kind of "negotiation with the dead" that Catholic doctrine had provided. A good deal of Prince Ham- let's guilty grief is owed, indeed, to his negotiations with his unquiet dead father, who pleads for remembrance, piety, and revenge. Greenblatt points out that this ghost's doomed night-walking "has now lasted four hundred years," bearing along with it "a cult of the dead," one which readers and writers have been variously "serving" ever since.[78] One finds a good deal of such debt ser- vice in Wordsworth, as well. Still, *Hamlet* cannot entirely account for the poet's particular conception of "a community of the living and the dead."

Part of Britons' search for alternative forms of social order involved a pro- nounced shift from a religious sense of universal destiny to what Ariès describes as "the sense of the other," with emotional affectivity concentrated "on a few rare beings whose disappearance could no longer be tolerated and caused a dramatic crisis: the death of the other."[79] Hamlet served as one exem- plar for a sensationalist, quasi-religious vogue of interest in grief and suffer- ing, typified by death scenes, by desired social intercourse with the dead, and by the mourning pangs of family or friends. Sentimentalism and aspects of gothicism reflected not only this renewed interest in death, especially in mourners' "enduring grief for . . . irreplaceable loved ones who have died," but also a broader desire, Joshua Scodel adds, "for intimate communion with . . .

the beloved dead."[80] Even Goody Two-Shoes' inscriptionless monument, "over which the Poor as they pass weep continually, so that the Stone is ever bathed in Tears,"[81] conveyed to readers how mourning could provide a "unifying focus" for community.[82]

Schor argues that at the center of the century's "culture of mourning" lay Adam Smith's *Theory of Moral Sentiments,* mentioned above, a work that focused attention "on the possible ways in which individual sympathies," especially grief, "might provide the basis for a public morality."[83] In a modern economy uneasily dependent upon paper currency and foreign credit,[84] Smith's moral theory, Schor argues,

> suggests that the dead become, as it were, the gold standard for the circulation of sympathies within a society; at a single stroke, Smith both provides a theoretical account of the relation between private morals and public morality and suggests a role for mourning in remediating anxieties attending the proliferation of paper money in the British economy.[85]

Smith's vision can be viewed as both typical and somewhat peculiar for its time given its emphasis upon grief and sympathy as ways of promoting egalitarian sociability in an alienating age of fervent self-interest. Alexander Pope's "Elegy to the Memory of an Unfortunate Lady," adapted by Wordsworth for his Hawkshead fragment "On the death of an unfortunate Lady," appears to have seized on much the same cultural anxiety, localizing the problem within its own generic horizons. Schor's argument obliges her to avert to other issues, but the social implications of Pope's "Elegy" are still conspicuous in her analysis: that the account books in a poetry of mourning do not balance; utterance leaves one in the red insomuch as the debt always exceeds and resists the tribute paid. Pope seems to have perceived in Britain's economy of debt a rising, deeply cultural dilemma. Wordsworth may in turn have perceived in Pope much the same power of grievous debt in the common tribute it exacts from the living.

Of course, Wordsworth may also have looked no further than his parish church. In the Christian rite of Communion, redemptive sacrifice likewise posits interminable debt, to be paid ever after with gratitude and faith, which is to say with mourning and a degree of debt sharing, too. In *Paradise Lost,* Satan rather understandably bristles at the "debt immense of endless gratitude" owed God.[86] And although he acknowledges "that a grateful mind / By owing owes not, but still pays, at once / Indebted and discharg'd" (4.55–57), his wording catches the haunted spirit of indebtedness *in perpetuum* to the Other. Ultimately, as with Satan and his omnipotent sovereign, this sense of debt is profoundly relational, establishing the very basis *for* relationship between other and self, "paying, still to owe" (53).

Wordsworth would draw upon and draw together the cultural capital of Smith, Pope, Milton, Shakespeare, and other writers, consolidating a social vision in which a negative balance of payments between the living and the dead could foster cohesion. His would be a society of debtors whose bond is that of the perpetuity of their mourning. At some level, Wordsworth sensed that the social possibilities of mourning lay less in sympathy than in insufficiency, which Schor somewhat differently defines as the "recognition of one's ability to be diminished *by a loss of that which lies beyond the self*."[87] That loss looms beyond but also deep within the mourner. Against her claim that Wordsworth's poetry is nonetheless complicit in Britain's turn-of-the-century commodification of mourning's value, Guinn Batten counters that his poetry is "neither complicit with an economy founded on the *work* of mourning nor ignorant of that economy's operations and questionable compensations." His poems instead emerge from a deep social "awareness of the *significance* of a fundamental but forgotten loss, a loss that persists as a 'nothingness' or absence that is in fact replete with irrecoverable but nevertheless emotionally charged presence."[88] Such mourning is a wrestling with the impossibility of mourning,[89] with what has been lost in or to mourning. Wordsworth in this way intuited the social potential of such impossibility: the power not just of mourning or of debt but of the debt of mourning, of "paying, still to owe," to gather together a company situated between the living and the dead.

But it was not to last, not entirely. Having perhaps lost some of his "confidence in social man" (*PW* 5: 117) and, more importantly, having come to desire a release from his own vexatious grief, Wordsworth became more satisfied, in the years after 1804, with the "true society" he had made in Grasmere, bolstered by a moral philosophy of stoic acceptance and a tradition-bound ideology of corporate identity and faith. By the second decade of the nineteenth century, if not before, for many writers the "the great social principle of life" (*2P* 2.438) had begun to give way, often to skepticism about idealized communities, as in the poetry of Lord Byron and Letitia Landon. Even Shelley's writings evince considerable anxiety about extending the self toward a group.[90] By the Victorian era the revivalist search was all but over. The glad dawn of Romantic community softly faded into the modern light of day.

IV. Summary

This study begins at the beginning, with Wordsworth's earliest poetry, and traces the development of his imagining of community from 1785 to 1814. With this movement from dawn to dusk, *Buried Communities* engages in a form of genetic criticism. It seeks, however, to avoid an overly organicist view of authorial development, rarely assuming, for example, that Wordsworth was entirely cognizant of what his poetical writings were formulating, and often finding in the poet's early and later works more recurrence than lock-step evolutionary progress. In this first respect, my approach resembles that of Ferry's *Limits of Mortality* or Richard Onorato's *The Character of the Poet,* which praises Ferry's study as revealing "a constellation of wishes" that "remained permanently at odds with many of the surface appearances of Wordsworth's poetry."[91] My readings similarly trace a particular path through the poet's writings. Referring as I do to Wordsworth's social "paradigm" of course lends a certain façade of unity and stability to what is fundamentally more like an underlying process or force, more verbal than nominative. But one needs to give the unseen a local habitation and a name of some kind, and many of Wordsworth's poems do in fact share an implicit structure or structuring of community focused upon mourning the dead, as the following seven chapters will show.

Chapter One opens by briefly demonstrating the extent to which Wordsworth's grammar-school poetry writing is concerned with death and mourning. His valedictory poem *The Vale of Esthwaite* demonstrates this fascination and, more significantly, uncovers the basis (and so lays the foundation) for the poet's later depictions of community: interminably indebted grief and its supplementation. Specifically, the *Vale* reveals how its speaker's lack of mourning for his dead father underlies the narrative's poetics and its repeated quests of retrieval. Although only hinted at, such mournful indebtedness promises to press the speaker to share with others his unbearable burden of grief, his debt of mourning owed to a "world of shades."

Chapter Two argues that Wordsworth's Cambridge-era works elaborate upon the nascent sociology of mourning adumbrated in the *Vale.* The four Evening Sonnets not only demonstrate the poet's abiding interest in grief but also connect that grief's "strange harmony" of elegiac remembrance and forgetting to a fraternity of past poet-mourners. In so doing, these poems provide a glimpse of Wordsworth's developing vision of community. Like the *Vale,* his *Evening Walk* seeks to cross a "dark and broad gulf" to revisit loss, signified by death-filled recollections that include the poet's first depiction of grief for another, a significant advance. *Descriptive Sketches* praises "an unknown power" connecting the living "to the dead" and, in representing the poet's continental travels as motivated by a "charge of woe," connects mourning even to political solidarity.

The Salisbury Plain poems, the focus of Chapter Three, thrust Wordsworth's connection between mourning and community into clearer expression. In *Salisbury Plain,* two wanderers' sharing of grief forms a community founded upon the poignant force of the dead, whose burdens these mourners bear and who haunt the "dead" locale. Moreover, by *misfitting* its romance form and its social-realist content, the poem exhorts readers to interrogate the problems and possibilities of English community and of literary and political representation. A response to the Terror's erosion of revolutionary fraternity, Wordsworth's revised text, *Adventures on Salisbury Plain,* shifts the action from romance quest to the realm of gothic frisson. And in depicting community as an effect of ghostly converse "consigned" to and *griding* out of "other worlds" within mourners, the poem discovers a mechanism for social cohesion prior to reason and agency, and to the would-be political heroes Wordsworth saw failing at home and abroad.

Chapter Four demonstrates that, like *Salisbury Plain, The Ruined Cottage* depicts dead-oriented, mournful conversation as the primary force behind social bonding. This narrative is the poet's most fully realized vision of a community founded upon the inefficacy and interminability of grief and upon mourners' desire for consolation. *The Ruined Cottage* is also his first work to introduce the competing paradigm of the "One Life," which forms the philosophical basis for the nature-loving pedlar figure's expostulations on the good that survives and toward which all things tend. But his listener's grief is irreconcilable with that doctrine, and the two men's contrary responses to mourning in turn produce a dialogical scheme in which neither grief nor consolation can prevail. Community becomes a form of social cohesion ever in need of supplementation inasmuch as its sources of mourning and consolation remain unresolved and perpetual, struggling in friendly dispute—this community's sustenance and lasting power.

Chapter Five examines *The Ruined Cottage*'s legacy in Wordsworth's explorations of community in the 1798 and 1800 editions of *Lyrical Ballads.* In response to his lost connection to Nature's prior "all in all" immanence, the elegiac poet of "Tintern Abbey" turns to his sister, to form with her a social covenant based upon their shared anticipation of loss and their mutual indebtedness. The "Lucy poems" and Matthew elegies, from the second edition, focus on the incommensurability between mourning and its object, while in "The Brothers" oral, supra-epitaphic conversation about the dead forges cohesion among the living, making the dead the invisible center of a community founded upon the absence of memorial signifiers. Concluding the second volume, the pastoral elegy "Michael" illustrates how the troubled relationship of elegist and elegized drives poetic representation, revealing both the ruination and textual parasitism that may underlie communities of commemoration. *Lyrical Ballads*' elegies and epitaphs in these ways focus upon the manner in which indebtedness sprung from mournful payment enacts and prolongs grief, and with it a desired legacy of social cohesion.

Chapter Six considers mournful community in the five-book *Prelude* and in *Home at Grasmere.* Although he praises nature as "the great social principle of life," even of "one life," *The Prelude*'s poet in fact is more elegist-mourner than nature-loving sage. His poetics and sociology are rooted in loss, as is especially evident in the elegiac five-book version of the poem, whose arc ends in a funereal conclusion. The Boy of Winander and the famous "spots of time" schematize community as a mournful, insistent bond between the living and the dead, one formed by forces of silence, death, and a frisson of fear. These texts suggest the disquiet on which such social cohesion is firmly based. In *Home at Grasmere*, written for *The Recluse*, eulogy and elegy are the twin discourses of inclusion in Grasmere's vale, and mourning is the currency for a community now to include animals as well as human beings. Yet the poet's mourning of a pair of swans (possibly killed by a local dalesmen) complicates his hope for inclusion, obliging him to retrench to retain the more limited, familial community his grief had previously vouchsafed. That retreat and retrenchment quietly signal the paradigm's imminent, yet gradual, decline.

The final chapter contends that the real blow to the scheme of the Dead ultimately comes less from *The Recluse*'s mandate of "Nature" than from the poet's altered view of mourning. After 1804, Wordsworth's poetry repeatedly evinces a desire to quell grief by turning from the troubling dead to new sources of consolation, including, notably, Christian faith. This tendency becomes pronounced after the death of the poet's brother John, the topic of "Elegiac Stanzas." Hence, although his ambitious later poem *The Excursion* is built upon the foundations of the old scheme, even as its culmination, the narrative reveals that model's diminishment. The central books are set in "The Churchyard among the Mountains," but their eulogies' recurrences to grief are mediated by quelling discourses of faith. The basis for social cohesion has shifted from troubled mourning to shared tradition, history, and religion, and to an inception of selfhood structured by institutions. A "new controul" is at work, although the paradigm of mournful community lingers on, arguably coming to a complete end only with the author's death.

1

A "World of Shades"

The Birth of Community in the Juvenilia

> Recoiling from a gloom too deep.
> —*The Vale of Esthwaite*

Wordsworth is quick to lead readers back to his early life as a source or cipher for his later poetical talent and preoccupations. He contends in *The Prelude* and elsewhere that his views on "Nature, Man, and Society" were shaped in those years, and describes his best piece of juvenilia, *The Vale of Esthwaite,* as containing "thoughts and images most of which have been dispersed through my other [i.e., later] writings" (*PW* 1: 318). Readers must of course proceed cautiously in undertaking so Romantic and vexatious a pursuit, of which Wordsworth himself was wary: "Who knows the individual hour in which / His habits were first sown, even as a seed . . . ?" (*13P* 2.211–12). Yet in the writings of Wordsworth's youth one does in fact find traces of the poet's mature views and interests, including traces integral to his later conception of a "spiritual community binding together the living and the dead."

That social formation is for the Wordsworth of these early years very much "something to be labored upon and worked through,"[1] to be haphazardly articulated in the morning light of creation. He will not provide the model its clearest realization for a whole decade, in *The Ruined Cottage.* Yet, although Wordsworth's later, mature conception of "spiritual community" is relatively undeveloped in the poems he composes between 1785 and 1787, certain of its crucial elements nonetheless take root during this "fair seed time" of his life. They become established in childhood experiences of death and familial fragmentation; in a milieu of social, political, and economic transformation; and in Wordsworth's extensive reading of ancient and modern literary works treating death, melancholy, and lamentation. In these experiences his views of the social power of death and memorialization take their start, to become thereafter a shaping force in his poetry and its unfolding sociology.

I. "Never Ceasing Moan[s]": Death and Mourning in the Hawkshead-Cambridge Poems

During Christmas vacation of 1784–85, the first anniversary of his father's death and nearly six years after his spotting of the drowned schoolmaster's pile of clothes beside Esthwaite Water, Wordsworth composed his first self-motivated poem. The verses have not survived, but Kenneth Johnston deduces they likely treated the subject of change, turning "compulsively on changes in his life" occasioned by his father's death, in keeping with "the majority of his verses surviving from this period" (*HW* 96). A year and a half after the death of his father, in 1785 Wordsworth undertook his first significant poetical task, composing celebratory lines for the bicentenary of Hawkshead School. Two years later he had composed his second "public" poem and his first published work, the sensationalistic "Sonnet, on seeing Miss Helen Maria Williams weep at a Tale of Distress" (1787), which appeared in *European Magazine*. Although the evidence does not suggest prodigious writing on Wordsworth's part, these works, along with his other surviving writings, attest to his seriousness and ambitiousness as a fledgling poet. Under the guidance of Hawkshead's encouraging, poetry-loving schoolmasters Taylor and Bowman, and with such praise from an older student who asked, "How is it, Bill, thee doest write such good verses?" (*WL* 31), Wordsworth seems to have taken to poetry writing with a measure of enthusiasm. And while it is arguably true that neither of the above-mentioned poems gives an "indication of what was really promising in Wordsworth's schoolboy writing," Stephen Gill is right in observing that other of his Hawkshead poetry shows considerable promise (31).

Admittedly, aside from a few poetical fragments jotted by Wordsworth in his brother Christopher's notebook, and two public poems, little survives of Wordsworth's early poetry that can definitively be dated to before his matriculation at Cambridge in October 1787 (*EPF* 24–25). But of the finished poems recorded in his much prized leather-bound notebook, since labeled DC MS. 2, a number may have been composed during or before the summer and fall of 1787, the time of his departure from the vale.[2] One of the earliest of these Hawkshead poems (the notebook's first pages are missing), "Anacreon

Imitated" is a school exercise dated by its author, probably to its time of composition, "August 7, 1786." Carol Landon and Jared Curtis, the editors of Cornell's edition of Wordsworth's *Early Poems and Fragments, 1785–1797,* conjecture the poem to have been copied from another manuscript (MS. 4), where
it is accompanied by three other poems also probably composed between 1786
and 1787, and of more interest to this study for their marked interest in death:
"Sonnet written by M^r _____ immediately after the death of his Wife," a
short imitation of Alexander Pope's "Elegy to the Memory of an Unfortunate
Lady" entitled "On the death of an unfortunate Lady," and the four-line
Thomsonian "Fragment of an Ode to winter." The titles paint a fair picture of
Wordsworth's fascination not just with death but also with mourning. That
image becomes clearer still in a list of all but three of the works recorded in
the notebook: "The Death of the Starling" (one of two translations of Catullus), a *Lycidas* imitation titled "The Dog—An Idyllium," a ballad, and, from
around January 1788, two dirges, two epitaphs, a "Tale" about a grief-mad-
dened woman, and extracts from the death-haunted narrative of *The Vale of
Esthwaite.* This list well supports Duncan Wu's observation that most of the
poems Wordsworth wrote between his first attempts at poetry and his 1787
departure "are concerned with death."[3] The writings moreover reveal the
young poet's fascination with the lingering inadequacy of mourning, an
important facet of his mature social scheme of "spiritual community." His
translation of "The Death of the Starling," for example, strips Catullus's poem
of all its irony, taking seriously the poet's lament for his lady's loved pet and
lamenting, as in "The Dog," the absence of the forces or personages—gods,
nature, fellow poets—required to mourn the dead sufficiently.

Of these varied works from the Hawkshead era, one other poem apart
from *The Vale of Esthwaite* merits closer attention for the manner in which it
discloses a kind of outline of its author's emerging and developing views about
the dead. Like the contemporary *Vale,* this early work deserves to be read as
more than just the autobiographical lament of a grieving or morbid schoolboy,
however much its subject matter may have arisen from Wordsworth's person-
ally felt losses. Composed in March of 1787, the sentimental "Ballad" ("And
will you leave me thus alone") appears to have been modeled on David Mallet's popular Revival ballad "Margaret's Ghost" in Percy's *Reliques* anthology,
and on Thomas Tickell's similar "Lucy and Colin," which follows that text in
Percy.[4] Wordsworth's kindred tale of a lovelorn abandoned woman, named
Mary, was likely also based upon Ann Tyson's account of her Lakeland neighbor Mary Rigge, who had, like her fictional counterparts, been deserted by her
lover and then pined away, dying at age twenty-one.[5] "Ballad" is chiefly concerned with unrequited love, abandonment, and with a lover's inability emotionally to let go of her cruel beloved—topoi of the sentimental ballads on
which the poem was modeled. But it is the less obvious answer to the maid's

opening question to her lover, "And will you leave me thus alone . . . ?" (*EPF*, l. 1), that in fact guides the narrative and reveals its social meaning. That answer to Mary's appeal comes, belatedly, in her memorialization:

> Her knell was rung—the Virgins came
> And kiss'd her in her shroud
> The children touch'd—'twas all they durst
> They touch'd and wept aloud.
>
> The next day to the grave they went
> All flock'd around her bier
> —Nor hand without a flower was there
>   Nor eye without a tear.——
>
> (57–64)

Here the dead draw the living to flock around them, consolidating what seemed elsewhere to be lacking. In doing so, the living form an ad hoc community comprised of those now shepherded together by mortal loss and its memorialization. Of course, Wordsworth scarcely invented either lingering loss or the communal powers of mourning; they are stock elements of elegy, ballad, epitaph, and even the Eucharist. "Lucy and Colin" itself relates that often at its deceased couple's shared grave "the constant hind / And plighted maid are seen."[6] The same can be said for ballads like "The Bride's Burial" or "A Lamentable Ballad of the Lady's Fall."[7] Wordsworth might also have carried over this element from his personal experience with loss or from having observed Lake District funerals. All the same, "Ballad" attests to its author's fascination with the motif of interminable grief.

Behind Mary's deathbed recollection of a prophecy that her "head would soon lie low" (42) are the dying words of Hawkshead master Taylor. *The Prelude* records that "[a] week, or little less, before his death" he said to Wordsworth, "[m]y head will soon lie low" (*13P* 10.501–2). James Averill argues that Wordsworth interpolates Taylor's prophetic words "to exploit their deep, if personal, emotional significance . . . to endow a conventional and imitative fiction with tragic emotions" (*PHS* 43), much as the poet did with the story of Mary Rigge. One may also argue that he sought to connect the poem not only to his own life but also to Lakeland social history, as one of those "tragic facts / Of rural history" to which the 1799 *Prelude* will refer. Wordsworth in effect is indirectly memorializing Taylor as well as Rigge, painting a social scene of loss much as he will do with schoolmaster Jackson in the Drowned Man episode. This topos of communal grief may appear commonplace or trivial, but, as the allusion to Taylor's loss suggests, it was for Wordsworth an element of considerable importance. As readers find in the poet's later writings, a wrong or inadequacy connected with mortal loss has the power to draw a poem's speaker to mourn and to bond with other mourners, and thereby form a community.

The persistence of mournful observance, and of its social and poetical effects, is one of the implicit, and at times relatively explicit, subjects of Wordsworth's finest composition from this Hawkshead-to-Cambridge period: his valedictory narrative *The Vale of Esthwaite*. But although the *Vale* is chronologically next in line for analysis, it is best approached by way of the poet's translation of a portion of Virgil's *Georgics* IV, jotted at Cambridge in 1788 in the same notebook (MS. 5) as two of the "Various Extracts" from the *Vale*. Wordsworth's translation, titled "Orpheus and Eurydice" by Ernest de Selincourt in *Poetical Works* and listed as "Georgics Translation IX" in the Cornell edition, is by far the most sustained and ambitious of the poet's renderings of selections from Virgil's bucolic poem, and its thematic similarity to the *Vale*, which Wordsworth was then revising, makes its pairing and use as a prolegomenon of sorts appropriate.

Bruce Graver helpfully describes Virgil's Orpheus epyllion as the tale "of a bereft spouse who is destroyed both psychologically and physically by the intensity of [his] grief."[8] Wu, for his part, speculates that what Wordsworth found so "compelling" about this particular portion of Book IV was Orpheus's "grief at his failure to restore Eurydice to the physical world"[9]—in other words, this hero's troubled mourning of her loss. In Wordsworth's rather loose translation, Orpheus, upon returning from Hades to the world above,

> Felt his dear wife the sweet approach of Light
> Following behind—ah why did fate impose
> This cruel mandate—*source of all his woes*[?]
> When [   ] a sudden madness stole
> His swimming senses from the lover's soul. . . .
> He turn'd and gaz'[d]
>   And thrice a dismal shriek
> From Hell's still waters thrice was heard to break. . . .
>   (18–22, 27–29; original emphasis)[10]

This originary elegiac poet is described as thereafter singing his "[tale] of sorrow o'er and o'er" (45) in a lament likened to the forlorn nightingale's mourning "with low sighs and sadly pleasing tongue" (52). Wordsworth's translation likely follows Dryden's rendering of these lines, associating Orpheus's "sighs," as Virgil does not,[11] with the mourning elegies of the nightingale. Wordsworth's verses more directly connect the bird, by her "low sighs," to her human antitype's repeated sighs, stressing, Graver argues, much "more emphatically than Virgil the ways in which the bird is a poet like Orpheus, whose magical power springs from the rending pain of grief."[12] In fact the phrase "o'er and o'er" appears to be Wordsworth's, not Virgil's,[13] echoing to Wu's ear as to my own *The Vale of Esthwaite*'s important repetition of "sighs . . . o'er and o'er."[14] "Orpheus and Eurydice" and the *Vale* indeed both "construct comparable myths designed," Wu says, "to satisfy the . . . drive towards retrieval" of the dead.[15]

"Twice robbed of his wife" (*Georgics* IV.504), Orpheus mourns a double loss owed to losing Eurydice in the very act of retrieving her. He may find solace in the survival of his dying poetic lament, but that lament and its perpetuity stem from the irredeemable and interminable character of her death. Singing "o'er and o'er" his elegiac "tale of sorrow," Orpheus in this way epitomizes an open-eyed refusal to negate or replace the dead. His grief characterizes him, in Freud's binary scheme, not as the typical mourner, who declares "the object to be dead" by accepting a substitute for it, but as the melancholic, who "struggle[s]" with "ambivalence" (*SE* 14: 257), acknowledging loss while resisting all mediating symbolic substitutes. Much like the minstrel of "Ballad," Orpheus refuses to replace the lost beloved with a substituting trope that would, as Freud himself conceded, as a substitute remain "at an essential remove from what it replaces."[16] Nonetheless, Kathleen Woodward rightly argues that Freud "leaves no theoretical room for another place, one between a crippling melancholia and the end of mourning."[17] It is on this middle ground that many of Wordsworth's protagonists stand, as Orphic mourners who resist substitution and its cessation of grief. That resistance indeed produces and further defines Orpheus's quest-like lamentation and song—a song linked not just to Eurydice's loss but to his failure to retrieve her, to translate her lost presence somehow back into life rather than into the repeated, mediating echoes he hears and, in death, becomes. As the *Vale* suggests, "o'er" is, in this way, *more*. Orpheus's troubled grief over a death no material mediation can recover, as a debt no tribute can pay, thereafter becomes the focus for a lineage of others' elegies of loss, including Wordsworth's own, as in that best piece of his Hawkshead-era poetry.

II. *The Vale of Esthwaite*'s Secret Promise

> Come thou for I know what kind
> of grief is heavy at my heart's core . . .
> oh exert all thy art for grief at
> my heart.
>
> —Fragment
> (*Vale* Affinitive Piece [AP] VIII)

Wordsworth recalled *The Vale of Esthwaite* to have been "[w]ritten . . . in the Spring and Summer" of 1787 (*EPF* 149). Certainly begun, at the latest, by the eve of his departure from Hawkshead for Cambridge, the valedictory poem was by far his most ambitious composition to date, and is for its readers today by most any measure "an altogether more interesting prelude to his mature work" than anything else he had written (*WL* 31). Yet, since the text's belated publication in the 1940s, in an appendix to the first volume of *Poetical Works*,[18] it has largely either been dismissed as juvenile scribbling or been plundered for the few biographical clues it could provide about its author's developing psychology. This was in part the case with Geoffrey Hartman's psychological reading of the *Vale*, which for years remained one of the poem's few extended analyses and is to this day still one of the most convincing (*WP* 76–89).[19] But in recent years the poem's literary stock has risen, owed in part to the injection of critical capital by new, even more persuasive advocates. Wu, for one, has focused much-needed attention on the work's imagery and dynamics, while Johnston has examined the *Vale*'s generic form and the poem's "compulsive" reiteration of gothic horrors that remain "intensely personal" (*HW* 106–7). John Turner has persuasively argued that the emphasis on "the capacity to mourn" which so typifies Wordsworth's great poem of the dead, *The Ruined Cottage,* can be traced back to the *Vale*'s own "mighty debt of grief."[20] Landon and Curtis's edition of the juvenilia promises to attract still more attention to this early, intriguing poem. After all, as mentioned above, the poet himself described the *Vale* as containing ideas "dispersed" throughout his later work. And a good number of these ideas and topoi, some of them markedly social in character, can be gleaned from the poem, despite the surviving text's fragmentary state.

That text certainly presents challenges to the reader or editor. In the notes to his premier edition of *The Vale of Esthwaite*, de Selincourt argued, for example, that a "good deal of the [original] poem is lost," and speculated the missing pages might have been added to the later, similarly locodescriptive narrative *An Evening Walk* (*PW* 1: 368). Wordsworth recollected an original "long poem" of "many hundred lines" (*FN* 6), which may or may not have extended beyond the surviving text. In a laudable but problematical attempt to reconstruct that long-lost *Ur-Vale* of MS. 3, where seven pages seemed to have been "cut out," de Selincourt interpolated several passages culled from two other manuscripts (MSS. 2 and 5), conjectured by him with some cause to have "probably [been] a part" of those lost pages' contents (*PW* 1: 273). Especially significant among these added portions are twenty-eight lines of a gothic episode copied along with lines nearly identical to those recorded in MS. 3 (*PW*, ll. 240–67; cf. *EPF* Extract XVI, ll. 31–58). This text follows nine lines about "the tempest's dirge," which perfectly fit back in the latter manuscript (at line 160, as de Selincourt saw), whence they may well have originated.[21]

The passage is of considerable importance to understanding *The Vale of Esthwaite*'s oddly convoluted narrative, and needs to be read in closer conjunction with the bulk of that text than its relegation to an "extract" in the Cornell edition may suggest.[22] With this in mind, I treat these twenty-eight *Vale* lines (preserved in MS. 5) as a piece of Wordsworth's original composition.

The MS. 3 text of the *Vale* can be divided into three sections (*EPF*, ll. 1–132, 133–272, 273–379), to which the Cornell edition appends the manuscript's succeeding tributes to Dorothy (380–87) and to Wordsworth's Hawkshead friend John Fleming (388–97)—and to which I follow de Selincourt in appending the succeeding "Adieu" to Hawkshead (*EPF* AP V). The narrative can further be divided into approximately thirteen parts, three of which are gothic episodes and one a paternal elegy followed by further elegiac reflections. The three gothic scenes and the elegy alternate with, and rather "knock askew" (*HW* 106), locodescriptive portions written along the lines of Milton's *L'Allegro* and *Il Penseroso*. I refer to the gothic descents as Episodes one, two, and three—Episode two being comprised in part of those above-mentioned twenty-eight lines—and to the elegiac lines as Episode four.

The *Vale* opens with fairly typical eighteenth-century locodescription, describing its lone speaker's wanderings amid his beloved "landskip's varied treasure" (*VE*, l. 2). But the ensuing, broadly topographical lines are concerned less with terrestrial description of Esthwaite's pastures than with the speaker's melancholy travels and, especially, with his three subterranean descents into "gloomy glades" (25). As Johnston observes, just about wherever the reader "slices into" this most "compulsive text," he or she will find "the same poem," for like an anxious dream the *Vale* "is highly repetitive" (*HW* 106).[23] The three gothic episodes indeed are even at first glance so similar as to suggest they may allegorize the same underlying thing. And of them the second episode most clearly and temptingly directs the reader to a "treasure" beneath its textual surface, and so serves as a helpful point of entry into *The Vale of Esthwaite*'s intricate (some might say disordered) narrative structure. In this decidedly gothic scene, a specter leads the poem's speaker from a "haunted Castle's pannel'd room" down

> to [a] dungeon deep
> And stopp'd and thrice her head she shook
> More pale and ghastly seem'd her look
> [   ] view'd [*shew'd*]
> An iron coffer mark'd with blood[.]
> The taper turn'd from blue to red
> Flash'd out—and with a shriek she fled. . . .
>
> (Extract XVI, 32, 48–54)[24]

Terrified, the speaker attempts to flee "[w]ith arms in horror spread around," only to find some "form unseen . . . / Twist round my hand an icy chain / And drag me to the spot again" (55–58). In Wordsworth's day, as now, the word *coffer* meant a "strongbox" or "chest" containing treasure ("coffers"). But a more obscure sense survived: a "coffin."[25] Such a connection makes sense in this context of a "ghastly" and bloody "spot," in a poem that concerns not just ghosts but the death and burial of the speaker's father, along with the son's guilty feelings about that loss.

While the ironclad coffer begs (or "shrieks") to be deciphered, its ambiguous description nonetheless largely conceals its function in this scene and whatever contents it hides from view. Still, it seems reasonable to read the coffer as a safe containing "treasure" of some kind or, what is even more likely given the scene's gothic locale and the poem's ghostly, elegiac character, as a blood-stained coffin concealing a corpse. In either case, however, the coffer hides *what* it hides but not entirely *that* it hides, and so insinuates the possible presence of some secret treasure concealed within, a treasure associated with revisitation and with the "unseen" hands and binding chains of the dead. That the *Vale* opened with the speaker's appreciation of the landscape's "treasure," that at the poem's midpoint (Extract XVI) he discovers a hidden "iron coffer," and that the narrative concludes, in MS. 3's trailing passages, with his imminent descent into "Mammon's joyless mine" (AP V, l. 14), suggests not only that the coffer is the container of some withheld treasure but also that such a subterranean container or content is connected to the narrative's repetitions and revisitations. After all, the poem's poet-speaker[26] is not just ushered to this ghoulish locale; he is physically forced back to it, specifically to the coffer's highly charged *spot*. Whether one reads the coffer's undisclosed treasure either as a corpse or as something merely associated with death (with ghosts and blood), the episode's dead serve as the dreaded object of descent and as a force of visitation.

The poem's fourth episode, similarly recounted in Book 9 of the 1805 *Prelude,* presents a further vantage for the narrative's decoding. In this scene, the poet recalls events of December 19, 1783, and of succeeding days. Impatiently waiting on a ridge above Hawkshead for a horse to take him and two of his brothers home for the Christmas holidays, the anxious boy endures the inclement weather, little knowing what is to come:

> One Evening when the wintry blast
> Through the sharp Hawthorn whistling pass'd
> And the poor flocks all pinch'd with cold
> Sad drooping sought the mountain fold[,]
> Long Long upon yon steepy [*naked*] rock
> Alone I bore the bitter shock[;]

> Long Long my swimming eyes did roam
> For little Horse to bear me home[,]
> To bear me[—]what avails my tear[?]
> To sorrow o'er a Father's bier.—
>
> (*VE* 274–83)

In a text of repeated descents, where repetition is itself a structural principle and key, the repeating of the word "long" focuses attention on the narrator's anticipation of the horse and on the duration that marks not just death but also the "shock" of loss. The narrative indeed surfaces *because* of this past "bitter shock," a seizing, self-consuming kind of *affect* ("bitter" <OE. *biter*, "biting")[27] that causes the event and its objects to linger, like the "lingering" treasures of the poem's opening lines, and to resurface as haunting intimations, repeated descents, and cryptic, poignant recollections. Moreover, by forming an analogy between being *borne* by a horse and *bearing* the father's "bier" (<OE. *beran*, "to bear"), Wordsworth's text establishes a typology in which being borne prefigures bearing the dead, as a bearing that must itself be borne (i.e., be lamented and recollected). Such a prefigurative paradigm would of course have been familiar to one at all versed in the Anglican liturgy, as was Wordsworth. The landscape of "whistling" and "rustling Boughs" (68), and of other prefigurative and refigurative treasures, takes its allegorical start from this hidden mine of paternal death. Yet, if the poem's melancholy poet is "playing over" some sort of lingering past trauma owed or at least connected to the dead,[28] it might well be asked just what that trauma is and why it appears here to be so strangely significant. In short, what burdensome "treasure," linked to bearing the dead, has been coffered away?

The answer is to be found in subsequent lines of this same passage, where the poet, still lingering over the memory of his father's death, tells how the narrative's tears give his

> soul [*heart*] relief
> To pay the mighty debt of Grief
> With sighs repeated o'er and o'er[;]
> I mourn because I mourn'd no more . . .
> Nor did my little heart foresee
> —She lost a home in losing thee[;]
> Nor did it know—of thee bereft
> That little more than Heav'n was left.
>
> (286–95)

The speaker's remembrance of the events preceding and following the loss of his father elicits tears that "ease" the "mighty debt of Grief" he feels. His words echo Lord Lyttelton's *Monody*—"I now may give my burden'd heart relief, / And pour forth all my stores of grief" (cited *EPF* 446)—and to some extent Adam Smith's debt analysis of mourning and the ensuing exchange of sympathies.[29] At the same time, however, the narrator's elegiac payment of tribute is in the form of repeated "sighs" paid not because of the dead's troubles, the case in Smith's model, or really even to unburden his heart, as in Lyttleton, but because the poet himself "mourn'd no more."

These lines more closely recall another poem, one important enough to Wordsworth that he later enlisted it as evidence for his claim, in the Preface to *Lyrical Ballads* (1800), that there is "no essential difference between the language of prose and metrical composition" (*LB* 253). The poem, likely read by him at Hawkshead, is Gray's "Sonnet on the Death of Richard West," the closing couplet of which expresses the melancholy lament, "I fruitless mourn to him that cannot hear / And weep the more because I weep in vain."[30] It is easy to see why these lines, singled out in the Preface, remained so memorable for Wordsworth: as with the above lines from the *Vale*, they treat a predicament of mourning "in vain." Yet, however much Gray's poem may be credited as having influenced Wordsworth's lament,[31] there are also pronounced differences between the poems' mourners and their predicaments. As Peter Manning states,

> To read Gray's poem is to experience complete stasis; the paralysis of imagination by grief. . . . Without West to share his burden of grief, Gray is driven back into a solitary death-in-life. . . . Gray's grief feeds on itself and perpetuates its own condition: he weeps the more because he weeps in vain. Gray becomes the tomb of his loss, his immobility the counterpart and representation of West's death.[32]

Gray's grief arises from West's inability to hear his elegist's mourning, creating for the speaker a self-perpetuating cycle of mourning driven by its distance and alienation from its object. His mourning is "fruitless" and "vain" because its loved object cannot perceive its proper actions.

The case is considerably different for Wordsworth's grieving poet, who mourns not because the deceased cannot perceive him but because his mourning is itself insufficient. Either in the *amount* he mourns his dead father ("no more" than he did) or in the *duration* he mourned ("no more" as "o'er," as not "long" enough), there was and is for him a troubling insufficiency in this experience.[33] Thus the ostensibly similar situations for these two mourners could hardly be more different. Although each mourner's mourning is troubled, incessant, and in some manner "vain," for Wordsworth's poet his mourning's troublesome character is marked by insufficiency. That inadequacy is suggested by the semantic ambivalence of "more," a doubling that, like the speaker's second loss of a heart's "home" ("in losing thee"), shifts toward a more overt language of tropes, in a manner that then links that tropology to a prior, traumatic loss.[34] The poet's repetition of "sighs" emphasizes their materiality, as does his later reference to the overtly poetical "pensive sighs of Gray" (317), an allusion to "Elegy Written in a Country Churchyard" and its "tribute of a sigh" (l. 80), a phrase that similarly implies debt, with sighs paid as tribute.

That the text enlists a heart's or soul's lost *home* as a metaphor also suggests that holding to a too literal interpretation of these lines—prompted, say, by the fact that Wordsworth did lose a home as a result of his father's death—risks losing sight of the deeper connection between mourning and this Orphic loss "in losing." Indeed, the logical antecedent for the line's oddly non sequitur "Nor" is the directly preceding lament of mourned past mourning. The poet's summation of a trauma that cannot be summed situates the text's enigmas in the metaphorical equating of one type of mourning with another. It does so in a manner analogous to the prior association of horses and biers (both vehicles of conveyance) but with the key difference that it represents the original death-related trauma as lost and unaddressable. Mourning becomes in this sense a privative rather than a restorative signifying mode (to mourn mourning is not the same as to mourn death), the repetition, in Paul de Man's words, "of a previous sign with which it can never coincide, since it is the essence of this previous sign to be pure anteriority."[35] Whether quantitative or qualitative, this "more" is, as the passage's play of meanings suggests, "no more," a fundamental lack. The poem's allegorical narrative leads back, via mediating textualized sighs and repeated ghostly descents, to a problem rooted in the process of mourning itself.

In *Mémoires* Jacques Derrida argues that all such allegories of mourning are written "to the memory of mourning," which is "why there can be no *true* mourning."[36] And, as Derrida elsewhere observes, not only is such mourning "interminable" and "impossible," but, equally importantly, it is also the mourner's "object and . . . resource, working *at mourning* as one would speak of a painter working *at a painting*."[37] This basic impossibility of the poet's fulfillment of mourning cryptically structures the *Vale*'s coffered narrative, as an interminable debt (and an irretrievable possibility) that enunciates his text's repeated Orphic attempts to mourn. It is not a corpse, then, so much as a missing corpse, and more precisely a missing or lost relationship to the dead, that is coffered away in the poem's ghostly "spot[s]." In this respect the reader may mark a further difference between the poets of Wordsworth's and Gray's elegiac texts. For despite all the *Vale* poet's gothic descents, retreats, and melancholy wanderings, the death he mourns is for him an occasion not for ending or paralysis but for beginning and movement (for poesis, narrative), albeit for recursive beginning and repetitive movement.

This mourning of a prior, foreclosed mourning is touched upon in *The Prelude*'s depiction of this same scene of paternal loss. Wordsworth here recalls how, before having been but ten days

> A Dweller in my Father's House, he died
> And I and my two Brothers, Orphans then,
> Followed his Body to the Grave.
>
> (*13P* 11.366–68)

This passage underlines in a few words the poet's shift in status from a "dweller" not just to a homeless orphan but to a funereal figure following the corpse "to the grave" (were a despondent spouse so described one would assume he or she had "followed" the departed in death). Such death is not literal death—the speaker has lived to write the tale—but a falling or following into an inauthentic relationship between self and (deceased) other.[38] The poet mourns, but like Orpheus he cannot see his lost beloved or feel directly his original loss. Such a counter-logic or "counter-spirit," to borrow Wordsworth's coinage (*PrW* 2: 85), subverts its host-referents, for if to mourn in the first sense (one subsequent to death but prior to narrative) is to grieve death, then to mourn "mourning" is to grieve not the death of a body but the death or deathliness of one's relationship to the dead.

A similar situation exists between the living and dead in Wordsworth's later Fragment of the *Gothic Tale* (1795–96), in which two men descend to a dungeon "where feudal Lords of antient years / The vassals of their will in durance bound" (*B*, ll. 102–3). This gothic descent reveals a subterranean social form of organization associated with binding, prolonged confinement ("durance" points to duration) and "antient" feudal obligation to which the subject "vassal" is bound but, like the *Vale* poet, unable to pay. His is a "durance" that confines and determines him, a debt and duration owed to an unpayable debt. And it is just such a quest for recuperative reconnection that serves in the *Vale* to establish an important promissory relation between the dead and the mournful living. For the interminability of (failed) mourning makes an encrypted poetry of return, revisitation, and recuperation not just possible but also necessary. In this way, the undisclosed, coffered dead linger, haunting the poet and calling him, as his vocation, to follow them to these treasured, secret spots. Desired mourning thereby leads to the basis both for poetic production and for the *Vale*'s nascent imagining of community.

A reading of the most prominent of the *Vale*'s descents, Episode three, helps to expose this mournful foundation of Wordsworth's poesis and sociology. Here the narrator recalls being terrified to find at his hand a "[tall] thin Spectre" who "bore / What seem'd the poet's harp of yore" (219, 226–27). This figure at once led him down a "narrow passage damp and low" to Mount Helvellyn's "inmost womb" (233, 243), where, the speaker tells us, the ghost

> made a solemn stand[,]
> Slow round my head thrice waved his [hand]

And cleaved mine ears then swept his [lyre]
That shriek'd terrific shrill an[d] [dire]
Shudder'd the fiend. The vault a[lo]ng
Echoed the loud and dismal song.
'Twas done. The scene of woe was o'er[;]
My breaking soul could bear no more[.]
[?] when with a thunderous soun[d]
That shook the groaning mountain round
A massy door wide open flew
[?] [   ]
That spirit [   ] my grisly guide
Each night my troubl'd spirit ride[s.]

                            (244–57)[39]

In this visit to Helvellyn's Underworld it is evident that, as Jonathan Wordsworth claims, "some kind of initiation ceremony is taking place."[40] The poem's poet and his "grisly guide" stand in the "inmost womb" of the mountain, and at the scene's conclusion a "groaning" sound is heard just before a door flies open. The problem of burden bearing represented in Episode four's "little Horse" scene is literalized as ghostly reproduction: a macabre enunciation of one's vocation as a producer of texts representing this haunting subterranean world. To be a poet is here to witness the production of poetry, which is to say to witness one's production as a poet bearing (birthing) a burden of sorrow and woe he cannot bear (carry, tolerate). This "scene of woe" initiates the speaker as a poet by representing to him and through him thereafter the cryptic (re)production of poetry out of the womb-like, haunted grave, in signs that localize the loss in his father's death, generalize it in terms of Helvellyn's regional Cumbrian history (and its dead),[41] and materialize it in a haunting language of tropes.

As becomes even clearer in subsequent lines, the episode represents poetry's production as stemming from and being owed to a burden of the dead, an unbearable debt beyond the self that is circulated "o'er and o'er" in an economy of loss and desire. The object of the *Vale* poet's initiating song will thereafter be a "Terror shapeless [that] rides" his "soul" as the latter is "hurl'd / Far Far amid the shadowy world," a terror that leaves a haunting legacy of the dead: "And since that hour the world unknown[,] / The world of shades is all my own" (267–71). The terror "rides" the poet's soul as if the latter were a horse or other beast of burden, placing him and his poetic discourse in a position uncannily like the horse of Episode four and like the "bier" that bore his dead father. The poet must bear his burden repeatedly, "Far Far" amid a "shadowy world" not unlike his shadowy burden itself: a "world of shades" that is more a legacy or vehicle ("all my own") than a place. Indeed, in each of the

Vale's gothic episodes the poet discovers and is bequeathed a ghostly source, a "dismal" origin for his burdensome vocation.

Similarly, in the poem's first gothic scene the wandering minstrel, "led astray" in the swamps, hears "Spirits yelling from their pains / And lashes loud and clanking chains" (53–55). Fleeing, like the poet, and startled to hear his harp suddenly "sigh[ing] . . . with hollow groan,"

> He starts the dismal sound to hear
> Nor dares revert his eyes for fear[.]
> Again his harp with thrilling chill
> Shrieks at his shoulder sharp and shrill[;]
> Aghast he views, with eyes of fire
> A grisly Phantom smite the wire.
>
> (58–64)

The vision's beginnings near a mansion's coffer-like "rusted door" (49), and the harp's ghostly "shrieks," connect this episode with those scenes already described. The connection between the episode and its mournful source is underlined by the minstrel's subsequent rousing by

> rustling boughs above
> Or straggl'd sheep with white fleece seen
> Between the Boughs of sombrous green. . . .
>
> (68–70)

The lines intriguingly refigure and repeat the "little Horse" scene's poignant "sharp Hawthorn," through which the wind "whistling pass'd," and the nearby "poor flocks" of sheep. In this way the episode similarly alludes to the father's death and his son's troubled mourning, representing its trauma of "lost" homes and haunted poetic recollections. The poem depicts death, and the distinct problem of mourning it initiates, as an inspiring ghost that haunts the Hamlet-like poet, "smit[ing]" his minstrel's harp with the "dismal sound" of "sighs" and "dismal song[s]," repeating a ghostly poetry. According to Jonathan Wordsworth, "the Spectre of *The Vale of Esthwaite* lives on the other side of the border; he is a ghost, but like Hamlet's father, whom he frequently recalls, he is a troubled one."[42] As in Wordsworth's later Salisbury Plain poems, this first episode presents a poetry haunted and "thrill[ed]" by the dead, and for the very reason that the poet owes to them more than he can give. Such a poetics is the product of a following after the dead, through a "shadowy world" reproduced by a binding that is also a bearing, repeated "Far Far" from the mourning and the dead it seeks. It is a burden whose payment in representation structures the text we read, guiding the poem toward its social vision of self and other, in which the mourned dead tentatively serve as the foundation for a promissory kind of community.

Episode four contains an important additional detail: the poet's elegiac contemplation of the grave's promise of immortal reunion ("I soon shall be with them that rest" [303]) and of the relationship it effects between mourner and mourned: "Ah pour upon the spot a tear" (323). Following his recollection of paternal loss, the speaker rallies himself with the consolation that he and his father "again shall meet" (297). For, he says, often when

> from afar the midnight bell
> Flings on mine ear its solemn knell[,]
> A still voice whispers to my breast
> I soon shall be with them that rest.
>
> Then, may one [*some*] kind an[d] pious friend
> Assiduous o'er my body bend.
> Once might I see him turn aside
> The kind unwilling tear to hide[,]
> And may—
>
> (300–8)

In this homiletic, consolatory scene the "knell" leads to thoughts of mortality and of the restoration of lost presence. Yet, although this promise is entertained, what dominates the poet's vision of mortality in this section is the churchyard landscape, whose images draw upon lines from Gray's "Elegy." Wordsworth's poet envisions his friend bending over his grave in "pious" acts observed by the dead. The scene readily calls to mind one of Dorothy Wordsworth's later journal entries, describing how in a trench in John's Grove she and William

> lay still, and unseen by one another; he thought that it would be as sweet thus to lie so in the grave, to hear the *peaceful* sounds of the earth, and just to know that our dear friends were near.[43]

Sister and brother envision the grave as a site where the dead remain engaged in viewing mourners' acts of remembrance. In the *Vale* the poet's consoling thought that he will see his friend bend over his grave suggests a similar living-on, in which the deceased, bound to a grave and locale, exists as a resting body and a surviving surveillant mind (the implication is that to "be with them that rest" is to find both "sleep" *and* waking while in "peace beneath a green grass heap" [315]). The dead are in topographical and spiritual proximity to the living, not just as corpses but as listening, seeing, potentially demanding presences haunting the living with their hopes and desires for tribute.

Rather like in "We are Seven," the churchyard in the *Vale* integrates these consecrated "heap[s]" of the surveying dead into a social topography of children, friends, and family:

> What from the social chain can tear
> This bosom link'd for ever there
> Which feels where'er the hand of pain
> Touches this heav'n connected chain[,]
> Feels quick as thought the electric thrill
> Feels it ah me—and shudders still.
> While bounteous Heav'n shall Fleming leave
> Of Friendship [what] can me bereave[?]
>
> (388–95)

Landon and Curtis find no literary source for Wordsworth's image of this "electric" social chain, but ponder that the detail might bear some relation to the theory of the Great Chain of Being, "while signifying more specifically the 'social chain' linking man to man and especially, in this context, friend to friend" (*EPF* 454). They also rightly remark Dorothy's quotation of this line in a letter to Jane Pollard, in which she comments that "[n]either absence nor Distance nor Time can ever break the Chain that links me to my Brothers" (*EY* 88). In the *Vale*, death exposes a still wider "heav'n connected chain" binding together the living and the dead—a chain depicted in a subsequent extract as "world encircling." That "social chain" is described in terms that recall Episode one's "thrilling chill" of the Phantom's "smit[ing]" of the minstrel's harp, Episode two's "icy chain," and Episode three's "shrill" and "dire" sounds from the Spectre's "lyre." These *thrills* of death reveal to the poet the bond's existence as well as the mutability of the links of its chain. The reader is informed, moreover, that "loitering" children may impiously "disturb the holy ground" in the churchyard, violating the graves' sod with their footsteps (318–21) and thereby repeating, in displaced form, the poet's own lack of sufficient paternal reverence, while also making needed just such acts of pious caretaking.

This churchyard topography blends together the impious young's uninhibited play among the dead and the pious elders' commemoration of these same dead, making the intercessions of the friend necessary and, so long as the young remain forgetfully impious, in need of repeating. That the recollected or imagined dead are retrospectively or prospectively envisioned as desiring remembrance would seem in itself to attest to the insufficiency of their "rest" and to their need for supplementary intercessions. No wonder, then, that a mourner might feel their presence as expectant onlookers. The churchyard establishes or emblematizes this connection between the living and dead but also implies the lingering pains of such relationship, rising from loss and mediation, from thwarted desires, and from feelings of insufficiency regarding mourning and remembrance. Such lasting connection between the living and the mourned dead, and among the living themselves, finds in the churchyard its locale for a chain that binds the dead to the living and, potentially—and in the *Vale* only implicitly—the living to one another as indebted mourners. They mourn, owing their mourning as quasi-suffrages to the dead, who may or may not survey them but whose loss is felt, grieved over, and imparted all the same. Death and its dead create a desire for grief: not just for one's own (poetry is in a sense that already) but for another's, as well as for the other's grief for oneself. The *Vale* poet seeks an elegiac and communitarian "social chain" of mournful others and of "lingering look[s]" (359), his poem in this way envisioning a lineage of survivors recurrently tied to loss and to that loss's "world of shades."

Nevertheless, *The Vale of Esthwaite* hardly seems to end on an optimistic communitarian note, for its conclusion returns the poet to a subterranean, crypt-like place:

> And that full soon must I resign
> To delve in Mammon's joyless mine[.]
>
> Your hollow echoes only moan
> To toil's loud din or sorrow's groan[.]
>
> (AP V, 13–16)

The biographical event described is Wordsworth's imminent departure for Cambridge, and in particular his rejection of advice from his relations to concentrate on more practical matters than poetry (chiefly the law), substituting Mammon for art. But in terms of the poem's thematics, the speaker's "resign[ed]" descent to a "joyless mine" signals the narrative's return to the grief of its previous subterranean allegories. As the Miltonic allusion to the devil Mammon suggests, this last descent advances the prospect of mining such veins of gold to forge an infernal society of the dead.[44] And, to judge from the *Vale* poet's experience, the hidden coffered ore of such society, both of its foundations and of its social bonds, is grief: the lingering, interminable character of "Sweet Melancholy blind / The moonlight of the Poet's mind" (5–6).

In *Home at Grasmere* Wordsworth likens his poetic investigation "into the mind of Man" to a descent into "The darkest Pit / Of the profoundest Hell" (*HG*, MS. B, ll. 989, 984–85). The analogy is apposite, for it implies that the prerequisite for his poetics—its "haunt" (990) and what it is haunted by—is an Orphic *katabasis* to recover a "living [Elysian] home" crafted by the "delicate spirits" of the dead (991–97). To be a poet is to descend or to desire to descend into the grave. Yet, at the same time, neither *Home at Grasmere* nor *The Vale of Esthwaite* reduces death merely to a problem of language as "prison-house"; nor does the *Vale* reduce its mourning only to a "linguistic predicament" of difference or indeterminacy underlying some mystified poetics of retrieval.[45] For the *Vale*'s foundations of poesis are rooted in mourning the dead, requiring not just death but an experience of loss that is not reducible to language and mediation. Figuration accentuates and perpetuates such originary loss, as an echo that is never quite the thing itself nor ever just an echo. It is a mournful economy that makes poems not just possible but necessary, as the products of a burden neither silently nor singly to be borne.

Although the poet figure of the *Vale* nonetheless remains to some extent isolated and confused about his status, the poems Wordsworth composes over the next few years will come closer to imagining a "spiritual community" structured between "the living and the dead." As subsequent chapters show, mournful narrative increasingly becomes a meeting place of sorts, where tributes of grief are exchanged as the currency of community. At Cambridge, Wordsworth will especially begin to envision the ways in which an "awful grief" can proffer salutary "social rays." By the time of his graduation and departure, the poet's implicit paradigm of community will nearly be complete.

2

Grief and Dwelling in the
Cambridge Poems,
including *An Evening Walk*

An unknown power connects him with the dead.
—*Descriptive Sketches*

As Mary Moorman observes, Wordsworth's leather-bound Hawkshead note-book (MS. 2) "went with him to Cambridge" (*WW* 86). So did his develop-ing sociology. Tucked in his bags with the notebook was *The Vale of Esthwaite* (MS. 3) and likely a few pages containing other of his Hawkshead works, including "On the death of an unfortunate Lady," "Sonnet written by M^r _____ immediately after the death of his Wife," and "Ballad." We can-not know just how much Wordsworth continued to work on *The Vale of Esth-waite*; his dating of the poem to "Spring and Summer 1787" (*EPF* 76) attests at least to its relative completion. But his interest in the poem clearly con-tinued as he now set about reducing the long narrative to a series of "extracts." His interest in death and mourning continued unabated, as well, as writings in the leather notebook evince: notably "Dirge Sung by a Min-strel" (for a boy), one of two such dirges composed during his first months at Cambridge. In the notebook he also recorded "A Tale" (whose grief-mad-dened woman anticipates figures of the Salisbury Plain poems and *The Ruined Cottage*), the previously completed "Ballad," two epitaphs, and the bulk of *Various Extracts* from the *Vale*.[1] In two other contemporary manu-scripts, he translated Virgil's "Orpheus and Eurydice" (MS. 5) and Moschus's elegy, "Lament for Bion" (MS. 7).

As this list of titles suggests, the sense (and the sensibility) of grief that had dominated Wordsworth's Hawkshead poetry continued to shape his poetic and social vision at Cambridge. And this list does not include the most important, and surely the most impressive, of the poet's college-era writings: his four so-called Evening Sonnets and his first significant published poems, the topographical diptych *An Evening Walk* (1788–93) and *Descriptive Sketches* (1792–93). Taken together, they and his other Cambridge works reveal signs of Wordsworth's poetic maturation and of the development of his social views. Notably, there is now an increasing emphasis upon a social desire for dwelling—not so surprising, perhaps, given Wordsworth's recent departure from the Tyson cottage and his brothers' company, his disappointment with school life at Cambridge, and political events on the world stage.

Yet, in a period rife with talk of revolution and of reform, Wordsworth's Cambridge poems have little to say about politics, excepting *An Evening Walk*'s mention of the past war with America and a few such lines in *Descriptive Sketches*. Although almost certainly inspired by the French Revolution, the latter poem's decrial of oppression and its praise of liberty, freedom, and justice noticeably skirt recent continental history, and may be read as suggesting the impact more of Wordsworth's reading than of the explosion of revolution. At the same time, however, the decrials and social interests of the Cambridge poems suggest their timeliness: the extent to which they respond to ideas and problems both in Wordsworth's personal life and in British society. These college writings focus upon isolated human figures affected by the era's economic and social changes, upon landscapes that promise to heal the wounds of alienation and melancholy, and, finally, as an emerging and increasing concern, upon the foundations of society. In these works, Wordsworth's desire to articulate fundamental bonds of social cohesion really begins to make itself felt, advancing from the shadows of the poems' picturesque landscape details— from the Lakes to the Alps—to glimpse the first "social rays" of mourning.

I. The Evening Sonnets' "Magic Path"

Likely composed between 1789 and 1791, the four Evening Sonnets[2] follow in the sonnet and nocturne traditions, echoing William Bowles's recently published *Fourteen Sonnets* and in fact borrowing the poems' rhyme scheme. They also reveal the influence of Charlotte Smith's popular *Elegiac Sonnets* (1784–89), Helen Maria Williams's vogue sonnets in *Poems* (1786), Milton's *Il Penseroso,* Thomson's *The Seasons,* and William Collins's and Joseph Warton's respective odes to evening (*EPF* 676)—to list only the most prominent literary works. But as much as the sonnets show Wordsworth glancing behind, they also show him looking ahead.

Wordsworth's Evening Sonnet IV, "How rich in front with twilight's
tinge impressed," is best known in its revised form in *Lyrical Ballads,* under the
title "Lines written near Richmond, upon the Thames, at Evening." For the
volume's second edition the text was divided in two and retitled "Lines written when sailing in a boat at evening" and "Lines written near Richmond
upon the Thames," still later titled "Remembrance of Collins. . . ."[3] The original version probably dates from the second half of 1789, the date assigned it
in *Poetical Works* (1836–37), although Cornell editors Carol Landon and Jared
Curtis conjecture the poem could have been composed as late as the latter part
of 1791, when Wordsworth graduated from Cambridge (*EPF* 684). The only
surviving text of this poem is recorded, sans a final couplet, in the Racedown
Notebook (MS. 11), and so may contain some later, minor revisions from
1793–95. Thinking back to his sonnet's origins, Wordsworth recalled that the
poem had arisen from his "solitary walk on the Banks of the Cam," but that
he had later shifted its setting to that of "the Thames, near Windsor" (*FN* 36).
That locale was certainly the more appropriate one given the sonnet's conspicuous nod to Collins's "Ode Occasioned by the Death of Mr Thomson,"
Thomson having been buried near the Thames, at Richmond.

The scene described in Wordsworth's elegiac sonnet is, as in Collins, a
river at dusk, along which a lone man gently rows a boat. From the shore a
"dreaming loiterer," the poem's speaker, watches the boat's easy progress:

> How rich in front[—]with twilight's tinge impressed
> Between the dim-brown forms impending high[,]
> Of [s]hadowy forests slowly sweeping by[—]
> Glows the still wave, while facing the red west
> The silent boat her magic path pursues
> Nor heeds how dark the backward wave the while
> Some dreaming loiterer with perfidious smile
> Alluring onward[,] such the fairy views
> In [   ] colouring clad that smile before
> The poet [thoughtless] of the following shad[es.]
> Witness that son of grief who in these glades
> Mourned his dead friend[—]suspend the dashing oar
> That[4]

As in the poems culled from this sonnet, Wordsworth's image of the oar
alludes to Collins's ode of remembrance and commemoration, specifically to
its plea to "oft suspend the dashing oar / To bid his [Thomson's] gentle spirit
rest."[5] But there is something much more mysterious and more interesting
going on in Sonnet IV than a poetical nod to Collins or to Wordsworth's
enduring grief. For in Wordsworth's poem the poetically emblematic boat,

akin to Dante's *barca*, is, as Duncan Wu observes, "navigated by 'magic' . . . towards some otherworldly destination" of its own, in an advancing darkness that seems to be "not exterior to the experience but integral to it."[6] The sonnet's wording indeed suggests that these "following shad[es]" are what conduct the boat along its "magic path," as a phenomenal, empowering force looming "suspend[ed]" between the observer and what he observes.

How to explain such shadowy "magic"? The answer lurks in the speaker's temporal and psychological suspension between ignorance and awareness. Having before been "thoughtless of the following shad[es]," now, in the diagetic present, he becomes sufficiently conscious of them to narrate and critique that past thoughtlessness. As in the *Vale*, these looming shades are not just shadows but ghosts of the (un)remembered dead, and herein lurks the source of the boat's and the poem's "magic." Wu, who also reads these shades as ghosts, recalls a telling line scrawled by Wordsworth on the inside cover of his notebook: "the dead friend is present in his *shade*," likely adapted from Rogers's *The Pleasures of Memory* ("the lost friend still lingers in his shade").[7] Another of the notebook's fragments describes the dead persisting as ghostly shades in twilight shadows: "the Spectres are busy in shrouding the vale with wan white mist, shrieking and wailing and every dreary hou[r] is heard the solemn knell of the Curfew" (*EPF* 551).[8] In Wordsworth's sonnet the dead's lingering shades, and the responses they incite, are the haunting "magic" that powers the poem and that underlies its depicted elegist's actions, as is clarified by his ostensibly unmotivated turn, at the fragmentary sonnet's end, to "that son of grief," Collins.

This turn to a past mourner is in one sense of course a highly textual, intertextual one, in which description—the seeing or hearing or writing of an oar—echoes a previous text's trope of suspension as tribute. The allusion helps to explain the poem's seemingly non sequitur leap from the perceived scene to thoughts of that "son of grief." On the one hand, this leap may be read as associative: the raised oar simply recalls a similar past oar-raising qua rite, coloring the elegist's perceptions of the boat and shadows even before the turn is itself apparent. On the other hand, however, one may view that leap as motivated rather than as haphazardly associative: initiated by the speaker's grief, which precedes his visit to the darkening glades. "[M]ore is meant than meets the ear," Milton declares in *Il Penseroso*.[9] By this account, the poet's turn to Collins occurs because he, too, mourns a "dead friend" made "present" to him in haunting shades. Far from being "thoughtless," he is, through his ex post facto representation of thoughtlessness (set in contrast to pious grief and tribute), instead a thoughtful "witness" to grief and to its acts of memorialization. Those hints of motivation suggest that his fraternal turn to the other son arises from an impulse not just to grieve but also to amend or supplement his own previous lapses of grief. Fraternity, much in the air given the Revolution's grand triad of guiding principles, is the communitarian result—at least the elegiac prospect—of this magical recursive path of mourning and tribute.

Two other of the Evening Sonnets lend support to such a reading of the poet's grief and to its social significance. The first of these texts, Sonnet I in the Cornell edition, is reproduced from Wordsworth's leather-bound notebook and probably dates from the period 1789–90. It has a setting consistent with that described in Sonnet IV and serves as something of a sequel, detailing the subsequent twilight of the river scene and its boat. My interest is focused principally upon the closing couplet, which presents yet another non sequitur leap, apparently sparked by the speaker's hearing of those echoing sounds of the now "unseen oar":

> When slow from pensive twilight's latest gleams
> "O'er the dark mountain top descends the ray"
> That stains with crimson tinge the water grey
> And still, I listen while the dells and streams
> And vanish'd woods a lulling murmur make;
> As Vesper first begins to twinkle bright
> And on the dark hillside the cottage light,
> With long reflexion streams across the lake.—
> The lonely grey-duck, darkling on his way,
> Quaakes clamourous—deep the measur'd strokes rebound
> Of unseen oar parting with hollow sound
> While the slow curfew shuts the eye of day—
> Sooth'd by the stilly scene with many a sigh
> Heaves the full heart nor knows for whom, or why—

The sounds the poem's speaker describes are, as Wu states, ones "whose sources can only be inferred: the oar is 'unseen,' as is the lonely duck, which, like the nightingale in Milton's Eden, 'Sings darkling.'"[10] The scene's aural effects are disconnected from their "vanish'd" sources. Because of these sounds and picturesque sights, even because of their separated or lost status, the speaker's heart heaves "with many a sigh"—for whom or for what, and for what reason, he cannot say. He is the familiar, already prototypical, Wordsworthian melancholic or *penseroso* who wanders amid a landscape that brings both relief and unrest, the latter owed to a grief that is "clamourous" and yet "unseen," like the locodescription it inspires. His grief's eruption indeed suggests that the sonnet's presentation of landscape detail is *guided* by his looming grief. This causal relationship transforms the natural scene's details into allegorical sighs—psychological signs—of a mourning that exceeds the poet's depicted consciousness but that also unconsciously determines it. Filled with a "darkling" grief, his heart overflows with sighs that, like the "unseen oar parting with hollow sound," are empty and yet profoundly commemorative, representing a grief once submerged and now clamorously recalled, overflowing in perceptions and markedly psychological verse.

The third Evening Sonnet, "On the [   ] village Silence sets her seal," circa 1788–91,[11] was first printed anonymously in the *Morning Post* of February 13, 1802, under the title "Written at Evening" (with the opening line "Calm is all nature as a resting wheel"), and then revised and republished as "Written in very early Youth" in *Poems, in Two Volumes* (1807). It, too, takes up the topic of inspiring yet ambivalently registered grief, and does so in a manner that further establishes the composing poet's grief and its effects. I quote the text from line five, omitting the locodescriptive opening:

> a timely slumber seems to steal
> O'er vale and mountain; now while ear and eye
> Alike are vacant what strange harmony,
> Homefelt and homecreated[,] seems to heal
> That grief for which my senses still supply
> Fresh food. [For never but when Memory
> Is hush'd, am I at peace: M]y friends[,] restrain
> Those busy cares that must renew my pain[:]
> Go rear the [sensitive] plant—quick shall it feel
> The fond officious touch and droop again.[12]

In the growing darkness, as "the last lights die," the speaker's senses are obscured, with nearby "kine" now only "obscurely seen" (2–3). The "fresh food" that had fed his grief is withdrawn with the light, but such sensory suspension only "*seems* to heal," quieting his perceptions and darkening his memory for the time, albeit with the certain knowledge that grief must return. Indeed, grief is still present as a memory of past grief. To perceive is here to remember, and to remember is to grieve.

Between the poem's original composition and its publication in *Poems*, Wordsworth would revise the phrase "must renew my pain" to its opposite, "would allay my pain," implying that the "busy cares" of the world are mere distractions from the "strange harmony" of grief, even of the "homecreated" desire for the company of friends such griefs provoke. In the revised text these "cares" are to be shunned, but not because they reinvoke pain; rather, they are to be shunned because they could eliminate or tranquilize that pain. These contradictory revisions underline the ambivalent character of tributary legacies. Both versions of the poem suggest that it is grief as much as its suspension that provides this harmony of tension and relaxation, remembering and forgetting, tranquillity and painful tribute. As Wu observes, this "strange harmony" derives "from forces beyond" the poet,[13] muse-like forces (like the *Vale's* "world of shades") of a liminal grief, a play of presence and absence that inspires and guides the poem's excursive narrative. In this way, Sonnet III, like Evening Sonnets I and IV, describes the condition not of being "hushed" or "at peace" but of being ill at ease: of answering and of answering to uncannily "homefelt" desires of grief and of a desire *for* grief, to which home and its social virtues will continue to be linked in Wordsworth's writings.

To return to Sonnet IV, one better sees in its text that to be a poet is to be a "son of grief": to be the heir of grief, one who, as the preposition "of" here implies, is born of and yet also separated from grief. In these sonnets the "harmony" of thoughtlessness and its memorial supplementation, of a grief responsive to its absence or lack, provides the basis for tribute and its payment to the "following" shades of the dead. In this sense, poetry in Evening Sonnet IV arises from one's grief at grief's absence, a mourning of absent or insufficient mourning, similar to that troubled mourning lamented in the *Vale*. Mourning the "following" dead, responding to the dead who haunt us, elicits the "magic" that conducts the poem's tributary vehicles. Unlike Shelley's *Adonais*, in which the dead await the elegiac poet's boat, here the dead—or, more precisely, the mourner's feelings for the dead—darkly drive it on.

Nor, finally, is poetry the sole product of this lapsed grief. Its "magic path" also founds a fraternity of grieving sons linked by their mourning and its patrimony of loss passed from deceased father to son (that women, too, participate in this "patrimony" becomes clear in *An Evening Walk* and its textual descendants). And in an important sense that fraternity is bequeathed from mourning itself. Mourning links the poet to other mourners—specifically to one other mourner—similarly virtuous in offering obsequies to the dead. In this way, mourning constitutes a community of bearers of the burdens of the dead, a community that will become more developed and more central in Wordsworth's mature works. In enlisting the tradition of elegy (the tradition of tradition, really, with all its inherent sense of lineage and fraternity), the Evening Sonnets manifest within their poetics the forms of mournful connection the poems "darkling" seek and that lurk and linger in the channels of Wordsworth's early writings. Mortal loss, and the desire it provokes, will likewise conduct Wordsworth's poet of *An Evening Walk*, leading him both to flee and to desire the "strange harmony" mourning produces, along with its "homefelt" dwellings and company.

II. "SOCIAL RAYS" IN *AN EVENING WALK*

Wordsworth composed *An Evening Walk* (1793) between October 1788 and the spring of 1790, before he left Cambridge for summer touring.[14] In the poet's estimation the poem then was "huddled up" with *Descriptive Sketches* and sent "into the world in so imperfect a state," with the hope that it nonetheless might show that its author "could do something" (*EY* 120). In the wake of its tepid reception, the author continued to revise the poem in 1794, in a cottage shared with Dorothy at Windy Brow. James Averill describes *The Vale of Esthwaite* as "a kind of proto-*Evening Walk*" (*EW* 3) and so implies that *An Evening Walk* is in some manner a *Vale* redux. So does Kenneth Johnston, and for good reason (*HW* 150). The poet of each narrative wanders through a darkening Lakeland landscape "in search of interesting poetic material" (*EW* 3), although of the two texts the *Vale* is more interested in the supernatural and macabre, *An Evening Walk* in the sentimental and quotidian.

Despite the fact that Wordsworth was just nineteen in the summer of 1789, *An Evening Walk* stands up, in Jonathan Wordsworth's estimation, as "an accomplished and professional late eighteenth-century poem . . . full of pleasurable allusion—to the Milton of *L'Allegro* and *Il Penseroso,* to Thomson's *Seasons,* to Gray, Collins, Goldsmith, and many lesser figures of the day."[15] One could add to the list Shakespeare, Spenser, Burns, Beattie, Langhorne, and Dyer. The poem also brims with picturesque detail and theory, influenced by William Gilpin's *Observations on the Picturesque Beauty in Cumberland and Westmoreland, 1786,* Thomas West's *Guide to the Lakes,* and James Clarke's *Survey of the Lakes of Cumberland.*[16] Stephen Gill argues that the text's "melancholy reflection on past and present," its depiction of a "mind accordant to the promptings of Nature," and even its "address to an absent loved one" are such common eighteenth-century tropes that one might indeed suspect the author to have "conceived of the poem's dominant tone just by turning the leaves of his favourite authors" (*WL* 42). At the same time, however, despite all this "poetical stock-in-trade," Gill finds *An Evening Walk* to be a credible depiction of Lakeland topography, "bringing into the compass of one imagined walk a survey of Lake District life, its occupations, its variety of wood and vegetation, its dangers as well as delights," and also "bringing into focus what were currently the most painful and inchoate aspects of Wordsworth's life" (43). In fact, Toby Benis argues that the poem significantly departs from conventional topographical writing "by introducing speakers who identify with traditionally ornamental homeless people, even as that identification arouses anxiety and physical danger."[17] Although the poem parades its literary influences boldly, at times awkwardly,[18] it reveals elements later fundamental to Wordsworthian community, elements that become more manifest, and manifestly political, in the Salisbury Plain poems.

An Evening Walk entered the world on January 29th, 1793, just eight days after Louis XVI's execution. The years of revolution that preceded the king's death likely account for the poem's few topical references to revolution and war, although these are only to the American Revolution and war of the previous decade. What motivated Wordsworth to mention this past struggle and not its current, news-making successor is unclear. It seems unlikely that he feared government reprisal (a more reasonable concern the following year of 1794).[19] It may simply be that until his sojourn in France in 1792, when he had already completed most of *An Evening Walk,* the Revolution had not yet fired his imagination. It also bears mention that although much of the poem was written two months after the Revolution's advent (*WCh* 7), the plan likely had been settled upon a year or more before. Hence, like other of the juvenilia, *An Evening Walk* responds to a largely pre-gallic crisis, perceived by the poem's author through the lens of a late eighteenth-century British culture of sensationalism and reform. The poem may not display its author's new political colors, but it nonetheless does reflect the fact that at the time he was, as Gill puts it, "under pressure from events which were beyond his control, grand happenings on the world stage which made his own anxieties seem both insignificant by contrast and yet also more intense" (*WL* 68).[20]

By 1793, when the poem was published along with *Descriptive Sketches,* the Revolution had been destabilized by foreign invasion and by internal division, and there were by then also personal circumstances with which Wordsworth had to reckon: his French mistress, Annette Vallon, was pregnant—a prospect that argued for career compromises on his part—he had no income or home, and he was now alienated from his only benefactors, the Cooksons (no doubt in part because of Annette), and hence in some measure also from Dorothy, the probable addressee of *Evening Walk.* In terms of domestic politics, what faith he had in English institutions and the old social order had been shaken by recent political events. It was enough to make anyone anxious or nostalgic and yearn for a better world. Enough even to prompt one to seek to "do something": to look, in a time of separation, alienation, and loss, to discover bonds to unite a disunited world. In such an enterprise Wordsworth followed sociopolitical revisionists like Rousseau, whose ideas resound in *Salisbury Plain.* But he also followed his own lead, drawing upon more intuited notions of connection based not on revolution and the new so much as on loss and restoration—themes explored in the Cambridge sonnets but given different shape in *An Evening Walk,* with envisioned social prospects that extend beyond those poems' more exclusive elegiac fraternities.

An Evening Walk's opening lines proclaim its catalogue of landscape details to be linked to the "memory of departed pleasures," and reveal its narrator's feeling of separation from "[f]air scenes" looked on (in lines that anticipate "Tintern Abbey") "with other eyes, than once" (*EW,* ll. 16–17). This sense of being alienated from a familiar topography is the result of the latter's defamiliarization by memories that, Geoffrey Hartman argues, remind the poet of past personal loss, despite the fact that "no vivid and *Prelude*-like retrospects occur" in the poem (*WP* 93).[21] The poet-speaker's return to Grasmere triggers the memory of youthful pleasures, when "no ebb of chearfulness

demand[ed] / Sad tides of joy from Melancholy's hand" (21–22), a time before
the tidal ebbing and mixing of joy and grief that now characterizes his experience. This decline of cheerfulness opens the floodgates for a melancholy joy
stemming from loss and grief and for a tale whose secret stores are conveyed
by the hand of melancholy. The mixed metaphors of sea and body, of natural
and anthropomorphic forces, also suggest something more, and not just their
author's inexperience: that these "tides" are hand-delivered *tidings* of sorrowful joy, elicited from loss and producing such excursions and histories as we
here read. Such tides are in a sense, then, also *tithings to* loss and to the elegiac sensibilities such loss inspires.

The poem's nostalgic remembrances are made the more poignant by
the aforementioned mutability of the recalled landscape, a terrain which
reveals that,

> Alas! the idle tale of man is found
> Depicted in the dial's moral round;
> With Hope Reflexion blends her *social rays*
> To gild the total tablet of his days;
> Yet still, the sport of some malignant Pow'r,
> He knows but from its shade the present hour.
>
> (37–42; emphasis added)

The poet's lamenting of the mediated nature of perceptions and thoughts
underlines a more important assumption: that the past looms as a "shade" coloring people's understanding of "the present hour," gilding the book-like
tablet of hopes (as the "hand" from which hopes and joys come). One may
usefully compare this passage with its prose predecessor, a fragment from the
same manuscript containing "Orpheus and Eurydice":

> Human Life is like the plate of a dial, hope brightens the future,
> Reflection the hour that is past—but the present is always mark'd
> with a shadow—
>
> (*EPF* 663; *PrW* 1: 10)

The fragment clarifies Wordsworth's main point above: that, as the dial's
shape suggests, the past is a "shade" that determines the present and its gilt
anticipations. Because of the allegorical character of this marker of life's
delimited round—a "tale" written in light and shade—as in the Cambridge
sonnets such *shade* is more than just the occlusion of daylight. It is the persisting, even "malignant," shade of one's past, specifically of those melancholy
losses and events that have bestowed one's shadow-marked identity. As in the

Vale and the Evening sonnets, in *An Evening Walk* the persistence of loss is the first cause and prime mover of "idle tale[s]." The "simplest sight" provokes from the poet "unbidden tear[s]" (49, 44) owed to his past and leading, as an alternative to static despondency, to the excursive "history" conveyed both in its stead and as the product of its empowering, haunting shade. For the narrated present is, by this model of the dial, always a history impending from the past and its histories.

And what a melancholy and suggestive "history of a poet's ev'ning" it is. At the outset the "wan noon" is "brooding," the clouds "deep" and "embattl'd"; beneath, in the late-day heat, herds gaze longingly on the "tempting shades" here "deny'd" them (53–57). "Unshaded" horses stare in "mute distress" while in the parklands even the free deer appear "troubl'd" (63–67). Such oppressive conditions oblige the poet, too, like the later narrator of *The Ruined Cottage,* to seek the "twilight shade" (80) until the sun "sinks behind the hill" (174). Thereupon, after witnessing how the local "Druid stones their lighted fane unfold" (171), he recalls having heard of other apparitions: of "desperate" horsemen upon the cliffs and hills, superstitiously observed by the inhabitants (which Wordsworth notes Clarke's guidebook "amus[ingly]" corroborates[22]). These advancing, pursuing, and retreating dead are literal and symbolic eruptions of a violent, death-filled history. As such, the shades again point, via the landscape, to the navigating force of the past and its shadowy dead in the poet's "history."

From this later point in the narrative, the poet presents a favorite local scene, a family of swans. They are animals seemingly secure from harm and care: "No ruder sound your desart haunts invades, / Than waters dashing wild, or rocking shades" (237–38). Yet the poet's observation in fact is a response to his perception of their safety *from* the sounds they hear of the "hound, the horse's tread, and mellow horn" (234), sounds that suggest the swans' vulnerability to hunting, later represented as a very real threat to the swans of *Home at Grasmere.* At his lonely excursion's midpoint this (in)secure domestic scene leads the poet to contrast the birds' relatively carefree, relatively unthreatened life to the harsh existence of those "hapless human wanderers" compelled to throw their "young on winter's winding sheet of snow" (239–40). Such is the hard lot of a nearby vagrant mother widowed by the American war.

Having seen these same swans and "call'd the[m] bless'd," she must travel on through the storm; one

> Who faint, and beat by summer's breathless ray,
> Hath dragg'd her babes along this weary way;
> While arrowy fire extorting feverish groans
> Shot stinging through her stark o'erlabour'd bones.
> —With backward gaze, lock'd joints, and step of pain,

> Her seat scarce left, she strives, alas! in vain,
> To teach their limbs along the burning road
> A few short steps to totter with their load . . .
> And bids her soldier come her woes to share,
> Asleep on Bunker's charnel hill afar. . . .
>
> (242–50, 253–54)

This maternal "wretch," whom the poet proceeds to contemplate at length, is, like her important successor in *Salisbury Plain,* a figure of homelessness and social alienation, forced to wander over "the lightless heath, / Led by Fear's cold wet hand, and dogg'd by Death" (285–86). She desperately clasps her children to her breast and shouts (sensationalistically, á la Lear) to the storm, "Now ruthless Tempest launch thy deadliest dart! / Fall fires—but let us perish heart to heart" (291–92). Hers is no pleasant evening excursion like the poet's but the dark socioeconomic underside of Lakeland life, nature, and wandering.

In a note to the revised text of *An Evening Walk,* Wordsworth reports that the episode "relate[s] the catastrophe of a poor woman who was found dead on Stanemoor . . . with two children whom she had in vain attempted to protect from the storm" (p. 148). Whether or not based in historical fact (Averill finds no record of the event), the scene clearly draws upon contemporary fictional accounts of destitute widows and vagrants, particularly Langhorne's *Country Justice* and Joseph Warton's *Ode to Fancy,* both of which Wordsworth may have read at Hawkshead.[23] Mary Jacobus contends that *An Evening Walk* indeed represents the female beggar "in terms of grotesquely exaggerated torment—first burning, then freezing"—depicting not a real contemporary beggar but instead only Wordsworth's "distance from his subject."[24] Such suffering figures of course are typical of eighteenth-century topographical poetry, which Averill argues "exploit[s] material only too available in the wretches who wandered the countryside" (*PHS* 63). But although the poet no doubt in part drew his vagrant from stock representations in Langhorne and Warton as well as in Knox, Thomson, and Smollet, his use of this shelterless beggar figure (who, Benis points out, does *not* beg[25]) is more than simply a capitulation to some generic topos, as his note to the revised text affirms. Indeed, Alan Liu reads both the swans and the beggar woman as "characters whose full-scale treatment stands out strikingly in a poem where other entities are fortunate to deserve a single verse."[26] The vagrant, "always threatening to emerge through the [text's] surface of repose,"[27] notably occupies over sixty of the narrative's four hundred-plus lines, unlike any other observed figure, prospect, or event.

The poet's account continues with his imagining of the vagrant mother and her children's plight in the growing darkness:

I see her now, deny'd to lay her head,
On cold blue nights, in hut or straw-built shed;
Turn to a silent smile their sleepy cry,
By pointing to a shooting star on high:
I hear, while in the forest depth he sees,
The Moon's fix'd gaze between the opening trees,
In broken sounds her elder grief demand,
And skyward lift, like one that prays, his hand,
If, in that country, where he dwells afar,
His father views that good, that kindly star;
—Ah me! all light is mute amid the gloom,
The interlunar cavern of the tomb.

(257–68)

"[D]eny'd to lay her head," the vagrant leads a life of forced wandering, lamenting the absence of her soldier husband, whose uncertain status—asleep or dead upon Bunker Hill—leaves her, too, in an uncertain position, as fully neither wife nor widow. The indeterminate status of the absent beloved will become a significant aspect in Wordsworth's articulation of mournful community in *The Ruined Cottage,* although it here seems to be presented as yet another pathetic detail. The scene is one of marked social failure, in the tradition of Langhorne's and others' protest poetry: the failure of a colonial policy that ends in war and of national, regional, and local policies that end up producing the neglect and dislocation of war widows like the vagrant. "For hope's deserted well why wistful look?" the poet asks her (and his readers) via biblical imagery from Ecclesiastes, "Chok'd is the pathway, and the pitcher broke" (255–56).

According to Liu, Wordsworth wishes "to describe a landscape in repose; but in the slips, swerves, and stutterings of his poem, he regresses to landscape haunted by story."[28] That story is not only of the American war and of the English widows and orphans it created, nor of the war's historical analogue in the French Revolution, nor only of lower-class impoverishment during the war years and in the several years of the poem's composition. It is also, as just mentioned, a story from Ecclesiastes, to which the image of the broken pitcher alludes and which the poet will revisit in *The Ruined Cottage* a few years later (a related allusion to a "golden bowl," from this same portion of Ecclesiastes, also appears in *Descriptive Sketches*). The passage, from the twelfth chapter, refers to old age and to times of scarcity and social adversity, when "mourners go about the streets" and "the pitcher is broken at the fountain" (12:5–6).[29] They are days when prosperity ebbs and the waters that had nourished and united people have become dried up. Community has collapsed, save for the actions of peripatetic mourners. Wordsworth's allusion thus subtly implies social decline, when "the doors on the street are shut" and "the sound of the grinding [of grain] is low" (12:4); a time when, in the wake not just of decrepitude but of social and economic depravation, man longs to go "to his long home" (12:5). One recalls the similar wording of the *Vale*'s "long long home." Such is the poet's desire, and certainly the vagrant's: she who is denied a place "to lay her head" by the absence of dwellings, human compassion, and the sort of social safety net later proclaimed in "The Old Cumberland Beggar" to be woven together only by a real community. But, aside from peace and charity or the good fortune of a home, does Wordsworth's poet reveal or even glimpse any reasonable means of restoring such lapsed or failed community as the vagrant's "broken" plight reveals?

The poem's poet is driven by his lingering feelings of loss and by his gilded desire for a cottage and the company of his "friend" (419); such is the basic "round" or "bound" of his evening walk. That grief leads him to iden-tify with the vagrant and her history, something unparalleled in Wordsworth's poetry up to this time, excepting his Evening Sonnet's turn to Collins, but that will come to typify his art in the Salisbury Plain poems, *The Ruined Cottage,* and "Resolution and Independence." While by no means himself a vagrant, having the luxury of a melancholy "joy" of wandering, this poet is depicted as being at least able to feel some of the anguish the vagrant experiences languishing over loss and wishing her husband would return, "her woes to *share.*" Like the poet's, her history arises out of a shadowy round of loss. And he is drawn to her tragedy not only because he wanders in the same landscape but also because he is himself in some measure enabled by loss to share her grief. His narrative of the vagrant family's "moral round" of travail ends as elegy, lamenting the sad yet noble history of the homeless mother and children's death from exposure, unaided and alone in a beguil-ingly beautiful landscape.

From her plight the poet retreats to the "Sweet . . . sounds that mingle from afar, / Heard by calm lakes, as peeps the folding star" (301–2). Her suf-fering and history now seem to vanish from his thoughts, leaving one to won-der if his meditations on her life and death were, along with his protestations against social injustice and inequality, but set pieces for an eighteenth-century melancholy wanderer. Or were they, as Liu argues, eruptions of history in a narrative of denial? One might well wonder were it not for the passion with which Wordsworth has invested her story, for the number of lines expended on her history, and for the poet-speaker's "vacant gloom" and the "shuddering tear[s]" he continues to express after her death. In fact, two lines that shortly follow the scene are intriguingly ambiguous in this regard: "While, by the scene compos'd, the breast subsides, / Nought wakens or disturbs it's tranquil tides" (309–10). The subsiding "breast" of course chiefly refers to the poet's troubled state. But it also alludes, and arguably cannot help alluding, to the frozen "breast" of the vagrant described nine lines before. What is so intriguing about these lines, then, as John Williams observes, "is the way in which Wordsworth—perhaps subconsciously—has left the presence of the dying woman hovering over the formal tranquility of th[is] latter section."[30] From this vantage the poet's looming yet unspecified grief is given a potential object and source in the death of another, a death that in turn awakens in the poet-mourner some half-forgotten grief. In this way, the scene of the vagrant marks a significant development for Wordsworth's implicit sociology, as will become clearer in the next chapter's reading of the Salisbury Plain poems.

That landscape to which the poet of *An Evening Walk* returns is a haunting play of light and shade, where sadness threatens as before to erupt: "still the tender, vacant gloom remains, / Still the cold cheek its shuddering tear retains" (387–88). Out of such "vacant gloom" over loss and death arise the poet's desires for dwelling, companionship, "history," and epistolary address:

> —Ev'n now she [Hope] decks for me a distant scene,
> (For dark and broad the gulph of time between)
> Gilding that cottage with her fondest ray,
> (Sole bourn, sole wish, sole object of my way;
> How fair it's lawns and silvery woods appear!
> How sweet it's streamlet murmurs in mine ear!)
> Where we, my friend, to golden days shall rise. . . .
>
> (413–19)

The poet's consciousness stems from and continues to develop through hauntings from the past, a past now opened to more recent events and deaths. The repetitive, circuitous "round" of the dial again signifies the extent to which consciousness is defined by an unlit past of loss. Wordsworth's ostensibly hackneyed text formulates a peculiar and particular subjectivity, one different from the philosophical, resilient *penseroso* and from that of the more static melancholic of Gray. For Wordsworth's subject is bound and illuminated by his own past of grief. This new consciousness is moreover a social one, defined by its sense not just of loss but also of the "social rays" of sympathy. The poem's is a "homeward way" (434). But although it is founded upon what for Wordsworth will remain among the most cohesive and consistent of social forces, this "way" is, for the time, mostly a gesture *toward* shared loss, shared mourning, and shared histories. As Benis states, "he is homeward bound," but to a home that for now "can only be imagined . . . as a 'distant scene.'"[31] This symbolic social gesture is suitably underlined by the poem's epistolary frame of address to a "friend," presumed to be Dorothy. In an important sense, it is a "way" that, for all its desires, remains solitary and dislocated. But Wordsworth's social-elegiac history of the vagrant nonetheless operates to urge discursive exchange and foster desired connection to a friend with whom the poet would like to dwell. This structure of Wordsworthian community, now nearly formed, becomes further articulated in *An Evening Walk*'s revision the next year.

III. "An Awful Grief": *An Evening Walk* of 1794 and *Descriptive Sketches*

Wordsworth accomplished his first revision of *An Evening Walk* in that longed-for cottage shared with Dorothy, overlooking Lake Derwentwater at Windy Brow. Unlike the MS. 9 revisions, which provide the text for the Cornell edition's "Expanded Version of 1794," these MS. 10 additions can be dated with reasonable certainty. With regard to the former revisions, John O. Hayden argues, to my mind persuasively, that the MS. 9 writings, dated by Averill and others to 1794, be given a revised date of spring 1798 or even later.[32] Until a more convincing argument for 1794 comes along, I defer to this dating and, because I am interested in the development of Wordsworth's views of community, the following pages restrict their scope to the spring 1794 MS. 10 revisions of *An Evening Walk*, most of which differ little from the later version. According to Averill, these Windy Brow revisions are especially significant because in them the 1793 text's conventional locodescription becomes a *paysage moralisé* (*EW* 14).[33] In fact, their ostensible innovations are a return to the allegorical *paysage* of the *Vale* and, in some measure, to the implicit "moral round" of the 1793 text of *An Evening Walk*. In innovating, Wordsworth draws upon and draws out meanings and prospects implicit in his early verse. Most illuminating about these revisions is the manner in which the narrator's grief now more clearly has a cause—a mortal, death-related cause—arising "in mortal minds from mortal change" (*EW*, p. 161).[34] The Windy Brow additions in this way make explicit the 1793 version's looming sense of mortal loss and grief, helping readers to spot the poem's emerging communitarian horizons.

In the MS. 10 text of *An Evening Walk* "an awful grief" conveys "passions, of a wider range," into the speaker's mind, leading him to wander, "conducted," as in the *Vale,*

> by some powerful hand unseen
> Led where grey cots unfrequent intervene[,]
> I seek that footworn spot of level ground between
> Close by the school within the churchyard[']s bound[,]
> Through every race of them who near are laid
> For children[']s sports kept sacred from the spade[;]

> Such the smooth plot that skirts the mouldering rows
> Of Graves where Grasmere[']s rustic sons repose. . . .
>
> (161)

The course taken by the poet, guided by this "hand unseen," leads him along paths where "many a scattered hut . . . unfrequent intervene[s]" to the morally and mortally leveling sacred ground of the churchyard (161). His trek past gray huts to "mouldering rows / Of Graves" takes him into a topography not unlike the *Vale*'s. His "awful grief" similarly urges and conveys him into the proximity of those of "Grasmere's rustic sons" who "repose" in the earth, amid a topography "skirt[ed]" by dwellings. In some respects this of course is a traditional enough depiction of human mortality, reminiscent of such eighteenth-century authors as Gray, to whose Eton College Ode these lines allude. Where better to contemplate death than in a rural churchyard, among "tribes of youth" unaware "how near / Their sensible warm motion [is] allied / To the dull [earth] that crumbled at their side" (161)? The topography of huts and graves connects terrestrial and subterranean demographies in a mortal pageant from youthful ignorance to the awareness of death and finally to mortal decline and admission into the local fraternity of reposing sons. The poet's grief over "mortal change" evokes recollections of his own prior, youthful ignorance of mortality and mutability, with the churchyard serving as a perfect setting for just such graveyard-schoolish meditations, especially given its enticing prospect of "little victims" for whom, Gray famously observed, "'Tis folly to be wise."[35]

A second scenario, however, locates the objects of the poet's desire in these huts and graves themselves and in the corporate whole they compose in the topography's interrelating of the living (the innocent playing children and adult cottagers) and the dead of Grasmere. The "grey cots" by this reckoning find a place in the poet's excursion because they "intervene" in it as desired objects—objects connected to the churchyard. The topography signifies connection to the dead and to the dwellings they provide the living, as the mournful center around which the circumference of skirting huts has sprung. The poet describes this interlinked world of living and dead, and the communal proximity of the dead to human dwelling, as an "endless chain / Of Joy & grief[,] of pleasure and of pain" (163).[36] Like the hub of a wheel or dial, the dead are the point from which other desirous projections stem. They are the "domestic train" or chain of "care[s]" to be "duly share[d]" (163) between dwellers on the skirting margin of the dead. And it is these dead, and mourners' mourning of these dead, that binds together the living.

More explicitly than in 1793, Wordsworth's 1794 text associates enduring grief with excursion and with the dead-oriented dwelling and connection it seeks. Yet, like that of its predecessor, *An Evening Walk*'s 1794 excursion is toward but not at a "home" and community. The poet does not linger near the vagrant's corpse, nor in subsequent lines does her death appear to occupy his thoughts more than in the 1793 text.[37] These developments lie in future works. At the same time, one finds in these revised lines both a trace of the interconnection of the living and the dead and a clearer sense that the "bourn" toward such interrelationship arises out of grief, even out of the mortality *of* such grief in "mortal minds" and their memories and feelings. That "round" of excursion leads back to the dead and to the dwellings they link and secure. Although the churchyard huts are here but a temporary stop along the poet's excursive path, now more than in previous poems such travel has community momentarily in sight: as that gilded cottage and its minimal, mournful society, the "sole bourn, sole wish, [and] sole object" of the poet's "homeward way."

This chapter concludes its own round with a brief consideration of *An Evening Walk*'s topographical companion, *Descriptive Sketches,* composed after Wordsworth's walking tour of the Continent. The poem is of less importance to the formation of Wordsworthian community but merits consideration for the sociological vistas it still presents, vistas with clearer social and political implications. Although intent upon describing Switzerland's sublime alpine scenes, *Descriptive Sketches* emphasizes the Swiss political qualities of freedom, justice, and liberty—qualities that of course had added resonance given recent events, to which the poem alludes. That said, even though some of the poem was actually written in France (*WCh* 14), and despite the fact that the narrative shows considerably more political zeal than does that of *An Evening Walk,* the text treats the Revolution, Gill observes, "at such a level of generality" as to make its concluding call for renovation "applicable to all political situations, or to none" (*WL* 65). The explanations may accord with those already offered about *An Evening Walk*'s own historical omissions. Or it may be that Wordsworth tended, then as later in life, not just to view political events in terms of their underlying causes but also to focus on what he felt generally connected human beings together—in 1792 as in 1388, in the case of *Descriptive Sketches*' reference to the Swiss battle at Naeffels.

Given *An Evening Walk*'s fixation upon dwelling and grief, it is not surprising that this second half of the diptych reveals similar interests, lamenting the presence or, in places, rejoicing in the absence of "social suffering" and loss (*DS,* l. 197). Sufferers include the isolated gypsy in the sublime landscape's forbidding "waste" (189) and the beggar "moan[ing] of human woes" (304)— the latter thankfully *missing* from the locale. Dwellings are again a focus for man, the "central point of all his joys" (571), toward which and for which he struggles through a stormy landscape of "mournful sounds, as of a Spirit lost" (334). In these ways, *Descriptive Sketches* and *An Evening Walk* are very much a diptych, and a decidedly social one, with much more to reveal than its author's fascination with the picturesque and the sublime.

In his descriptive sketch of Underwalden, Wordsworth not untypically first dilates upon the death of a local inhabitant in these mountains, whose corpse "in future days" his son may chance to find, "Start[ing] at the reliques of that very thigh, / On which so oft he prattled when a boy" (412–13). Wordsworth may be far from England's north country but his preoccupations travel with him. The lines recall those of Hamlet for Yorick, who "hath borne me on his back a thousand times" (V.i.185–86; the play is directly quoted—or, rather, misquoted— fifty lines later), and so slyly resituate Wordsworth's text in the father-haunted, melancholy terrain of *Hamlet* and the *Vale*. The scene presages *Descriptive Sketches'* subsequent praise of "[a]n unknown power [that] connects [Man] to the dead" (543) in an alpine landscape of "unsubstantial Phantoms" (374), "images of other worlds" (544), and a "death-like" silence (376)—perceived by a mind traveling under its burdensome "charge of woe" (193). Moreover, the mention of that "power," hailed in the context of praising the ancient Swiss struggle against "Oppression" (541), connects the dead to social-political struggle and solidarity, and more generally to the above-mentioned sense of "social suffering." Although the lines may sound Burkean in their regard for the dead and for tradition, the specific context of the father's death contextualizes that "power" in terms of grief and its own magic rather than of patriotism or conservative piety (granted, Burke also espoused the virtue of the domestic affections). In *An Evening Walk* and the Evening Sonnets as well as in *Descriptive Sketches,* human beings' feelings for the dead and for mourning the dead are what "connects" them to those dead and to one another.

Descriptive Sketches' final lines might as easily have concluded *An Evening Walk* had the wandering poet but gained a place to rest for the night:

> To night, my friend, within this humble cot
> Be the dead load of mortal ills forgot,
> Renewing, when the rosy summits glow
> At morn, our various journey, sad and slow.
>
> (810–13)

Following John Turner, Cornell's editor Eric Birdsall hears in this last line an echo of the end of *Paradise Lost,* in which Adam and Eve, upon leaving Paradise, "with wand'ring steps and slow, / Through *Eden* took thir solitary way" (12.648–49; cited *DS* 118). As with that mortal pair, "Wordsworth's narrator hopes that he and his companion might find a way to build the paradise that does not now exist."[38] By addressing his friend, Wordsworth appears to be suggesting, for Birdsall,

> an alternative response to the social evils the poem describes. No existing political structure can completely eliminate poverty and oppression, so solutions to

these problems must be sought within the more personal relationships of
friendship, family, and community. . . . The poem's conclusion . . . gestures in
an important new direction even as it confirms the failure of the poet's
quest . . . [:] irreducible, enduring human values emerge from small gestures in
humble cots.[39]

The journeys to such cots or huts, and the virtuous gestures shared along
them, stem from grief for the dead; those griefs serving as the bonds for transmortal connection. From the "strange harmony" of shadowy "awful grief[s]"
come the "social rays" of desired mourning, dwelling, and, faintly traced in *An
Evening Walk* and in these closing lines, community, predicated upon the
binding but "unknown power[s]" of the dead.

In the socially and politically conscious Salisbury Plain poems, written
in the following years, this trace of mourning-founded community will
become clearer and bolder. Wordsworth will struggle to weld his developing
sociology of mourning to the rusting edifice of a Britain fractured by revolution, domestic repression, and war. In this endeavor, mourning the dead shall
play a defining role, as will the poet's potent deployments of genre, crafted
for troubled times.

3

Genre, Politics, and Community
in the Salisbury Plain Poems

Human life has been said to resemble the situation of spectators in
a theatre. . . . It is only when the business is interrupted . . . that
[each] begins to consider at all, who is before him or who is behind
him, whether others are better accommodated than himself, or
whether many are not much worse.

—William Paley, *Reasons for Contentment*[1]

In the tumultuous years between 1793 and 1795 Wordsworth was a republican
under stress, living in a London convulsed by political, social, and economic
crises, now including war with France. By autumn of 1793 he was also watching the horrifying specter of the Terror destroying the very ideal of universal fraternity that he had embraced during his first visit to France in 1791. As a
restorative to his confused and often melancholy feelings of being "cut off / And
toss'd about in whirlwinds" (*13P* 10.257–58), he, like a good many of his disaffected and fearful English contemporaries, sought solace and, eventually, rural
"retirement." Regina Hewitt's *The Possibilities of Society,* following much the
same critical path as John Williams's *Wordsworth: Romantic Poetry and Revolution Politics,* claims that many such "sympathizers with the French Revolution
and other critics of British government policies periodically retreated from London when prosecution seemed imminent, biding their time or revising their
strategies in the relative safety of the countryside."[2] It was a countryside that in
England as in France had come to symbolize republicanism, as is evident in
Wordsworth's pro-republican "descriptive sketch" of Swiss alpine communities
and in his later depictions of English rural communities in *Guide to the Lakes.*

Seeking solace for his acute political and social despair, and perhaps seeking as well to revise his strategies, Wordsworth undertook a West Country walking tour in July 1793 with his Hawkshead school friend (and semi-pupil) William Calvert. *Salisbury Plain* (1793–94), revised as *Adventures on Salisbury Plain* (1795–96, 1799), was an important result of that tour. The poem arguably took its start when, according to Dorothy Wordsworth, Calvert's horse "began to caper one day in a most terrible manner, dragged them and their vehicle into a Ditch and broke it to shivers" (*EY* 109). Calvert rode the horse to friends in the north while Wordsworth oddly elected to cross the waste of Salisbury alone, passing its Cathedral and the ruins of Stonehenge en route to a friend in Wales (*WL* 74).[3] It was a fortuitous decision. By Wordsworth's estimation the impressions formed by that "lonesome Journey" (*13P* 12.359) across Salisbury Plain rekindled his smoldering creativity and remained with him throughout his life.[4] Indeed, according to Paul Sheats that waste's ruined monuments sparked the poet's desire "to compare past and present societies" in *Salisbury Plain*.[5] Kenneth Johnston in turn reminds us that the plain was and still is, moreover, "one of the most desolate open spaces in England, with . . . few human habitations of any kind." Gilpin called it "'one vast cemetery,' full of 'mansions of the dead'" (*HW* 346–47). It was a fitting place to contemplate homelessness and the absence as well as the basis of community. As Stephen Gill states, the plain provided Wordsworth's pensive imagination "with a focusing image through which he could express much of what he had been feeling so impotently about the nature of man in society" (*SPP* 5).[6] That vast waste offered a topography in which he could examine and stage the social exchanges of a specific place, on the margins of Britain's political world.

The "Advertisement" to *Guilt and Sorrow,* the final version of *Salisbury Plain*, describes the original poem as having been written with the "American war" and "revolutionary France" "still fresh" in its author's memory, but also as having been inspired by those "monuments and traces of antiquity" scattered across the plain (*PW* 1: 94–95). Mary Jacobus calls *Salisbury Plain* the "most impressive protest poem of its time," but argues against those who would reduce it merely to polemical pamphleteering.[7] In so doing, she follows in the tradition of critics like Geoffrey Hartman, who has found the poem to be "haunted" more "by a concern for a specific place" than by "humanitarian or political concerns," although Hartman has acknowledged these as being significant forces in the text (*WP* 118). Recent criticism has, with some justification, set its sights on the poem's implicit and explicit politics, and has tended, despite Jacobus's appeal to the contrary, to view it as a work of social protest.[8] At a time of the Terror, impending war, domestic political repression, and social upheaval owed to poor harvests, inflation, and stagnant reforms, Wordsworth had much to protest and consider.[9] Indeed, as Toby Benis points out, the reactionary Pitt government had clamped down hard on dissent, repressively "broadening the categories of political crime" while at the same time polarizing political expression "as either loyalist or traitorous, leaving little maneuvering room for critics." The result was that in 1793, the very year of *Salisbury Plain*'s composition, "there were more prosecutions for seditious words and libel . . . than in any other year in the 1790s."[10] The poem's staunch criticisms of governmental oppression as well as of socioeconomic inequality and injustice must appear all the more bold, then, and one wonders about the poem's likely reception had Wordsworth found a publisher (a severer fate would certainly have attended the publication of his contemporaneous, likely seditious *Letter to the Bishop of Llandaff*).

Add to these social and political conditions Wordsworth's personal feelings of alienation, guilt, and aimlessness, being himself in some manner homeless and without an income (the publication of *An Evening Walk* and *Descriptive Sketches* having attracted little attention), and it is little wonder that he sought to ameliorate his country's and his own poor circumstances. As David Collings observes about *The Prelude*'s record of these times, Wordsworth appears to have felt that he had stepped off the "'self-same' path . . . into 'another region,' one unknown to him, or as if some external force had suddenly stripped him of his 'station,' his secure unmoving social identity."[11] The "revolution" of sentiments (*13P* 10.237) experienced from foreign and domestic turmoil left him longing all the more for forms of stability and social cohesion. It may account for his coming to embrace, briefly, one of the reformist age's most influential philosophies of social and political change: the rationalist utopianism of Godwin's *Political Justice*. And yet Wordsworth's path was one that, even at this juncture, ultimately led him away from rather than toward Godwin's philosophy.

Indeed, although Godwin's influence can certainly be detected in *Salisbury Plain,* not least in its narrator's reformist and rationalist declarations and in the narrative's emphasis upon human benevolence, Wordsworth is pursuing a social course more his own. It is one based upon emotion rather than upon Enlightenment reason, and on the imperfection of the past rather than on the dream of some perfectible future. Michael Friedman argues that, "having lost faith in the French Revolution and the community of brotherhood it had seemed to hold out, Wordsworth found his way into a new community," one composed "of people poor in effective power but rich in affective power."[12] This community is founded upon the social powers of mourning. But the poet's interests also lead him to experiment with the stock of literary genres at his disposal, using romance to frame the narrative of *Salisbury Plain* and the gothic genre to re-envision that poem's plot and meaning as *Adventures on Salisbury Plain.* These deployments enable Wordsworth to devise communities well suited to a country in social decline and political crisis. He pursues this course by considering even more deeply the relationship of "the living and the dead" as well as by discerning, more than ever before, the force of literary form itself.

I. THE SOCIAL DEEP:
SALISBURY PLAIN'S "THRILL" OF COMMUNITY

> Hard is the life when naked and unhouzed
> And wasted by the long day's fruitless pains,
> The hungry savage, 'mid deep forests, rouzed
> By storms, lies down at night on unknown plains
> And lifts his head in fear. . . .
>
> *—Salisbury Plain*

In "Public Transport: Adventuring on Wordsworth's Salisbury Plain," Karen Swann poses a simple but provocative question: why should Wordsworth have composed his most ambitious and significant poem to date, *Salisbury Plain,* in one of the most taxing of metrical patterns, the Spenserian stanza? "Why choose this obdurate stanza," she asks, "and thus revive endless repetition, [and] court the visitations of the dead?"[13] Swann answers that Wordsworth deploys this "unmasterable" form in the hope of returning to himself a "power of repetition" able to "mobilize the public."[14] Her argument usefully focuses on *Salisbury Plain*'s "gothic" elements of transport, compulsion, and return, but in so doing grants rather less attention to the poem's romance form than one might expect given the text's Spenserian-romance metrics and other conspicuous romance elements (more on these below). To argue that the young poet's use of Spenserian stanzas "marks his poem as gothic" because in the eighteenth century any poem so written was "in the spirit of the Gothic revival" to my mind ignores the prominence of romance in the Revival, not to mention the close connection between Spenserian metrics and Revival-romance form.[15] In point of fact, while for readers of our day *Salisbury Plain*'s Spenserian and other romance elements might not so obviously distinguish the poem as a romance, for Revival readers such formal characteristics would have been familiar.

Indeed, while gothic and romance shared much in the decade of the 1790s,[16] there were clear distinctions to be made between them, as Wordsworth's later adoption of revivalist ballad over "frantic" gothic attests (*LB* 747). Ian Duncan contends that although gothic and romance both evoked for Revival readers "a past that was other and strange," gothic signified "a more adversarial [and] . . . militant anti-classicism," a "fragmented" rather than unbroken historical genealogy.[17] No less a patchwork of lost origins than was the gothic, romance by contrast posited a logic of return and of imaginative transformation and future possibility,[18] a logic not offered by gothic. Revival gothic in fact was the death of such possibility, an opposing pole of dislocation, fetishization, and compulsion. Wordsworth's selection of Spenserian romance to frame a social narrative of two of England's homeless must not, then, be hastily dismissed as mere Revival trendiness or as some journeyman exercise.

Wordsworth himself nonetheless remained silent about his motives for casting *Salisbury Plain* as a romance.[19] In looking elsewhere for clues about what it meant to adopt the genre in the late eighteenth century,[20] the beginnings of an answer may be found in Thomson's prefatory note to *The Castle of Indolence* (1748), which declares Spenser's romance "style" and "measure" to be "appropriated by custom to all allegorical poems written in our language."[21] In so stating, Thomson implies that there might be more tenor to romance and to one's choosing of romance than can be explained by the genre's mere popularity, antiquity, or sonority. His poem bears out his description of most eighteenth-century English romances as allegorical[22] and suggests Revival-era romance was to be read, in what was then considered the *spirit* of Spenser, as a form whose different registers of meaning were to convey moral or other social themes cast in the guise of alternative times, places, and societies.[23] Like Thomson, and like Beattie, West, and other contemporary neo-Spenserian writers, Wordsworth deploys romance genre as a moral-didactic form intended both to influence readers and to intercede in society. Unlike his predecessors, however, he does so in large part by contriving within the text a subtle generic conflict, aptly described by F. W. Bateson as an "unco-ordinate collocation" of romance form and "eye-on-the-object" social-realist content.[24]

In telling a social-realist narrative of British poverty and war, Wordsworth nonetheless unambiguously stamps *Salisbury Plain* as a romance, employing not just Spenserian romance's traditional stanzaic structure of eight lines of iambic pentameter and an Alexandrine but, like Thomson and Beattie, many of the genre's key motifs,[25] most notably in the poem's numerous allusions to *The Faerie Queene*. These intertextual romance allusions begin from the start, with the "Plain" of *Salisbury Plain*'s title (one of the first words also of Spenser's poem) and continue until the concluding lines' markedly Spenserian appeal to all "Heroes of Truth" to drag "foul Error's monster race" from their dark dens into the light to die (*SP*, ll. 541–47). Moreover, for all its realist elements, *Salisbury Plain* has at its core that defining characteristic of romance: the "difficult road" taken by the protagonist to a place of refuge, transformation, and renewal (in this case, a healing Spital).[26] Such elements cast the poem's two protagonists as romance-quest figures, and with considerable "unco-ordinate" tension, pointing their travels toward romance's generic trajectory of spiritual and social transformation[27] rather than toward the much more likely outcome for a homeless man and woman in eighteenth-century Britain.

Escapism was of course part of the appeal of both romance and gothic to antiquarians and lay readers. Walpole himself confessed to having written his seminal gothic-romance, *The Castle of Otranto*, as an escape from politics.[28] But, as has been suggested, in the 1790s romance was the genre par excellence not just for the supernatural and escapist but for the psychological and social as well, being arguably the premier literary form of political improvement.[29] Romance's associations with imagination and history well suited it to framing representations of the French Revolution, an event so unprecedented and transformative as to have appeared to Southey to inaugurate "a visionary world" of a regenerated human race.[30] In similarly romantic terms, in *The Prelude* Wordsworth describes the Revolution as having lent to the "stale, forbidding ways / Of custom, law and statute. . . . / The attraction of a Country in Romance," a land "regenerated" and yet of "the world / Of all of us" (*13P* 10.694–96, 244, 725–26). In fact, it took little time for romance's motifs to become the principal ordinance in the tropological arsenals of Jacobins and anti-Jacobins alike. Warring writers like Paine and Burke deployed its images to conjure up polemical pro- or anti-gallican associations of the natural or unnatural, the historical or fantastic, and so on.[31] In the 1790s, romance tended to be perceived and utilized as a nostalgic or optative mode divided between conservatism and progressivism and set in contrast to the nightmarish and labyrinthine nontransformational mode of gothic as well as to the vogue, Newgate-brand pessimism of social realism. Either way, romance was the genre of old and new possibilities—possibilities often associated with a more corporate (e.g., feudal and sacral) rather than individualistic (e.g., privatized and secular) English social world.

I am not arguing that Wordsworth necessarily employed romance in *Salisbury Plain* to enter into the contentious debate about the Revolution and its principles, about which he was himself feeling increasingly disconcerted. I am arguing only that the form, in addition to being allegorical and didactic, was also politically, if ambivalently, charged. In a decade of escalating social and political tension (Habeas Corpus was suspended in 1794), when, as Gertrude Himmelfarb points out, changes in technology, economics, politics, demography, and ideology made England's "poverty more conspicuous, more controversial, and in a sense less 'natural' than it had ever been before," and when the numbers of the poor, unemployed, and homeless were steadily rising,[32] romance form offered Wordsworth a much-needed strategy and course of action. That course was less openly polemical, and arguably less politically and legally risky, than the more staunchly realist paths being forged by Mary Wollstonecraft, George Dyer, and the authors of the many pamphlets on pauperism and the so-called "poor laws," seeded by reform debates on the rising rates of the poor and the unemployed.[33] But it offered him a political course nonetheless, in an era when Britain's institutional and other reforms were viewed with increasing dismay and skepticism. The need to cope with the rising tide of English poverty would culminate in the Poor Bill of 1797 and, arguably, in *Salisbury Plain,* inspired as it was by Wordsworth's time in London, his travels in the southwest,[34] and his professed desire to intercede in the nation's circumstances of poverty and war.

It is not so surprising, then, that of the genres at his disposal to represent England's homeless, Wordsworth should have chosen a form currently being deployed precisely in the politically charged pro- and anti-revolutionary rhetorics of natural versus unnatural social orders and rights, a form participating in the very social-political world that to us it might appear to elude or deny. And although growing despair over the possibility of cultural return[35] or rebirth may well have been responsible for the popularity of the gothic (the death of such promise), in the 1790s such despair also served to rekindle the alternative genre of romance, in order "to locate . . . unrealized possible futures."[36] Esther Schor's analysis of David Hume's preference for the "popular . . . and widely circulated literary form" of romance shows, moreover, that romance emphasized conversation,[37] in marked contrast to epic or tragedy— or for that matter, to gothic. Such social intercourse proves essential to *Salisbury Plain*'s imagining of community, and suggests the suitability of the genre for a narrative in which "converse"—specifically mournful conversation about the dead—figures so importantly in the plot and its social aims. Taking the poem's form as evidence, then, of Wordsworth's aim to frame *Salisbury Plain* as a romance and to have it and its Revival-era readers be governed by the genre's rules and expectations,[38] this chapter considers the pressures the form exerts within the text, including the extent to which the poem's genre engages readers in interrogating both the problems and the possibilities of English community, political engagement, and literary and political representation.

Salisbury Plain opens with its reformist narrator decrying the disparities of England's capitalist, class-based system. In order to exemplify that system's inequality, he tells the tale of a traveler's search for shelter on the desolate plain, a search whose travails show modern life to be worse even than primitive human existence. For the life of one like the traveler is a life not of shared primeval hardships, as is the case even for the "unhouzed" savage who shares "his hard lot" in "wild assemblies" (ll. 1, 16–17), but of disaffecting inequalities and inequities, where alienated individuals

> in various vessels roam the deep
> Of social life . . .
> Beset with foes more fierce than e'er assail
> The savage without home in winter's keenest gale.
>
> (32–36)

This nautical tropology of "vessels" roaming across an enigmatic "deep" recalls a similar motif used by Spenser in *The Faerie Queene* to describe the course both of his romance narrative and, within it, of its questing figures.[39] Wordsworth's extended metaphor likewise signals a semiotic disjunction between surface and depth, vehicle (or vessel) and tenor, form and content. It also suggests the narrator's desire not only to represent the plight of social mariners who "roam" with unfulfilled desires but also to plumb the social depths—the causes, meanings, and connections—that underlie economic and political existence amid these eddies of modern life's "turns of chance" (33). John Rieder sees these latter lines as exploiting a "politically charged" eighteenth-century commonplace, that of "comparing the physical suffering of savages to the more thorough misery of those who are destitute in the midst of civilization,"[40] a disparaging vision of modern life that likely echoes Rousseau's *Discourse on Inequality* and Hobbes's theory of the war-like state of nature.[41] Kenneth Johnston indeed finds Rousseau's disturbing paradox lurking here: namely, "that increased civilization leads to increased human inequality and mental suffering" (*HW* 350). Collings provides perhaps the most compelling reading of all, arguing that the passage suggests, like Rousseau's Second Discourse, that "the Hobbesian state of nature, of devastating violence and brutality, is not a precultural but a postcultural condition." *Salisbury Plain* in effect "cancels the difference between culture and the state of nature,"[42] leaving in its place a sociological void. That abhorrent vacuum cries out to be filled, and it *will* be filled by an alternative social model dependent upon the uneasy relationship between present and past, culture and grief, the living and dead. The opening lines' description of social difference and alienation can be read as an allegory of the text's implicit search for a means to transgress social limits and thereby discover a means to diminish inequality and suffering. The poem seeks to envision a place where moderns can truly be at "home"; hence the passage's conspicuous rhyming of "rouzed" wandering with the "unhouzed" condition that prompts it (1–3).

Lacking a home, the poor traveler of *Salisbury Plain* struggles to spot on the plain some "trace of man" or human dwelling, but no "homeward shepherd" or cottage can be found in the unhomely waste (43, 50), only a Janus-faced "naked guide-post's double head" (107) pointing to nothing. The sight of crows "homeward borne" along the "blank" horizon of the "vacant" plain brings tears to his homesick eyes (58, 41, 62). Finally, "Worn out and wasted, wishing the repose / Of death," the traveler comes to a spot

> where, antient vows fulfilled,
> Kind pious hands did to the Virgin build
> A lonely Spital, the belated swain
> From the night-terrors of that waste to shield.
> But there no human being could remain
> And now the walls are named the dead house of the plain.
>
> (120–26)

The Spital recalls the "Hospitall" in *The Faerie Queene*'s House of Holynesse (I.x.36) and is, like that sanctuary, a romance topos of recuperation and change. Its "pious" religious affiliation underlines its generic status as a shrine for those seeking shelter within its walls. It is a "dead house" to some extent of course because it is a non-house where "no human could remain." But it is also so named because of the quasi-purgatorial power it possesses to effect the regeneration of those socially or spiritually "dead" and "plain" souls who meet within it upon the "vacant" waste.

Significantly, the traveler's encounter with the "dead" ruin involves his first hearing from within it the haunting voice "of one that sleeping mourned" "in sorrow's throes" (136, 135). Moreover, when he first glimpses the female vagrant, this mournful voice's author, she appears in a "dead light" (140). Prior incidents in the traveler's lone trek across the plain suggest that such perceptions of loss are in fact characteristic of him. Before arriving at the Spital he had been startled by the perceived "mournful shriek" of a bustard (70) and had longed to see a "line of mournful light / From lamp of lonely toll-gate" (116–17). Such repetitions of mourning-related and death-oriented sights and sounds around the traveler argue for a common source within him, owed to a past loss displaced outward into signs, in which "imagery imitates desire"[43] and mortal loss entails quest. Nor is he alone in his preoccupation with death and mourning. The vagrant also has experienced loss, as she reveals in her poignant recollections of sufferings centering around her father's dispossession of their home and land, her loss of husband and children in the American war, and her subsequent decline into vagrancy. The traveler reads her voice as mournful and ghostly, then, for much the same reason that she perceives him as one of the dead's company and is herself referred to as a "mourner" (351): they are already assembled by their status as mourners and by their transferring of mourning and death onto one another.

We learn from the female vagrant's narrative, as told by her to the traveler, that as a child she had lived a life of "thoughtless joy" (231), accompanied by her cottage's "humming wheel and glittering table store" and by "well-known knocking at the evening door" (247–48). But having lost their home and lands to the greedy actions of a neighbor, her family was forced to resettle in a new town, enjoying there a modicum of new-won happiness until greater events again shattered their domestic life:

> For War the nations to the field defied.
> The loom stood still; unwatched, the idle gale
> Wooed in deserted shrouds the unregarding sail.
>
> (295–97)

Such intrusion precipitated her transport over the social seas, as one of "a poor devoted crew" of husband, wife, and children (her father having already died), "dog-like wading at the heels of War" in America (306, 313). Amid the war's slaughter, the family "perished, all in one remorseless year" (320)—all save the (soon-to-be) vagrant, who after "[s]ome mighty gulf of separation passed" (370), found herself back aboard a transport ship en route to England. But once disembarked on English soil she watched her condition go from bad to worse, as one now "homeless near a thousand homes" (386). It is as this homeless vagrant that she wanders still, enduring the hardships of a social world produced by political failure. Yet, as bleak as this picture is, the poem envisions a modicum of hope for the likes of the vagrant and this traveler she meets, a "thrill" of community that arises from a social-political breach.

Elsewhere upon Salisbury Plain there is a macabre model for the poem's economy of mourning and exchange. Before discovering the "dead house," the traveler had neared the ruins of Stonehenge, where a ghostly voice warned him to turn away:

> "For oft at dead of night, when dreadful fire
> Reveals that powerful circle's reddening stones,
> 'Mid priests and spectres grim and idols dire,
> Far heard the great flame utters human moans,
> Then all is hushed: again the desert groans,
> A dismal light its farthest bounds illumes,
> While warrior spectres of gigantic bones,
> Forth-issuing from a thousand rifted tombs,
> Wheel on their fiery steeds amid the infernal glooms."
>
> (91–99)

Through their sacrifice of living victims these druid rites effect a reciprocal power to transform the dead, "issuing" them forth with birth-like "moans" from "rifted tombs." Stonehenge in this light is an uncanny social structure organized around death and resurrection,[44] symbolizing the power of the dead to (re)produce and consolidate a society of the living. Of such supernatural powers the female vagrant has heard tell, too: of a swain who from a height saw the druid dead

> Thrilled in their yawning tombs their helms uprear;
> The sword that slept beneath the warriour's head
> Thunder[ed] in fiery air. . . .
>
> (186–88)

The significance of the term "thrill" will be addressed in a moment. For now, what I wish to emphasize is the text's revisiting of this resurrective and transgressive power to awaken the dead to social (here "warriour") life. It is not so much druid violence as this transformational romance economy of sacrifice and resurrection that these lines accentuate, in terms transferable to the dead house and its "dead" as a state of sleep, with tombs aptly depicted as "yawning" sites of awakening (Paine for one had loosely figured the poor as "dead"). Stonehenge's paradigmatic status is further suggested by other tales the vagrant has heard, concerning how the ruin's dead compose vast "assemblies" in the desolate wilderness, their awe-inspiring "files / All figured on the mystic plain" they have "charmed" below (195–98). The transformations wrought by these "mystic" druid "files" show Stonehenge's mysterious "figures" to have a power to "charm" (<L. *carmen*, "song," "incantation," "poem") the plain and its inhabitants; terms like "files," "traces," and "figures" suggesting, with the "blank[s]" and "marks" of prior lines, a transformative and regenerative power in dead-oriented words themselves. Stonehenge's economy models the power of dead-oriented narratives such as those exchanged by the "plain" vagrant and traveler, a power to break forth what is hidden and thereby resurrect the spiritually or socially dead. Hence, *The Prelude* describes such assemblies' druid priests as the musicians and bards of a ritual "pomp . . . for both worlds, the living and the dead" (*13P* 12.335–36).

To return to the term "thrill" and its connection to the power of mourning and mournful discourse, when the traveler first entered the ruined Spital, the startled vagrant's fatigued "spirits" had failed,

> Thrill'd by the poignant dart of sudden dread,
> For of that ruin she had heard a tale
> That might with a child's fears the stoutest heart assail.
>
> (141–44)

The vagrant's *thrill* of dread is due, we learn, to her having heard a ghost story about the Spital, describing how a visiting traveler's frightened horse had with "ceaseless pawing beat" upon the floor stones, which when "half raised" had disclosed "the grim head of a new murdered corse" (148, 151–53). She applies the tale to the traveler, whom she casts as the murdered corpse while she in turn becomes, as Swann states, "stony, like the discloser of the dead, like the stone covering the dead, and like the corse."[45] The vagrant's horrified response emblematizes the power of the dead to rise up from the past and transform the present. Rather than locked away in stony tombs, they exert a "poignant," piercing transformational power. It is of no little significance that the tale is presented close upon the traveler's experience at Stonehenge, for it serves, as the vagrant's descriptions of the American war will later serve, to bring the ancient sacrificial murders of Stonehenge's rituals into the narrative present (the corpse is "*new* murdered") and its words of mourning. The tale also functions to associate death with dwelling, the dwelling for which the "corse" is a foundation and *core,* as a death that physically underlies the foundations of this most basic and yet dead of dwellings. This "dead house," as Collings observes, indeed "is a haunted house, an unclosed tomb in which the unquiet dead can cause an agitation so fierce it shakes the walls,"[46] making it another version of Stonehenge and its powers. Set between the living and the dead, the Spital functions as a site of mourning, a house of and for the revisited and revisiting dead, where people like the vagrant and the traveler mourn, converse, and find protection and healing. It is also a site where, to quote again from Collings, "the dead may not only return but may cross over into a living body," where the dead may "wander not only on the plain but in the spaces of narrative and in the relations between people."[47]

Gill rightly argues that this use of the word "thrill" to describe the raising of the dead owes much of its metaphorical sense to an older meaning, to "pierce," used by Spenser in *The Faerie Queene,* although, according to Gill, Wordsworth's use of this term fails "to respect th[is] metaphoric use" (*SPP* 25). But Gill may not take sufficient account of the exact character of this "poignant dart of sudden dread" that thrills the vagrant's body and mind. For the use of "dart" signifies precisely the kind of penetration and "poignant" sting the term "thrill" would suggest in its traditional romance meaning. It is easy to miss the way this second use of "thrill" insinuates itself into the female vagrant's response as the "poignant," mnesic sting of Stonehenge's resurrection of the dead, and hence easy to overlook the manner in which this thrill associates a transformative romance power with the mournful narrative the vagrant unravels in the "dead" Spital.[48] Rather than losing the romance meaning of *thrill,* then, these lines repeat and broaden that meaning, in such a way that the Spenserian term inserts Stonehenge's transformational, quasi-purgatorial economy into what might otherwise seem only to be the vagrant's pathetic, gothic loss of consciousness.

Whereas the sensational frisson of gothic form effects a loss of speech and sensation, isolating the self, the romance *thrill* functions differently, as suffusion or influx. As the poem's descriptions suggest, the cause and principal effect of the vagrant's "thrill" of "dread" concern not her oblivion and isolation but a form of what she elsewhere has called "transport" (230, 371): a trope of transformation within and of connection to a larger world (via a thrill that is never wholly one's own). It is a romance world she both recalls and enters, in which death prefigures awakening and transcendence rather than gothic paralysis and annihilation. The female vagrant's "thrill" of "dread" in this way connects her to a transformational economy. It also importantly connects her to the traveler, who intrudes like these obtruding memories of past tales. The connecting thrill of influx and transport thereby extends Stonehenge's economy to the humble goings-on inside the ruined Spital, reinforcing and expanding the former's status while underlining the Spital's own transformational nature as a "hospitall" by its metonymic connection to these transportive romance thrills of the dead.

The "thrill" serves, in the Spital as at Stonehenge—and still more powerfully as the linkage of these two sites—to dilate and bind rather than to contract and fragment. Hence, in these lines the revived romance repetition of "thrill" shifts from an isolated reality of individuals to an arena not so unlike that of Stonehenge, where people are linked by corporate experiences of death.[49] Similarly, in *The Vale of Esthwaite* Wordsworth had associated a shuddering, "electric thrill" with a "social chain" of friendship, "link'd" by loss and grief (388–92; see Chapter One). It is as a proleptic sign of social transformation from isolation to community that, as the traveler and female vagrant converse within the Spital, outside

> the churlish storms relent;
> And round those broken walls the dying wind
> In feeble murmurs told his rage was spent.
> With sober sympathy and tranquil mind
> Gently the Woman gan her wounds unbind.
>
> (199–203)

The vagrant's Lazarus-like unbinding of her "wounds" is followed by her unraveling of her autobiographical narrative. She is in her tale-telling a mourner of "never ceas[ing]" tears (270) owed to a loss that can be signified in words only incompletely and never be assuaged, let alone ended. Such perpetuity accounts for much of her mourning's peculiar power. Her "unbinding" of this past loss enables her and the traveler to "convers[e]," and it is their conversation that in turn converts them from solitary wanderers to "comrade[s]" in mourning (160, 341).[50] The narrator's term "comrade" is apposite, for their relationship cannot really be characterized as friendship. They are bound to each other by virtue of their mourning and to some extent also by their poverty and isolation, not, it would seem, by any particular other attraction. Cathy Caruth, in her study of trauma, argues that such scenes of "listening to the voice and to the speech delivered by the other's wound" are the basis of trauma and of "its uncanny repetition," as well as the story of psychoanalytic theory itself.[51] And it is this trauma of mourning, of expressing and sharing grief, that bonds the traveler and vagrant, forming them into the most minimal and fundamental of communities.

In *Salisbury Plain* ghostly converse exhibits a potency akin to what Walter Benjamin describes as "a *weak* Messianic power" to awaken the dead in a "now" filled "with chips of Messianic time."[52] For the power of the narratives shared in the Spital lies in the poignant force of the past events and persons they both recollect and, in some manner, ghostily recuperate: to awaken the listener and, through the exchange of mournful narratives, release his or her private history into a public, communitarian field of discourse. The "mystic" romance plain on which these exchanges occur is again not unlike Stonehenge's own setting, and is represented as being capable, too, of resurrecting the marginalized "dead" back to social life. The traveler and the vagrant's "Night Journey" (*WP* 123) of death and rebirth depends upon these transformative powers of mourning and its conversations of loss—powers framed by *Salisbury Plain*'s romance form.

II. THE POETICS AND POLITICS OF DISJUNCTION

> To learn to live with ghosts, in the upkeep, the conversation, the company, or the companionship . . . of ghosts. To live otherwise, and . . . more justly.
>
> —Jacques Derrida, *Specters of Marx*[53]

Traveling in search of food and shelter, as "Day fresh from ocean wave uprears his lovely brow" (333), the two wanderers pause midway in the female vagrant's narrative. They view a recuperative vista presenting a very different world from that of the previous night, with a

> lengthening road and wain
> Descending a bare slope not far remote.
> The downs all glistered dropt with freshening rain;
> The carman whistled loud with chearful note. . . .
>
> (343–46)

This symbolic shift from "ruinous" night to "fair" morning is typical of romance (330, 335). The shift is underlined by yet another sign of the social revitalization of these comrades: their sighting of a "lengthening road" leading down to a cottage. These locodescriptive cues point to a "dawn of gladness" (337), in keeping with romance's traditional structure. That dawn implies a *post hoc ergo propter hoc* causation by which the poem's Revival readers are encouraged to see the vagrant's healing narrative as having itself "charmed" and revived the dead world inside and outside the Spital, instigating the regenerative scene that follows closely upon it. Such signs of revitalization as accompany her and her new comrade indeed augur something more than mere diurnal or climatic transformation: a spiritual restoration effected by the power of mournful and poignant tale-telling, by a discourse able to lead the past and its dead out of darkness and thereby force the dawning of community. But to be raised up like the sun and to raise up a world from spiritual and social death requires for Wordsworth also that one descend, in the manner of the romantic night journey, into the entombing medium of mournful words. The vagrant "unbinds" a "tale of woe" that brings her mourned dead out from the "grave" to disrupt the present and its isolating disconnections, with the promise of joining the living to one another as mourners who awaken and in turn are awakened by the dead.

Although Wordsworth's poem in no way presents the restoration of all that these paupers have lost, such romance signs suggest that the two have gained for their shared deeds (that is, for their mournful and sympathetic conversations) a shared homeward journey. The traveler and the vagrant's journey stands at a symbolic midpoint between isolation and community, accompanied by sounds of a "chearful" song and by signs of a pastoral topography romantically transformed from the gothic "waste" of the previous night. The world that had shunned them appears almost to beckon, along a road that is a product of the narratives that will still occupy its traversal. Hence, for all this story's pathos and for all the indications of a failure of British society, the traveler and female vagrant's night journey concludes, as readers of romance might well expect, with signs of hope. Indeed, as if to add to the already favorable environs that have greeted the pair, no sooner has the vagrant concluded her account of hardships than

> The city's distant spires ascend
> Like flames which far and wide the west illume,
> Scattering from out the sky the rear of night's thin gloom.
>
> (394–96)

The fiery images from the previous night's tales of sacrificial pyres and Celt resurrections now reappear as symbols of rebirth. Like the living dead of Stonehenge, the traveler and vagrant are figured on a "mystic plain" of intermingling natural and supernatural transformations and possibilities, where social laws may, like the physical laws of life and death, be "charmed" away or suspended. It is their mournful "discourse" that creates "confidence of mind / And mutual interest" (*ASP* 256–58), a condition of sympathy that bonds them in an intimate community based upon shared understanding and, especially, upon a mutual bond of mourning.

The signs are evident as the pair proceed, for

> now from a hill summit down they look
> Where through a narrow valley's pleasant scene
> A wreath of vapour tracked a winding brook
> Babbling through groves and lawns and meeds of green.

> A smoking cottage peeped the trees between . . .
> While through the furrowed grass the merry milkmaid strays.
>
> (*SP* 406–10, 414)

By the agency of their mournful narrative the traveler and the female vagrant have journeyed from the "dead house" to a "smoking cottage" of social regeneration and hope. Like the rites of Stonehenge, the pair's narrative transformations point to a transgressive breach in the hierarchies of life and death, past and present, rich and poor (for instance, that of romance knight and modern peasant, here disruptively conflated). Conversation, rather than law or commerce, bonds together these alienated moderns into an "assembly." The text in this sense proffers less the "light" of reason called for by the poem's Godwinian-reformist narrator (545) than a romance means of effecting social transgression and the sympathetic reconnection of bonds that transform the self in its relationship to another.

Hence, at the end of the female vagrant's narrative, having identified and sympathized with its account of past and present sufferings, the traveler is led to strive "with counsel sweet" to "chear" her "soul" (403), like Arthur in *The Faerie Queene,* who offers "[f]aire feeling words" to soothe Una's "sorrow" (I.vii.38). *Salisbury Plain*'s intertextual allusion to a romance and political exemplar reinforces the traveler's status as being more than that of a beggar— a marginal and dismissible character of the time—as does the vagrant's comparison to the regal Una. In fact, it is at this very moment that, in apparent reward for the traveler's sympathetic identification with another, the two wanderers spot from their "hill summit" (406) the longed-for cottage, a cottage they will "share," its "board . . . piled with homely bread" (417, 420). *Salisbury Plain*'s romance form casts this vision as a summit of recuperation, setting its protagonists within a framing structure of permanence and renewal that contrasts with the narrative's "ruinous" social world. Like the Red Cross Knight and Una of Spenser, the traveler and female vagrant share in a passage from unaccommodated isolation toward the social reward of what Anne Janowitz calls "moments of community."[54]

Even *Salisbury Plain*'s pessimistic narrator affirms our estimation of these wanderers as allegorical romance figures by his appraisal of all modern social existence as "like this desert broad" on which they have just been treading, "[w]here all the happiest find is but a shed . . . 'mid wastes interminably spread" (421–23). In so doing, while he limits the scope of the summit the pair has reached—as but a shed or spital—the narrator makes their social lot universal and applicable to the reader's own. Moreover, given the reality of a world of social wastes and their temporary, ruined dwellings, the comradeship achieved by the vagrant and the traveler can be viewed all the more as the summit of a homeward quest, and their romance-framed mourning-work as the primary means of its attainment. Unlike Southey's similar *Botany Bay Eclogues,* Wordsworth's poem is able to imagine, Benis argues, that such wanderers can be "independent agents" capable of experiencing a "healing, communal feeling" between them—"the only kind of 'homes' the[se] homeless or perhaps anyone can be sure of."[55] Against all such affirmative readings, James Averill argues that the poem's sea change from dark isolation to sunlit dwelling is little more than a "radical transformation within the traveler's mind" (*PHS* 77). But in fact this alteration is a product more of romance signs that frame reading than of character psychology.

The readers of *Salisbury Plain* have been invoked from the outset, by a narrator whose main hope is to call their "soft affections from their wintry sleep" (29). Wordsworth's readership was in this case more addressed than reached, as an envisioned reading public attuned to the poem's issues regarding British war and poverty and to the poem's conspicuous Revival form. In *Salisbury Plain,* as in any such work, genre is a social construct between writer and reader, calling the latter into the form's particular system of requirements, limitations, and expectations. As Marlon Ross states, "a genre names a community of readers, who learn to practice rituals, which mark their relation to the text as binding."[56] That *Salisbury Plain*'s narrator returns at the poem's end again to address his readers makes explicit their involvement as those who frame and are framed by his text and its form, a text whose "summit" is shaped by readers' adherence to romance's revisited rules and possibilities. Drawn into the genre's horizon of expectations[57]—what Stuart Curran calls "the imperatives of genre," the primacy and inescapability of a "logic within fixed formal patterns"[58]—the anticipated reader of *Salisbury Plain* would expect that the narrative's summit of a cottage portend, at this difficult road's envisioned end, a more significant result than a meal. Yet Janowitz rightly points out that, in contrast to such ameliorative social trajectories, *Salisbury Plain*'s narrator instead proclaims the "irrecoverability of . . . habitation" for moderns like the traveler and vagrant.[59] And it is clear that, according to the narrator's perspective, if such "poor benighted mortals" as these are ever to "gain the meed / Of happiness and virtue" (511–12) it will be not by their own words and deeds or by any charity offered them but by the virtuous "labours" of social and political "sage[s]" (510). More realist political reformer than romance poet, the narrator dismisses this modern pair's summit as "but a shed" in a social "desart" without the possibility of ascent.

As already mentioned, Bateson years ago criticized this "unco-ordinate collocation" between *Salisbury Plain*'s "supernatural" romance "horror" and its "eye-on-the-object realism," adding that "like oil and water, the two elements . . . do not mix."[60] He was right. In point of fact the respective voices of narrator and narrative frame, "shed" and "summit," are at odds, rather like that double-headed guidepost revealed to the traveler by a flicker of light. Thereupon one stumbles over a problem of reading. Are readers to believe the teller of the poem's tale and therefore look no further than his vantage, or are they to adhere to the hermeneutic logic of the tale's generic frame? While there may be no satisfying resolution to this interpretive dilemma, such a formal contradiction raises at least the possibility of irony: that of a limited, intrusive narrator at odds with the tale he tells or of a framework that exaggerates, even to the point of contradicting, the hardships of the impoverished moderns it represents. So which context does the reader allow to intervene? Certainly there is no reason to take the narrator's assessment of the tale as gospel—Wordsworth's later narrators often are limited—nor is there, given the prominence of the poem's romance genre, much reason not to accept the summit reached by the traveler and vagrant as at least in some way symbolic of their new or renewed condition. By this reckoning, the traveler and vagrant are rewarded for their sympathies by the attainment of their quest's goal: a dwelling amid "the terrors of our way" (432). And yet this symbolic summit has been achieved in no small part by the overdetermining pressure of genre on interpretation, which is to say by an act of reading that constructs a literary "summit" over the historical "desart" through which the poor couple desperately travels.

One might then argue that, despite such claims for the powers of a comic romance universe of social transformation and mournful progress, the imaginative sympathies of the poem's readers are enlisted in a context in which romance genre simply does not fit.[61] Readers are left either to fill in or ignore the gap between the poem's lofty structure and its representation of disaffected and marginalized vagrants it cannot be said really to represent. Romance thus gives the lie to a social reality of "benighted mortals" like the traveler and vagrant, whose plight is intended to call attention to the need for social reform and who are, after all, no knight and damsel. In this light, Wordsworth's deployment of romance might be seen to demonstrate "the poverty of [his] political theory" at a time when both revolution and reform had to his mind failed.[62] Rather than place his characters in their real historical milieu, Wordsworth returns to a hackneyed albeit vogue generic paradigm (what amounts to a feudalistic order of predetermined, static social positions), using romance as a nostalgic "refuge from the waking world," a literary evasion of political and other pressing realities.[63]

But I have already suggested that Wordsworth may employ this romance frame in order to structure a resolution to late eighteenth-century social ills, one of the key values of *Salisbury Plain*'s romance genre being its aforementioned corporate rather than individualistic nature and another its potential for representing alternative social and political possibilities. Such a system works to link the poem's protagonists to each other in order to emphasize the communal character of their shared mourning and sympathy and also, again, to lure readers to structure for them an ameliorated world in a poem explicitly about the harsh character of modern social life. If romance form does not fit the text's realist content, such misfitting can be read as the generic subversion of a representational social and political universe ill suited to the trials of such alienated and unaccommodated wanderers as these. By both courting and frustrating readers' sympathies, framing the simple and impoverished of society in (the) terms of the exalted and valued, Wordsworth's narrative interrogates the social basis for its frame. In doing so, the text engineers a subversion of generic qua social categorization, a point underlined by *Salisbury Plain*'s hybrid generic nature. More even than in romance's contemporary pro-revolutionary deployments, its decidedly "unco-ordinate" use in Wordsworth's experimental poem strains against that which it obdurately and hauntingly structures.

Such an ironic vantage paints in a different light the narrator's position vis-à-vis his subject. If *he* is misfitted to the narrative and its generic effects, then it may be the case that his transferring of social-political progress from the oppressed themselves into the hands of a few wise Godwinian-reformist "sages" might itself be misfitted and suspect. As a result of such generic tension, one may be led ultimately to accept neither the nostalgic frame of the narrative nor the declarations of its progressivist narrator. Instead, with both ends of the text mooted as representationally inadequate, readers are left with literary, social, and political gaps to try to fill. One significant generic effect of this textual subversion of romance is then that it motivates the poem's readers, today much as in 1794, to desire such social amelioration in its absence and to question the basis of literary and political representation right along with the structures and assumptions of past and present social models and reforms.

As Michael Wiley points out in *Romantic Geography*, Wordsworth's initial denominating of this landscape "Sarum's plain" (l. 38), a rotten borough, situates the two travelers in "a place that represents no one," a place notorious for having no one for its MPs to represent.[64] The poem's setting, like its genre, seems incapable of representing the impoverished, needy pair, who all the more clearly lack representation. And, in short, it is by a misfitting of form that *Salisbury Plain* is able to effect a polemic that illuminates both the dignity and poverty of Britain's poor while at the same time pinpointing the deficiencies of the poet's and his readers' discursive means to represent them—a point that circles back to the opening lines' ill-fitting figurative vessels on social seas. As Rieder states, such poetry constructs "a fantasy of community," drawing in readers through their "play of participation and detachment in the literary experience itself," providing them with "a place to exercise judgment, recast convention, revalue tradition."[65] What *Salisbury Plain* demonstrates perhaps most in its duel between romance and social realism is the power of genre itself: its power to exert hermeneutic force upon reading, romancing history and subtly historicizing romance.

In a decade of contentious debate not only about the Revolution but also about the domestic reform of a system of poor relief that seemed to some to create as many problems as it solved,[66] *Salisbury Plain*'s uncoordinate generic dynamics effect a covert means of political mobilization, focused on and by acts of reading. In so doing, the poem's romance form provides its author and readers with the means to signify both reformist skepticism and republican hope, alternative registers of dissatisfaction and idealized romance vision.[67] As Wordsworth's well-known contemporary William Paley observed, in the epigraph to this chapter, in the theater of modern life it is only when the mesmerizing "business" of the stage and its tantalizing fictions are interrupted that the spectator "begins to consider at all . . . whether others are better accommodated than himself, or whether many are not much worse." *Salisbury Plain* similarly functions to startle its reading audience into momentary awareness in order to effect its agenda about the disparate accommodation of England's rich and poor. By doing so, Wordsworth's poem serves to broaden our understanding of the politics of genre in general and specifically of the complex interplay of genre and polemic in the late Revival, in which, Duncan reminds us, romance plots served to represent "a transformation of life and its conditions, and not their mere reproduction."[68] All in all, it is a potent romantic formulation and strategy, well fitted to oppressive times.

That Wordsworth, a soon-to-be self-proclaimed "man speaking to men," should find social and political power in his ability to affect the better natures of his readers is characteristic of him. But that he should deploy a particular genre by virtue of its dissonance from social reality, as a tactical (and tactful) means to challenge Revival readers' attitudes about English poverty, society, and culture, is more surprising, and intriguing. Although it is true that this strategic experiment with generic resistance[69] seems to be all but revised away in the following year's *Adventures on Salisbury Plain*, the poet would nevertheless return to romance form and to its rules and expectations: in "Peter Bell" (1798–99), "Resolution and Independence" (1802), the 1805 *Prelude*,[70] and his Spenserian romance *The White Doe of Rylstone* (1807–8). These and other poems attest to Wordsworth's continuing interest in romance form and its generic effects. Yet their deployment of genre is more muted than is the case in the experimental romance of *Salisbury Plain*, producing neither that poem's disjunctive mobilizations nor its haunting visions of a summit as yet unattained in a world of social deserts and deeps.

III. Margins of Society in *Adventures on Salisbury Plain*

And groans . . . [to] make a dead man start.

—*Adventures*

At Racedown cottage in 1795 Wordsworth undertook revising the unpublished, and to his estimation unpublishable, *Salisbury Plain,* now derided as being but a "first draught" (*EY* 159). The resulting narrative, suitably retitled *Adventures on Salisbury Plain,*[71] was "almost . . . another work" (159), stripped of much of its predecessor's "explicit political argument" (*HW* 483) and re-envisioning the traveler as a homeward-bound sailor with his own hidden, Godwinian story of personal suffering and injustice. Sheats points out that the "goal of hope in 1793, the cottage, effectively vanishes from the poem and becomes the invisible center" around which the poem's haunted protagonist "circles."[72] Although *Adventures* retains *Salisbury Plain*'s integral Spenserian metrics, it sheds many of its romance motifs and most all of its romance trajectory[73] in favor of gothic repetition, pessimism, and circularity. The resulting narrative emphasizes its impoverished characters' persisting alienation and, in the case of the tormented sailor, unrelenting guilt; hence, the published 1842 version's title, *Guilt and Sorrow.* Given such dark gothicism and pessimism it is small wonder that Mary Moorman could view *Adventures on Salisbury Plain* as likely "the bitterest, most unsparing indictment of social injustice that he [Wordsworth] ever wrote" (*WW* 295). Benis points out that even the exchanges between the traveler and vagrant now are "tainted by concealment and uneasiness," in keeping with the current treason trials' political aftermath. In fact, as Wordsworth undertook revising *Salisbury Plain,* Parliament was debating Pitt's bills on Treasonable Practices and Seditious Meetings.[74]

Wordsworth intended his poem, he said, "to expose the vices of the penal law and the calamities of war as they affect individuals" (*EY* 159). Jacobus speculates that Wordsworth heard of the "crudely sensational" confession of one Jarvis Matchan, "a sailor who had murdered a drummer-boy in 1780 and six years later confessed to his companion as they tramped across Salisbury Plain in a storm" Matchan feared to be "divine wrath."[75] Arnold Schmidt contends that the poem also evokes the politically charged hanging of the Nore Mutiny's leader, Richard Parker, an understandable evocation for a "maritime family" like the Wordsworths and for the likes of a poet still appalled by the war and yet at the same time increasingly ambivalent about political commitment.[76] But, as Sheats states, the poem's principal concern is that arch-Godwinian theme of a man "goaded into murder" by unjust social forces,[77] without *Salisbury Plain*'s stirring appeal to the equally Godwinian "heroes of Truth." Like Sheats,

Jacobus situates the poem in the milieu of *Political Justice*, "where crime is represented as the result of intolerable social oppression."[78]

Godwin's vision was influenced not just by revolution and war but also by the popular genres of protest and crime, as was Wordsworth's own. Gill remarks the poet's "resourcefulness" in interweaving into *Adventures* elements of protest culled from popular magazines and from such influential works as Langhorne's *The Country Justice* and Southey's *Botany Bay Eclogues* (*WL* 98). The resulting poem represents a world in which the "state that should be the bulwark of society is its undoing"[79] and where men and women "can do nothing more than foster kindliness to one another when they can" (98–99). It is a starkly gothic social sea of unrelenting violence and injustice, a place where, Collings points out, no one, not even Wordsworth, can escape guilt, "implicating the protagonist and himself in the savagery of the plain." Having renounced the Godwinian faith that reason will necessarily kill error—a faith subject to irony even in *Salisbury Plain*—Wordsworth has become a "poet of the whirlwinds, of errancy, of dark romance."[80] He is now more the poet of Godwin's *Caleb Williams,* to which the poem alludes,[81] and his poetry that of the gothic, experimenting with that Revival genre's powers much as had been the case with romance in *Salisbury Plain.*

Despite the narrative's focus upon its traveler's guilt and eventual grisly punishment, the narrative of *Adventures* has its own transformative social elements and its own intriguing, gothic formation of community. The poem may speak, as Collings claims, "forever of society's traumatic, irreversible dislocation from itself,"[82] but it is really the dislocation of *Gesellschaft,* with the alternative potential of *Gemeinschaft* still to be represented. Indeed, for all the poem's gothic horror and frisson, the stormy social sea depicted in *Adventures* has deeper currents of sympathy and ghostly connection. *Adventures* reveals a phantom communitarianism, in yet another tale of haunting burdens, a community-to-come grounded in death and mourning, set amid a gothic waste.

Adventures opens with its nameless protagonist crossing the plain, searching, like the traveler of *Salisbury Plain,* for some sign of a "cottage" or a "shepherd's ragged thorn" (*ASP,* ll. 65, 68). We learn this man is a veteran who, having served at sea and then in the American war, had upon his return to England endured the final insult of being denied his pay. Nearly in view of his home, the disillusioned sailor robbed and murdered a stranger, then fled the scene and, along with it, his home. Now, years later, still haunted by his crime, the veteran falls into hysterical trances whenever something brings it to mind. Like the traveler of *Salisbury Plain,* he is driven to seek shelter, and does so in a spital occupied by a soldier's widow (née the female vagrant) who tells him her story. In the morning, again as in *Salisbury Plain,* the two of them seek food and shelter. But in *Adventures* their tale does not end here.

Instead, they cross a plain made "even grimmer by day than . . . by night,"[83] eventually coming to an inn where the sailor is uncannily reunited, in perverse romance fashion, with his abandoned and now dying wife. At her death, his remorse exceeding fear for his life, he departs for the city to confess his past crime, and the poem concludes by describing the grisly image of his gibbeted body displayed above a holiday crowd. These events might suggest that, in light of the Revolution's anti-fraternal progress and of the advent of war and of domestic repression, Wordsworth had lost faith not just in existing society but in the potential even for a modicum of community. But in fact, as mentioned, one finds evidence in *Adventures* that his belief in the socially cohesive powers of the dead had not abated, certainly not entirely. Likely owing to his growing despair about any political means for improvement, it has instead turned inward and been made less dependent upon human agency and will.

Venturing "on the skirt of Sarum's Plain" (1), the traveling sailor overtakes "an aged Man with feet half bare," a fellow veteran whose "ragged coat scarce showed the Soldier's faded red" (2, 9). For the next mile he shares the "short-lived fellowship" (33) of this comrade, who tells

> how he with the Soldier's life had striven
> And Soldier's wrongs; but one who knew him well
> A house to his old age had lately given.
> Thence he had limp'd to meet a daughter driven
> By circumstance which did all faith exceed
> From every stay but him: his heart was riven
> At the bare thought: the creature that had need
> Of any aid from him most wretched was indeed.
>
> (20–27)

The veteran's recollection of his "Soldier's life" and its "Soldier's wrongs" foreshadows the traveler's hidden history of lamented wrongs and lost domestic connections. In fact, the poem devotes much more attention to this soldier's winning of a house than to his life as a soldier, about which we learn next to nothing.[84] This vision of domestic recuperation and reunion is set on the farthest margins of society, between a social world symbolized, as in *Salisbury Plain,* by the Cathedral's fading "spire" (48) on one side and a "houseless moor" (227) on the other. In parting company with the old veteran and stepping from this social border into the "vacant" waste of the plain, the sailor indicates his distance from such community.

Having "daily . . . survey'd" in war "Death's worst aspect" (83), upon returning to England the sailor had found himself unjustly "spurn'd" as an "unfriended claimant" by "the slaves of Office" (91–92). With no hope left of

> Bearing to those he loved nor warmth nor food,
> In sight of his own house, in such a mood
> That from his view his children might have run,
> He met a traveller, robb'd him, shed his blood;
> And when the miserable work was done
> He fled, a vagrant since, the murderer's fate to shun.
>
> (94–99)

One cannot miss the irony that the sailor's objectification of this other traveler precipitates his transformation into the equally anonymous "traveller" of the poem's first lines. At the same time, in Godwinian fashion Wordsworth's poem lays the blame for this violence on the doorstep of corrupt government. The sailor is driven to commit murder as "Death's minister" (84) not only on foreign soil but also, as Godwin predicted, in his native land. And yet, despite being the product of a violent system, the sailor is hypocritically held responsible by that same system for the actions it had driven him, and had for that matter also taught him, to do. "Death's worst aspect" precipitates his socioeconomic metamorphosis from homeward-bound veteran to homeless, fleeing criminal. Such death, rather than serving as a force for community, works instead to undermine it, transforming one of English society's "kind and good" (761) into this tormented and marginalized wanderer subject to the "murderer's fate." *Adventures* in this way distinguishes between a gothic "worst aspect" of death—a repetitive economy of death for death and "minister" for "minister"—and an implicit *better* vision of death, characterized by an ameliorating escalation of mourning and sympathy. The narrative thereby reveals a dialectic that, although unable to alter the legal "fate" of a criminalized figure like the sailor, is able to detour his story for a moment from this deterministic cycle to glimpse at least a promise of community.

IV. THE GRIDING DEAD

After the sailor and widow leave the spital to seek food and shelter, they encounter a peasant family picnicking on the plain. The picnic at once erupts into violence when the five-year-old son takes his father's "place" after he moves to get a pitcher of drink, and "when desired to move, with smiling face / For a short while [the son] did in obedience fail" (622–25). The father cruelly beats the boy, "as if each blow had been his [son's] last" (627), leaving him with a "batter'd head" whose "streaming blood . . . dy'd the ground" (642–43). The oedipal outburst signifies the violence and breakdown of patriarchal society, akin to Mortimer's murder of Herbert in Wordsworth's dark tragedy *The*

Borderers. As a result of the sailor's witnessing of this event, so reminiscent of "the spot where he [the sailor] that deadly wound / Had fix'd on him he murder'd" (644–45), through the sailor's brain

> At once the griding iron passage found;
> Deluge of tender thoughts then rush'd amain
> Nor could his aged eyes from very tears abstain.
>
> (646–48)

The sight is a gothic mise en scène of his murder of the stranger, "iron" being associated since *The Vale of Esthwaite* with the dead and their "griding" power over the living. But iron is here also associated with an act of near filicide and so with the sailor's quasi-murder of his family (through the harm indirectly inflicted upon them by local rumor and suspicion). The gruesome scene represents the power of the dead to gride into the mind—*gride* being one of the few new Spenserian terms in *Adventures*—or, as the text's ambiguous language also suggests, to elicit crypt-like "griding iron" from *out* of the mind. The "iron" coffered presence evoked by this scene of violence grides through the sailor's mind from inside to outside, from repression to representation, to find expression as an outward "voice [in] which *inward* trouble broke" (656; emphasis added). The previously incorporated *other* thereupon attacks the self's consciousness. As Nicolas Abraham and Maria Torok observe, such an incorporated other, once encrypted in the self, begins to ventriloquize it, haunting its host, "the keeper of the graveyard, making strange and incomprehensible signs."[85]

This relationship between the remembered or unremembered "inward" dead and the external living is touched on early in the narrative, when the traveling sailor hears a "sudden clang" as

> chains along the desert rang:
> He looked, and saw on a bare gibbet nigh
> A human body that in irons swang,
> Uplifted by the tempest sweeping by,
> And hovering round it often did a raven fly.
>
> (112–17)

The gibbet is, we learn, a sight with the power to arrest any traveler who encounters it, in a gothic version of the epitaphic *Sta Viator* ("Pause, Traveler"):

> It was a spectacle which none might view
> In spot so savage but with shuddering pain
> Nor only did for him at once renew

> All he had feared from man, but rouzed a train
> Of the mind's phantoms, horrible as vain.
>   . . . a terrific dream in darkness lost
> The dire phantasma which his sense had cross'd.
>
>   (118–22, 130–31)

The spectacle elicits from him a "shuddering pain," owed not just to the punishment he "fear[s] from man" but also to other forces, described as a ghostly
"train / Of the mind's phantoms." These phantoms are "rouzed," as if waking
from a pre-existing sleep of repression and "cross[ing]" from "darkness" into
consciousness—or nearly so, for, as they awaken, the sailor lapses into unconsciousness, lying "without sense or motion" (125). The word *phantom* or *phan-
tasm(a)* can, like the synonym *apparition,* refer either to an illusory appearance
or to an actual specter or ghost (*OED*). Wordsworth provides enough detail in
the narrative to support either meaning of "the mind's phantoms," and arguably
to merge the two definitions as memories of the dead, which reside until beckoned from oblivion into liminal consciousness. As Paul Fry has observed, in
Wordsworth's poetry "memory harbors phantoms,"[86] and in this scene the
causes of the sailor's trances and visions are these "dire phantasma" of "a terrific
dream in darkness lost," rather than, say, the physical form of the corpse.

   Schor argues that in this light the scene can be read as another example
of the Burkean sublime, specifically of sublime terror and of the potent fear it
produces. The phantasms provoke a fear "so paralyzing as to 'cross' the sailor's
sense, disabling emotion" and the powers of sympathy, via a "paralyzing implo-
sio[n] of consciousness" that, Schor believes, thwarts *Adventures'* envisioned
"community of sorrow."[87] Yet one can read the sailor's trance differently, and
locate in it more promise of community than Schor's vantage affords. For the
gibbeted form elicits in the sailor not only a reciprocal, symptomatic loss of
animation but also a phantasm within his internal "darkness," a tomb-like
place of loss connected to such "dire phantasma" as now cross his senses. The
dead in this way evoke other dead, with the mourner's unconsciousness serving as the limit point of ghostly expression. The scene comes to represent
more than psychic paralysis owed to legal interpellation or to religious fears
about the body's resurrection (still believed at the time to be reserved only for
entire bodies, Benis notes).[88]

   As in *Salisbury Plain,* in *Adventures* a ghostly burden is socially productive, producing a "train" of recollections and identifications, and connecting
not just the living and the dead—the traveling sailor and gibbeted criminal
and in turn the gibbeted sailor and traveler—but also people like the widow,
who seek companionship because they too are haunted by a ghostly, phantasmal legacy and its burdens. Rieder holds that "if the larger political and economic communities are mediated by violence and self-interest, then the sym-

pathetic community of the poor comes together through their speaking and listening to one another."[89] And what these poor speak of, what they in some measure are *driven* to speak of, is their dead. Hence, at the poem's conclusion the above-mentioned second traveler, fleeing a storm and chancing upon the executed sailor's gibbeted corpse "hung high in iron case," at once himself "drop[s]," as his "kindred sufferer" the sailor "once dropp'd, in miserable trance" (820, 825–28). For he, too, is struck by this contagion of death and of those dead looming inside and outside himself, "phantoms" who seem to occupy all who are "kindred" individuals. In this sense, the poem's conclusion presents what amounts to a form of serial community (similar to that later depicted in Coleridge's Wordsworth-influenced ballad, *The Rime of the Ancyent Marinere*), mediated by the powers of the dead to possess and guide the living.

The epigraph that opened the last section comes from the vagrant widow's narrative of her recuperation in a hospital, where she endured "careless cruelty . . . / And groans, which, as they said, would make a dead man start" (493–95). On the one hand, those "groans" in this quasi-spital speak to the power of the sick and dying to move sympathizing others—even the dead. On the other hand, the phrase turns on the power of the dead themselves to awaken, and not just to "start" but, from the same etymological root, to *startle*: to "start" and to startle readers, instilling or (re)awakening in them a frisson. The widow's remark points to the possibility of a griding passage of ghostly communication, "the commerce without commerce of ghosts,"[90] between the dead and the living or dying. It is a coinage and an economy based upon the poignancy of suffering and death, and especially upon the piercing power of those dead entombed within the mind. A similar crossing over of the dead into the living occurs inside the Spital, where (as in *Salisbury Plain*), startled by the sailor's entrance, the widow recalls the tale of a "grim head of a new-murder'd corse" discovered under one of the Spital's floor stones (216). The stony corpse is transported from this ghostly gothic narrative into her body "bound" by "[c]old stony horror," conveying into her form its haunting presence and inducing her "fail[ed]" "spirits" and "stony" corpse-like motionlessness (204, 220). Swann asks if "what frightens is perhaps not so much murder as one's vulnerability to the shocking return of the dead. Here the dead come back in story—the kind of story that figures its own effects as the return of the dead."[91] The phantom "corse" of the "dead house" crosses, as the corpse's "dire phantasma . . . had cross'd" into the sailor's mind, from the absence of death into bodily presence. According to Theresa Kelley, the widow in fact represents "how figurative interventions can bring what is hidden," in this case one's memories of the dead, "momentarily out of hiding."[92]

The widow's attempt to detour her listener from the dead of the dead house instead leads to further converse about those phantoms "of other worlds

consign'd" (224): "ghostly wanderers" able to cross into narrative as easily as
they cross Sarum's plain "on nightly roam intent" to confront travelers
(407–9). The encrypted phantom is fundamental to such "ghostly" communication, as its basis and motivation. Just as the widow's mind clings to the murdered "corse" of the Spital and to others lost to the murder of war, so the
sailor's mind "cleav[es] to the murder'd man" of his past (597). And this cleav-
ing attachment is associated, as the scene of the beaten boy suggests, with a
hidden "spot" to which and from which the griding "iron" of sensation (of
grief or guilt) finds "passage." The coffer-like iron case of a gibbet or other
marker is able to pierce into or out of the spot wherein the corpse is encrypted.
Such phantasmal presences thereby exert a double representational effect,
making their life-in-death traces felt in darts and other poignant signs.

In death the sailor is himself transformed not just into a grisly legal signifier but also into a phantom able to gride inside and outside of another haunted
mortal's mind and body. In reading this passage, Swann calls upon Abraham's
"Notes on the Phantom: A Complement to Freud's Metapsychology" and its
account of a patient "haunted by a phantom, itself due to a tomb enclosed
within the [unconscious] psyche of the father."[93] This ghost-effect qua psychic
affect lies similarly coffered away in the stranger's psyche, as an otherness that
both exceeds and underlies the self and that on occasion will find expressive
transport out of its mental "darkness." Derrida's reading of Abraham and Torok's
analysis of Freud's case study of the "Wolf Man" determines such a hidden psychic tomb to be at bottom a primary, prelinguistic encryption. It is one that
"forms a contradiction, enclosed, entombed, encysted within the Self," as an
affect that comprises the self but that is also other. That buried thing "is always
a living-dead," whose incorporation "always marks an effect of impossible . . .
mourning."[94] In *Adventures* the dead serve in much this same way to bridge and
inscribe otherness in a dream-like topography where ghosts "cross" into the
haunted borders of being. The sufferer viewing the gibbeted sailor is affected
because he, too, bears a hidden mark whose stimulation causes a contagious
mimesis. The contradiction is that precisely that which connects should be so
markedly and necessarily other to the self, and that the self should be transported into this sort of waking communitarian life by those dead entombed
within it. Yet that haunted self desires to express its hidden burden of ghosts, at
the cost even of consciousness itself. It is a form of subjectivity and social cohesion perhaps best dubbed "gothic communitarianism," fit for Otranto, for Elsinore or Inverness, and certainly for the disillusioned Britain of the mid 1790s.

An uneasy hero or spokesman of truth, in life the sailor is doubly placed
by his present words and past deeds both at the story's moral center and at its
legal margins. He also stands upon the foundations of the poem's scheme of
community, as in these "homely truths" prompted by his viewing of that violent family picnic:

> Then with a voice which inward trouble broke
> In the full swelling throat, the Sailor them bespoke.
>
> " 'Tis a bad world, and hard is the world's law;
> Each prowls to strip his brother of his fleece;
> Much need have ye that time more closely draw
> The bond of nature, all unkindness cease,
> And that among so few there still be peace:
> Else can ye hope but with such num'rous foes
> Your pains shall ever with your years increase."
>
> (658–66)

The "inward trouble" cannot but recall and be associated with the "dire phantasma" that gride through his mind into expression. Here internal woes and griefs prompt not paralysis but discourse—a discourse not dissimilar to the opening preamble of *Salisbury Plain* and its social seas of injustice and inequality. The sailor perceives and describes a modern world bereft of community—a Hobbesian state of war, scarcely a *Gesellschaft*—where animalistic prowling humans prey upon each other, having forgotten the uniting "bond of nature." That bond is in part one of consanguinity but also more loosely one of fraternity: a bond of our common nature as human beings. It is a bond that *Salisbury Plain* and *Adventures* represent as one of shared yet singular mortality and, especially, of shared yet singular grief: of the shared burdens caused by the dead who break out from within. The sailor's burden of grief—irrepressible, uncontainable, and interminable (hardly characteristics of social stability)—generates a desire for the *core* of Wordsworthian society: a translation of remorse into narrative or expressive trance.

In this way *Adventures* reveals a power of the dead at best latent in *Salisbury Plain*: their power to arise within the living from the crypts of the unconscious. The dead gride into corporeal representation as fits and starts, driving the living not just to fall into paralytic gothic trances but also to feel empathy and to desire to share their and others' mournful burdens. As in the *Vale*, these forces of the liminally remembered dead exceed and determine their mourners' consciousness and, through these hauntings, the foundations of community. Such discourse constitutes a community of mourners related by and to a shared cor(s)e. The guilt-ridden mourner is connected, less as agent than agency, to other mourners in similar need of converse. Community shifts from the genre of romance and its agents of light to that of gothic frisson and its more passive, tormented participants, becoming the dark product of a desire of which the self cannot be wholly conscious (for the dead *other* exceeds it). Such potential community is to be based, arguably more than anywhere else in Wordsworth's poetry, upon the subjection of the living to the haunting dead. It is tantamount to the dead speaking, to a converse "consigned" to and griding out of "other worlds" of shades (of a "world of shades") coffered within mournful selves.

Wordsworth's experimentation with genre once again structures a means for Revival readers to interrogate the grounds of community, chiefly because those readers find themselves implicated in spectatorship and its identifications with others and with the dead. They do so with little or no reliance upon institutions or, for that matter, even upon Enlightenment notions of human agency. One thereby finds in *Adventures on Salisbury Plain* a novel rearticulation of the foundations of society, laid out in a markedly unRousseauian, anti-rationalist manner, resting not in assent but in an abiding of the dead in the living. In doing so, Wordsworth salvages a mechanism for cohesion a priori to and other to those would-be social-political heroes he saw failing both at home and abroad. Yet for all *Adventures'* generic pessimism and circularity, its social cohesion follows from earlier works and anticipates the (less gothic) re-envisioning of community to be found in later poems, notably *The Ruined Cottage*. This point of linkage in *Adventures* treats death as a burden of phantoms whose "homeward" road conveys the narrative's protagonists, along with their Revival readers, toward the threshold of community. The path leads through a topography of ruins and crypts that lie on the Appian margins of society, as its furthest boundary and, deep within the haunted heart of the social, as a phantom content exchanged between the living and the dead.

4

The Shades of Mourning and the
One Life in *The Ruined Cottage*

> Give me a spark of nature's fire,
> Tis the best learning I desire.
>
> . . . . .
>
> My Muse though homely in attire
> May touch the heart.
>
> —Epigraph to
> *The Ruined Cottage,* MS. B[1]

By June of 1797 William and Dorothy were ensconced in Racedown Lodge, said by Dorothy to have been the "first home [she] had" (*EY* 281). But despite the profound happiness the two siblings shared dwelling in their home and viewing its Dorsetshire surroundings, all of course was not right with the world around them. The war with France had resulted not just in continental carnage but in domestic repression, spying, inflation, and paupery, with "shoals" of unemployed and homeless people wandering through England's countryside, much like those vagrants depicted in *An Evening Walk* and in the Salisbury Plain poems. Despite the rise of Robespierre and the ensuing Terror, Wordsworth had been able, for a time, to continue to trust "in the ideas of the early Republicans and [to share] the conviction of all radicals that the war could have been avoided" (*WL* 107–8), such that he penned his *Letter to the Bishop of Llandaff* (1793) defending Louis XVI's execution and other recent revolutionary events (the letter would almost certainly have been viewed as seditious, and was left unpublished). But by 1795, matters had changed considerably. As Stephen Gill states, with France's imperial aims now

> becoming more and more apparent, especially after the rejection in 1796 of
> British peace feelers and the triumphs of Napoleon's Italian campaign, it was
> no longer possible to believe that the war was being prosecuted solely from
> the malevolence of the Pitt government or even to have faith that some-
> where amidst the turmoil in France the ideals of the Revolution remained
> intact. (*WL* 108)

In France, and increasingly at home in England, reason itself appeared to have
failed, entrapping its former "heroes" in a quagmire of contradictions, cold calculations, violence, and irreversibly dashed expectations. In *The Prelude*'s
recounting of these tumultuous days, Wordsworth depicts himself as one who,
"wearied" by the "contrarieties" exposed by his quixotic quest "to probe / The
living body of society / Even to the heart," had finally "[y]ielded up moral
questions in despair" (*13P* 10.874–76, 899–900). In a "melancholy waste of
hopes o'erthrown" and of good men fallen (2.449), rationalism and revolution
had failed him.[2] So, like other English radicals, Wordsworth too began to
entertain social and political doubts, doubts that extended to his prior belief
in Godwin's philosophy of the gradual but inevitable progress of reason, predicated upon what now must have seemed an overly optimistic view of human
nature. By 1796, with this last utopian gasp of Enlightenment confidence and
hope largely expired, Wordsworth no longer had a "clear-cut creed to
announce, not even the counter-creed of the one-time zealot who had lost his
faith" (*WL* 108). And he knew it.

One of course must exercise care in trusting Wordsworth's poetical representations of his development, but I find little reason to doubt him regarding his sense of personal crisis in the mid 1790s. He likely did turn away from
Godwin around the time he and Dorothy had reunited at Windy Brow in
1794, as the topsy-turvy *Adventures on Salisbury Plain* attests, representing in
place of enlightening reason the necessitarian forces of gloom, superstition,
and unrelenting guilt. Even in *Salisbury Plain* Wordsworth's use of Godwin-
ism had been ironically delimited in a dialogical conflict between reformist-
rationalist realism and emotive romance, as if to hold the system at arm's
length to consider its limits and possibilities, the better, perhaps, to harness
them both. By the time of *The Borderers* (1796) progressivist rationalism likewise appears to have inspired only a pessimistic critique of the immorality or
amorality of abstract reasoning. Wordsworth's revisions to *An Evening Walk*
(MS. 9) similarly suggest his shift in orientation and, importantly, his ensuing
search for a philosophical system to explain and lend aid to troubled times. As
Dorothy wrote, theirs was, indeed, an "age of systems" (*EY* 180). And, as
H. W. Piper reasons, between 1795 and 1797 her brother William "desperately needed to find a religious system in which to believe."[3] Readers may
wonder with James Averill whether Piper does not overstate matters (*EW* 15);
that Wordsworth sought at the time a specifically "religious" system seems

particularly questionable. But that in these years he was seeking after some sort of system seems clear enough. He continued, and for moments appears even to have concluded, that search within the binding powers of his paradigm of mournful community.

In fact, as the last chapter argued, the Salisbury Plain poems very nearly succeeded, via that scheme, in piecing together the full framework of Wordsworthian community—of which the lost, June 1797 version of *The Ruined Cottage* was, so much as one can infer from the scant surviving manuscripts, in many ways the culmination. The poem was Wordsworth's great work of mourning, and is scarcely less so in its surviving versions.[4] It certainly represented a departure from the communitarianism of *Adventures on Salisbury Plain*, which focused upon the power of the dead to act as haunting forces able to compel community—a turn that may well have reflected Wordsworth's dissatisfaction with the scheme's reliance upon human agency. In June of 1797, however, with his composition of *The Ruined Cottage*, the poet steadfastly returns to mournful conversation as the primary means of social bonding, at the same time transforming *Adventure's* depiction of the dead's power into a more messianic, less gothic force. Such power of the dead is really the last piece Wordsworth articulates in this implicit sociology, albeit one to some extent implicit all along, most notably in the ghost-driven *Vale of Esthwaite*. But, as this chapter shall show, in its many revisions *The Ruined Cottage* also brings Wordsworth's social scheme under new pressure, from the social and religious "system" of pantheism. This novel paradigm, although frustrated by and frustrating to the narrative's work of mourning, in fact itself proves to be socially significant, producing communitarian results beyond the powers of either paradigm on its own.

I. The Seeds of Mourning

A frequently taken because useful approach to deciphering *The Ruined Cottage's* implicit workings traces the poem's beginnings to two fragments. These are recorded, along with the earliest version of *The Ruined Cottage*, in Racedown manuscript "A" of 1797, available in an appendix to the Cornell edition. Titled by Ernest de Selincourt "Incipient Madness" and "The Baker's Cart," the two fragments have been regarded as the "basis,"[5] "germ,"[6] and "origin"[7] of *The Ruined Cottage* itself. They certainly anticipate its key concerns. The lines that compose "Incipient Madness" provide the early setting for the poem (indeed, Wordsworth attempted to incorporate the lines into the MS. A text[8]), hearkening back to the Salisbury Plain poems' lone traveler and dead house—here a ruined "hut." "The Baker's Cart" adds to the mix the figure of a destitute woman (forerunner of *The Ruined Cottage's* Margaret), her

fatherless children, and a broken pitcher, plus "the pathetic moment of dialogue."[9] These two fragmentary texts serve well to lay the ground for my
reading of *The Ruined Cottage,* revealing as they do the rudiments of community over which Wordsworth apparently was mulling at Racedown.

The narrator of "The Baker's Cart" recalls seeing a mother and her "[f]ive
little ones" ignored by the local bread-wain:

> I have seen the Baker's horse
> As he had been accustomed at your door
> Stop with the loaded wain, when o'er his head
> Smack went the whip, and you were left, as if
> You were not born to live, or there had been
> No bread in all the land. . . .
> The wain now seen no longer, to my side
> [   ] came, a pitcher in her hand
> Filled from the spring; she saw what way my eyes
> Were turn'd, and in a low and fearful voice
> She said, "That waggon does not care for us."
>
> (A.1–16)

Given how the name "Margaret" fits metrically into the manuscript's lacuna,
Peter Manning speculates that her name might have been this mother's own,
although she is but one in a "series of sorrowing mothers in Wordsworth's
poetry of the 1790s." Drawing from the waters of psychoanalytic theory,
Manning reads the pitcher as a displaced symbol for the lost maternal breast,
an equation corroborated, he argues, by the symbol's occurrences in *An
Evening Walk,* with its broken "pitcher," and in *Adventures'* oedipal scene of a
son usurping his father's place when the parent retrieves a similar container.[10]
More to my purposes, the metaphorical connection between pitcher and
breast and its metalepsis from breast to loss suggests that the germ of this
germ of *The Ruined Cottage* lies in a past experience of troubled loss and grief,
as has been the case with the seeds of other of Wordsworth's poems. Whether
or not one reads the pitcher in Manning's psychoanalytic terms, then, the
result is much the same: the pitcher symbolizes loss.

Like Ecclesiastes' emblematic broken bowl, the pitcher in "The Baker's
Cart" is particularly associated with a loss of life sustenance, what is at bottom
a failure of community. John Turner argues that the mother's words reveal her
"need for fellowship,"[11] a need underlined by her ambivalent use of the word
"care" in her pointed lament that the local bread wagon "does not care for
us"—"care" meaning both to *like* and to *minister.* Were the swain or others in
this rural society to care more about this woman and her children, would he
or they then be more inclined to care *for* them? Could or should economics

follow upon sympathy and feeling? This connection is central to the narrator's indictment of a local community that ignores the mother and her children as if they "were not born to live, or there had been / No bread in all the land." Caring's constitutive elements—its sympathy, identification, and solicitude—are, like the children's father and like the carman, absent where they need to be present. "The Baker's Cart" reveals not the seeds of community, excepting for the narrator's sympathies, but rather what comes of an absence of community and its sustaining bonds of "care."

"Incipient Madness," for my purposes the most significant of these MS. A fragments, deepens the nature of this personal loss and grief, to the point even of grief becoming (or at least resulting in) a form of madness. The narrative begins, like its successor and like the Salisbury Plain poems, with a solitary traveler crossing a "dreary moor." On a clear night he comes to a long-ruined hut and, upon entering its interior, sees

> At a small distance, on the dusky ground,
> A broken pane which glitter'd in the moon
> And seemed akin to life.
>
> (5–7)

At this point the speaker pauses to observe that in such instances as these,

> There is a mood,
> A settled temper of the heart, when grief,
> Become an instinct, fastening on all things
> That promise food, doth like a sucking babe
> Create it where it is not.
>
> (7–11)

Hence, he confesses,

> From this time
> I found my sickly heart had tied itself
> Even to this speck of glass. It could produce
> A feeling as of absence [   ]
> [   ] on the moment when my sight
> Should feed on it again.
>
> (11–16)

Night after night the man is "obsessively drawn" to this "speck" out of a desire to see it glitter in the moonlight, "feed[ing]" on it rather as a child sucks on its

thumb. In fact, on this clear night he seeks not shelter per se but the realization of a memory, a fetishized memory associated with past loss. That loss has
produced a deep-seated "grief, / Become an instinct," the source of his compulsion for revisiting the cottage's glimmering reflections of lifelike presence.
As mentioned in the Introduction, Wordsworth may have been influenced in
this regard by Locke's discussion of the phenomenon of "incurable sorrow," a
condition owed to a peculiar association of ideas. The melancholic victims of
such a "wrong connexion" thenceforth spend their "lives in mourning, and
carry an incurable sorrow to their graves."[12]

   An example of such "incurable sorrow" can also be found in "The Thorn,"
discussed in Chapter Five, and in *The Borderers,* in which the villain Rivers
(falsely) reports of the obsessive funeral rites an abandoned woman performs
nightly for her dead infant:

> But every night at the first stroke of twelve
> She quits her house, and in the neighbouring church-yard
> Upon the self same spot, in rain or storm,
> She paces out the hour 'twixt twelve and one,
> She paces round and round, still round and round,
> And in the church-yard sod her feet have worn
> A hollow ring; they say it is knee-deep——
>
> (*B* I.iii.16–22)

With its quasi-incantation of repeated phrases, the narrative enacts rhetorically
a similar sort of repetition complex as that acted out by the female mourner in
her diseased resistance to loss. Although the Iago-like Rivers in fact has fabri-
cated this sorrowful tale to serve his own selfish motives, he nevertheless understands grief's constitutive value and appeal for others; hence his manipulative
employment of just such devices and tales. As John Rieder points out, Rivers

> attempts to bind Mortimer to himself by means of seizing the power of
> death over another, making of that other a sacrificial victim whose execution
> produces the communal bond of a shared guilt. The play lets us know that
> this procedure is nothing new, that it is, in fact, things as they are.[13]

Rivers understands the nature of shared guilt: the manner in which death can
bond the living as comrades, even as partners in crime. It is a perverse version
of what Wordsworth saw elsewhere to be the basis for social cohesion among
the living.

   The roughly contemporary "Incipient Madness" plays out a similar scenario
through its traveler's visitations to an occluded absence. Paul Sheats reads the
flickering "life" the traveler seeks in the abandoned hut as phantasmal and there-

fore wrongheaded: "spurious, projected on a broken shard of the past by emotions that, though unnamed, are clearly compulsive and related to the human life this cottage once sheltered."[14] Turner better diagnoses the traveler's condition as "a depression which *cannot* grieve."[15] But such grief is, I think, best read as a "sickly" species of a now familiar Wordsworthian grief *for* grief. A disturbing and unrelenting sense of loss, the death of a beloved inhabitant of the hut or some similar dwelling, draws the traveler to revisit an enigmatic spot associated with pleasure and pain, life and death, presence and absence, desire and loss. This spot typifies less the loss of a beloved, the case in Locke's pathology, than the fetishizing of and longing for loss and grief themselves, the mourning of mourning.

"Tied to dead things and seeking sympathy / In stocks and stones" (*RC*, p. 467)—to borrow from several lines scrawled ambiguously between "The Baker's Cart" and "Incipient Madness"—the traveler's grief has become psychologically disturbed, "settled" in its shadowy realm of "instinct" and fetish like an infant "fastening on all things / That promise food . . . where it is not." It in fact is not life that he finds so alluring but instead his kinship with a grief that itself desires to "feed," a kind of genius loci that is only a "feeling as of absence." The broken pane's lifelike play of light and dark is not an adequate substitute for the lost object (but what would be?) or even for absence (it produces a "feeling *as* of absence"); it only points to a loss "where it is not." In this way, Wordsworth's second fragment explores what comes of incomplete or unshared mourning: an incipience of isolation, alienation, and madness.[16] At the same time that the text shows what can come of disrupted, "broken" mourning, it illuminates grief's power to spark and instill desire: the desire for the lost grief it would reconstitute, for the dead it would reclaim and who claim it still, and, potentially, for forms of burden sharing, in the absence of which the fragment's self-enclosing madness is the topsy-turvy gothic result.

Like "The Baker's Cart" fragment, this seed of *The Ruined Cottage* reveals the origins of narrative to lie in loss and mourning—and in a troubled form of mourning at that. A trauma of loss underlies revisitation, and hence also underlies the structure of travel (as quest) and, potentially, of narrative. As in these poems, community in *The Ruined Cottage* is woven from the threads of vexed mourning, produced by mourners' shared but unfinished, ceaseless grieving for the dead.

II. READING AND MOURNING IN *THE RUINED COTTAGE*

> I have written 1300 lines of a poem in which I contrive to convey most of the knowledge of which I am possessed. My object is to give pictures of Nature, Man, and Society.
>
> —to James Tobin, 6 March 1798

The Ruined Cottage was the first work Wordsworth recited to Coleridge when the latter visited Racedown, "leap[ing] over a gate and bound[ing] down a pathless field" to the cottage on June 6, 1797 (*LY* 3: 1263). Subsequently, Dorothy glowingly described Coleridge to Mary Hutchinson, adding that their new friend "was much delighted" with the poem (*EY* 189). The visit understandably marked an escalation in affection, intimacy, and intellectual exchange between the two poets, whose mutual debt of influence had already begun to accumulate in late 1796.[17] Still, there is little evidence of a direct debt to Coleridge in those lines for *The Ruined Cottage* likely composed by the time of his visit, when he arrived at Racedown doubtless excited to impart his philosophical, political, and sociological views. Those views would, however, have a pronounced impact on the poem's course from that day forward.

Like "Incipient Madness" and the Salisbury Plain poems, *The Ruined Cottage* opens with a lone traveler crossing a deserted common:

> Across a bare wide Common I had toiled
> With languid feet which by the slippery ground
> Were baffled still; and when I sought repose
> On the brown earth my limbs from very heat
> Could find no rest nor my weak arm disperse
> The insect host which gathered round my face
> And joined their murmurs to the tedious noise
> Of seeds of bursting gorse which crackled round.
> I rose and turned towards a group of trees
> Which midway in the level stood alone,
> And thither came at length, beneath a shade
> Of clustering elms that sprang from the same root
> I found a ruined Cottage, four clay walls
> That stared upon each other.
>
> (B.18–31)

It is unclear whether the June manuscript read to Coleridge began with this traveler's discomfort or, as Dorothy summarized matters in a letter that included lines from the poem, with the "Poet suppos[ing] himself to come in sight of some tall trees on a flat common" (*EY* 200). It may simply have opened with the phrase "I found a ruined Cottage." The poem read that day was certainly shorter than the 528–line MS. B text produced between January and March of 1798 at Alfoxden Park and was probably lacking, Jonathan Wordsworth conjectures, MS. B's opening (lifted in part from the MS. 9 revisions of *An Evening Walk*), its biography of the pedlar, and its moral transition between the narrative's two principal sections.[18] In the first months of 1798 Wordsworth composed addenda to that revised text, "surrounding" it, Rieder states, "with additions that swell[ed] it to some 900 lines."[19] The result of still further revisions commenced in early 1799 at Goslar, *The Ruined Cottage* of MS. D concludes with lines incorporated from the second of those addenda but eliminates most all of MS. B's interpolation of the pedlar's history, later used as the basis for the expanded *Pedlar* (1803–4). Hence, although the core of the surviving MS. B narrative likely resembles that of the poem read under the trees at Racedown, the story's framing is considerably altered, making the overall poem quite different from what Coleridge probably heard. The MS. D text, with its sedative conclusion, presents a further departure or progression from the relatively stark June version.

There has been considerable discussion among scholars about the preferability of one or the other of these two complete manuscripts of *The Ruined Cottage*, MS. B of 1797–98 and MS. D of 1799, the debate often centering on the appropriateness of MS. D's "reconciling addendum" (*RC* 20).[20] Both texts are presented in James Butler's Cornell edition, and, as I see it, form part of a larger compositional matrix that incorporates all surviving versions of the poem and its addenda.[21] Mindful of Gill's rejoinder that any version of *The Ruined Cottage* is at least in some manner an editorial construction[22]—the poem not having been published until its inclusion in Book First of *The Excursion*—for my purposes I treat both the "B" and "D" versions and the addenda as integral parts of the poem. Hence, although my focus is on the earlier of the two complete versions, MS. B, I do not hesitate to supplement that reading with passages from the addenda and from the MS. D version. Indeed, in places my reading is based upon Wordsworth's considerable revision of the poem between 1797 and 1799, notably his introduction of the philosophy of the "One Life" as the basis for MS. B's consoling addenda and for MS. D's reconciling conclusion.

The above-quoted MS. B text likely represents Wordsworth's attempt to craft a suitable prologue or preliminary frame to the core narrative of the June *Ruined Cottage*,[23] a key aspect of the poem's opening being the solitary traveler's condition of alienation from nature and society. This opening motif of isolated wandering in a hostile and wearying locale, midway in a journey between life and death, presages the narrator's spiritual crisis and progress: the expectation that, rather like Dante in the *Commedia*, he is in need of moral improvement, which he will gain from a guardian who will lead him, via some sort of descent, to see what he now does not see. This is in part what happens. Adjacent to the ruined cottage, "a super-annuated Pedlar"—so Francis Jeffrey called him[24]—rests in the shade of the stand of elms. The traveler greets the itinerant, with whom he shares a lesser or greater acquaintance depending upon which of the manuscripts one consults. Advanced in years and with an "iron-pointed staff" (B.39) by his side, the pedlar is an appropriate Virgil to lead the traveler into the narrated past of the ruin. Fittingly, the traveler first describes him in death-like terms: "[s]tretched on a bench," the latter all "studded o'er with fungus flowers" (37–38). The elderly sage's "way-wandering life" has led him to the outskirts of society, and to become well acquainted with the last inhabitants of this cottage.

Unbidden, the pedlar proceeds to recount these tenants' sorrowful history. He tells the traveler of Margaret, who had lived in the cottage with her husband Robert and their two children. But with the American war's impact on the cottage-weaving industry, coupled with disastrous harvests and her husband's sudden but doubtless related illness, the family was ruined. Robert abandoned them, enlisting, Margaret believed, to provide them the bounty paid recruits. She was left to await his return. Five years later, having "gone to pieces like her cottage"[25] and having watched her children waste away, Margaret, too, died, "[l]ast human tenant," the pedlar concludes, "of these ruined walls" (528). And with that the MS. B version of the poem dramatically ends, as likely did the June version, leaving the traveler and pedlar to mourn.

Spurred by the consolatory agenda of *The Recluse,* in which Wordsworth and Coleridge soon determined *The Ruined Cottage* was to figure prominently (see below), Wordsworth sought to compose a more suitable, consoling conclusion to the poem. Hence, in MS. B's addenda the narrator reveals himself to have been much affected by Margaret's history, in such a way that he has become "a better and a wiser man" (*RC,* p. 257). Likewise, in the conclusion to the MS. D manuscript of 1799, adapted from MS. B's "Not Useless" addendum, the pedlar makes it clear that his responsive listener has served the "purposes of wisdom" (D.511), a change signaled at the text's end by the two men's departure to a "rustic inn" (538). As Jonathan Wordsworth observes, these wanderers symbolically enter the scene "separately, with their separate attitudes," but leave it together, as comrades bonded by the pedlar's story and with a pleasant sojourn, and even a dwelling, before them.[26]

Indeed, of primary importance to *The Ruined Cottage*'s social vision is the development of their friendship. Readers familiar with the poem might of course reasonably object that the narrator and pedlar clearly are already friends at the outset. After all, upon seeing the old man, the traveler feels himself to be "no stranger to the spot" (B.51) because of his familiarity with the itinerant and the latter's "talk of former days" (52). The pedlar subsequently calls him "friend" (130, 526), and in MS. D the narrator describes himself and the itinerant as having been "fellow-travelers" (D.41). How, then, can their actions be said to consolidate community if the principal form of association of such community, namely friendship, in fact preexists it? The answer is that the two wanderers' relationship is altered by the pedlar's narrative of Margaret and by their different responses to it, as MS. D's symbolic conclusion suggests and as is suggested also by Wordsworth's various attempts to conclude the poem in MS. B. Furthermore, the earliest manuscripts of *The Ruined Cottage* demonstrate that the author initially conceived of the two wanderers as strangers. In the June 1797 text, for example, to judge from Coleridge's quotation of the poem's last lines in a letter to John Estlin, the pedlar distinctly called the narrator "Stranger" (*RC,* p. 95). Similarly, in the poem's first surviving manuscript the pedlar hails him as "Sir" (MS. A.170) and, significantly, needs to provide an account of his livelihood as a "wanderer among the cottages" (191). Even in MS. B the narrator is occasionally addressed as "Sir" (311), a formal salutation that, although perhaps attributable in some measure to class differences, is more suggestive of the two men's passing acquaintance than of past friendship. In addition to these wanderers' intertextual progress from the strangers of June 1797 to the "fellow travelers" of 1799 in MS. D,[27] there is also the previously mentioned intratextual progression, signaled in the latter manuscript by the two men's joint departure.

How, then, did the strangers of June 1797, the quasi-strangers at the opening of MS. B, come to be the comradely friends depicted departing together at the close of MS. D? As will be shown, the answer is that their social conversion is effected by their conversation of the dead, similar in this way to the eighteenth-century epitaphic topos of the "stranger" implored to become, through what Joshua Scodel describes as "an emotionally charged, dialectical relationship," a new "friend" to the deceased.[28] In *The Ruined Cottage* Wordsworth locates the agency of such conversion in mourning's unique bonding of the living and dead as well as in the differences in individual mourners' approaches to mourning those dead. Like mourning, in the poem friendship is localized and specific, based not on univocal abstract ideals or attachments—as had been the Revolution's (failed) ideals of universal benevolence and fraternity[29]—but on particular sources of loss, shared by particular people in a specific place.[30] These friendships do not become subsumed into a universal substance and yet they are predicated upon something intangible that lingers between the particular and universal, looming beyond even the affections of the mourners themselves while remaining tied to their own mourning and discourse. In *The Ruined Cottage* such mourning of the invisible dead ever remains the ne plus ultra of camaraderie and its resulting community.

In explaining to the narrator the secret character of the ruined cottage's enigmatic "spot," the pedlar describes himself as one able to see "[t]hings which you cannot see": a place where

> that which each man loved
> And prized in his peculiar nook of earth
> Dies with him or is changed, and very soon
> Even of the good is no memorial left.

> (B.130–34)

Yet such history recapitulates not just objects lost to time but also the grief that underlies or accompanies their loss. The pedlar proceeds to draw the narrator's gaze to the adjacent spring, whose waters "if they could feel / Might mourn" Margaret's death (135–36). But, he relates,

> They are not as they were; the bond
> Of brotherhood is broken—time has been
> When every day the touch of human hand
> Disturbed their stillness, and they ministered
> To human comfort.
>
> (136–40)

The spring waters signify the breaking of this "bond / Of brotherhood," a social breach that alienates nature from ministering to "human comfort." Yet the tale of the ruin and its last occupants is unfolded not simply because human beings abhor a memorial vacuum but because they are preceded by a store of blocked and unfinished mourning, eliciting the text's belated repetition of elegiac history in the absence of any proper "memorial."[31]

In terms of the underlying nature of this mourning, to which the pedlar's history responds, we learn that Margaret's melancholy was owed chiefly to her uncertainty about her husband Robert's fate. After his surreptitious departure to America,

> she had learned
> No tidings of her husband: if he lived
> She knew not that he lived; if he were dead
> She knew not he was dead.
>
> (435–38)

As a result of Robert's indeterminate status as one awaited or mourned, Margaret "lingered in unquiet widowhood, / A wife, *and* widow" anxiously "shaping things" in "the distance" in anticipation of his return (483–84, 492; emphasis added). One can see from the description of her sufferings that her tragedy lies less in her husband's tacit abandonment of her, or for that matter in the economic conditions that precipitated his departure, than in her uncertainty about his fate. She is able to reject neither alternative about him being alive or dead, and so is condemned to being not a wife *or* a widow—the resolution of her ambivalence—but the wife *and* widow of one unable really to be mourned. Her mourning of Robert is blocked, resulting in her melancholy condition and its debilitating listlessness, self-neglect, and reveries of reunion.[32]

Margaret's troubled mourning is revealed in this way to be the raison d'être of the poem as a whole, in all its versions, for the narrative is occasioned and produced by the conversation of the two travelers at a "ruin" owed to (and signifying) her inability to mourn. The force of her personal tragedy of non-mourning is what elicits the pedlar's narrative of her, and what here provides the implicit basis for tale-telling, dialogue, and the travelers' resultant association as kindred mourners. Hence, as in that Rosetta stone of Wordsworthian desire, *The Vale of Esthwaite*, in *The Ruined Cottage* the haunting desire for memorialization takes its start from a past disruption of mourning that becomes, in its need for supplementation, the predicating ground or seed of subsequent mourning and conversation. Community in this way is founded upon the underlying inefficacy and interminability of past and present mourning. A gathering of readers responds not just to a death but, more importantly, to a reserve or a lack associated with it: a loss responsible, in its incompleteness, for the mourners' desire for mourning and consolation.

This break between present and past, and within the past itself, is symbolized in *The Ruined Cottage* by the neglected waters. Their former disturbance by "the touch of human hand" had signified a communitarian bond, but now in their stillness the waters signify its loss. So, too, the "deserted" well's "useless fragment of a wooden bowl" (141, 145) signifies the loss of community. The latter line at first sounds so commonplace that, as Jonathan Wordsworth has pointed out, readers might not recognize "the pitcher broken at the fountain in Ecclesiastes," although there can be little doubt that Wordsworth, here as in both *An Evening Walk* and "The Baker's Cart," "had in mind this archetypal image of life stopped at its source."[33] This previously mentioned figure of the broken pitcher is in Ecclesiastes one of a metaphorical series lamenting economic scarcity and old age, a series comprised of the "loosed" "silver cord" of the lamp, the broken "golden bowl," and the "wheel broken at the cistern," along with the white almond tree and the lagging grasshopper (12:5–6).[34] The series of geriatric figures describes waning physical and sexual vitality, symbolized by the loosening of the wick of sexual potency and by a break in the bowl of life's waters, as well as by the gray hair and bent gait of old age.

Ecclesiastes' lament extends to man's final journey "to his long home," and to mourners who thereupon "go about the streets" to mark his passing (12:5). The sign of a lost bond of community in *The Ruined Cottage*, "still" water signifies a wished-for animating and reactivating of mourning; in other words, a desire for mourning. The ruined cottage's waters in this way register a double symbolic coinage of loss and desire, of a break between man and man (viz. "the touch of human hand") and of a desire for a mourning that, although "broken," would restore a degree of social connectedness and continuity, since lapsed in "evil days" (12:1). As a textual sign, then, the bowl is no longer exactly "useless," for it connects the "deserted well" to a "regained home" (12:5)—for Wordsworth a sure sign both of presence and of social cohesion— and to those who would mourn mortal loss, like those pastoral elegists to whom the pedlar later refers, who "call upon the hills and streams to mourn [the departed]" (D.75). Reactivation of broken mourning becomes in this light the hallmark of a community organized to mourn death, loss, and mourning itself.

Indeed, for all this ruinous spot's elision of human cultivation and culture, its surviving signs speak volumes of what has been lost. They offer to those readers possessed of an elegist's "creative power" and "human passion" (D.78–79; <L. *patior*, "to feel" and "to suffer") an opportunity to read *and* to mourn: to come to see reading as a form or means of mourning and to see mourning as the registering and reading of a lack or loss of mourning. The pedlar's description of Margaret symbolizes this hermeneutic project: how, along a nearby path,

> There, to and fro she paced through many a day
> Of the warm summer, from a belt of flax
> That girt her waist spinning the long-drawn thread
> With backward steps.
>
> (B.495–98)

More than her weaver husband, Margaret is depicted not just as a flax-wasted spinner but as a figure of the memorializing poet, "spinning the long-drawn thread" which since the Greeks has symbolized poetic process. She is also figured as a type of historian who retraces "with backward steps" the "thread" of difference and loss that leads back into a temporal "distance" she has shaped: "her eye . . . busy in the distance, shaping things / Which made her heart beat quick" (491–93). In this sense she is fundamentally a figure of the elegist, whose vocation is the textualizing of what has been lost. Her melancholy "shaping [of] things" arises in response to her inability to leave what is distant—a life or a death, a body or corpse—*in* the distance. In fact, no amount of backward steps will lead her back to Robert or to her proper mourning of him. They will only measure, like poetic meter, her distance from that loss.[35]

Karen Swann observes that the pedlar, in his repeated laments, "recognizes and elegizes Margaret as a lost fellow poet, changed into something strange, dead before her time."[36] Indeed it is clear that Margaret's strange grief and death are the foundation for the pedlar's own poetic practice. Her errant movements and fantasies emblematize the manner in which he spins out her tale as a narrative line extending into the past—the tale of a spinner-weaver occasioned by his spotting of a spider's web stretched across a well, no less.

Margaret serves as the genius loci, the long-suffering saint and muse, of this ruin and its narrative.[37] Her mourning inaugurates and haunts poesis as mourning-play and is the focus for the rehearsals of grief that compose most of the poem and effect the changing relationship of its interlocutors. The poignancy of her suffering as a mourner and textualist, its insistent insufficiency, forges the primary link of identification between the mourners who retrace her thread of irremediable grief. Hence, the pedlar is "not seldom" drawn by the thread of her tragedy to envision her as "destined to awake / To human life" (D.368, 372–73), while the narrator, in response to the old man's own "busy" eye's textualizing of distant things, reviews those details as a still-surviving, ghostly "secret spirit of humanity" (503). Margaret is the flickering focal image of a lost yet "busy" grief, recalled in a tale about the very production of tales, a metapoetic marker of poetics as the supplement to an unfulfillable, infecting loss caught by those who rehearse her history. It can be said that in *The Ruined Cottage* history is elegy: an attempt to reconstruct through reading a "broken" bond of "brotherhood" that "human passion" desires to mend. The details of the ruinous garden "plot" (B.116) compose a script that allows or obliges readers to read and mourn, deciphering and to some extent recapitulating a broken mourning ghostily locked within a landscape of decay.[38] That topography's deathless spirit is the measure and product of a loss that lives on in its insufficiency: as a potential force, a piece of lingering, unfinished, ever-busy human activity and history.

III. "To Virtue Friendly": Mourning and the One Life

At the midpoint of his narrative, the pedlar pauses to ask "Why," amid all the "repose and peace" of nature, Margaret's history should still cause there to be "a tear . . . in an old Man's eye?" (B.250). Nature's peace and beauty ought to be enough. Such a vantage is to be expected from the poem's proponent of the consolatory "calm of Nature" (256).[39] But before I consider his distinctive and quite contrary vantage, a bit of background concerning the provenance of his pantheist views is needed, specifically concerning Wordsworth's borrowing of the "One Life" from Coleridge, likely around the time of that friend's first visit to Racedown.

By June of 1797 Coleridge had already formulated his version of One Life doctrine, predicated upon the radical Enlightenment notion of an all-pervading, single energy or spiritual presence underlying all the earth's natural and intellectual matter—what William Ulmer describes as the immanence of divinity, with all of nature existing as "modulations of the Universal Mind."[40] That pantheist vision was already exemplified in lines Coleridge composed in the autumn of 1795 for the (later titled) "Eolian Harp":

> And what if all of animated nature
> Be but organic harps diversely framed,
> That tremble into thought, as o'er them sweeps
> Plastic and vast, one intellectual breeze,
> At once the Soul of each, and God of All?
>
> (44–48)[41]

Coleridge reformulated traditional pantheism's material monism as a more intellectualized and spiritualized "omnipresent Mind, / Omnific" (*Religious Musings*, 105–6). He appears also to have embraced the philosophy's inherent determinism, in 1796 proclaiming himself to be "a compleat Necessitarian," and arguably sticking to this meliorist aspect of the One Life until nearly 1799,[42] despite his reservations about pantheism's monism, which posed problems for the orthodox Christian tenet of a transcendent deity.[43] Wordsworth's new friend almost certainly brought with him to Racedown this exciting conception of "the one Life, within us and abroad, / Which meets all Motion, and becomes its soul."[44]

Despite its problematical implications, One Life doctrine was attractive to both poets for its ameliorative vision (chiefly made possible by the monism and determinism that troubled it).[45] As Ulmer states, to subscribe to the One Life and its tenet of God's immanence in nature was also to believe "in the gradual approximation of all things to ultimate goodness."[46] So Coleridge promoted the One Life as the philosophical basis for a consoling, hope-restoring philosophical epic to mend the dejection, pessimism, and cynicism his countrymen were experiencing as a result of the Revolution's failure. To Coleridge's mind, a fall of sorts indeed had occurred, and as a result respected radicals like John Thelwall and fellow republicans like Wordsworth were disengaging from political activity and seeking passive rural retirement. The question was what could be done to correct their pessimism and despondency. The projected master poem of *The Recluse* was intended, as Kenneth Johnston states (echoing Coleridge), "to keep the best minds of their generation from recoiling *too far* into domestic concerns, in their reaction against the failures and excesses of the French Revolution."[47] I am not going to address here the problems the project of *The Recluse* presented for Wordsworth once he had agreed to take on the onerous task of writing this ambitious poem,[48] except to say that this decision had immediate repercussions for the seemingly hopeless (rather than hope-filled) *Ruined Cottage* of June 1797. Enter the One Life into the planned "moral and Philosophical Poem" (*EY* 454) and, more to my purposes, into the revised text of *The Ruined Cottage* as one of its two alternative social vantages: the one tied to shared mourning and the other to the confidence and equipoise proffered by a compensating pantheist view of nature and death.

One may speculate that in those summer months of 1797 Wordsworth first attempted to articulate some of this dazzling new system's principles in his revisions of *An Evening Walk,* which had previously been revised at Windy Brow. These added lines' references to ambiguous "social accents" and "a secret power" recall the transmortal "secret power" of the dead praised in *Descriptive Sketches,* and suggest that Wordsworth's pantheism was even then as much social as religious in its key tenet that "[f]rom love of Nature love of Virtue flows" (*EW* 1794, l. 261). In these and prior lines, *An Evening Walk's* eighteenth-century locodescription veers toward a more interactive model of mind and nature. John O. Hayden's positing of a later date than 1794 for this revised text lends weight to Jonathan Wordsworth's prior argument that, as Robert Ryan summarizes, "Coleridge was the primary influence on Wordsworth's doctrine of the 'one life' that mankind shares with the rest of nature, and that this influence was brought to bear most effectively . . . in 1797 and early 1798."[49] If, in the time following Coleridge's visit, Wordsworth was not yet casting himself as *The Recluse's* exemplary *philologus*—described in Coleridge's *Table Talk* as "a man in mental repose, whose principles were made up, and so prepared to deliver upon authority a system of philosophy" (*CWSTC* 14: 1.307)—he certainly was grooming his pedlar for the part. Now the itinerant would proclaim that "In all forms of things / There is a mind" (*RC,* p. 123) and be described as having himself found in "all shapes" in nature "a secret and mysterious soul" (B.83–84). In Coleridge's words, such a man, living "in contact with external nature," would serve to reveal to "the present state of degeneracy and vice . . . a redemptive process in operation, showing how this idea reconciled all the anomalies and promised future glory and restoration" (1.308).

For the pedlar, this pantheistic vision of nature produces a mood of "easy chearfulness" (although that is not the case in the tearful instant of his query), as nature does in the narrator, too, for a time, "[stealing] away" his own mournful despondency (259–60). But could this ruinous topography really be expected to counteract the sorrow of a history that has revealed it to be a site of loss and its locodescription to be elegy?[50] In fact, the pedlar's attempt to interpose his brand of restorative "natural wisdom" (253) ultimately fails to reconcile the narrator, and, for that matter, fails even to stay his own tears. Although in light of the old man's cheerfulness the narrator turns from Margaret's tragic yet "simple tale" and its "restless" effects (256) to view the natural scene around him, he does so only for a moment. Soon he restlessly returns to his contemplation "of that poor woman," a woman he has come to behold "as . . . one / Whom I had known and loved" (265–66). For her elegist-historian

> had rehearsed
> Her homely tale with such familiar power,
> . . . that the things of which he spake

Seemed present, and, attention now relaxed,
There was a heartfelt chillness in my veins.

(266–71)

Thus finding himself staring at the "tranquil ruin" not with the pedlar's natural tranquillity but with "a mild force of curious pensiveness," the narrator
seeks out the old itinerant, asking "that for my sake / He would resume his
story" (276–79). Here the hope of the MS. B text's epigraph achieves fruition:
that the poem's "homely" muse might "touch the heart." The narrator has
identified with the homely tale's dead protagonist not as he would a stranger
but as one he "had known and loved," to the point even, in the reconciling
conclusion to MS. D, of reviewing her sufferings, in a place now ruinously
marked by the absence of "brotherhood," with a new-found "brother's love"
(D.499). It is an act that, for Esther Schor, underlines the extent to which the
traveler has himself become "an initiate" of Margaret's "somber magic."[51]

The narrator has developed an identity closely resembling that of the
Wedding Guest in Coleridge's roughly contemporary, partly Wordsworth-
influenced narrative *The Rime of the Ancyent Marinere,* wherein that guest
becomes, through hearing the Mariner's sea tale of death and insufficient
atonement, both "a sadder and a wiser man" (*LB,* 1. 657). As Sheats observes,
this too is the lot of the pedlar's listener, who becomes "a humble initiate and
a 'better and a wiser man'" able to display "compassion for Margaret."[52] Like
the Guest's moral improvement, the speaker's progress is, James Chandler
points out, a "consequence of the narrative he has just heard related."[53] Indeed,
more explicitly than in the case of the Guest, *The Ruined Cottage*'s narrator
becomes a further teller of tales of and for the dead. Margaret's "broken"
mourning sparks his anguished "impotence of grief" (D.500), a paradoxically
potent impotency whose force lies in its own troublesome status as a mourning at a "distance" from its object. As was similarly the case with mourning in
the *Vale,* the result of such a keenly felt "impotence of grief" is, in Schor's
words, that "grief accumulates,"[54] increasing without abating. Mourning compels in the pedlar a "passion" to rehearse the mournful tale (like the Ancient
Mariner), as evidenced by the poem we read, and it makes its listener "a better and a wiser man" by binding him to the living and the dead.

Such stress on the narrator's moral progress provides an intriguing context for the following lines from MS. D, in which the pedlar, nearing the end
of his history of Margaret, explains to his sorrowing listener that:

It would have grieved
Your very heart to see her. Sir, I feel
The story linger in my heart. I fear
'Tis long and tedious, but my spirit clings

To that poor woman: so familiarly
Do I perceive her manner, and her look
And presence, and so deeply do I feel
Her goodness, that not seldom in my walks
A momentary trance comes over me;
And to myself I seem to muse on one
By sorrow laid asleep or borne away,
A human being destined to awake
To human life, or something very near
To human life, when he shall come again
For whom she suffered. Sir, it would have griev'd
Your very soul to see her. . . .

(361–76)

This enigmatic scene has been variously interpreted: as a "moment of apoca-
lyptic insight" into "the quickening power of love" (*WP* 223), as a less-
worked-through "imaginative fantasy" of Margaret's "return to life,"[55] as a
fairy-tale "fantasy of reunion with the lost mother,"[56] and, in the words of
Averill, as a "version of Christian immortality," insofar as the

> phrase, "he shall come again," while it refers to Margaret's husband, has res-
> onances of resurrection and apocalypse. Similarly, "for whom she suffered"
> recalls Christ's sacrifice for mankind. From musing on Margaret's suffering,
> then, the Pedlar would appear to claim a vision of immortality much like that
> contained in the Christian promise. (*PHS* 133)

Wordsworth's wording indeed draws on Christian associations of resurrection
and sacrifice,[57] and represents a secularization of the supernatural powers associated with Christian apocalypse and Judaic messianism. So much has the
poem's focus been on the narrator's improvement, however, that in the pedlar's
revelation that his "spirit clings" to Margaret's spiritual "presence," such that
she seems "destined to awake . . . when *he* shall come again," the latter pronoun can be read not as, or certainly not just as, Robert or even Christ, but as
the narrator himself. It is, after all, for his "sake," he declares, that Margaret's
sufferings have been "rehearsed" and are being rehearsed still, and it is his
grief-stricken "heart" and "soul" that suitably bracket the pedlar's revelations.
The episode may also recall Jesus's words to his disciples: "where two or three
are gathered together in my name, there am I in the midst of them" (Matthew
18:20). The pedlar and narrator's shared discourse of Margaret invokes her
posthumous presence—or, rather, the clinging force of her absence and of her
incomplete grief. Margaret's status as a saint-like martyr underlines her con-
nectability to and exchangeability between those who invoke her as this

eucharistic "secret spirit" whose sufferings, unable to be ended—and so never and always to be worked through—hauntingly continue. The pedlar's visits to the cottage "both prophesy and allegorize Margaret's propensity to return, unbidden, to his thoughts" as a kind of apparition.[58] In their eternal, trans-missible character, her sufferings become the basis for others' sense of con-nection to her and to those who share in the sufferings' rehearsal.

The Ruined Cottage is, after all, not just the tale of Margaret's suffering and death but a tale told by a pedlar "emotionally involved in her sufferings to a lis-tener who becomes increasingly so."[59] It is a transformation owed to the narra-tive's resurrective power for making absent "things" seem "present," which is to say to the transmissive character of that which cannot be worked through and concluded, as is perhaps reflected in the MS. B *Ruined Cottage*'s numerous and problematic endings. We learn from the pedlar's biography that he has in fact long possessed a facility for finding "In all shapes . . . a secret and mysterious soul, / A fragrance and a spirit of strange meaning" (B.83–85). That disposi-tion produces in him a state of mind that others might mistake for

> madness—[and] such it might have been,
> But that he had an eye which evermore
> Looked deep into the *shades of difference*
> As they lie hid in all exterior forms . . .
> And by an unrelenting agency
> Did bind his feelings even as in a chain.
>
>   (93–103; emphasis added)

These lines are the principal presentation of the pedlar's *lived* One Life phi-losophy, the "forms" being chiefly those of nature—"a stone, a tree, a withered leaf" (97)—in which the itinerant finds an animating, unified "soul" or "spirit." At the same time, Wordsworth's text betrays other concerns, including a con-cern for death, as with the dying "withered leaf," which anticipates the pow-ers of Margaret and her ruin. In the context of the One Life, one might read such shades of "difference" as being shadowy because they are mere appear-ance: the illusion of difference, individuality, and distinction. Yet the lines as written suggest it is difference (distinctness and otherness) that is to be fer-reted out of nature's humble objects; that in objects, including ruins like this one, there lurks "a spirit of *strange* meaning," a "spirit" hardly kin to Berkeley's unified *anima mundi*. Hence, in Wordsworth's first attempt at providing a consoling conclusion to his MS. B tale the emphasis is upon the "spiritual presences of *absent* things," related to "tender," heart-rending "lesson[s] . . . / Of human suffering or of human joy" (p. 263; emphasis added). Spiritual dif-ference, not sameness or unity, becomes the key element in the almost magical powers of the mourned dead. Although the itinerant's focus may be upon natural forms, then, the strange secret "spirit" he uncovers has a more immediate objective correlative or source in the remnants of the ruin.

The narrator, the poem's proponent of incessant grief, insistently torques such differential narrative power, and its play of absence and presence, back toward the dead. We find him connected to a ghostly absence able to induce "chillness" and "restless thoughts" (B.256), much like the stark scenario represented in "Incipient Madness." It is the elegist's "passion" for the unmourned or unmourning dead that induces restlessness, discernible in the narrator's and pedlar's lamenting of that which resists or exceeds representation, its memorials, and mourning itself. Witness the pedlar's elegiac lament that he "cannot *tell*" the way Margaret at one point pronounced his name (312; original emphasis) and the fact that her sufferings are made "present" to the narrator through a "tale of silent suffering, hardly clothed / In bodily form" (292–93). One might well ask how it is that a *silent* tale of shadowy "things" that resist or exceed the clothing of words can nonetheless be "rehearsed" in such a way as to induce chills and a "curious pensiveness" in the listener. How can the dead's "silent suffering" be conveyed? The answer is that, although the pedlar's fantasy concerns Margaret's immediacy, the bulk of his digression treats her power as one "borne *away*" by a sorrow that, although the death of her, is not the end. Her melancholic suffering continues as a muse-like, inspiring potential (hence the pedlar's trance-like reveries), as an elegiac "need to retell."[60] Margaret's ghostly return to "human life" is associated less with christological resurrection than with the silent spiritual force inherent in such sufferings as they are rehearsed. The pedlar's "countenance of love" for his subject, and the "familiar power" (267–68) with which he relates its tragic details, corresponds to the narrator's acquired sense of loving the dead woman. Theirs is a community of mourners, triadically formed by the powers of a discourse staged against the shadowy "spiritual presences of absent things" (p. 263) as well as against the absence in things liminally present but "not as they were." The sense of commonality here established between the traveler and the pedlar is ultimately owed not to the formal subject positions of elegiac dialogue but to these crossings over of mourning from the dead to the living. Mourning is revealed as a force of insufficiency and unfulfillable loss that, in its debt to those dead who exceed it and by that debt's payment in conversation, forges a different kind of subjectivity, always with a shadowy remainder of "difference."[61]

In response to the narrator's consuming responsiveness, the pedlar informs him that

> It were a wantonness, and would demand
> Severe reproof, if we were men whose hearts
> Could hold vain dalliance with the misery

> Even of the dead, contented thence to draw
> A momentary pleasure never marked
> By reason, barren of all future good.
> But we have known that there is often found
> In mournful thoughts, and always might be found,
> A power to virtue friendly. . . .
>
> (B.280–88)

The pedlar's praise of an emotional reaction to his elegiac history of Margaret is instructive, especially because it comes from one who provides consolation and equipoise to such depressing scenes as this one. "Dalliance" *is* "vain"— idle, wasteful, trifling—and it is against such vulgar enticements that the pedlar holds up an appropriate response, which will find in "mournful thoughts" a "power to virtue friendly." The adjective "friendly" itself reveals something important about the character of this "virtue" in mournful thoughts of the dead. The tale is to be recited for the listener's "sake," which is to say for the moral "good" these rehearsals and revisitations promote. Such good is "virtuous" to the extent that it is "friendly": a discursive power to "touch the heart" and transform strangers, by their mournful thoughts, into friends.[62] From singular "I"s they are changed into a common but inherently differential, intersubjective "we," the pronoun signaling the traveler's entrance or, as Jonathan Barron and Kenneth Johnston put it, his "election" into a community with the pedlar.[63] Barron and Johnston's wording is apposite, for it is a community forged *with* the pedlar through a shared struggle with grief, not a community *of* the pedlar or of his particular philosophical vantage or school.

The pedlar's comments suggest the way in which in *The Ruined Cottage* a "passion" of mourning registers a force "laid asleep or borne away" yet "destined to awake" to the "human life" of the present. These memorializing words describe a form of low messianism[64] in which a past potentiality is recuperated in narration as a lack or insufficiency, effecting a desired "power to virtue" that was missing in its past. "He" for whom Margaret suffered will not come, yet the poignant force of the return and lack of return of mourners and mourning carries across to that narrating "he" who, in the present of narration, is himself both able and unable to mourn. Hence, in an addendum to MS. B, having heard the pedlar's narrative, the poet awakens "from the silence of . . . grief" (p. 257), restored to a consciousness that makes him that "better and . . . wiser man." His moral resurrection is raised up from the ruins of Margaret's life and death, all the more clearly associating him with the "he" promised to return in fulfillment of her sufferings, supplementing that which remains incomplete and unending. It is in these lingering powers of the dead, realized in the exchange of narratives of grief, that Wordsworth's wanderers receive the gift of their community. Far from the quiet, enduring dead described in Adam

Smith's moral philosophy, and far from the happy immortals later beloved by Victorians,[65] the dead of *The Ruined Cottage* endure with considerable disquiet, as the force of an unfulfilled history that makes possible these quasi-eucharistic relationships of mourning.

IV. "Not Useless": Community and Uneasy Détente

> From a clear fountain flowing he looks round[;]
> He seeks for good & finds the good he seeks. . . .
> —MS. B Addendum

In the "Not Useless" addendum to *The Ruined Cottage*, lines of which are quoted in the epigraph above, the pedlar proclaims that the "quiet sympathies" inspired by such a jubilant vision of nature will inspire in men a "kindred love" and a related seeking after of that which is "good." To do so will in turn help to cure the present maladies of "disquietude," "vengeance," "hatred," "execration," and "contempt" (pp. 260–61). His litany of course lists precisely the forms of post-revolutionary disillusionment that *The Recluse* was intended to counteract via its depictions of suffering and of corrective hope-inspiring and kinship-inspiring pantheism. For by 1798 Wordsworth had apparently come in part to agree with Coleridge that, as George Wilbur Meyer puts it, sufferings like those of Margaret needed to be used not to indict the political system, thereby risking further despair and aversion, but to stress "the serenity and benign influence of nature and the good which resides in the human heart."[66] The lines of "Not Useless" suitably detail the pedlar's doctrine of the healing powers of the One Life, reminding mourners of the good that survives and toward which all things tend. The spiritually rejuvenated person will accordingly find his harsh "feelings of aversion" for humankind to be "softened down," and will himself not just seek "for good" but also "find the good he seeks." Subsumed into the context of nature, Margaret's sufferings thereupon acquire a different moral force, such tragedies as hers providing the pedlar and others with the means to drink in the very "soul of things" (271).

In lines from the "Not Useless" addendum included in the MS. D *Ruined Cottage*'s "sedative" conclusion,[67] the pedlar recalls an insight owed to a previous visit to the cottage and his spotting of tranquil spear grass on the garden wall. He proclaims that, for him at that moment,

> what we feel of sorrow and despair
> From ruin and from change, and all the grief
> The passing shews of being leave behind,
> Appeared an idle dream that could not live

> Where meditation was. I turned away
> And walked along my road in happiness.
>
> (D.520–25)

The pedlar encourages the poem's narrator to do likewise, and the version of these lines in MS. B's addenda, nearly identical to those above, concludes with the narrator's report that he and the pedlar had thereafter "chearfully pursued our evening way" (p. 279). *The Ruined Cottage* was amended to incorporate this vision, and in fact the lines are among the few from the addenda to be retained in the MS. D text, suggesting their importance to the *Recluse* scheme as it evolved at Alfoxden and Goslar as well as their significance to the poem's intended consolation for the travelers' griefs. The lines were to do so in a way that would go beyond the moral benefits merely of experiencing suffering as the growth-promoting antipode to joy or as an expression of humankind's natural private affections, or even as a means of emotional catharsis.

But this new way ended up presenting considerable problems for *The Ruined Cottage* and ultimately for *The Recluse*. According to Ulmer,

> The metaphysics of the One Life afford consolation for Margaret's death by denying that death demands incessant mourning. . . . Wordsworth's "Not useless" lines make awareness of an eternal spirit immanent in nature . . . the ground of belief in a final transcendence of human pain and mutability. The human problem of time, the anguish occasioned "From ruin and from change," ends by seeming almost illusory, "an idle dream" occasioned by the passing "shews" (semblances) of life. . . . The true reality is the One Life, and to that all-healing force Margaret has been assimilated by death.[68]

Mortality is in this light only the illusion of annihilation. In reality, death is a return of the self to nature's inspirited oneness. As in the Hindu notion of maya, the world of change and death is viewed as a veil, a misperception of the nature of things. Therefore, one need not prolong one's grief, or even grieve at all—so the logic would follow—because death is merely a false show. In contradistinction to her transmissive, ghostly mobility, Margaret is proclaimed to sleep "in the calm earth," with "peace" being "here" amid her natural surroundings (D.512). But such subsumption comes close to making the poem's mourning itself "useless," conflicting with the mourning-oriented dynamics of the twin texts of manuscripts B and D. "In effect," Edward Bostetter concludes, the pedlar's closing observations "repudiated the story as he . . . told it."[69]

The narrator's grief proves to be irreconcilable with the pedlar's pantheism, undermining the very reasons for the philosophy's incorporation.[70] For Sheats, the pedlar's "naturalism" and the narrator's mournful "humanism" produce not equilibrium but "disequilibrium," and so obliged Wordsworth to reframe the MS. D text's conclusion.[71] In short, the two social models clashed. They therefore could not at the level of moral philosophy provide the consolation Wordsworth and Coleridge had deemed appropriate for the poem and its impending spot in *The Recluse.* The paradigm of mournful community brought no *end* to mourning, no consolation other than friendship—and at that a friendship based not upon a totality or essence but upon incompleteness and absence. The One Life nearly made that foundational mourning useless, despite Wordsworth's attempts in the addenda to have it function otherwise, and so proved to be irreconcilable with the pedlar's tale. Wordsworth may also have grown troubled with the One Life's monistic, necessitarian, and anti-individualistic aspects, but it was this more textual or dramatic problem of disequilibrium that likely prompted him to readjust the philosophy's status in the poem. The MS. D version's reduction of the pedlar biography and the pantheistic "Not Useless" addendum may thus be the result of the author's decision to provide equilibrium to the unbalanced narrative by equalizing its competing "pantheistic and pathetic" moral visions (*PHS* 138).

By doing so, Wordsworth ultimately contrives for his troubled poem a dialogical scheme, similar in this sense to that produced in *Salisbury Plain* but here dependent upon the inherent irreconcilability and incompleteness both of grief and of the travelers' contrary responses to that grief. Sheats indeed views the poem as revealing—I would instead say *staging*—a moral conflict between its narrator's humanism and the pedlar's "naturalism," with the former character's "human compassion for Margaret" compensating the inadequate "'cheerful' necessitarianism of the pedlar."[72] Alan Bewell likewise holds that in fact Wordsworth's finest mature poems

> had their genesis in his antagonism toward this philosophical model [of Nature], in his attempt to write within and at the same time to displace, submerge, or repress the very paradigm that had initially authorized them.
>
> (*WE* 5)

Bewell adds that "the relative poverty of some of the later poetry" ultimately "may have less to do with a falling away of poetic power than with the poet's weakening resistance to this paradigm" (5). In fact, both completed versions of *The Ruined Cottage* hold the One Life at a certain distance, in MS. B by abruptly ending the poem with Margaret's death and in MS. D by reducing the pedlar's status, strategically diminishing, as Ulmer has shown, both the presence and the force of his pantheism. The MS. D text does so mainly by reducing the pedlar's biography—the textual foundation for his One Life pronouncements and for their moral authority—and the number of pro-pantheist lines included in the reconciling conclusion, while at the same time subtly increasing the narrator's resistant sorrow, now to some thirteen lines. For Ulmer these changes, however undramatic, diminish "the Pedlar's prestige as a pedagogue" and enhance comparatively the importance of the narrator's "need to mourn Margaret's death."[73] Wordsworth's alterations in this way achieve an important, tense détente between the poem's two social paradigms, the new balance of viewpoints discretely advancing *The Ruined Cottage*'s tacit aim to structure a community between the two wanderers. And it does so by emphasizing the social function and importance of their shades of philosophical difference.

Hence, in the reconciling conclusion to the MS. D text the narrator resists being consoled. Even in the "Not Useless" addendum, although he is obedient to the necessitarianism of his sage interlocutor ("my spirit had obeyed / The Presence of his eye, my ear had drunk / The meanings of his voice" [275]), the grief-struck traveler "*still* [turns] towards the cottage" to "trace with nearer interest / That secret spirit of humanity" that "still survived" amid an entropic nature's "oblivious" and obliterating "silent overgrowings" (276–77; emphasis added). Still sorrowing—in a sense arrested, made still by Margaret's and his own troubled mourning—he declines the pedlar's grief-abating sedative vision of nature, finding instead the perdurance of a differential "secret spirit of humanity" rather than that of a unified, divinized nature. The pedlar greets this resistance with further words describing a nature in which death and grief are but "an idle dream." His and his listener's responses are instructive not just concerning Wordsworth's apparent resistance even in the addenda to the grief-denying ramifications of the One Life, but also concerning the poet's developing, responsive vision about the formation of community. For that community is achieved and maintained by this dialogical clash of doctrines about the dead, with the narrator's understanding of community ultimately depending upon his recognition of "the limits of his informant's perspective."[74] So Regina Hewitt observes (about the poem's revised form in *The Excursion* of 1850). She moreover describes Wordsworth's sociological project as being in part a response to the distinct differences in vantage and occupation that he perceived to exist between country folk, differences that then challenged him "to ask how society can hold together when members seem to have little in common," in short, as a community produced and characterized by its individuals' "solidarity by difference."[75]

The results of this apparent shift in Wordsworth's strategy and social vision first appear in the concluding lines of "Not Useless," which, with the exception of the final line, are later reproduced almost word for word in the conclusion of MS. D (from which I interpolate a few missing marks of punctuation). The lines already evince an equalization of the friends, made the more prominent in the MS. D text's aforementioned adjustment of the pedlar and narrator's relative prominence:

> Admonished thus, the sweet hour coming on
> A linnet warbled from those lofty elms,
> A thrush sang loud; and other melodies,
> At distance heard, peopled the milder air.
> The old man rose & hoisted up his load.
> Together casting then a farewell look
> Upon those silent walls, we left the shade
> And chearfully pursued our evening way.
>
> (p. 279; cf. D.530–38)

The traveler reports having felt, like the pedlar, chastised by the fading sunlight as it fell upon them on their bench. Given the pedlar's pronouncements, one might understand why the poet should feel admonished by the signs of a becalmed and concomitantly becalming nature. But why should the pantheist pedlar himself feel "admonished" by the "sun declining" (279)? Is it just that the waning daylight signals the men's practical need to depart to seek lodging, as the last lines of MS. D imply? "And ere the stars were visible [we] attained / A rustic inn, our evening restingplace" (D.537–38). The admonishing "sweet hour coming on" may be interpreted as sweet, then, inasmuch as it is ripe. In this light (this waning light), the pedlar's pantheist sentiments serve to soften his and his friend's grief such that the two men can bring themselves to leave behind that which "clings" to them, lest they end up traveling in the dark. But the "sweet" admonishment also signals that both men have in some way erred: that they have wandered off the narrow path of equipoise and happiness. For all the pedlar's words of consolation, he is in much the same spot as the narrator, standing nearly as much in need of the consolation his pantheism proffers. As Richard Matlak observes, while the pedlar perceives his auditor's "need to learn" from Margaret's story, he also shares (like the Mariner) "a therapeutic need to tell" that tale.[76] The friends' bond is a double one, doubly forged by grief, as is attested by their shared "farewell look" to the "shade" and to the cottage's "silent walls," and especially by their mutual need for the "rest" such turning away promises to provide.

In the MS. B addendum, Wordsworth interestingly has crossed out the simple word "road" in the phrase "chearfull[y] pursued our road" and added in its place the (previously quoted) words "evening way," planting an allusion to *Paradise Lost*'s closing description of how, as the "Ev'ning Mist" rose, the exiled Adam and Eve "[t]hrough *Eden* took thir solitary way" into a new world of suffering and death (12.629, 649). Given the similarly lost home and befouled garden of *The Ruined Cottage*, not to mention the poignant history of death and loss the pedlar has detailed, the allusion is apposite. Indeed, like the narratives of Milton and Genesis, and much like the envisioned project of *The Recluse*, the pedlar's tale has attempted to explain why we find the conditions of death and ruin we do—a type of Fall. The allusion to the original human pair's departure suggests, moreover, not just that the narrator and pedlar must leave the ruined garden but also that they are a pair whose "solitary" paths are joined and are, symbolically, on the same proper path. The friends' struggles with each other, and with themselves as mourners trying to come to terms with loss, make their community possible. As it turns out, the One Life is finally situated in the narrative not as the subsumption of that turning away but as its expression, as a turn toward a form of consolation ultimately, and necessarily, unable to trump the death and grief it confronts, making revisitation and the renewal of bonds possible.

Consolation, as a turning away, even as a means of forgetting, is in this way represented as necessary to the community forged by the travelers. But there must also be something to *be* reconciled, turned from, forgotten. Hence, although the two men's philosophical differences contribute to the communitarianism of *The Ruined Cottage,* it is their mourning of the dead, and their desire for mourning, that fundamentally provides the ground for social cohesion and (as) a harnessing of difference, linking mourner to mourner and mourners to mourned. Their talk of the dead is finally *virtuous* inasmuch as it aims to consolidate "friendly" grounds of relationship within the "ruined walls" of representation and its "shades of difference" between self and other, mourner and mourned, and grief and consolation, in which mourning's troubles remain the focus for revisiting a "common tale" of mourning on a deserted "common." That the commonality the men achieve is both "common"—recurrent, shared—and "homely"—familiar, domestic—is owed to the tenacious and poignant character of the troubled sufferings of the ruin's lingering "tenant" (<L. *tenere,* "to hold," "to endure," "to bind," "to inspire"). Margaret's tenancy persists as the ghostly presence of an absence but also, importantly, as the absence of a "he" or memorial to come. As the object of acts of mourning, the dead's interminable holding-on forms the basis for the mournful travelers' dialogical bond of commemoration and hesitant leave-taking.

In sum, the friends' progress is occasioned by and predicated upon their shared yet different experiences of grief and its "sweet" troubles: by the obsessive mourning of the narrator and by the sedative gestures of the pedlar. Each speaker, and paradigm, corrects and draws from the other. The two proponents thus manage, through their differences, to forge a community that remains ever in need of supplementation insomuch as it is unfinished, unresolved, and even in dispute—its raison d'être and source of strength. "Opposition," Blake wrote, "is true friendship." It appears to be the case in Wordsworth's poem, in which each vision struggles with the other and in the process remains resistant, untriumphant, incomplete, and unfinished. The dead in this way become a socially constitutive legacy for the living, uniting without dissolving the "shades of difference."

For Johnston, *The Ruined Cottage* is ultimately a species of Romantic poetry because it presumes "a dissatisfaction with available solutions, such as those invoked by De Quincey in his . . . hysterically conservative reaction to the poem."[77] Wordsworth's text admits something much more difficult to bear: that political, legal, religious, and other solutions often as not are "too little and too late for the likes of Margaret."[78] Recent neo-De Quinceyan new-historicist readings of *The Ruined Cottage*'s ideology and submerged milieus arguably miss the poem's subtler communitarian workings, refusing, Johnston argues, "to accept Wordsworth's . . . search for human community in the terms he proposes,"[79] or really in any terms save those of denial or evasion. *The Ruined Cottage*'s narrative suggests its author not only to have been dissatisfied with reformist and more radical solutions to economic and social inequality, but also, much as in the Salisbury Plain poems, to have been seeking deeper sources of social connection, with men's very differences being harnessed as an additional, constitutive element of social cohesion. That desire allows the poem's narrator, and the poem, both to entertain and to delimit the pedlar's reconciling philosophy of the One Life.

In its treatment of mourning and difference, *The Ruined Cottage* discovers contagious forces for linkages between the living and dead and between the living themselves—those of the present and, as the chain of elegist-historians and histories continues, of the future. Readers may accordingly discern in the poem a desire not so much to be free of the past as to amend and revisit it. Community in this way remains necessarily unfinished and imperfect, vitally based upon the "sweet troubles" of mourners' differing griefs for the dead. How long do these new friends travel before resuming their conversation about Margaret? How long before their excursive digression from mourning returns them to grief and to their struggle with mourning? Readers cannot know, of course. Yet the traveler's insistence upon the lingering character of his grief, and the pedlar's rehearsal of his own melancholy revisitations, suggests that such conversations of the dead will resume, and that they will carry with them a sustaining spirit of community.

Wordsworth had circuitously attained his social vision, but as the next chapter shows, the communitarian work of the poet's great decade was far from over. During the last years of the eighteenth century and through the first years of the next, Wordsworth's poetry will continue to explore the foundations of collectivity. And his poems will do so in a manner that, for all the influence of the One Life and for all the poet's newfound emphasis upon nature and its healing effects, pursues the circuit with which Wordsworth's poetry of mourning and community began. Can grief be situated in nature, even in an inspirited nature, and still serve its social aims? The poems of *Lyrical Ballads* suggest Wordsworth to be seeking and considering answers while at the same time continuing to explore and refine his implicit sociology of mournful community.

5

Elegies, Epitaphs, and Legacies of Loss in *Lyrical Ballads*

[T]he poet binds together by passion and knowledge the vast empire of human society, as it is spread over the whole earth, and over all time.

—Preface to *Lyrical Ballads* (1802)

The writing for the first edition of Wordsworth and Coleridge's *Lyrical Ballads* began at Alfoxden in the spring of 1798. The final poem, "Lines written a few miles above Tintern Abbey," was composed in July after the rest of the first edition was in the hands of the publisher. In their Cornell edition of *Lyrical Ballads*, James Butler and Karen Green describe Wordsworth's contribution to the first and second volumes (1798, 1800) as "in part a long digression from *The Recluse*" (*LB* 30), as similarly does Kenneth Johnston.[1] The 1798 edition's loose make-up of generically mixed ballads and other poems certainly provided Wordsworth with a holiday from, and perhaps a means of "sympathetic resistance" to, the by then already onerous *Recluse* project (*WL* 172). Even a partial list of the first edition's topics suggests the extent to which the author was happily using the opportunity to explore a variety of interests, including abnormal and child psychology, education, superstition, indigenous peoples, social outcasts, and, by no means least, death and community. In fact, one finds in the 1798 volume easily as much death as nature.

Stephen Gill and other recent readers describe the still more dead-oriented, two-volume *Lyrical Ballads* of 1800 as a work closely focused upon moral and social reform,[2] including altering the current views of "the legislating, voting, rate-paying, opinion-forming middle class" (*WL* 141). Much the same may be said of the first edition. Such social aims help to explain the volume's focus upon the plight of economically and socially marginalized persons and its stand against poor reforms that threatened to undermine or destroy traditional Northern community-forging acts of charity. Those aims may account in part for the conservative Francis Jeffrey's attack on the Lake School, including the authors of *Lyrical Ballads*, for their blatant "discontent with the existing institutions of society." Aggrieved by "the sight of poor men spending their blood in the quarrels of princes," these poets blamed the "present vicious *constitution of society* alone . . . for all these enormities."[3] In the first edition, Wordsworth does in fact pursue an agenda focused upon representing much the same disaffected and alienated socioeconomic class as did the Salisbury Plain poems and *The Ruined Cottage*. Also like those works, the poems of both volumes of *Lyrical Ballads* strive to represent and consolidate communities, those gained through the auspices of nature as well as those approached along the older, more haunted paths of the dead. Hence, John Rieder finds many of the best poems of the expanded second edition—"Hart-leap Well," "The Brothers," the Lucy poems—to "concern themselves in varying degrees with delineating a coherent rural community that holds together youth and age, nature and humanity, even *the living and the dead*."[4] Alan Bewell's reading of the post-1797 poetry concurs with the tail end of Rieder's assessment, for it demonstrates the extent to which, amid all the poet's proclamations about beneficent nature, *Lyrical Ballads* subtly devises an anthropology of death (*WE* 187–234). Wordsworth's poems in the *Lyrical Ballads* of 1798 and 1800 explore the death-shadowed territory of his paradigm of mournful community (a.k.a. the Dead), and do so now with a greater emphasis upon the scheme's discursive and other limits, on its varied mourning-based forms, and on the socially cohesive powers of indebtedness.

My previous discussion of two poems from the first edition, "We are Seven" (see the Introduction) and "Lines written near Richmond" (see Chapter Two), showed these works to schematize Wordsworth's implicit sociology of mournful community. "We are Seven" is particularly important in this regard, enough to merit a brief reiteration here. As stated, this deceptively simple ballad implicitly proposes a model of community, indeed a schema for community, organized around the dead. The deceased are an integral part of the locale's history, affections, and environment, as attested by the child's habit of sitting and singing to her dead siblings and on occasion even taking her "porringer" to eat supper atop their graves (ll. 44, 47–48). For her, as for others in this small community, social being is predicated upon physical and psychological proximity to the dead. Hence, the girl's repeated assurances to the stodgy narrator that the number of her siblings is to be calculated as "seven" and not five despite two of their deaths demonstrates, in Wordsworth's later wording, the existence of "a spiritual community binding together the living and the dead" (*PrW* 1: 339). The living dwell in the midst of the dead, and the dead, as the girl's narrated words and actions attest, dwell among the living, as a cohesive force in their families and community.[5] In this rural district the dead's presence indeed forms the basis for community.

"We are Seven" and "Lines written near Richmond" (with its depiction of elegiac grief and tribute) are by no means the only works from the first edition to evince such social meaning. "The Thorn," considered in the second section of this chapter, certainly does so, as does an extract from the then still unpublished *Salisbury Plain*. Although the truncated form of the excerpt, titled "The Female Vagrant," belies much of its sociological function *in situ* within the entire narrative of *Salisbury Plain*, the extract reveals considerably more than just the lamentable absence of community in a Britain where a destitute woman stands "homeless near a thousand homes" (*LB*, l. 179). For this widow, "by grief enfeebled" (181), is the "more welcome, more desired" (216) by an outlaw band of gypsies whose "warm-hearted charity," Gary Harrison argues, "offers a foil to the calculating niggardliness of the mainstream community."[6] In fact, these outlaws are moved to such charity by their sympathy for the female vagrant's grieving condition. Her grief's "perpetual weight" (270) becomes the basis for a fleeting community formed between her and these outcasts, a community forged not by illegality, ethnicity, class, or cultural otherness, as in the model of the out-group, but by the gypsies' sympathetic reactions to mourning. Although the vagrant ultimately rejects the outlaws for their lawlessness, the poem nonetheless presents here a microcosm of *Salisbury Plain*'s communitarianism, founded upon mourning and the sympathetic bonds it forges as well as upon the basic commonality and difference that grief evokes, trumping such other interests as profit, secrecy, and security.

Other poems from the first edition, and many more from the second, similarly treat these social powers of grief. Like *The Ruined Cottage,* some of these works attempt to situate mournful community within nature, making nature a locale of the dead, and do so at least in part to move beyond the former narrative's troubled (if socially cohesive) clash between grief and nature-oriented consolation. In this light, the relationship of the Dead and Nature in *The Ruined Cottage* casts a very long shadow, shading much of the poetry that follows, especially in *Lyrical Ballads*. In some ways, Wordsworth never *stops* writing *The Ruined Cottage*. Some of his finest works of these very productive years, such as "Tintern Abbey," "Lines written in early spring," and "Hart-leap Well," are variations on its form and themes as well as being attempts to explore and resolve its difficulties. As *Essays upon Epitaphs* and other later works attest, well into the first decades of the new century this putative "poet of nature" remains a poet of "the living and the dead." Until at least *The Excursion* (1814), Wordsworth's poetry subtly reiterates the impulses and problems that instigated and drove its sociology decades before.

I. "The Shadow of Death":
Mourning and Murmuring above Tintern Abbey

> It was a grief,
> Grief call it not, 'twas anything but that,
> A conflict of sensations without a name. . . .
> —*The Prelude*

The Ruined Cottage's antithesis between the Dead and Nature informs Wordsworth's effort to integrate the two paradigms in the precisely titled, death-shadowed "Lines written a few miles above Tintern Abbey, on revisiting the Banks of the Wye, during a Tour, July 13, 1798." A paean to nature's One Life-like "motion and a spirit, that impels / All thinking things, all objects of all thought, / And rolls through all things" (101–3), this work is also fundamentally a poem of loss and desired recompense.[7] Revisiting the picturesque locale above Tintern Abbey after five years' absence, the poem's speaker laments his inability to "paint / What then [he] was" when "nature . . . was all in all," was for him "a feeling and a love, / That had no need of a remoter charm, / By thought supplied" (73–76, 81–83). The situation is in this respect similar to that dramatized in *The Ruined Cottage*. In a variation on that poem's story line and sociology—now all but synonymous for Wordsworth—the narrator visits a landscape haunted by suffering, ruination, and death as well as by consoling, pantheistic intimations. The recollections evoked precipitate his turn to another, his "dearest Friend," producing a promissory form of mournful, spiritual community poised between presence and absence, past and present, and between the living and the dead.

Rieder rightly hears in the poem's opening "Once again" lines (4, 15) an echo of *Lycidas*'s famous elegiac refrain, "Yet once more, O ye laurels, and once more / Ye Myrtles brown." The allusion is a significant one, for it frames Wordsworth's locodescriptive narrative as a form of eighteenth-century self-elegy.[8] It does so in a subtly elegiac tone Rieder describes as being "muted, attenuated, but still hauntingly present"—this despite the poem's dominant, subordinating "tone of triumphant consolation."[9] Of course, there is a reason for this attenuated grief. In response to his feelings of persisting loss, of his difference from an earlier time when he felt himself to be one with nature's immanence and interconnectedness, the speaker proclaims:

> Not for this
> Faint I, nor mourn nor murmur: other gifts
> Have followed, for such loss, I would believe,
> Abundant recompense. For I have learned
> To look on nature, not as in the hour

> Of thoughtless youth, but hearing oftentimes
> The still, sad music of humanity,
> Not harsh nor grating, though of ample power
> To chasten and subdue.
>
> (86–94)

That oft-heard "music," David Bromwich contends, is "the cry of human suffering and human need: the same cry that Rousseau in his *Discourse on
Inequality* had heard as the original motive for a society founded on nature."[10]
Mary Jacobus hears in this same music similar strains of the "painful perplex-
ities" of life, of an admission of human suffering that *The Ruined Cottage's*
pedlar, in his aforementioned reference to a "secret spirit of humanity," ultimately had, she says, "refused to admit."[11] "Tintern Abbey"[12] elegizes not just
nature but, within or lurking behind that nature, the "sad" sufferings of men
and women like those nearby "vagrant dwellers in the houseless woods" (21),
whose presence the speaker surmises. In doing so, the poem implicitly also
elegizes the recent sufferings of Wordsworth's disaffected, formerly revolutionary peers.

The *Recluse* was intended of course to address the pessimism and disaffection caused by the perversion of the Revolution's grand ideals, including
the promise of liberty, equality, and, linchpin of all, fraternity. "Tintern
Abbey," although arguably on holiday from *The Recluse's* philosophical task,
treads similar social and political terrain, and so may be said not really to be
on holiday at all. The poem discretely suppresses and slyly invokes the current
social-political troubles at home and abroad, in part to console the post-revolutionary philosophical and social sufferings *The Recluse* (deferred) was meant
to heal and in part to address what Johnston calls the poet's own "honest
doubts" (*HW* 595). For Wordsworth's speaker the loss of connection and opti-
mism, troped as "nature," is in part to be compensated by his now hearing and
understanding this saddening social "music of humanity." More significantly,
that loss is to be assuaged by his and his friend's (his sister's) articulation of a
community predicated upon loss and its "still, sad music." That music was well
attuned to the poem's contemporary readers, many of whom could be expected
to recognize the historical significance of this topographical poem's banner
headline of a title, with its specific temporal and geographical coordinates.

July 13, 1798, Bastille Day eve on the revolutionary calendar, of course
marked the ninth anniversary of the age's greatest promise of community, heralded by the storming of the Bastille prison by partisans on July 14, 1789.
Although "visible only to readers already acquainted with [Wordsworth's]
life,"[13] the date also marked the eighth anniversary of the poet's first visit to
France, whereupon, according to *The Prelude's* account, he "did soon / Become
a Patriot, and [his] heart was all / Given to the People" (*13P* 9.124–26). In that

blessed dawn, Wordsworth became an ardent supporter of the Revolution and its ideal of loving "Man . . . / As man" (313–14), a phrase Evan Radcliffe persuasively argues was "linked to universal benevolence in denoting an attachment free from reasons of personal, national, or class connections" (more on this below).[14] That Wordsworth came to believe in the Jacobin ideal of fraternity was not surprising for one who had already thirsted for community (and who would thirst long after these waters dried up). "Five years" before also marked to the day the assassination of Jean-Paul Marat, whose *L'Ami du peuple* championed the Revolution and whose martyrdom symbolically marked the cause's own ugly betrayal. Thereafter the Revolution was of course transformed, first into the Terror and then into Napoleonic imperialism and conquest. One may reasonably conclude, then, that the poem's precise dating is more than serendipity or a byproduct of the fashion for lengthy locodescriptive titling.[15] In fact, for most readers of Wordsworth's day, the title's date must have been irrepressibly provocative, recalling the Revolution's origin nine years before, Federation Day of July 14, 1790, the five-year anniversary of Marat's death,[16] and along with these dates the Terror, the ongoing war, and, for some, Britain's anti-revolutionary domestic policies. The cries of suffering the speaker hears are thus artfully framed to resonate with cries from revolution and war and from their collateral effects on travelers and vagrants. Such "still, sad music of humanity" soberly colors, even as it motivates, the speaker's turn to nature and his desire for solace. It quietly tolls a lament of lapsed ideals of liberty, equality, and fraternity—*too* quietly for some recent readers, who have found in this turn evidence of authorial suppressions and evasions of history.[17]

For what "Tintern Abbey" explicitly elegizes is a lost, more innocent and immediate relationship not to revolutionary ideals and their promise of fraternal cohesion but to nature's "all in all" communion. The relationship ostensibly lost is not that of the blessed Gallic dawn of brotherhood Wordsworth experienced five or more years before but of a form of immanence he in fact did not discover before first taking up *The Recluse* in late 1797. As Gill and other readers point out, in 1793 it was of course Jacobinism (and his French lover, Annette Vallon) exciting his passions, not nature. Then, having returned from France, while living in London the author still "had been a radical patriot, his heart given to the people and to the French cause" (*WL* 153–54) as well as to that cause's ideals of brotherhood, liberty, and republicanism. Witness the poet's unpublished defense of the untoward events in France, in his *Letter to the Bishop of Llandaff*. For that matter, his first visit to the landscape above Tintern Abbey had been troubled: preceded by his sighting of the British fleet preparing for war with France and by his lone trek across Salisbury Plain and his viewing of the ruins of Stonehenge (see Chapter Three).

It is a writer's prerogative to elaborate upon and diverge from personal experience, and readers must therefore necessarily tread carefully when traversing from *life* to *text*. "Tintern Abbey"'s announced date, as well as its speaker's apostrophe to his "dear" sister-friend, certainly prompt such interpretive crossings from poetry to biography. The poem downright beckons to be read as the (in part falsified) record of Wordsworth's revisiting of Tintern Abbey's environs on or before July 13, 1798, which he indeed did. We modern readers do well to remember that *Lyrical Ballads* was, however, at the authors' request, published anonymously. For those first readers, who would the poem's speaker then have been? For that matter, "Tintern Abbey" is more drama than documentary, more generalized lyric or ode than autobiography,[18] more like a fictional film than a home movie. Helen Vendler indeed condemns as a "canard" the assumption that the speaker is "coterminous with the historical Wordsworth."[19] According to Anne Janowitz's *Lyric and Labour in the Romantic Tradition,* "no matter how much one knows about the particularity of Wordsworth's situation and locale in the poem, the 'I' continually exerts its force as an abstraction or model of consciousness above its presence as any set of particulars."[20] Although himself a topographical poet—of these very "lines written"—the speaker is scarcely more his flesh-and-blood author than is the myopic narrator of "We are Seven," a poem also based upon Wordsworth's experience.

Yet, as David Chandler points out, Wordsworth's depiction of himself (or of his poet-speaker) as "a nature-worshipper in 1793" does not "fully erase the memory of . . . wartime vagrancy, of a fugitive self with danger's voice behind."[21] Likewise, Bromwich argues that despite the poem's "picturesque placement" its title's specific dating must recall the disquieting, *nearly* excluded subject of France.[22] Nor, I would add, was the poem likely intended to erase or displace such recent political history, contrary to Marjorie Levinson's and Jerome McGann's new-historicist claims about the text's witting or unwitting displacements and omissions. I agree in part with William Richey that such displacements can be interpreted instead as signals to a disillusioned post-revolutionary readership during a time of government censorship. From the *Georgics* to Sir John Denham's "Cooper's Hill," locodescriptive poetry had itself been, after all, and was still, a potential "site of politicized discourse in which poets would draw from the landscape lessons that applied to the social conditions of their times."[23] Dating the poem on Bastille Day eve signaled the narrative's social-political vantage, and specifically that vantage's overview of recent political events in France.[24] In the presence of nature the speaker thus "still" hears a "sad music of humanity" associated with social and political sufferings. Social history is not to be elided or substituted by nature—itself mourned and murmured about by the poet. History's elegiac strains murmur in the title's dating and, at least as powerfully, in the poem's siting "a few miles above" the ruins of a Cistercian monastery.

"Tintern Abbey" surveys what Denham's "Cooper's Hill" had long before described as a Catholic chapel despoiled by Henry VIII. As C. John

Sommerville states, following the Act of Dissolution, Henry had confiscated church lands and sought to level the remaining shrines and break up all "wonder-working images."[25] Henry's Act thereby became an anti-Catholic project of "monotheistic occultation," eliminating worldly shrines of the polytheistic divine and in their place installing a transcendent, unified *Being* withdrawn from Britain's ever-more secularized world.[26] Christopher Saxton's commissioned country maps contributed to this royal erasure of Catholic landmarks: the "paths of pilgrimage, the shrines that had tapped into grace and health, the monasteries that [had] sheltered travellers and beggars."[27] Such sites as ruined rural abbeys were thereafter resistantly sought by pilgrims "to compensate for the loss of saints' shrines."[28] To be above a site such as Tintern Abbey, even to be as many as a "few miles above" or below it, had been for recalcitrant pilgrims to be in or near the (elided) presence of the divine. From this disappearance of shrines, Sommerville argues, was born a "historical consciousness, a sense of a break with the past,"[29] best expressed in Webster's *The Duchess of Malfi*: "I do love these ancient ruins: / We never tread upon them but we set / Our foot upon some reverend history" (V.iii.9–11). Even at a distance of some miles the ruined abbey and its environs are a poignant correlative for lost immanence, for an elided past, and for lapsed community.[30]

In her well-known, now nearly infamous new-historicist reading of "Tintern Abbey," Levinson argues, rightly in part, that the poem's siting reiterates the standard Protestant history of the conversion, whereby "collective worship by the isolated and exclusive religious community was replaced by private . . . acts of communion performed outside the institution and in forms defined by impulse and individual invention."[31] According to Levinson, that history is revealed by the surveying speaker's envisioning of a hermit's hut (putative source of a nearby plume of smoke): the symbolic "substitute for . . . the abbey or monastery and for the socioeconomic relations that gave rise to those institutions."[32] In his history of the confiscations, Sir Henry Spelman himself contended that up until Henry VIII's actions England had required no poorhouses, for the monasteries and other religious houses had provided for the impoverished (a disputable claim, no doubt).[33] Levinson cites the historian F. A. Gasquet's own connection of Henry's destruction of such monasteries as Tintern Abbey to the destruction of Englishmen's "sense of corporate unity and common brotherhood, which was fostered by the religious unanimity of belief and practice in every village in the country . . . centred in the Church with its rites and ceremonies."[34] She observes that in Wordsworth's poem the Cistercian ruins below the speaker signify this "loss of a meaningful collectivity, a brotherhood of the self-elect, subsidized by the whole society."[35] James A. W. Heffernan argues, furthermore, that for Wordsworth "this monastic charity went hand in hand with the sanctity of monastic contemplation." King

Henry's dissolution of the monasteries was therefore indeed much to be lamented, and was "at once late-medieval and modern: as old as the Reformation, as new as the French Revolution."[36] After all, the National Assembly would confiscate its own share of church real estate, prelude to the foreclosure of the Revolution's promise of community.

Moreover, as Stephen Greenblatt has recently argued, the Catholic doctrine of Purgatory had itself entailed in pre-Dissolution Britain a "communal commitment to caring and assistance that conjoin[ed] the living and the dead." Those who offered suffrages for the dead in Purgatory could hope that these dead would, once in Heaven, reciprocate with prayers for them. The living and dead in this way formed "a perfect community of mutual charity and interest," in which "the border between this world and the afterlife was not firmly and irrevocably closed."[37] In "Tintern Abbey" a similar model of reciprocity plays a fundamental part in establishing Wordsworth's secularized, quasi-sacral (vaguely Catholic) community above these ruins. The poem's survey of ecclesiastical and political change in these ways has as its prospect and retrospect a history of ruins, insinuated by the text's siting as well as by its casual mention of local vagrants and imagined hermits. As Heffernan succinctly concludes, "the ruined abbey of the title subtly informs everything that follows."[38] The ruins, vagrants, visitants, and hermit, along with the strains of human suffering, all represent, and in their way all map, a loss of community.

"Nature never did betray / The heart that loved her" (123–24), the speaker pronounces, as if to contrast the fraternal revolutionary "errors" by which he had, less fatally than Marat, been "betray'd" (*13P* 10.882). For the poet, nature symbolizes both the lapse and the potential recovery of communal presence, transferred from abbey ruins to natural-sacral surroundings, with the poem's pantheism signifying not solitariness but collective worship and social cohesion. For in the poem it is the eucharistic worship qua mourning of nature, predicated upon nature's loss, that promises to bind friend to friend—poet to sister—in a community of remembrance. "Tintern Abbey" thus quite appropriately surveys the ruins of a fraternal community whose destruction could be directly or symbolically linked to an increase in poverty and alienation, typified by the locale's alienated vagrants dwelling in the "houseless woods" and its solitary hermit sitting "alone" by a secluded fire (21–23). Much as in *The Ruined Cottage*, the poet seeks to form a compensatory community upon or above a defunct one. And he does so by means of a sacred rite of election: convoking a fraternity of mourners whose main bond will be based upon troubled responses to a sorrowful legacy of loss, including the loss of brotherhood.

Near the poem's end, the speaker's turn to his sister for consolation indeed appears to occur *because* the consolation he desires is lacking in his revisitation of this site of former joys. For him, nature in this locale above Tintern Abbey is both present, as the landscape he and his sister visit, and absent, as the object of a relationship that no longer exists. He is haunted by that loss and by a resulting grief he cannot assuage. So, in need of solace he turns, suddenly it may seem,[39] to his "dearest Friend" (116), introduced first by this gender-neutral noun and only thereafter as his "sister."[40] This addressee is, Alan Grob states, to be not just "his 'dear, dear Sister' bound to him by ties of blood, but also his rationally chosen partner and companion, a 'dear, dear Friend.'"[41] Radcliffe moreover points out that in the 1790s the revolutionary idea of universal benevolence had come to be opposed to Burke's espoused values of the family and the domestic affections. Wordsworth likely did not go so far as Godwin in believing that "ties of kinship, affection, and gratitude simply inhibit us from . . . proper action."[42] And yet, Grob notes, the poet's contemporary ballad "The Old Cumberland Beggar" pointedly lauds charity "to one who has no personal claims on us" over love "bound by the private affections."[43] One may wonder whether in 1809 Coleridge chose to name his newspaper *The Friend*—a term reminiscent of Marat's ultrarevolutionary, denunciatory periodical—to reclaim, by revaluing, this diminished (too-) universalist conception (rather, say, than simply to call up connotations of the Society of Friends). The speaker's hailing of his sister as "friend" is highly charged, signifying a good deal more than simple familial attachment, to which the term frequently was opposed.

The poet turns to perceive in his friend's eyes as she witnesses the vista, on this her initial visit, some sign of his "former pleasures" (119) amid a happier world. His present lack of unmediated, "all in all" interconnectedness with nature is to be supplemented by her immediate (unmediated) experiencing of the scene. Significantly, he allusively hails this savior of sorts in the words of the twenty-third Psalm: "For thou art with me, here, upon the banks / Of this fair river" (115–16). He could as nearly say, and very nearly does say, "here, in 'the valley of the shadow of death.'" His friend serves a redeeming role, as a divinized "thou" who promises pastoral care. She does so in a landscape shadowed by death and characterized, in the absence of divine or other superintendence, by considerable want, as well. That this past immediacy is to be recovered by the speaker's reading of joy in her eyes (120) suggests the problematical character (and troubling *nature*) of his turn. Unlike the psalmist, who takes comfort in pastoral presence—"The Lord is my shepherd; I shall not want" (23:1)—and finds solace in the prospect of "dwell[ing] in the house of the Lord forever" (6), the poet seeks at best a temporary, temporal fix for loss, via the mediation of representation: "Oh! yet a little while / May I behold in thee what I was once . . . !" (120–21). The insufficiency of his seeking of comfort from this sororial *thou*, amid a world of post-revolutionary betrayals, "evil tongues, / Rash judgments," and "sneers of selfish men" (129–30), steers the text from pastoral consolation to elegy and from the One Life to spiritual and natural "decay" (114), in what is really a mourning and seeking of something lost in "the light of setting suns" (98), the shadow of death. The speaker may pray to recover immediacy between mind and nature and between present and past, but in his acknowledgments of suffering and loss he "mourn[s]" and "murmur[s]," as the psalmist ultimately does not.

Although the latter figure takes comfort in God's spirit-preserving presence, he is himself nonetheless in need, seeking assurance through prayer and, implicitly, through reaffirming the covenant between God and a chosen people. "For thou art with me." Without such need there is no turn to the other, and no community. The poem's speaker similarly seeks consolation, and he does so likewise through prayer: "this prayer I make, / Knowing that Nature never did betray / The heart that loved her" (122–24). Now alluding to God's instructions to Moses for the latter's benediction for Aaron and sons (Numbers 6:22–27),[44] the poet prays on his sister's behalf:

> let the moon
> Shine on thee in thy solitary walk;
> And let the misty mountain winds be free
> To blow against thee: and in after years . . .
> Thy memory be as a dwelling-place
> For all sweet sounds and harmonies; Oh! then,
> If solitude, or fear, or pain, or grief,
> Should be thy portion, with what healing thoughts
> Of tender joy wilt thou remember me,
> And these my exhortations!
>   . . . Nor wilt thou then forget,
> That . . . these steep woods and lofty cliffs,
> And this green pastoral landscape, were to me
> More dear, both for themselves, and for thy sake.

(135–60)

Brother and sister are to be bound to one another both in joy and, more importantly, in what will live on as the nostalgic memory of their visit. She, like her brother, will assuredly find herself far from this place, in the midst of alienating "solitude" or "grief." As with his turn to her for consolation, she then will turn to him, perhaps at a time when he no longer is able to hear her voice or "catch from [her] wild eyes these gleams / Of past existence" (149–50). He may be living elsewhere; he may even be dead. Importantly, she will, he believes, find solace, amid her vagrant-like wanderings, in the remembrance not so much of the locale's "steep woods and lofty cliffs" as of his happiness at her pleasure in viewing them. Like her brother, she will thereupon find or at least seek to find recompense for present sorrow, owed to her memory of this past experience of shared joy and of shared grief at departed pleasure and lost presence.

His prayerful prediction that she will "remember" him and his benediction to her situates him discursively between God's proffered prayer—"The Lord make his face shine upon thee" (6:25)—and Jesus's parting injunction to his disciples, "this do in remembrance of me" (Luke 22:19). It is a curious but appropriate mingling of testaments, both covenantal and eucharistic. In addition, the allusion to God's benediction associates the poet's prayer with an earlier verse in Numbers mandating the law of those chosen few who "shall separate themselves to vow a vow of a Nazarite, to separate themselves unto the Lord" (6:2). Given the brother and sister's distance from the corrupting city, and Wordsworth's claim, propounded more clearly in *The Prelude,* to be himself a "chosen Son" of Nature (3.82), this biblical allusion becomes all the more fitting for its mandate of selected individuals' shared election, separation, purification, and consecration. Like the poem's indirect references to the Cistercian brotherhood and to the Revolution, this signpost of sorts functions as an emblem of community, in concert with those other registers framing the poet's desire for social cohesion.

The poem's odd weaving of these biblical allusions also functions, in keeping again with the ideal of fraternity, to equalize, with the brother figured both as psalmist to his sororial *thou* and as instructing Lord to her benediction-receiving Moses or Aaron. The chiastic structure of these figures situates brother and sister each in the place of guide and disciple, of nature's God and God's Nazarene priest. In this way, the allusions structure and unstructure hierarchized relationships, laying the ground both for election and for the equality of fraternity. And it is a fraternal bond based upon this: that the speaker's sister will remember and, in her physical and temporal distance, have empathy for her brother's grief and hope on July 13, 1798. She will thereby be placed in the similar position of an elegist, and so feel a similar sense of loss and connection: of connection to him for this gift of blessings and happiness (at her joy), and of loss at what has passed and must pass away. Each one in need will find consolation, and a bond, in the other, drawing upon a covenant of anticipated loss and remembered joy. Their community relies upon this model of reciprocity, a fitting secularization of the suffrages associated with the once Catholic locale.

As David Simpson notes, in this prayerful turn the poem "acknowledge[s] access to a community,"[45] an interpersonal compact Richey sees as being akin even to "a social contract."[46] One is reminded of Mona Ozouf's analysis of the Revolutionary festival as serving not only to promote "collective unity" but also to construct the "new sacrality" of "an eternal society," its decadence "conjure[d] away."[47] Wordsworth similarly employs discrete religious troping here to establish a post-revolutionary, earthly, nonsubsuming community. And the covenant of that community is these two friends' mutual anticipation of each other's absence and feeling of loss. Do this, the poet implies, recall this time of gladness and sadness, and I shall be with you. Do this, the pair's new implicit covenant urges, and we shall be a community of recollection and its inherent mourning, here and now as there and then, "for thy sake" and mine. The allusion to the Eucharist and its formation of community is yet a further emblem of this fraternity the poet desires, as well as being a sign of that community's foundation in loss. Simpson ponders whether the text's "community of experience" may be possible only between the two siblings, "if it is possible at all," and regards "Tintern Abbey" as anything but "the record of a highly affirmative moment in Wordsworth's life."[48] One should reiterate, however, that the poet first addresses his sister as a *friend*, a far more general and potentially much more reproducible basis for relationship and social cohesion. This is one reason why Wordsworth's micro-communities[49] (so often of two) bear the structural promise of being not just reproducible but expandable, if never quite universal because always particular and, here as elsewhere, historical. In addition, as this poem makes so clear, such community is necessarily *to come*, bracketed in a futurity that is its promise and its limit, even for the poem's speaker and his sister-friend. That promise (of communion without immanence) is made present whenever one friend accedes to the imminence or inevitability of loss and death posited by the other, rather like the model of the sundial in *An Evening Walk* (see Chapter Two). Through this trope and vantage of prospective retrospection the addressee comes to mourn, here and now, what passes away, even while experiencing the pleasure that is to pass.

One might of course read this turn to another as an instance of Wordsworth's "egotistical sublime," in the words of Keats's famous formulation. Some readers go further, condemning the poet for his inability to allow his sister to feel and sustain a joy he himself cannot, as well as for relegating her to what seems a voiceless, passive status. As with the poem's representation of history, from the plight of the poor to Wordsworth's own situation, Dorothy's putative depiction has become a contentious site (even a *locus in quo*) of scholarship. James Soderholm goes so far as to say that her "place in the poem encapsulates the positions of the major critics of romantic poetry."[50] Informed by a long line of feminist and new-historicist critiques of Dorothy's silent treatment in "Tintern Abbey," Judith Page's *Wordsworth and the Cultivation of Women*, to take but one example, holds that she "is denied her own narrative in the context of Wordsworth's masculine narrative of loss and desired restoration."[51] I largely agree with Heidi Thomson that disparaging and affirming interpretations alike too often fixate on what they see as the speaker's individualist character, "*en route* to individual selfhood," to the exclusion of his interlocutory, dialogical subjectivity and its "web" of community.[52]

Readings that focus on the construed dichotomous relationship between
William and Dorothy in the poem, although often revealing in terms of the
poem's gender dynamics, tend to reduce the poet's apostrophe merely to "a
form of narcissistic projection," overlooking the depicted siblings' deeper,
more social relationship.[53]

In their intimations of loss, brother and sister realize a bond responsive to
social turmoil and to the remembrance of what is past and what must pass
away. The pairs' covenant is their mutual, fundamentally equal future-made-
present anticipation of loss, arguably leading each to elegize even joy, in a cir-
cular temporality of mourning (then as now as then) that, via this play of presence and absence and past and present, forms one of Wordsworth's most
peculiar and most historically and politically charged visions of mournful
community. The locale above Tintern Abbey is thus described, to borrow a
line from Geoffrey Hartman, "as if it were a monument or grave,"[54] a signifier
of commemorated loss. As Levinson, too, sees, "Tintern Abbey" depicts
nature as "a guardian of ground hallowed by private commemorative acts."[55] It
is a nature, or rather an experience of nature, that is *mourned,* a nature tied to
powers of loss and remembrance in this picturesque valley of death. In these
terms, "Tintern Abbey" comes as close to structuring a community of both
nature and mourning as any poem Wordsworth would write, at least in part
because its depicted nature is so muted and its grief is made so insistent. Such
community is realized only as a prospect and retrospect to be glimpsed, anticipated, enjoyed, and mourned. Bequeathed a legacy of joy lost and, this day, of
indebtedness for recompense, the poem's poet bequeaths to his sister the same
basic troubled inheritance of lack and supplementation, of shadows of death
and their promised reward.

As Wordsworth prolonged his holiday from *The Recluse* in order to compose, in addition to the two-part *Prelude,* poems for the two-volume edition
of *Lyrical Ballads,* that legacy of the Dead and of its problematical compati-
bility with Nature remained with him. Indeed, the scheme of mournful community is even more evident in the second volume of the 1800 edition, which
includes enough elegies that it could have been entitled "Elegies and Pastorals" or, better, "Elegies and Epitaphs," to borrow a section title from
Wordsworth's later collection of his poetical works. "The Brothers," examined
in this chapter, and "Hart-leap Well," considered ahead in Chapter Six, are
two such examples of the way Wordsworth mines much the same poetical ore
unearthed in *The Ruined Cottage* and, deeper still, in *The Vale of Esthwaite.* But
he does so now with a pioneering difference. The same can be said for the second volume's "Matthew" elegies and "Lucy poems," elegies that also explore
the social foundations, legacies, and limits of grief. These new works advance
while variously refining *The Ruined Cottage*'s and other poems' explorations of
community, with less emphasis on the healing possibilities offered by natural

consolation. In this sense, the second edition of *Lyrical Ballads* presents an attenuation of Nature's influence and an increase of the social and poetical significance of mourning.

II. "OH! THE DIFFERENCE": MOURNING LUCY AND EMMA

> The memory of what has been,
> And never more will be.
>
> —"Three years she grew"

The poems of the second edition of *Lyrical Ballads* were mostly written in Germany between October 1798 and February 1799 and, upon the poet and his sister's return to England, at Dove Cottage in Grasmere. This Goslar-Grasmere poetry, Butler and Green observe, "differ[s] significantly from what appeared in the *Lyrical Ballads* of 1798," emphasizing as it does not ballad but pastoral (*LB* 26). Stephen Parrish indeed argues that most all of the new poems of the 1800 edition appear to be variations on Wordsworth's version of pastoral form.[56] These generic experiments were undertaken at least in part because they were deemed, Butler and Green aver, to be "honorable apprentice work for the would-be epic poet, *even* for the poet of *The Recluse*," the latter opus being intended to include, Coleridge remembered, "pastoral and other states of society" (*LB* 26; emphasis added). Butler and Green's qualifying "even" above is apt, for although many of Wordsworth's pastoral experiments are in a genre he probably considered to be appropriate to that sociological project, the second edition of *Lyrical Ballads* reflects, like the first, his wide-ranging interests, including those concerning mourning and death. His version of pastoral in fact is, for its part, really a form of *elegiac* pastoral, with that genre's tone and generic concerns being very much in evidence in works like "The Brothers," "Hart-leap Well," and "Michael," as well as in the Matthew elegies and the several "Lucy poems."

This last set of elegies narrates the death or envisioned death of a girl named—or, in the case of one of the works, commonly presumed to be named—Lucy. Never collected together by Wordsworth, this group is comprised of the three untitled texts known as "Strange fits of passion," "A slumber did my spirit seal," and "Three years she grew," plus the simply titled "Song," later titled "She dwelt among th' untrodden ways." Many scholars also include with these a Lucy poem from 1801, "I travell'd among unknown Men," with some justification as Wordsworth at one time reported it to have been earmarked to follow "A slumber" in the 1802 edition of *Lyrical Ballads* (*EY* 333).[57] A few other critics add to this group the narrative poem "Lucy Gray,"[58] as do I. Like the first four works above, this poem is from the 1800 volume of

Lyrical Ballads, and yet, perhaps because it is arguably more ballad than lyric (with "too much story," according to Pamela Woof[59]), "Lucy Gray" has tended to be excluded from the grouping. The poem certainly fits in with the other texts given its concern with death and with death's aftermath for the living, not to mention its attribute of elegizing a dead girl named Lucy—not the case in "A slumber."[60] Paul de Man in fact dubbed the whole series the "Lucy Gray poems."[61] For my purposes, I examine the four poems Wordsworth *nearly* grouped together in the second edition of *Lyrical Ballads,* in which "Strange fits of passion," "She dwelt among th' untrodden ways," and "A slumber did my spirit seal" appear in tandem and "Lucy Gray" arrives two poems later. However problematical any grouping of Lucy poems must be,[62] I find these four elegies to hold together well as a group *of sorts* because of their shared attitudes about death and loss.

In *Wordsworth's Poetry,* Hartman situated the Lucy poems, sans "Lucy Gray" and "I travell'd," in a discursive realm "between ritual mourning and personal reminiscence" (*WP* 158).[63] Bewell similarly characterizes the Lucy group, including "Lucy Gray," as "innovative experiments in the mythic representation of death," focused upon human beings' "primal linguistic struggle to deal with death" (*WE* 202). These four, five, or six poems (one could add still others, such as "Among all lovely things" from *Poems*) reflect Wordsworth's continuing and seemingly inexhaustible interest in mortality and, particularly, in death's aftermath for the living. The grouping only hints at the deeper workings of the poet's social scheme of mournful community, but merits consideration for the extent to which the poems focus upon important aspects of the paradigm. In the end, the Lucy poems indeed effect an intriguing analysis of the social model as it is reformed and re-envisioned through the genre of elegy, much as the scheme had previously been revised and advanced by romance, gothic, and, conceptually, by revolutionary fraternity and by the One Life. The poems are also intriguing instances of Wordsworth's turn away from the model of Nature (especially the One Life), for in them when nature is considered at all it is envisioned either as an entropic force or, in "Three years she grew," as a Hades-like entity responsible for stealing Lucy from the living. Those living are left, as in most all of the Lucy poems, to mourn and elegize the girl's loss.

In the case of the well-known elegy "A slumber did my spirit seal," the elegist laments having been oblivious to Lucy's mortality: "She seem'd a thing that could not feel / The touch of earthly years" (*LB,* ll. 3–4). Like the other Lucy poems, this text is a meditation upon the legacy of mortal loss and is focused more upon mourner than mourned. The lingering character of its elegist's mourning of Lucy (assuming the girl in fact to be named Lucy) is suggested—indeed it is paralleled and signified—by her own lingering: "Roll'd round in earth's diurnal course / With rocks and stones and trees!" (7–8). Lucy's odd interment poignantly attests to the power of her loss for the speaker (these are, after all, his terms and surmises), who discerns her presence among nature's turbulently rolling objects. Hardly a consoling image of the One Life.[64] And in fact this elegy's sociological core rests nearer the haunting dead than it does nature and natural consolation. "A slumber" ultimately represents the power of the dead to affect the living, especially those who, having insufficiently mourned or anticipated death ("I had no human fears" [2]), become mourners living on in a state of irrevocable, perhaps even guilty, loss.[65] It is a by now familiar Wordsworthian motif of indebtedness to the dead, in a poem David Ferry provocatively locates "at the powerful centre of the poet's art."[66]

Like many of my readers, I frequently teach "A slumber," and on occasion a student will express dissatisfaction with the poem's melodramatic tone, heralded by the concluding line's exclamation point ("rocks and stones and trees!"). My response is that this punctuation, later revised to a stoic period,[67] not so subtly shifts the lament's meaning away from that of nature-derived consolation—of consolation on a par with that offered by the old pedlar in *The Ruined Cottage*—and toward what the speaker represents as the overwhelming perpetuity both of Lucy's loss and of his mourning-work. The disconcerting incongruity between the poet's Newtonian observation of her lack of "motion" and "force" and his emotional registering of her turbulent terrestrial rolling testifies less to her posthumous status than to his own condition as a decidedly unstoic mourner. "Oh! / The difference," the elegist of "She dwelt" more explicitly laments. "A slumber" figures the perpetual nature of mourning as, and as proportionate to, Lucy's ubiquity and concomitant lack of location. Which rocks and stones, one asks? Not those of headstones, nor even those of some stone heap, as in the volume's concluding pastoral elegy, "Michael."

The best answer of course really is *all* rocks, stones, and trees, and hence no particular, locatable, localizable stones or other potential markers. Lucy's lack of location thus makes her absence the more felt and contributes to her death's impact on the elegist-mourner's awareness of mortality. At the same time, her mourner's grief amplifies her absence, for it is *his* feelings and understanding that the text chiefly concerns. As Marlon Ross observes, in fact the poet has clearly gained from Lucy's loss.[68] Hartman, too, reads the aftermath of Lucy's death as being more than only loss, "for it brings . . . to birth" a "new consciousness" of death (*WP* 161). Perhaps it was this very sense of the poem's representation of loss and of a type of reward from that loss which led Coleridge to hail "A slumber" as a "most sublime epitaph" (*CLSTC* 1: 479), an epitaph with no monument on which it could be inscribed.[69] "Sublime epitaph" becomes sublimely haunted elegy: elegizing the distance between the living and dead that an inscription on stone would symbolically bridge. For it is Lucy's unrecoverability, her distance from the living and her resistance to being located by them, that sustains mourning and the second-order mourning-work of a poetics of loss.

Similarly, "She dwelt among th' untrodden ways" explores the capacity of the dead to provoke lingering grief in the living. Lucy's death makes all the "difference" to her elegist (12) and of course more than a little to Lucy herself, as more than one parody has observed.[70] Mary Webb holds that "all the grief at a great gulf of absence is expressed in that simple exclamation" by the narrator.[71] One thinks of Wordsworth's later lament in "Elegiac Stanzas": that, after his brother John's death, a "deep distress . . . humaniz'd [his] Soul" (*PTV*, l. 36). In "Three years she grew," as well, despite the poem's obvious nod to the Orphean myth of Persephone,[72] Lucy's death has the principal effect of evoking from her mourners a profound sense of "irredeemable loss" (*WE* 204) and difference, "The memory of what has been, / And never more will be" (*LB*, ll. 41–42). Although the Lucy of "She dwelt" is, we are told, "in her Grave" (11), like the girl of "A slumber" she lingers on in the mind of her elegist and in the minds of others. Lucy "*liv'd* unknown" (9; original emphasis) and so died relatively unknown: "few could know / When Lucy ceas'd to be" (9–10). But, as the emphatic "*liv'd*" signifies, her ceasing "to be" has made all the "difference" in terms of the speaker's and others' awareness. Lucy's loss is an ongoing fact to be communicated and reiterated by her elegists as a mournful legacy, one that makes a gathering of the "few" (or many) who mourn her possible and, as in so many past poems, necessary, too.

Such ghostly, lingering powers of the dead are even more clearly the topic of "Lucy Gray," in which another Lucy has died, specifically from having slipped off of a bridge and drowned.[73] So, at least, her last footmarks suggest, ending as they do in the middle of one of the wood planks. Yet death proves not to be the end of this Lucy, less so even than for her nominal kindred. As the poem's elegist adds,

> some maintain that to this day
> She is a living Child,
> That you may see sweet Lucy Gray
> Upon the lonesome Wild.
>
> (57–60)

"Trip[ping] along" (61) in death much as in life (the pun neatly if macabrely reiterates the child's death), Lucy's ghost lingers on as an intermittent yet persistent presence among the living, who talk of her sightings and now and then hear her "solitary song . . . whistl[ing] in the wind" (63–64). This Lucy is a more obvious, fairy-tale emblem of the dead's persistence.[74] According to Bewell, in the "interpolative layers" of mythopoesis contained within the poem's narrative, we readers discover "how a commonplace event, which can be explained without reference to supernatural intervention, has been taken up and revised over the course of its history by an interpretive community" (*WE* 205). At the same time, it is uncertainty about Lucy's loss, with its sense of unfinished business, of mournful incertitude, and of the limits of interpretation, that elicits such narrative from mourners and mythographers.

Lucy is, in Bewell's terms, one of Wordsworth's "unburied dead." Here likely following upon Hartman's reading of *katabasis* in Wordsworth (mentioned in Chapter One), Bewell finds "Lucy Gray" to be structured by three Orphic quest-descents "to the silent realm of the dead" (*WE* 205–6). In the first such descent-retrieval Lucy is sent for her mother to light her way home from town through the "stormy night." The parents then in turn search for Lucy in the darkness, as does the narrator, subsequently, in the dark of local folklore. Readers at this point are not so far from the Orphic quests of *The Vale of Esthwaite* or, for that matter, the quest of "Orpheus and Eurydice." Such mournful quests of retrieval, undertaken, in the various disappearances of these Lucy figures, by parents, villagers, lovers, mourners, elegists, and readers, compose not just a mythographical life-in-death for the deceased in the unfinished, unfinishable work of death. Together these descents describe another, familiar and uncanny form of Wordsworthian community, located in the uneasy and unending relationships of the living and dead. For in death Lucy is unfinished, looming but unlocalized, dwelling ever *between* the living and the dead. Like the Lucy of "A slumber," she lingers on as one and many, a ubiquitous, unburiable "thing."[75] Such critics as Hartman, de Man, J. Hillis Miller, and Frances Ferguson find this group of poems to focus or occasion a focus principally upon the inadequacy of language to represent Lucy.[76] But these poems can, I believe, be said to emphasize mourning and its troubles more than only language's own.

The dead's ghostly, "untrodden" dwelling is why the Lucy poems concern not the peace the deceased attain in gaining heaven or in being reintegrated back into nature and its processes but the power their loss exerts upon the living. As Wordsworth makes clear in an early draft of "Song," Lucy's power derives from her loss. In life she was "[d]ead to the world" (*LB*, p. 163), including to the slumbering poet himself. Only in her afterlife does she in some sense *live* in terms of mattering to others, and in mattering become the basis for an interpretive community of mourning. In this way, Wordsworth's Lucy poems are archeologies of the buried foundations of community, like those that underlay community in the Salisbury Plain poems and in *The Ruined Cottage*. The powers of the Dead are, by this accounting, scarcely in decline, let alone at an end, in the Goslar period. The dynamics of mourning, and this poet's visions of mourning as a troubled inheritance, are arguably intensified, and their elements more closely scrutinized, during the cold German winter of 1799.

Also from the second volume of *Lyrical Ballads* of 1800, "The Two April Mornings" serves here in part to bridge the Lucy poems' paramount concern with the power of the dead's indeterminacy and the clearer social vision of mourning represented in "The Brothers." Yet, were the poem's mourned girl, Emma, but differently named, "The Two April Mornings" might fit well in the Lucy group.[77] The first of two Matthew elegies (following upon an epitaph for Matthew, "Lines written on a Tablet in a School"), the poem recalls one of its speaker's walks with his friend the village schoolmaster, during which the old man suddenly was stricken with grief for his long-deceased child. This narrative of an outburst of grief is in this respect similar to that of *The Ruined Cottage*'s grieving pedlar and his impromptu recollection of Margaret, erupting even amid the beauty of nature. "[F]rom thy breast what thought, / Beneath so beautiful a sun, / So sad a sigh has brought?" the narrator asks Matthew (ll. 14–16). As Matthew himself observes in the companion poem, "The Fountain, a conversation," the birds of nature for their part are happy, never "wag[ing] / A foolish strife" with what they cannot change (41–42). Should not nature's beauty be enough for human beings, too? That is the elegy's question. In this duel between recidivist mourning and natural consolation the answer, more clearly even than in the pedlar's narrative of Margaret, is no.

On that April morning Matthew responds that nature, specifically the "purple cleft" of a cloud, has reminded him of a similar sky seen on an April morning thirty years before, under which he had found himself standing at his nine-year-old daughter's grave. His heart had brimmed with love for Emma, so much so that it had seemed that not "till that day / I e'er had lov'd before" (39–40). "[T]urning from her grave," he then had chanced upon another girl, who "seem'd as happy as a wave / That dances on the sea" (41, 51–52). But although Matthew took a certain delight in a child "so very fair" (47) and doubtless so much like his daughter, the sight had not prompted joy. Rather,

> There came from me a sigh of pain
> Which I could ill confine;
> I look'd at her and look'd again;
> —And did not wish her mine.

The narrator then adds to Matthew's sad account the following elegiac coda:

> Mat[t]hew is in his grave, yet now
> Methinks I see him stand,
> As at that moment, with his bough
> Of wilding in his hand.—

(53–60)

Like Lucy's death, Emma's loss remains singular, and Matthew's mourning of her refuses the easy reparative joys the sight of the living girl presents. In "The Fountain" we learn that indeed he "Mourns less for what age takes away / Than what it leaves behind" (35–36), which is to say that he experiences an ongoing sense of loss: of being "glad no more" behind a "face of joy" (46–47). As so often in Wordsworth, loss is represented as being both irreparable and unending.[78] The narrator's impassioned, compassionate plea that Matthew think of him as "a son to thee" is dismissed by the old man's melancholy reply that "Alas! that cannot be" (62, 64). Matthew resists these proffered symbolic substitutes for Emma, acting the part of the unrelenting Orphean melancholic to the narrator's (proto-Freudian) request for a mourning-work of substitution, as he similarly had that April morning to chance's fleeting offer of the girl as a proxy for his child. Yet this sharing of mortal loss between the two men is not without its "virtue friendly," to borrow words from the pedlar. Just as Matthew's grief recalls to him a past loss and grief, the first of two April mo*(u)*rnings (to my ears the homonymic pun is irrepressible), so the narrator is led, by a similar mnemonic conjunction of sights and sounds, to recall Matthew's own death.

   The situation in this way repeats much the same scenario and social scheme as that of *The Ruined Cottage*. But for one thing: that "The Fountain" and "The Two April Mornings" examine even more closely the limits of such mournful society, and not just those presented by mourning. The younger of the poems' "pair of Friends" ("Fountain" 3) of course cannot substitute himself for the elder mourner's lost beloved. As his request suggests, he remains on the borders of his friend's loss. Only in Matthew's death and in his elegist's commemorative gesture of tribute does their community become manifested. Now Matthew is one of the dead, and his elegist-pupil must direct his own grief to his readers, recapitulating the difference that both precipitates and limits, and even defers, such community. Friendship and community can be founded upon shared grief, but such mourning is in some degree never generalizeable, and can never fully be shared. In that shade of difference is part of mourning's peculiar power. As with Wordsworth's discussion in the Preface to *Lyrical Ballads* about the origins of poetry, the communicated grief is always only a "species" of the emotion and loss felt in the heart of the mourner. At the same time, such communicated griefs as these, and the rites of mourning they effect, are in "The Two April Mornings" and "The Fountain" the fixed marks of comradely friendship. That friendship is memorialized by Wordsworth's depicted memories of Matthew, a figure who, like Margaret, seems almost present in the insistent nature of his mourning: "yet now / Methinks I see him stand, / As at that moment." Never the equivalent of Matthew's grief for Emma, the narrator's grief for his friend still binds them, with considerable interstitial tension and difference, as one of a transmortal community of mourners mourning different dead in different ways. Such is their legacy and bond, and such is their community, emblematized in the narrator's recollection not of his own mourning but of Matthew's on that second April morning.

Wordsworth's unpublished additions to this elegiac series further signify the endurance of the mourning that perpetuates a community of elegizing remembrance. In one, the narrating poet proclaims to "suspend / Thy [Matthew's] gift this twisted oaken staff" in their favorite thorn, and in that tree's trunk, near where the schoolmaster's bones had been buried, to "engrave thy epitaph" (*LB*, p. 297). The former gesture is a means of still further tribute, à la the suspended wooden oar of the elegy to Collins revised for *Lyrical Ballads*. The gesture is one of a supplementing epitaphic writing (its own form of suspension) offered in addition to this one elegy, to the other Matthew elegies, and even to whatever epitaph has been engraved on the headstone in the churchyard to which Matthew's corpse has since been moved—suggesting the passage of considerable time. A further sequel records that "with a master's skill" the poet later carved Matthew's name "on the hawthorne tree," but that, despite such tribute, he has since written yet again of his dead friend because he "owed another verse to thee" (330). Still more verses follow, including "Dirge," which in elegiac fashion calls upon Matthew's other grieving survivors to mourn: "Both in your sorrow and your bliss / Remember him and his grey head" (302). *Lyrical Ballads'* "Lines" epitaph for Matthew closes with a key question and lament (and at least potential intimation): "and can it be / That these two words of glittering gold / Are all that must remain of thee?" (ll. 30–32). Wordsworth's inadequate series of published and unpublished, written and not-yet written elegies reveals, in a manner that sheds light on the Lucy poems as well, not just the relentless persistence of grief but also the promise that incessant mourning offers for social bonds between troubled mourners.

As in *The Ruined Cottage,* these elegies from the second volume of the second edition of *Lyrical Ballads* depict grief and its underlying loss erupting into the diagetic present, as aspects of an experience that cannot be put behind, be put by, or otherwise be concluded. Matthew and his poet-friend are linked insomuch as each man holds onto and has lasting *tenancy* with the dead: Matthew with his dead daughter and the narrator with deceased Matthew. Each mourner elegizes a loss become a memory, and each is bound by his reiterative memorializing of beloved dead who resist being located in a grave—or even in an elegy.[79] Those dead then become the foundations, and also the far limit, of a transmissible community comprised of mourners bearing a legacy of remarkable and persisting griefs.

III. Epitaphic Society in "The Brothers" and "The Thorn"

rude stones placed near . . . graves. . . .
            —*Essays upon Epitaphs*

In the first of the *Essays upon Epitaphs*, written in late 1809 and early 1810 for Coleridge's journal *The Friend*, Wordsworth defines an epitaph as being "a record to preserve the memory of the dead," inscribed in part "for the common benefit of the living" (*PrW* 2: 53). In the second of the *Essays*, considering the positive effects that epitaphs can have upon the living, the poet laments that the inhabitants of some parishes have only "small knowledge of the dead who are buried in their Church-yards." Such ignorance about the deceased of a place "cannot fail to preclude," he argues, "the best part of the wholesome influence of that communion between living and dead which the conjunction in rural districts of the place of burial and place of worship tends so effectually to promote" (66). Earlier in the same essay, Wordsworth proclaims that under appropriate conditions those same churchyards indeed may serve as the "eye or central point" of community—not of an idealized "rural Arcadia" but, he implies, of real locales in England (64). Churchyards certainly do so in some of the topographies depicted in his poetry, as in "We are Seven" and also, from the second volume of *Lyrical Ballads,* in "The Brothers," in which "communion" of the living and the dead is the basis for community. In fact, for all the *Essays'* Christian assertions of an afterlife (a revision of pagan ideas about mortality articulated in "We are Seven" and, more explicitly, in the Neoplatonic Immortality Ode), they show their author continuing, well into the second decade of the new century, to conceptualize community as a product of conjoining the living and dead. That conjunction is instituted by the propinquity of the two groups, but it is also, as the epitaphic focus of the *Essays* makes clear, forged by the reading and exchange of epitaphs: by epitaphic conversation among the living about the dead.

Although Wordsworth's poetry is, on the whole, more elegiac than epitaphic, its author's interest in epitaph was longstanding, and certainly pre-existed the *Essays'* aesthetic analysis of the genre. It is evident, for example, in his "Lines left upon a Seat in a Yew-tree," from the first volume of *Lyrical Ballads,* and in the numerous place-naming poems of the second volume of 1800. Wordsworth's schoolboy attempts in the genre, and mature texts like the Hanged Man spot of time from *The Prelude,* similarly touch upon epitaphic form, as "A Poet's Epitaph," also from *Lyrical Ballads,* does explicitly. This poetical epitaph intriguingly connects epitaphic writing and community, and also reveals Wordsworth's understanding of the ancient form's social powers. The prescribed reader of "A Poet's Epitaph," one who has discovered that truths lurk

hidden "[i]n common things that round us lie" (*LB,* 1. 49), is beckoned to
"stretch thy body at full length; / Or build thy house upon this grave—"
(59–60). Why should the ability to see into "common things" be the prerequisite for those who would build a dwelling upon or nearby the grave? The reader
approaching this epitaph and its implicit question by way of previous works
like *The Ruined Cottage* or the Salisbury Plain poems may discern the answer:
that such an ideal dweller—not to be found, the poet declares, among the traditional occupations of statesman, lawyer, moralist, theologian, natural scien-
tist, or soldier—has to be capable of converse with the deceased. Such a would-
be builder must be able to make a pact with the dead, dwelling in their midst,
upon the dead's very foundations, and be capable of perceiving those "shades of
difference" (to borrow again from the pedlar) that connect mourners to the
dead. This is, after all, a *poet*'s epitaph: an epitaph inscribed by a poet, to a poet,
and on behalf of those poets who will follow after him.

This communion beyond the visible, this exclusive form of "spiritual
community" of and beyond the epitaph, is the basis for community represented in "The Brothers." Here, epitaphic—or rather, supra-epitaphic—conversation of the dead forges social cohesion among the living, making the dead
again the invisible center of a community. Central to "The Brothers" is the
epitaph, or more precisely the eliding and superseding of churchyard epitaphs
in favor of a ubiquitous and intersubjective oral discourse. Conversations of
the dead, spoken around the foci of firesides and in the surrounding ruins of
the churchyard, serve as the principal registers of the dead. The living circu-
late oral epitaphs as the basis for very much the same kind of "communion"
praised in the *Essays*. In fact, although the focus of the latter prose works is on
written epitaphs and their aesthetic merits, Wordsworth all but concludes the
third essay with praise not of the elaborately crafted literary or even the more
humble rustic epitaph but of the minimal, almost nonexistent sort. The example he offers is one he claims himself to have spotted in a country churchyard:

> a very small Stone laid upon the ground, bearing nothing more than the
> name of the Deceased with the date of birth and death, importing that it was
> an Infant which had been born one day and died the following. . . . [M]ore
> awful thoughts of rights conferred, of hopes awakened, of remembrances
> stealing away or vanishing were imparted to my mind by that Inscription
> there before my eyes than by any other that it has ever been my lot to meet
> with upon a Tomb-stone. (*PrW* 2: 93)

Oddly, at the very point of concluding his three-part analysis of the English
epitaph, Wordsworth undercuts the aesthetics of epitaph he has promoted,
instead praising a minimalist form of the discourse that, although speaking
proverbial volumes, provides so little text as to be scarcely an epitaph at all.
But then Wordsworth had always tended to view mourners' signifying of the

dead in terms more of the "shades of difference" of loss, and in terms more of the powers of speech, than in those of epitaphic inscription. Why? As David Collings rightly observes, "because neither a name nor a mute sign is complete without its accompanying story." Each of them "depends entirely on the capacity of living people to explain what it means."[80] It is this dependence upon "the mutual acquaintance, affection or sympathy" of an oral-interpretive community, upon what amounts to epitaphic exchange, that, Collings argues, may account for Wordsworth's ambivalent feelings about literacy and about the written word itself.[81]

In "The Brothers" the emphasis upon oral epitaphic discourse is owed in large part to the fact that the poem's community is articulated in the discursive *exchange* of elegiac or epitaphic speech. And it would appear that epitaph, were it viewed as a complete rather than as a spare record, in need of supplementation, could attenuate or cancel such exchange and, with it, the promise or realization of community. Conversation requires at least two interlocutors, a teller and a listener, and so it is that for Wordsworth cohesion has at its center converse of the dead, qua mourning-work, and favors elegiac memorializing more than epitaphic recording as its principal discourse. "The Brothers" examines the extent to which a form of oral epitaph might serve as the cohesive discourse of a community staged much closer to the confines of that social "eye or central point" of the churchyard; indeed, as a panoptic eye overseeing the binding relationship of the locality's living and dead. In his note to the poem, Wordsworth held that nothing was "more worthy of remark in the manner of the inhabitants of these mountains than the tranquility, one might even say the indifference, with which they think and talk upon the subject of death"—thinking and talking prompted in part by the absence of mortuary monuments in Lakeland churchyards, some of which "do not contain a single tombstone" (*LB* 382).

The poem recounts the return of a mariner, named Leonard Ewbank, to his old village of Ennerdale, where he hopes to learn the fate of the younger brother he left behind. Fearing the worst, Leonard hesitantly surveys the churchyard, but in doing so he is mistaken for a tourist by the local priest, who wonders that such a stranger should "tarry *yonder*" in a churchyard that offers the visitor "neither epitaph nor monument, / Tomb-stone nor name, only the turf we tread, / And a few natural graves" (*LB*, ll. 12–15). Leonard does nothing to correct the once familiar vicar's mistake, and much of the poem's dramatic tension is produced by his repeated efforts to nudge the old parson into revealing his brother James's fate while at the same time retaining his own anonymity. For the most part, Leonard succeeds. He learns that after he had left Ennerdale "to try his fortune on the seas" (302)—his father's death having left the brothers orphaned and destitute—James had "pin'd and pin'd" for Leonard (336). He eventually died from mourning him, specifically from a curiously grief-related fall from a precipice. James had fallen asleep atop the rock and then, having previously contracted the somnambulist "habit which disquietude and grief / Had brought upon him" (391–92), had sleepwalked over the edge.[82] Now, with this brother's death confirmed, the inquiring "Stranger" departs, too grief-stricken to thank the parson, let alone to accept from him his kind offer of "homely fare" (403, 410). Stopping by a grove, Leonard reviews "[a]ll that the Priest had said" (417), much as the narrator of *The Ruined Cottage* had reviewed the pedlar's words. As a result,

> thoughts which had been his an hour before,
> All press'd on him with such a weight, that now,
> This vale, where he had been so happy, seem'd
> A place in which he could not bear to live:
> So he relinquish'd all his purposes.
>
> (419–23)

Traveling on, he tarries only to post a letter informing the vicar of his true identity and to seek forgiveness for his deception—owed, he confesses, to "the weakness of his heart" (428). He thereupon returns to sea.

Like Margaret in *The Ruined Cottage,* James died of grief and is elegized by an elderly man who knew him and observed his melancholy decline. And, as in that poem of mourning, upon which Jonathan Wordsworth contends "The Brothers" was modeled,[83] James's narrated loss draws the two men together, amid textual intimations that community is a product of just such mournful exchanges as this one. Yet "The Brothers" concludes not with that prior poem's image of camaraderie but with Leonard's feeling of alienation from his old village and from the company offered him by the priest. The poem's oddly somber finale may suggest Wordsworth's growing ambivalence about his paradigm of mourning-based community, his sense that grief can as easily separate people as link them together. But it more likely, and more positively, functions as a new means to analyze and pinpoint one of the inherent limits of dead-oriented community and of oral epitaph: the need for unrestrained conversation between those who, like the female vagrant of *Salisbury Plain,* poignantly share the "weight" of their mournful tales of the dead and those who listen to them. Leonard's "weakness" of heart, and that weakness's resulting reserve and outright duplicity, blocks the bonding that his queries and their answers might provide, as is suggested by the parson's offer of "homely fare" to this seeming (and dissembling) stranger.[84]

Although Leonard's questions and their answers focus attention upon grief and its lack of resolution, and although his and the vicar's talk ushers the two men into a closer relationship (to such an extent that the priest offers him aid and company and that Leonard feels compelled to reveal his identity and beg forgiveness), the main signs of community are arguably to be found elsewhere. Early in their graveyard dialogue the priest explains that he and his neighbors "have no need of names and epitaphs, / We talk about the dead by our firesides," and that in this way the dead "[p]ossess a kind of second life" in the thoughts of their survivors (176–77, 183). Conversation of the dead endows the latter with a form of continued existence (a notion of discursive immortality that of course dates back well before Homer's *Iliad*). That conversation of the dead forges and maintains this spiritual community in "The Brothers" is made clear by the vicar's words to his wife at the poem's opening and by the churchyard's special topography, specifically its significant dearth of epitaphs, monuments, and demarcated grave plots. The absence of such markers in this "total society"[85] underlines the importance both of the dead to conversation and social life for the living and of that conversation to the memorializing and quasi-living-on of the dead. The absence of headstones, footstones, and other markers of the dead signifies not a community "heedless of the past" (166), as Leonard duplicitously charges, but one mindful, and vocal, about its past and dead. And that community is articulated and maintained by oral epitaphic discourse transmitted beside firesides and other sites of conversation. Such speech serves not just to memorialize the dead (with gravestones and their epitaphs being viewed more as supplements to speech than the reverse) but also to organize a community bound together by "talk about the dead." The priest's conversation with Leonard exemplifies this epitaphic talk's socializing power: its tendency to evoke feeling, to lead people to ease mourners' burdens, and to provide in itself a remedy to social estrangement and wandering. Yet Leonard's resistance to revealing himself as a mourner, and as one with more than a passing interest in these dead, prevents him from being integrated or reintegrated into Ennerdale.[86]

At the same time, the poem's closing lines suggest the continuing circulation of Leonard's history (at least that portion concerning his departure) among this community: "This done, he went on shipboard, and is now / A Seaman, a grey-headed Mariner" (430–31). Susan Wolfson reads these words as sparely epitaphic.[87] For in speaking of the dead with the vicar, Leonard has unintentionally become a part of the community's exclusive economy of oral epitaphs, providing discursive fuel for the locality's social engine. The powers of epitaph and of mourning will have him, it would seem, whether he wills it or not. Leonard's incorporation into the discursive graveyard of the absent, even of the self-excluded, reveals the social cohesion of Ennerdale to be founded not so much upon mourners' physical propinquity to the dead as upon their distance from them, from those who are lost and yet maintained, liminally contained and (re)circulated, in an epitaphic economy. "The Brothers" reveals the fundamental needs less of mourners than of those communities they and their dead form: the social requisite of discursive exchanges among the living. Those who narrativize the lost or absent become the legislators or engineers of community in this dale.

Leonard may not himself be reintegrated into Ennerdale, but that certainly cannot be said to demonstrate a categorical failure of its epitaphic community, given the limits Leonard's ruse imposed. To be so integrated in this society the living must be willing to communicate their mourning-work to others and to have that grief and its dead be incorporated into the community's discursive economy. For Ennerdale is a community with one foot in the grave, a society organized, like the communities praised in *Essays upon Epitaphs,* around mourning and signifying—burying and reburying—the dead.

As with "The Brothers," "The Thorn" can also be read as an experiment upon the basic formula of *The Ruined Cottage,* centered on "a deserted woman who lingers around a spot made significant by her suffering" (*PHS* 171). In this distinctive narrative, likely the first major work to have been undertaken after the poet's 1798 additions to *The Ruined Cottage,* elegiac-epitaphic exchange is taken to its limit: reduced to mere gossip and hearsay, to what the pedlar condemned as "vain dalliance." "The Thorn" takes *The Ruined Cottage*'s scheme and, Averill argues, "distorts it into what would be parody if the fundamental undertaking were not serious" (173). The distortion is in large part owed to the poem's garrulous, rumor-mongering narrator, who reiterates a tale of inferences and local superstitions concerning the long-suffering, possibly infanticidal Martha Ray. Not surprisingly, his superficial discourse produces only a superficial, parasitical kind of community, based upon this poor woman's exploitation, subordination, and exclusion. Yet "The Thorn" does not only test and illustrate a model of community gone wrong. Like the tale of "The Brothers," this poem's narrative, more than its narrator, points to the social potential of mourning and loss. If we are to judge both from the words and from the disturbing inaction of the narrator, although Martha Ray's grief-derived sufferings and repeated cries of "O misery! oh misery!" (252) mainly succeed in attracting around her a community of voyeurs and gossips, they do nonetheless produce a form of social cohesion, one organized by her interminable mourning. It is of course also organized by the mystery concerning the status of her missing child—who, if it ever even existed, may have been born dead or been murdered by the husbandless woman and buried in the child-sized mound that lies beside the thorn.

Gossip is the predominant mode of discourse depicted in "The Thorn," and it is at bottom a generic perversion of epitaph and elegy. Yet, like those forms, the narrative textualized and exchanged by the village is dependent upon the mourning-work of others: upon their insufficient and interminable memorializing of the dead who rest so restlessly at this discursive community's limits, in rustic topographies astir with "voices of the dead" (174). Hence, even in a community like this, one which, like the poem's emblem of anthropomorphized moss pulling down a thorn, seems perversely intent upon dragging Martha "to the ground" (246), the dead are still the social core. It is to the grave-shaped spot that Martha Ray repeatedly returns to grieve, much like the absence-obsessed melancholic of "Incipient Madness" (see Chapter Four), and it is to that site as well that others repeatedly return either to see Martha grieve or else to view more freely and closely the symbol-laden scene in her absence. Her life is one of mourning, as, secondarily, are in some measure the lives of the members of this haunted community. And in this sense, for all its base gossip and predatory voyeurism, the poem's narrative is at bottom an almost incantatory elegiac recounting of Martha Ray's recurring mourning. Like her, and like the gossips of this society, readers are brought to stand on what is at the same time both the limit and foundation of community: that which constitutes it but also that which prevents it from including the poor, likely half-mad mourner around whom it so tenaciously organizes its thorn-like form.

Many of Wordsworth's communities appear to be built, like this one, upon the ruin(s) of another. And it could be argued that this extreme instance merely arrives at the violence inherent in his social paradigm. Yet it would also seem that an elegist like the pedlar, or even a fellow mourner like the female vagrant, could transform Martha Ray's personal tragedy and its grief into a more inclusive discourse of mourning (granted, the pedlar did little for Margaret while *she* lived; nor did the elegist for Lucy). In that elegiac converse, grief might bind together the living and include the living mourner, albeit within the limits of such inclusion, mourners being in an important sense always beyond the discourses that would include and represent them. Martha Ray's suffering, like most anybody's, exists for others, as Bromwich holds, only "by ascription: it cannot be fully known, not even surely known to exist."[88] And yet, despite the patent unreliability of the narrator's account of her sufferings, his narrative points to their permanence and to the potentially cohesive powers of grief and of the dead. The last words of the poem are Martha Ray's (narrated) words of grief, concluding the narrative with sentiments that loom between the genre of elegiac lamentation and, in their proximity to the dead, that of epitaph. "The Thorn" ultimately points to the limits of epitaphic economies and, through the very act of showing Martha Ray's exclusion, supports the pedlar's concern about "dalliance" with others' sufferings. The poem obliges readers to tread cautiously the ground that separates the living and dead: those who speak and those who are spoken of and whose legacy of epitaphs the living are entrusted to share.

IV. A HEAP OF STONES:
COMMUNITY AND NARRATION IN "MICHAEL"

In the pastoral elegy "Michael," the concluding poem of the second volume and edition of *Lyrical Ballads*, Wordsworth describes a dell above Grasmere's

Greenhead Gill, where he would direct the reader to "one object which you might pass by, / Might see and notice not" (15–16). That object is a ruined sheepfold, "a straggling Heap of unhewn stones" (17) that signifies a history of loss. The fold is a stark, wordless monument, a kind of epitaphic cairn, further described, in some early lines written for "Michael," as a "crowd" of stones

> That lie together, some in heaps and some
> In lines that seem to keep themselves alive
> In the last dotage of a dying form—
>
> (*LB*, p. 329)

As with the ruined cottage, these stones convey a presence of what has been lost and retained, as do the most basic of gravemarkers and tombstones. The stones are, like an epitaph, a fundamental "Register" of the dead, to quote again from *Essays upon Epitaphs* (*PrW* 2: 64). And as such a register they function to memorialize loss.

In the overtly Christian first essay of the above epitaphic group, Wordsworth contends "that without the belief in immortality . . . neither monuments nor epitaphs, in affectionate or laudatory commemoration of the deceased, could have existed in the world," essentially because people "respect the corporeal frame of Man, not merely because it is the habitation of a rational, but of an immortal Soul" (2: 52). Yet in the second of the *Essays* Wordsworth turns to focus upon the more mortal and mournful aspects of the dead and of their epitaphs. Thinking now less as the poet of the Immortality Ode and a member of Grasmere Church, and more like the poet of the Lucy and Matthew elegies, Wordsworth is "rouzed" from his "reverie" of the churchyard as an "Enclosure" devoid of "traces of evil inclinations." He detects instead a

> flashing . . . of the anxieties, the perturbations, and, in many instances, the vices and rancorous dispositions, by which the hearts of those who lie under so smooth a surface and so fair an outside must have been agitated.

Almost certainly writing here of his drowned mariner brother John, the subject of "Elegiac Stanzas," while also referring to Shakespeare's *Richard III* (and likely alluding to *The Tempest*), Wordsworth adds that, in contemplating such a location, for him

> The image of an unruffled Sea has still remained; but my fancy has penetrated into the depths of that Sea—with accompanying thoughts of Shipwreck, of the destruction of the Mariner's hopes, the bones of drowned Men heaped together, monsters of the deep, and all the hideous and confused sights which Clarence saw in his Dream! (64)

The pains of mourning, and mourning's less than "benign influence" on one's "contentment" and even "amity and gratitude" (64), ruffle and agitate Wordsworth's rather staid attempts to envision the churchyard as a source of virtue and stability. The model of mournful community doesn't work that way; such agitation about the deceased is not peripheral or superficial but central, at the very core. As Michele Turner Sharp observes of this same scene, "the passage below the smooth surface of the epitaph to the interior of the grave reveals not an image of a properly buried corpse, but the utter impossibility of burial." It is an image of horror; in her words, of "a death whose particular horror consists in the state of radical indeterminacy in which it leaves the deceased, a state in which burial, and hence resolution of mourning, is impossible."[89] The mourner, in other words, reaches no end of mourning. And whatever grave or heap the dead are buried under does not entirely quiet their stirrings, either, or quell their haunting of the living.

The intrusion of thoughts of dashed hopes and of bodies heaped on the "slimy bottom of the deep," propounded by Clarence in *Richard III,* with visions of jewels that "lay in dead men's skulls . . . in the holes / Where eyes did once inhabit" (I.iv.29–32), can be understood not just in terms of Wordsworth's fraternal desire to commemorate his brother. It can also be explained in terms of the poet's sociology, with its emphasis upon the irretrievable, unlocateable, ghostly nature of the mourned and of mourning itself, the mainstays of Wordsworthian community. So it is with the natural signs of Lucy's loss, with the ruinous or outright missing gravestones of "The Brothers," and with the *semai* of "Michael,"[90] which similarly point to a "history / Homely and rude," but which is told by the narrator "for the sake / Of youthful Poets, who among these Hills / Will be my second Self when I am gone" (*LB*, ll. 34–39). Better than in his well-known epistle to Charles James Fox, in a letter to Thomas Poole, Wordsworth describes his intention in "Michael" as having indeed been

> to give a picture of a man, of strong mind and lively sensibility, agitated by two of the most powerful affections of the human heart; the parental affection, and the love of property, *landed* property, including the feelings of inheritance, home, and personal and family independence. (*EY* 322; original emphasis)

The poet places emphasis upon the land, but it is with those tears that both he and his poem seem especially concerned. "Michael" had, Wordsworth tells Poole, "drawn tears from the eyes of more than one," and he was "anxious to know the effect of this Poem" upon his friend, as well (322). For "Michael" is a narrative not just of stoic pastoral endurance (attractive as such stoic patience would become to Wordsworth in later years) but of profound disappointment on the part of a father for his wayward son—and in some measure on the part of the elegist narrating that disappointment and loss on behalf of the dead and of a future, unfolding elegiac tradition.

The stones of the sheepfold were laid by Michael, we are told, as the beginning of work to be completed by him and his eighteen-year-old son, Luke, upon the latter's return from the city to which he was departing to earn money. In that city a kinsman, "[t]hriving in trade" (260), would aid Luke in finding employment, the earnings from which would save the "patrimonial fields" (234) Michael shunned to sell "to discharge the forfeiture" of another relative, his nephew (225). "[I]f these fields of ours / Should pass into a Stranger's hand," Michael laments, "I think / That I could not lie quiet in my grave" (240–42). So it is up to young Luke to preserve them along with his father's happiness and peaceful interment—and ultimately the family's pastoral patrimony, based upon the land they conserve on their posterity's behalf. For Regina Hewitt this household "shows a kind of solidarity by difference," with each member—Michael the shepherd, wife Isabel the spinner, and shepherd's assistant Luke—working at some defined task.[91] "Their bonds are strong," Hewitt argues (departing from such critics as Levinson and Karl Kroeber), "because each depends on the other for a particular contribution to their common welfare," a social reality that informs Michael's fateful plan to send Luke to the city.[92]

Michael and Luke lay the stones of the sheepfold to serve as the son's "anchor and . . . shield" in his travels; they are an "emblem of the life [his] Fathers liv'd" (418–20), a material reminder binding Luke to the pastoral values of the farm and of his agriculturist forebears. But when Luke descends into an urban life of "ignominy and shame" and is thereupon "driven at last / To seek a hiding-place beyond the seas" (454–56), the stones come to emblematize not life and futurity but death and the past, and to serve not as an "anchor" (Luke now being lost well *beyond* the seas") or even as a "shield" but as a memorial to and legacy of hopes overthrown. They become signs of loss, grave-like stones of a particular pastoral history and its core of Michael's mourning of Luke. Of course, in the poem the stones of the fold also attest to the Grasmere shepherd's rustic endurance. As Bromwich states, "Michael's feelings about his way of life have become so ingrained as to be unshakable even in catastrophe." But Michael's *hopes* are quite "a different thing,"[93] and they are dashed by Luke's loss. The incomplete sheepfold thereafter comes to signify both this paternal covenant and its breach, both hope and hope's disappointment. Pastoral fold becomes pastoral epitaph. Like "Tintern Abbey," "Michael" thus can be read as an attempt to discover, in response to loss, some means of social or other compensation, some form of recompense via narration. The text attempts to salvage from those pastoral ruins an elegiac history that will then in turn become the basis for a second(ary) formation of community as "mediated knowledge,"[94] articulated out of loss, through material and other auspices, and exchanged among the living.

To the heap of stones Michael will thereafter frequently bend his steps, adding to the enclosure for a "full seven years from time to time" (479) but leaving "the work unfinished when he died" (481). In fact, his continued "building of this sheep-fold" (480) was for him an act of mourning-work that could not have been completed and still have signified, and signify still, that paternal-filial breach. For with Luke's loss the sheepfold became a kind of monumental wordless text of "remains" (489), pointing back to a turbulent sea of grief and retaining in itself the semiotic power of its incompleteness. In this light, the old heap of stones was transformed or translated into a spare epitaph indeed, symbolizing the death of Michael's hopes for Luke and for the patrimony of the land: a "tale of lost hopes."[95] In time, the stones stand as the gravemarker and minimalist epitaphic text for Michael himself as well as for his family's disappearing way of life.

Tracy Ware points out that Michael's description of his love for Luke as repayment for the "gift" of love he had himself received from his own father, and his father in turn from *his* father, implies a "communal basis of morality," wherein Michael's relationship to his son is "governed by his sense of participating in the community of the living and the dead."[96] Like the sheepfold, the patrimonial lands bind one generation to another via a material history of dwelling and death, which is also to say via a debt owed by one generation to another: to the dead and to the living yet to come. The lands do so through a transmitted culture of indebtedness, the poem's great irony given that the debts of a kinsman necessitate, after all, Luke's quasi-sacrifice to the city. The name Luke may thus pun upon *lucre* and *luck,* playing upon Michael's failed gamble.[97] But, as Stuart Peterfreund notes, in English the name Luke is the masculine form of Lucy,[98] this offspring being indeed one more lost and mourned child, whose loss makes a great and lasting difference. And in the oedipal breach of that patriarchal covenant (binding one generation, by its debt, to a previous one) arise loss and lack and the opening of memorializing signifying systems: the piled grave-like stones and—the sole other surviving landmark—the oak clipping tree that grew beside the cottage door. Like those stones, the oak tree "no longer serves its particular human use, but remains as a marker of Michael's life and his death."[99] In addition to these signs, and as a means of supplementing them, second-order commemorating and memorializing discourses arise, including the pastoral-elegiac text we read.

"Michael" becomes a species of epitaph, as a historical record of loss, pointing to and in part explicating another record of loss, another allegorical ruin in need of material and exegetical elaboration. In so doing, as in other of Wordsworth's poems, a breach in the past becomes the basis for an interpretive community to come, salvaged by elegiac narrative.[100] Wolfson rightly observes that, as readers of "Michael," we perform the equivalent of reading the stones for the story they mark, and so join the community that can tell the tale. . . . Michael's doomed exhortation to his son—"do thou thy part, / I will do mine" (401–2)—is redeemed in the poet's covenant with his heir or "second self" (39), his listeners.[101]

It is a social compact emphatically focused upon reading and upon read signs of loss, with poetic vocation founded upon bare, grave-like *semai*. In "Michael" the spare, disordered stones of the unfinished sheepfold are minimally, too minimally, epitaphic: markers signifying a history of suffering, loss, and grief—a history that seems almost itself to suffer, and certainly to be in need. The stones are more (or less) than epitaphs insomuch as they are the signifiers *and* the material signifieds of that history. Into the discursive breach readers and succeeding poets go, to participate in its community of sorrow and, in part, to complete through supplementary acts "the story for which the 'unfinished Sheep-fold' is the only outward sign,"[102] the solitary epitaphic signifier, excepting perhaps the old oak tree, of a deeper, turbulent history.

As in *The Ruined Cottage,* history becomes its memorial, "living on as its own epitaph"[103] and, as in the Matthew elegies, in need of further memorialization. The sheepfold becomes a sign of the difference (of the loss and lack) between past and present, pastoral elegist and pastoralist elegized, and even, Bruce Graver argues, between poetic labor, exerted "in rural retirement," and "farm labor."[104] Accordingly, to its credit "Michael" does not assert an easy equivalence between poetic and manual labor; nor does this pastoral, or for that matter even its author's letter to Fox, "naively suggest" that poetry "might alleviate the plight of the working rural poor."[105] Instead, in Graver's view, the poem "dramatizes the ambiguous and necessarily uncertain relationship of the poet . . . at leisure" and the georgic realm of labor "in which even the most diligent of purposive labor is liable to fail."[106] Deanne Westbrook similarly argues that the poem "is not about repenting . . . and living, but about loss and death—the cessation of work and the death even of those proverbial of industry."[107]

A part of the greatness of "Michael" as an elegy, as a pastoral, and as a tacit protest tract is that it makes evident the cost of such a social vision and its desired poetical and sociological formations. In that light one can read Levinson's following assertion (and allusion to an earlier poem) otherwise than as a wholesale indictment of false consciousness or historical bad faith:

> the fact that Michael is dead when his spiritual victory occurs [as the basis for poetical memorialization] . . . is a detail that gives the narrator no pause. To him, it seems, life and afterlife are not intransigent opposites; they are positions on a single, self-enfolding continuum. This is to say, 'we *are* seven.'"[108]

Michael, rather like Luke, becomes the covenantal sacrifice for the poet and his community of living memorializers and memorialized dead.[109] But this transformation of loss into mournful gain does not obliterate history, which is still to be read in the poem and, more liminally, in those signifiers of the sheepfold, and it certainly cannot be said to elide Michael or Luke. Collings's reading of the ruined sheepfold as both an "incomplete altar" and an "incomplete tombstone" returns us to the grave-like stones as a site of cultural transmission and at least potential communitarian transformation: "[the] making of the covenant, at which the father hands the tradition of the dead fathers down to his son, implies a second ritual, in which the son buries his father, makes him one of the dead, and fully inherits the land."[110] The scene is much more than a mere replaying of the story of Abraham and Isaac, and not just because there is no symbolic substitution offered in place of the son. Wordsworth's pastoral tale is also about the fulfillment of unfulfilled, and in fact unfulfillable, inheritance, of a kind of prodigal transmission of value that the poet completes or compels through his bucolic-elegiac obsequies for the restless, nearly forgotten dead. As an elegist of pastoral, he earns his status through payment of poetic labor.

To reiterate, "Michael" insists upon the succession rather than upon the mere substitution of poet for son and of pastoral elegy for pastoralist labor, with the elegist himself, in lieu of that lost prodigal son, performing pastoral-elegiac rites for Michael and thereby inheriting a tradition and its patrimony. "[F]or thy children dead / I'll be a son to thee!" old Matthew's similar elegist pleads. As Susan Eilenberg argues, much like an inheritance "Michael" is an "attempt to repair and secure against the future something that has already been lost."[111] That the poem both foregrounds and disfigures tradition (and particularly oral tradition) may suggest its author's awareness that scenes of inheritance ever entail violence, difference, and loss. As Mark Jones states in "Double Economics: Ambivalence in Wordsworth's Pastoral," the poet's use of pastoral in "Michael" in fact "discourages the presumption that the real value of anything can be read by a single standard or from a single perspective."[112] Even at the time its first stones were piled together the sheepfold sparely signified, Eilenberg argues, "interruption, substitution, and . . . death," marking "a birthplace, an altar, and a tombstone all in one."[113] As with the pedlar's narrative, and its endless swerving between determinacy and indeterminacy, consolation and grief, the reader of Michael's pastoral history is left with ambivalence. One cannot finish with the narrative.[114] And this disfiguring of tradition (as meaning) points to a poignant sociological uneasiness with those specific forces that threaten to inhibit conversation and social conversion of the dead. That is the case in Ennerdale, where oral epitaph seeks to supplant writing, and it underlies the ambivalence about the written word in "Michael," whose elegist may become, in Collings's words, yet "another Michael, haunting the scene where texts unravel and hopes disappear."[115]

"Michael" mourns the cultural contamination it conveys itself, the death it bears as writing. In this sense, ruination and a kind of parasitism[116] lurk near the core of community, in "Michael" as in "The Thorn" and elsewhere among Wordsworth's elegies and epitaphs. But in their distance from what they elegize, these poems also engender and transmit considerable social power. It is in part as a result of their elegized lack and violence that Wordsworth's elegies and epitaphs leave behind a remainder of loss that circulates as debt, to be taken up and exchanged, time and again, as a legacy for, by, and among those who endure and mourn. As first glimpsed in the *Vale,* it is in this legacy of debt, of indebtedness sprung even from payment, that mourning is enacted and prolonged. For this reason, Michael's ruinous heap of stones will not be the last grief-suffused marker of Lakeland community, as the next chapter's readings of *Home at Grasmere* and the five-book *Prelude* demonstrate. These communities, too, necessarily have one foot deep in the grave.

6

Grieving and Dwelling in the
Five-Book *Prelude* and *Home at Grasmere*

> What dwelling shall receive me?
> —*The Prelude*

In the long cold winter at Goslar, during which Wordsworth composed the Lucy elegies and other poems published in the second volume of *Lyrical Ballads,* he was tentatively drafting a few autobiographical fragments. These narratives, including some of the well-known "spots of time," would soon help form the two-part *Prelude* of 1798–99, a poem whose concerns are much in keeping with the social views of his contemporary works in the *Lyrical Ballads* of 1800. *The Prelude*'s enigmatic spots of time and certain other of its scenes indeed attest to the endurance of the paradigm of mournful community in the darker passages of Wordsworth's art in these years (to draw upon Keats's wording). Much like the poet's poems in *Lyrical Ballads,* these memory fragments engage and investigate the parameters and permutations of his Orphic sociology of the Dead, despite the considerable pressures being exerted by the impending *Recluse* to cast himself as a "chosen Son" of nature. For "the poem to Coleridge," as Wordsworth frequently called his stop-gap "prelude" to the philosophical opus, provided yet another opportunity to digress as well as to revisit the sources of his poetical and social powers. Those sources were especially to be enlisted in the new poem's insistent quest for dwelling, sparked no doubt in part by William and Dorothy's current lack not just of a home but of a clear plan about where in England they would live.

One of the cornerstones of *The Recluse,* the topographical poem *Home at Grasmere* depicts Wordsworth's search for a home in that vale. More specifically, this foundation narrative explores the manner in which death and grief promise to sanctify dwelling and inclusion in Grasmere. Despite the poem's clear place in the larger plan of the magnum opus, as its first part's own first book, and its intent to represent nature's social and healing powers, Wordsworth seems throughout its narrative to be unable to imagine community otherwise than by enlisting the powers of mourning as its foundation. *Home at Grasmere*'s elegiac, at times notably eucharistic, verse of desired dwelling thus revisits much the same dead-oriented basis for cohesion that underlay the communities of the Salisbury Plain poems and *The Ruined Cottage*. But in conceptualizing Grasmere's vale as a community, Wordsworth's poem does more than reiterate past schemes of social bonding. It also broadens those sources of cohesion beyond the human realm of vagrants, pedlars, travelers, soldiers, and poets to include animals. Mourning these animals promises to form a "unity entire," but it also curiously and unexpectedly threatens to undermine such social cohesion and along with it the poem's foundational project.

I. Superstitious Company: Encountering the Dead in the Five-Book *Prelude*

> And I do not doubt
> That in this later time . . . unknown to me
> The workings of my spirit thence are brought.
>
> —Book 5

The communitarian importance of the dead persists in all the versions of *The Prelude*: in the two-part poem, in the five-book *Prelude* of 1804, and, in a proportionally diminished state, in the thirteen-book 1805 text and the authorized, fourteen-book edition of 1850. The paradigm in this way haunts the opus, even in that work's less dead-focused later incarnations. And it does so in part because this "Anti-chapel" to the gothic church-like *Recluse* (*Ex* ix) was to serve its author as a "pleasant loitering journey," a "sabbath" not to be bended to the "servile yoke" of that onerous task (*5P* 1.112–14). The poet's holiday was instead to be employed finding some other means of social utterance until he could develop the philosophical voice to undertake his and Coleridge's grand and taxing "determined aim" (124). Wordsworth tellingly explains away his vocational lassitude as but a poet's "unruly times," when "less quiet instincts, goadings-on," drive the mind "as in trouble through the groves" (144, 151–52). Yet in representing his vexed poetical faculty as a mythic hunter turned hunted, driven not by higher moral proddings but by hounding lower "instincts," Wordsworth's text reveals just such counter-aims to be operative.

The poet enlists Actaeon's mythic tale of ill fortune or hubris[1] to allegorize his less lofty, at least less philosophically proper, impulses—impulses already gratified by the diffuse character of the *Lyrical Ballads* of 1798 and 1800. Still prodded by his instinct-like desires, motivations, and inclinations from hidden sources, Wordsworth's poet-persona flies ahead, ambivalently fleeing into the poetical thickets. What dwelling—material, social, philosophical, poetical—will receive him and properly satisfy or situate his desire? The five-book *Prelude*'s and later editions' glad preambles of freedom and desired location proclaim "nature" to be the proper guide or guidepost for discovering a new home in the Lakes. And yet, such descried markers as "a wandering cloud" (18) seem uncertain blazings at best.

Despite his Actaeon-like troubles, Wordsworth tenaciously declares his "last and favourite aspiration" still to be to compose that too long deferred

> philosophic song
> Of truth that cherishes our daily life;
> With meditations passionate from deep
> Recesses in man's heart, immortal verse
> Thoughtfully fitted to the Orphean lyre.
>
> (228–32)

This second mythological reference explains a part of the dilemma: how to produce poetry of nature-oriented "brotherhood" (237) that would be "fitted" to the music of Orpheus? For Duncan Wu, editor of the reconstructed five-book text, the allusion invokes the view of Orpheus as the thoughtful figure of the philosopher and poet-musician (*5P*, p. 48 n33). And on one level Wordsworth's text surely enlists this meaning. But the hero of course was also a tragic one, who ended up, like Actaeon, being torn to pieces. More to the point, as mentioned previously, Orpheus is the mythic figure par excellence both of the elegist and of the prototypical resistant mourner who refuses to accept loss or mediating substitutes—the latter being, for Freud (in his dichotomous, therapeutic model) the basis of all successful mourning-work. Rather than accede to his beloved's death, Orpheus descends into the underworld and thereafter continues to mourn and wander, as the translator of "Orpheus and Eurydice" well knew (see Chapter One). The problem for Wordsworth's poet is not that of being diligent but of being recidivistically Orphic: more elegist-mourner, singing of and from those "deep recesses" of emotion, than nature-loving poet; hence the repeated "defraud[ing]" and silencing of his nature-poet's harp (1.104–5). Small wonder he should thereafter depict himself as one driven on by prodigal instincts, "Unprofitably travelling towards the grave / Like a false steward who hath much received / And renders nothing back" (267–69). For within *The Prelude* there lurks "a dark / Invisible workmanship" (350–51) rooted in loss and in the dead.

Wordsworth first specifically mentioned the five-book plan of *The Prelude* in a letter to Francis Wrangham in late January or early February of 1804 (*EY* 436). By March of that year he told Coleridge that within "two or three days time," upon completing the fifth book, he would "consider the work as finish'd" (452). In *Wordsworth and "The Recluse,"* Kenneth Johnston envisions the poet intently organizing that five-book text "on the theme of 'Books and Nature,' or nurture and nature, education and environment," making the new poem "an actual, plausible prelude or portico to *The Recluse*."[2] Yet by early March, mere days after completing the poem and only some eight weeks after its conception, the poet determined, Wu argues, "that five Books were inadequate to express everything he had to say about the development of the imagination that was prepared to compose *The Recluse*" (*5P* 14). Wordsworth likely became troubled by the five-book version's awkwardly diminutive plot of crisis and recovery; the only real crises being, Johnston states, his "disaffection with college and contemporary educational theories, some rather far-fetched fears about the perishability of books, and an overstated distaste for the claims of domestic life on a poet's time."[3] Treating his as yet unmentioned real crisis of hope, caused by the Revolution's failure, must have seemed the best answer—for other reasons, as well. After all, in a September 1799 letter Coleridge had pleaded with him to resume *The Recluse* on behalf of those fellow post-revolutionaries who, despondent, had "thrown up all hopes of the amelioration of mankind" (*CLSTC* 1: 527). Johnston surmises that Coleridge thereby inadvertently provided his friend with an opportunity to co-opt that rationale for *The Prelude*: to enlarge the poem and amend its crisis of college disaffection to one of political disillusionment figured as a type of fall followed by nature-induced recovery (*HW* 680). As William Ulmer puts it, "if Wordsworth could not fulfill Coleridge's hopes by producing *The Recluse,* he could at least placate his friend by producing a *Recluse*-related text on a suggested topic."[4] Expanding the poem to thirteen books was, moreover, also a convenient means to diminish the magnitude of the recidivist Orphean tones of mourning the dead. Whatever the precise reason, Wordsworth had barely completed the five-book *Prelude* before he abandoned it in favor of a vastly expanded plan, in which the older social model had a less prominent part.

And yet, as Wu states, for six weeks or more in 1804 that five-book text appears to have represented to its author "*The Prelude* in its ultimate form" (*5P* 20), with an Orphic narrative arc moving from the preamble's joyful birth to a funereal conclusion.[5] Fortunately, according to Wu, although the original manuscript is lost, a text approximating that of the one composed in 1804 can be reasonably reconstructed, with of course a degree of editorial conjecture.[6]

Fortunate, I say, because this prodigal text, ending at the grave as it does, is by far the most elegiac of the poem's four versions and so best reveals its author's "Orphean," still developing sociology, as in one of the poem's most well-known and enigmatic texts, with which I begin.

The last chapter passed over an important elegy in the second volume of *Lyrical Ballads*, "There was a Boy," a poem Wordsworth subsequently expanded and inserted in *The Prelude*. The elegy fit neatly in its original location, sandwiched between the elegiac pastorals "Hart-leap Well" (examined later in this chapter) and "The Brothers," and preceding the similar Lucy poems. But its situation within the rich context of Book 4 of the five-book *Prelude* (Book Fifth of the 1805 text), is also intriguing, preceding as it does the profoundly social "Drowned Man" episode. Originally composed in the first person (*NCP* 492), the "Boy of Winander," as the expanded, *Prelude* version is dubbed, indeed can be classed with the Drowned Man and the other spots of time. Like them, it is an enigmatic childhood memory ostensibly recalled for its connection to the growth or restoration of "imaginative power" (*5P* 5.285) and yet also curiously tied to death. In his preface to *Poems* of 1815 Wordsworth describes this elegy, in its earlier, separate form, as illustrating how "images of sound and sight [are planted] . . . in the soil of the Imagination" (cited *LB* 379). Following his cue, in *Wordsworth's Poetry* Geoffrey Hartman likewise determines the poem's intended theme to have been "growth and immortality, not death," imaginative growth being of course a theme well suited to the educational focus of the poem's subsequent siting. But Hartman also discerns that, especially in the expanded text in *The Prelude,* the "Boy" contrarily narrates the "mysterious" intrusion of a "supervening thought of death" (*WP* 20).[7] It is with this intrusion of death and ensuing grief, and with its connection to dwelling, that my reading of the poem is mainly concerned. For the Boy of Winander thereby represents the debts and troubles of an Orphic community where silence—muteness stemming from nature's disconcerting quiet—operates as a mysterious legacy and a decidedly social force.

The prodigious boy, we are told, was well known by the "cliffs and islands of Winander" (*5P* 4.473). He was accustomed to whistle to their owls through his intertwined fingers, his palms joined and "[u]plifted" (480), an image that, for all its accuracy in describing a quite literally handmade birdcall, emblematizes the child's pious, prayerful relationship to nature and its supernatural mysteries. As the narrator relates, through those pressed hands the boy

> Blew mimic hootings to the silent owls
> That they might answer him. And they would shout
> Across the watery vale, and shout again
> Responsive to his call, with quivering peals
> And long halloos, and screams, and echoes loud

> Redoubled and redoubled—a concourse wild
> Of mirth and jocund din!

>   (481–87)

The connection between the boy and the distant owls is forged by his imitative "hootings" and calls and by the answering owls' uncannily human
"halloos" and "screams." (One might ask who is imitating whom.) These
terms are doubtless meant to suggest not that the owls mimic the boy's
vocalizations but that they are "responsive," ending the silence that separated them from him. Yet, while this sonic interconnection of human and
animal realms is being suggested, the text proffers foreboding signs, too,
beginning with the owls themselves, "the fatal bellm[e]n" of *Macbeth*
(II.i.62), associated with ill omens and death, especially in a darkening wood
("Never halloo till you are out of the wood," the proverb warns). One might
conclude, with some justification, that although there are few other creatures to answer a good lad's halloo at twilight, the child is flirting with dangerous forces, near waters that glimmer with mysterious powers. Indeed,
succeeding lines describe another ominous lake, whose darkening waters are
directly linked to a man's death.

The Boy's elegist relates how, on occasion, it happened that "pauses of
deep silence mocked" the child's considerable mimetic "skill" (488). At such
times, while in the intervening silence the lad "hung," patiently

> Listening, a gentle shock of mild surprise
> Has carried far into his heart the voice
> Of mountain torrents; or the visible scene
> Would enter unawares into his mind
> With all its solemn imagery, its rocks,
> Its woods, and that uncertain heaven, received
> Into the bosom of the steady lake.

>   (489–96)

Readers witness a confluence of mind and nature, made all the more specific
by the narrator's surmise of another effect of such "pauses": the influx of "the
visible scene . . . unawares" into the boy's receptive yet passive, educationally
unhampered mind. Here the poem printed in *Lyrical Ballads* concludes, with
a natural scene of sublime education. Yet, to this image of influx and of unconsciousness, bordering on ego annihilation, *The Prelude*'s text appends elegiac
lines reporting that the boy thereafter "died / In childhood ere he was full ten
years old" (497–98).

The narrative is strangely silent about the details of the Winander boy's
death, curiously imitating the owls' own imposing silence and leaving the

reader to play the part of detective or coroner. Cynthia Chase suspects that the boy's prior act of "hanging" in suspense is itself a culprit in his demise, for the suspended action "suggests a coincidence between the 'pauses of deep silence' and the extended pause of death," a death by "accident."[8] For his part, David P. Haney deduces the boy's death—at least his voice's "death . . . in nature"— to be the "end result" of his "natural education."[9] Either way, with this intrusion of death the narrative becomes a story of something else, of that "supervening thought" more than of poetics or education, even natural education (one thinks again of Esthwaite's drowned schoolmaster). Readers discover a recurrence of Actaeon-like "instincts" driving poet and text toward what is at bottom a supernatural encounter, reminiscent of *The Vale of Esthwaite* and *An Evening Walk.* The owls' lack of articulation, and that lack's effect of opening the child's suspended consciousness to the all in all of surrounding nature, lurks as an explanation, the vaguest of explanations, both for the boy's death and for the elegiac poet's succeeding, supervening thoughts of mortality. The implication is that the boy has become a (sacrificed) part of Winander and of the Lakelands' dead, converged with those death-intimating, death-imitating owls and this void-like, heaven-reflecting lake.

As we shall see, the boy's loss beckons the poet's acts of memorialization, transmitting an extended circuit of absence and presence, lack and supplementation—a circuit inaugurated by the owls' ominous silence. This inadequacy of articulation, this haunting, mimicked muteness, explains *The Prelude* text's elegiac coda, which treats the speaker's own subsequent actions and consciousness:

> Fair are the woods, and beauteous is the spot,
> The vale where he was born. The churchyard hangs
> Upon a slope above the village school,
> And there, along that bank, when I have passed
> At evening, I believe that oftentimes
> A full half-hour together I have stood
> Mute, looking at the grave in which he lies.
>
> (499–505)

A lack of speech for or from the dead establishes a legacy of grief and its supplementation, in this case through elegiac obsequies that oddly mimic the boy's muteness in life and, now, in death. The poet's muteness, as he stands, *superstitio,* over the boy's grave (see below), responds to the deceased's haunting, superstitious force. That force is itself predicated, for the poet, upon the living child's death-in-life silence, itself in turn owed to the audible lack produced by the owls, and now mediated by (troped by) the entranced poet's mute rites of memorialization.

In each case a prior condition of muteness (an imposed or otherwise constituted silence) provokes a response, although in each the *nature* of that response is somewhat different. The boy's mimic hootings elicit (at times) the owls' silence, and his silence in death, or in life as he "hung," elicits not articulation but muteness, a supervening inversion of language and silence, a mute sort of elegy. "Looking at the grave," a monument inscribed to signify loss (the word "grave" being derived from *grafan*, "to engrave"), the poet responds by pausing in a manner like that dictated by the classical epitaphic summons, *Sta Viator*, "Pause, Traveler!" Michele Turner Sharp points out how the first of the *Essays upon Epitaphs* praises the ancient burial practice of burying the dead outside the city walls, where the traveler, "heeding the formulaic injunction to halt," would, "in the shadow of a funeral monument," quite "naturally be given to contemplate his own humanity and his ultimate destination."[10] The halted traveler would find there, along this or that Appian Way, "lively and affecting analogies of life as a journey" (*PrW* 2: 54). But more importantly, as the thrust of the *Essays* and of so much of Wordsworth's poetry suggests, he or she would not just confront mortality but also pay homage to the dead, standing in pious observance of the deceased, before or above the grave (a gesture the Latin term *superstitio* indeed denotes). Wordsworth finds such customs "counterbalanced" and effectively reiterated "by the custom of depositing the dead within, or contiguous to, their places of worship," which is to say in the churchyard (54).

It is with just such a scene of epitaphic pause, initiated in the environs of the dead, that the Boy of Winander closes. The *Sta Viator* of storied monument stays the poet's course and consciousness—in what almost seems an exaggerated parody of the classical summons—provoking in him a trance-like "mute" state in which the passage of time is rendered difficult to gauge, for one's self is no longer present. Unconsciously and contagiously mimicking the dead boy, and before him the silent owls, the entranced poet liminally becomes one of the dead and a part, at least a tributary part, of their surrounding, silent neighborhood. His "mute" response signals the haunting, supervening power this epitaphic play of absence and presence can cast over the minds of the halted living, reiterating and recuperating in them a social and poetic circuit of utterance and muteness, call and nonresponse—a circuit of writing and of community. The owls thereby become initiating elegists— or was it the boy who first initiated such mysterious conversation and intermittent muteness? The legacy of their collective death-like silence, and of death itself and the mute responses its silences and absences provoke, is transmitted from lake to cemetery, from the living to the dead and back again to the living, as an inheritance of loss, lack, and muteness, in the form of a serial community of utterance and silence, of turning away and of memorial tribute qua possession.

Subsequent lines indeed emphasize both the importance and the problematical character of such superstitious memorialization: the manner in
which, "[e]ven now," the poet envisions

> That self-same village church . . . sit[ting]
> On her green hill, forgetful of this boy
> Who slumbers at her feet—forgetful too
> Of all her silent neighbourhood of graves. . . .
>
> (506–10)

Wordsworth paints a picture of insufficient mourning, with Hawkshead
Church itself sitting "forgetful" of the corpse at its foundations, amid a similarly "silent neighbourhood of graves."[11] The use of the word "neighbourhood"
to describe the surrounding graves implies their power to bind together those
who participate, like the elegist, in the dead's culture of silence. The boy now
dwells among these neighbors, within a collective silence that signifies, much
like the owls' pauses, mute commemoration and silent danger—here chiefly
the danger of forgetting. The poet's superstitious muteness uncomfortably situates him among the forgetful and the forgotten, integrating him as an
entranced, tribute-paying visitor (*viator*) on the outskirts of this silent neighborhood. Nor does the poet's mute memorial remain entirely unarticulated.
As Haney points out, the elegist's narration of that "act of forgetting" enacts
his compensatory mourning-work of remembrance.[12]

As the boy's interaction with the owls exemplifies, silence beckons
response. Perhaps the answer is muteness, but, as mentioned, it may also be
offered as articulated sound and as writing—its own form of mute articulation.
Alan Bewell indeed reads the Boy of Winander's elegiac coda as illustrating the
complementarity of language and burial as "symbolic mediums that came into
being . . . for the same purpose—to deal with death" (*WE* 212). Such a lineage
does not end with mute observance at the graveside: there is the text we read,
the narration and reiteration of muteness in tribute to past silence and loss, deciphered by a series of readers themselves made mute before an inscription. Such
shared commemoration is the silent shibboleth for dwelling in a neighborhood
of graves, bonding poet and reader to the community of the dead. Muteness in
turn is then the basis for articulation, for memorial, and for grief. But such
silence also leaves the elegist hanging, like the boy, on the limits of language and
vocation, above an Orphean ground that suspends even as it invites elegiac tribute and speech. Muteness recurs, as a legacy of forgetting and memorializing—
even as the same legacy, rather as in the Evening Sonnets. Such is the cost and
debt of dwelling for one who, like the poet of "A Poet's Epitaph," perceives poesis and social cohesion to be products of building upon or in the shadow of the
grave, bearing the elegiac legacy of a silent but powerful "world of shades."

The Boy of Winander episode is followed by the "breathless stillness" of
the Drowned Man, a spot of time depicting yet another boy sporting upon the
shore of mortality. As stated in the Introduction, this text provides an important vision, even a schema, of Wordsworthian community. It does so via a
boat's corpse-retrieving "company" and, in a subsequent revision, an "anxious
crowd" of shoreline onlookers, who together compose a neighborhood gathered around the (un)located dead. The Drowned Man episode confirms the
Boy of Winander's representation of community as originating in ongoing
deeds of mute tribute for the silent dead. But the episode is by no means a
mere successor to that text. It is also as clear a depiction as any of the social
function of the dead in Wordsworth's poetry, as well as of the ambivalence that
attends such a community's formation around so "ghastly" an object and event.
So important a work is the Drowned Man in exposing these mournful foundations of Wordsworthian community that the Introduction's previous analysis of this episode merits partial reprise, along with further, more detailed consideration of the recollection's intimated legacies for the living.

Newly arrived in Hawkshead, this boy roves "up and down alone" at
dusk along the paths near Esthwaite Water (4.537). Looking across the lake,
he spots

> on the opposite shore
> A heap of garments—left, as I supposed,
> By one who there was bathing. Long I watched,
> But no one owned them; meanwhile the calm lake
> Grew dark with all the shadows on its breast,
> And now and then a fish up-leaping snapped
> The breathless stillness.
>
> (542–48)

The boy reads the scene to understand this enigma of unclaimed garments.
The sartorial detail speaks volumes, of course, if not to young Wordsworth at
the moment then later that evening to Ann Tyson or some other adult. As a
result, the next day

> Went there a company, and in their boat
> Sounded with grappling-irons and long poles.
>
> (550–51)

Thomas Pfau argues that "the actual discovery of the drowned man as a social,
communal event is detailed rather indifferently, almost as an afterthought."[13]
But although the evidence of such community is sparely conveyed, it is there.

As mentioned in the Introduction, the key word "company" derives from the Latin term *compania*, for people sharing bread, and has obvious communal denotations in English as well, denoting a group gathered for social or other purposes, including nautical ones, as in the case of this boat's crew. The word subtly underlines the social significance of this rite of pre-burial, as does Wordsworth's MS. A addition to the scene of an "anxious crowd / Of friends & neighbors" who, along with the curious boy, watch the men's progress from the shore (*13P* 2: 625). Other revisions refer to this "crowd" as a "Company assembled on the spot," in which some people stood "in anxious expectation on the shore" while others searched (625). One may read the "company" as including not just the few doing the actual searching but also those folk looking on and beginning to grieve, all of whom are congregated in observance and in service of the dead.

Once the crew prods the body loose from the reeds or from whatever else retained it, the corpse rises "bolt upright" with its "ghastly face" (*5P* 4.553–54). One might again recall the poet's ambivalent yet "favourite aspiration": to reveal an "awful burden" of truth recovered from "*deep* / Recesses" by "Orphean" verse. Those recesses may well include these watery coffers. As the first of the *Essays upon Epitaphs* implies, such acts of memorial are implicated in the very origins of culture, and of writing, particularly (*PrW* 2: 49–51). Moreover, Sharp argues that for Wordsworth this "return of the body to its proper place, giving it a proper burial, grounds the constitution of the ideal community."[14] One can state matters more strongly still with regard to this placing of the deceased. In Wordsworth, gathering the dead gathers community, providing the basis for social cohesion, which stems not from the living so much as from the displaced or misplaced dead themselves.

As revised for the five-book and later versions of *The Prelude,* this spot of time illustrates the power of imagination along with the power of reading (in the thirteen-book text the lines are included in Book 5, "Books"). The poem comes to demonstrate the manner in which the boy is protected from this unexpected image of "terror":

> And yet no vulgar fear,
> Young as I was (a child of eight years old),
> Possessed me, for my inner eye had seen
> Such sights before, among the shining streams
> Of fairyland, and forests of romance.
> Thence came a spirit hallowing what I saw
> With decoration and ideal grace,
> A dignity, a smoothness, like the works
> Of Grecian art and purest poesy.
>
> (4.555–63)

Just as Wordsworth's imagination and its sources in reading initially perceived the drowned man's body to be "ghastly" and spectral, so now imagination comes in aid of imagination, coloring over the gothic mise en scène with a "hallowing," sanctifying aesthetic "spirit" of romance and classicism, transforming, in reverse Pygmalion fashion, the schoolmaster's corpse into stone.[15] But the discomfort that attends the dead's presence and absence also suggests, as in *The Ruined Cottage* and even in the *Vale,* the need to turn from the dead, whether it is to books, to nature, or to religion. One needs to, and inevitably must, lose the dead. The episode's revision suggests the uneasiness provoked by the dead as well as by mourners' own acts of retrieval. Much as the Boy of Winander reveals the disquieting muteness that underlies and haunts loss and memorial, the Drowned Man implies the psychological pain of death, the burdensome quality the dead exert upon the minds of the living.

At the same time, the Drowned Man episode illustrates the extent to which the dead, for all their horror, are able to gather together mourners in a "company" of ritual observance, intent upon the enterprise of locating, localizing, and memorializing the deceased. Such death-bound community is, if Wordsworth the child is any gauge, ever turning from and returning to the dead, forgetting and remembering them, losing them and attempting, through memory and epitaphic or elegiac memorial—through and as the eucharistic rites of "company"—to recover them. The dead are lost into silence and then found; and yet, as with Orpheus's attempted retrieval of Eurydice, they are lost again even in the act of reclaiming them, evading the mourner's efforts to locate and preserve them. This recurrent movement fundamentally institutes and sustains community, as a legacy bequeathed from the dead and their silent domains, repeatedly depicted in Wordsworth from the *Vale* to *The Excursion.*

Tracing the spot of time of the Drowned Man of Esthwaite back to its original placement in the first part of the 1799 *Prelude,* the reader is led to a succeeding spot, one which then serves as the penultimate scene of the final, fifth book of 1804. The Introduction briefly considered this text of the Hanged Man, but this spot of time likewise merits a brief reprise in terms of its own legacies of mourning. The "urchin" Wordsworth, "disjoined" from his guide among the hills at Penrith (*5P* 5.291, 297), stumbles down into a valley bottom, to a site where

> in former times
> A man, the murderer of his wife, was hung
> In irons. Mouldered was the gibbet-mast,
> The bones were gone, the iron and the wood,
> Only a long green ridge of turf remained
> Whose shape was like a grave.

> (300–5)

Chase rightly describes the scene as one of "the erosion of the remnants" of an actual hanging, one that literalizes the figurative act of imaginative suspension in the Boy of Winander.[16] There is, after all, no sign of the gibbeted man other than the signifying "ridge of turf" poignantly shaped "like a grave." In the thirteen-book *Prelude* that ridge becomes a less minimal sign: a grassy epitaph of turf "engraven" with "the Murderer's name" in a "monumental writing," maintained "[b]y superstition of the neighbourhood" (*13P* 11.294–97), as must also have been that simple grave-like ridge. As stated above, the Latin term *superstitio* describes the pious act of *standing over* a grave, and the English derivation has a similar meaning in this episode. In either version of this spot of time readers find another instance of the epitaphic *Sta Viator*, and another community standing or hanging over the silent, perhaps absent, dead.

Like the Esthwaite company of the Drowned Man, the passage's implicit or explicit "neighbourhood" is superstitiously focused upon and articulated by its obligation to the dead, in maintaining the letters or the sod, or both. As Haney states, "the local citizens' ritual clearing of the grass . . . gives reverence to the actual letters carved into the ground, which are preserved and not allowed to disappear before their meaning as signs would."[17] These dwellers' rites of memorial intercession entail a divergence: a sacralizing of the profane and a concomitant binding together of the living not by exclusion but by inclusion, or at least by transforming the site into a minimal grave upon which the living are halted and obliged to remember. The demands of the dead for suffrage-like commemoration produce a culture, a tradition of haunting social coherence and its bonds of superstitious tribute—what become the fundamental rites of neighborhood.

One discerns in these scenes the haunting character of this form of community: its acts of pious observance and also its attendant fears. In the Drowned Man it is concern for the dead and a fear provoked by their loss and recovery; in the Hanged Man the dead of the neighborhood similarly provoke reverence as well as feelings and apotropeic actions of fear. Likewise, in the Boy of Winander the promise of an elegiac legacy, and of a memorial community, is predicated upon the relationship of the living to the dead, a relationship founded upon muteness, death. Such silence is dialogical, part of an economy of remembrance and forgetting, lack and supplementation, typified, even allegorized, by the Boy's intermittent vocalization and the owls' looming silence. These haunted communities wait upon the dead and their silence, and follow after them.

II. WAITING FOR HORSES AND FOLLOWING THE DEAD

> Long Long my swimming eyes did roam
> For little Horse to bear me home[,]
> To bear me[—]what avails my tear[?]
> To sorrow o'er a Father's bier.—
>
> —*The Vale of Esthwaite*

The opening of Book 2 of the five-book *Prelude* recalls the poet's schoolboy romps in the Lakelands, and praises "the home / And centre of th[o]se joys" of childhood: "A grey stone / Of native rock, left midway in the square / Of our small market-village" (2.33–36). Upon his return to Hawkshead from Cambridge, Wordsworth discovers the stone to have been "split, and gone to build / A smart assembly-room" (38–39). Johnston's biographical reading of the scene is instructive: that Wordsworth's return to the Lakes had "involved some new construction, as well as some recognition, of his own old foundations," the gray stone serving him as an "authenticating presence of old building materials under new."[18] I would argue, moreover, that in *The Prelude* the stone symbolizes the foundation for the "interminable building" of community. As previously noted, John Kerrigan avers that even "bare stones . . . are *semai,* signs,"[19] and although it would be too much to read this gray stone quite as a gravestone, it is all the same a signifier central to, and a central point of, the village's community and the "joys" of youth, having provided a younger Wordsworth with an early sense of "home." A focus of boyish activity, the gray stone represents more than simply juvenile foundations. That the stone is later used as actual building material for Hawkshead Town Hall indeed bespeaks its more fundamental significance, the old assembling point and center now becoming a part of the material foundation of that "smart assembly-room." But, as the poet makes clear in these same lines, the stone also signifies an older, "native" community organized around that primeval *stele* now "elbow[ed]" out by the town hall and its dissonant "fiddle scream" (40–41).

Wordsworth prefaces the scene by lamenting the "tranquilizing spirit press[ing]" upon his "corporeal frame," a subduing calm, a numbness, owed to his nagging sense of

> The vacancy between me and those days
> Which yet have such self-presence in my heart
> That sometimes, when I think of them I seem
> Two consciousnesses—conscious of myself
> And of some other being.
>
>   (27–33)

As in "Tintern Abbey," his awareness of this gulf between present and past, and between present and past selves, is figured as "vacancy" and otherness, and its effects as bodily tranquilization. The former metaphor intimates a desire both answered and frustrated by the missing home of the marketplace *stele.* The village square becomes unhomely, unfocused, and uncentered.

Yet, as is so often the case in Wordsworth, there is surmised recompense for loss, in the form of shared eulogistic or epitaphic remembrance:

> Yet, my friends, I know
> That more than one of you will think with me
> Of those soft starry nights, and that old dame
> From whom the stone was named. . . .
>
> (42–45)

All of this is to show, first, the extent to which the stone is, like the "grey huts" skirting the churchyard in *An Evening Walk* (1794), invested with social significance, as a stone upon which dwelling was built ("build thy house upon this grave," "A Poet's Epitaph" proclaims); and second, the extent to which the stone symbolizes absence and loss. It signifies death and the dead, as a "visible centre," like the churchyards praised in *Essays upon Epitaphs,* and as a marker whose very denomination is tied to the dead "old dame" whom it still signifies even in its absence. The old foundation discovered by this recollection is, as in the spots of time, thus not so much one associated with nature or its spirits as one connected to the dead and to enduring grief. For Wordsworth, the paradigmatic social center is a marker of loss, as potent in its absence as the eroded gibbet pole in the Hanged Man, the missing signs of domestic life in *The Ruined Cottage,* the omitted headstones in "The Brothers," and the ruined, incomplete sheepfold in "Michael."

As mentioned, the five-book *Prelude* culminates not with the transcendent ascent of Snowdon, narrated earlier in the poem's fifth book, or with ample praise for its poet's fellow prophet of Nature, but—remarkable to readers familiar with the poem's thirteen- and fourteen-book forms—with the grave-like spots of time of the Hanged Man and the Waiting for Horses episode. In this latter scene, briefly touched upon in Chapter One, Wordsworth recalls the enigmatic hours that preceded his impatient return home from Hawkshead one Christmas time, prior to his father's untimely death:

> The day before the holidays began,
> Feverish, and tired, and restless, I went forth
> Into the fields, impatient for the sight
> Of those three horses which should bear us home,
> My brothers and myself. There was a crag,
> An eminence, which from the meeting-point
> Of two highways ascending, overlooked
> At least a long half-mile of those two roads,
> By each of which the expected steeds might come,
> The choice uncertain. Thither I repaired
> Up to the highest summit. 'Twas a day
> Stormy, and rough, and wild, and on the grass
> I sate, half-sheltered by a naked wall.

> Upon my right hand was a single sheep,
> A whistling hawthorn on my left, and there,
> Those two companions at my side, I watched,
> With eyes intensely straining, as the mist
> Gave intermitting prospects of the wood
> And plain beneath.
>
>   (345–64)

There is an intriguing correspondence between the boy's condition—"feverish, and tired, and restless"—and the "stormy, and rough, and wild" landscape and its weather. As he is "feverish" it is "stormy," as he is "restless" it is "wild." Experience mirrors or else is mirrored by the local landscape; indeed it is uncertain whether it is the imaginative power (and memory) coloring the landscape or nature in some way guiding the mind. Impatient as the wind, the lad watches for those three horses to approach along one of two roads, "the choice uncertain." The text's wording is retrospectively poignant and apposite. As events soon show, young Wordsworth, too, is at a crossroads, poised uncertainly between life and death, dwelling and imminent homelessness. The scene's reflective, mimetic nature becomes visionary and proleptic: the boy and his brothers are symbolically already alone, "half-sheltered" (and then only by a "naked" wall) among the company of a lone, unshepherded sheep on one side and a funerary hawthorn all but "whistling" past or inside the graveyard on the other.[20] That solitary tree is later described as "blasted" (378), and hence as already dead.

As recollected, with all the retroactive, causal force remembrance conveys, the spot of time forebodes separation and death:

>   Ere I to school returned
> That dreary time, ere I had been ten days
> A dweller in my father's house, he died,
> And I and my two brothers (orphans then)
> Followed his body to the grave. The event,
> With all the sorrow which it brought, appeared
> A chastisement; and when I called to mind
> That day so lately past, when from the crag
> I looked in such anxiety of hope,
> With trite reflections of morality,
> Yet with the deepest passion, I bowed low
> To God, who thus corrected my desires.
>
>   (364–75)

His father's unexpected death retrospectively appears to the boy to have been the result of some divine "chastisement," a heaven-sent corrective to his impatience. This odd causality, whereby God smites poor William by slaying poorer father John Wordsworth, simply on account of the child's impatience to return home from school (or because of his anger at his father), appears to derive from a naïve species of *post hoc ergo propter hoc* reasoning not uncommon to children (nor to adult neuroses, one would suppose). But there is more afoot in these elegiac lines. James Averill notes the apparent oedipal character of the boy's guilty feeling of complicity in his father's death (*PHS* 248),[21] and Alan Richardson, in his psychoanalytic reading of the spots of time, similarly interprets the young man's "anxiety of hope" and his father's death as a drama reminiscent of that of Oedipus, set at "a crossroads (the 'meeting-point / Of two highways')," with the patriarch's demise the result of "the strength and impatience of [the son's own] desire."[22] Richardson observes how this curious association serves, here as in other spots of time, to convey both to the boy and to the older, recollecting poet a feeling of imaginative omnipotence that, as the 1799 text proclaims, "left a . . . power / Implanted in [his] mind" (*2P* 2.329–30). Johnston likewise reads the episode's power or lesson as chiefly residing in this potent representation of "archetype[s] of human imaginative expectation," of our "ability . . . to go beyond ourselves."[23] Yet in this scene that power is one not just of unbridled imagination but also of death, of a power that carries with it, Richardson adds, recurrent feelings of "guilt and sorrow."[24]

Adding more details to his recollection, Wordsworth recalls that on that inclement day at Hawkshead, while he and his brothers waited for horses,

> all the business of the elements,
> The single sheep, and the one blasted tree . . .
> The noise of wood and water, and the mist
> That on the line of each of those two roads
> Advanced in such indisputable shapes—
> All these were spectacles and sounds to which
> I often would repair. . . .
>
> (377–84)

Ernest de Selincourt detected in Wordsworth's recollection of mist-veiled "indisputable shapes" an allusion to Hamlet's address to his father's ghost: "Thou com'st in such a questionable shape / That I will speak to thee" (I.iv.43–44; cited *5P* 149 n68). The passage's language does describe an ominous experience associated with paternal loss, and in the 1805 text will furthermore recall to the reader the previously heralded, "unfather'd vapour" of the Imagination in the apostrophe that follows the missed crossing at Simplon

Pass (6.527). Wordsworth's recollection also signifies, as his allusion to *Hamlet* implies, a problem and a power in mourning. Indeed, for Lionel Morton a great share of the energy of the Waiting for Horses episode "is the energy of mourning, a fearful desire to make contact with the dead father who was not yet dead when the scene happened."[25] I find this desire to be associated less with the boy's premature or misplaced grief, as Morton does, than with the child's and later poet's Hamlet-like postmortem inadequacy as a mourner. Wordsworth's dilemma is one registered as guilt, one the *Vale* attributes, in its representation of this same event, not to complicity before the fact but to mournful insufficiency after it: "I mourn because I mourn'd no more" (*EPF*, l. 289). Like Prince Hamlet, who feels similarly chastised by the return of the dead, the *Vale*'s poet is troubled by the debt owed but inadequately paid the deceased.

This same haunting debt and guilt are registered in *The Prelude* through these very undertones of allusion, in the displaced, ante hoc energies of crime and punishment, and, most significantly of all, in the poet's description of having "followed" his dead father's body "to the grave." As remarked in the first chapter, such *following* in the path of paternal haunting suggests the legacy of mourning and of the dead's insistent powers, of what the *Vale* describes as a "world of shades" to which one is ever bound. Mortal loss becomes the funerary cornerstone of this most personal and ambitious, and arguably most recalcitrant and defiant, of pre-*Recluse* poems. For it is from loss, from looming absence rather than from natural or even imaginative presence, that, as Wordsworth states in the poem's concluding lines, "in this later time . . . unknown to me / The workings of my spirit thence are brought" (5.386–89). Those dark "workings" are conveyed from a world unknown, as a following after the dead.

Wordsworth closes his "prelude" with the hauntings of the dead because it is in the insistent force of mortal loss, in the mournful legacy it imparts, that his poetry takes its origin and that his communities of mourning find their foundations. For a poem ostensibly concerned with natural restoration and educational reform, it must have seemed, even to its author, a strange means of conclusion and closure, and was soon abandoned, ceded to the more buoyant finales of subsequent versions. Although death and "chastisement" may have served to mend his deeper sensibilities and to reveal the "workings of [his] spirit," such deep workings persistently rested not on the ground of Nature's instructive or healing powers but on the graves of the dead, on the endless mourning the deceased solicit from the living, in whose communities they hauntingly form the buried foundation and center. As in the Boat-Stealing episode, the most nature-oriented of *The Prelude*'s several spots of time, the dead mysteriously guide the actions of the guilty living, as internalized but "unknown modes of being[,] . . .

huge and mighty forms, that do not live / Like living men" (1.418, 423–24). Likewise, in the spot of time of the Discharged Soldier the dead triangulate community—here, by a dead-like border figure—from whom the living derive their key virtues and much of their identity. From this vantage, in *The Prelude*'s spots of time the fountainhead of "power" and of resulting community flows from lingering ambivalence: an impious turning from the dead followed by guilty, compensatory mourning, predicated upon insufficiency and its "chastisement."

By all accounts, the Waiting for Horses episode is a startlingly sober, sobering end to a work devoted, ostensibly, to Nature and education—an ending that, as I have said, revisits the earlier poetical site of the *Vale,* in whose predicament of mourning Wordsworth's poetics and sociology began. Following the father's body to the grave, Wordsworth finds himself bound, thereafter, to imagine and establish new and old communities (to draw upon his later wording in *The Excursion*). The poet retraces not just a primary trauma but also his poetic origination and elegiac genealogy, revisiting the foundations of his art and social vision, and in so doing structuring his trajectory from glad birth to grave. The arc of the five-book *Prelude* veers toward the Dead, however much the poet may have wished to establish more nature-oriented or imaginative and staid trajectories. Not all that surprisingly, Wordsworth ends close to where he began, raising his autobiographical edifice in the shadow of death.

But it was a dramatic ending that was not to last, excepting via relatively recent textual reconstructions that have reclaimed some or all of the lost poem of 1804. As mentioned, not long after writing to Coleridge of the five-book poem's impending completion (*EY* 452), the author determined to expand *The Prelude* to include his time in the Alps and France. In the process, perhaps as a result of his or his friend's discomfort with those darker powers of the Dead in his development, Wordsworth diminished the five-book version's typifying focus upon the dead—"the strength in what remains behind"—in favor of further emphasizing the restorative powers of nature and nature-inspired imagination. Yet in the years between 1800 and 1806, during which he composed *Home at Grasmere,* the poet nonetheless retained his almost instinctive sense of mournful community and of the necessary, mortal ground for dwelling in the world.

III. Community and Its Others in *Home at Grasmere*

> Must hear humanity in fields and groves
> Pipe solitary anguish. . . .
>
> —Prospectus to *The Recluse,*
>   from *Home at Grasmere*

Wordsworth's composition of the since lost, circa 1800 manuscript of *Home at Grasmere* was, like the full text recorded six years later in the surviving "B" manuscript, a clear return to the *Recluse* proper. Johnston sees that jubilant return of 1800 as having been indeed "more like a new beginning than a continuation" of previous concerns.[26] But, like Wordsworth's prior efforts inside and outside the parameters of *The Recluse,* amid all its seeming "freshness," his *Home at Grasmere* reveals older, insistent presences and desires. For all its exuberant descriptions of the vale's landscape and its proclaiming of Grasmere's community to be a "Whole without dependence or defect, / Made for itself and happy in itself, / Perfect Contentment, Unity entire" (MS. B.167–70), Wordsworth's narrative again predicates social cohesion upon the consolidating powers of the mourned dead.

Home at Grasmere opens with its speaker's description of his and his dear sister Emma's glad return to the vale to live. In December of 1799, the year prior to the poem's first period of composition, the Wordsworths' move to Grasmere had been typified both by their awe at its landscape's wonders and by the pair's hopes for their future as dwellers in its environs. So it is, too, with the siblings of the poem.[27] As Johnston points out, in relocating to Grasmere, William and Dorothy were "returning, brother and sister, aged twenty-nine and twenty-seven, to the general neighborhood of their childhood, reentering after long absence a childhood dream," that of "the re-formation of their family."[28] In fact, they "were not returning home to Grasmere but going to Grasmere *as if* it were home."[29] That at least is the presupposition for much of the adapted drama of *Home at Grasmere,* reminiscent of the *Aeneid* in this regard. In Wordsworth's auto-narrative of inclusion, such new dwelling is augured by the speaker and Emma's road-to-Damascus vision experienced during their journey into Grasmere's inclement vale.[30] Social foundation recurs to death and grief, which is to say to a loss that, in its insistence and its persistence, becomes for human mourners a promise of social beginning.

Wordsworth's text halts, as the pair of travelers halted then, at the site of Hart-leap Well, a hallowed, haunting spot that intimated to them a "milder day" and a "fairer world" to come (B.238–39). This locodescriptive passage is also an intertextual one, alluding to and in fact borrowing from the first poem of the second volume of the *Lyrical Ballads* of 1800.[31] That ballad, "Hart-leap Well," describes the medieval knight Sir Walter's famous—or infamous—pursuit of a deer. The beleaguered hart eventually kills itself in its last of three bold but desperate leaps, leaving the site thereafter "curs'd" (*LB,* l. 124). According to Raimonda Modiano, "by voluntarily leaping to its death" the heroic stag ultimately transformed Walter's hunt into a sacrifice, symbolized by that hunter's ritualistic erecting of three stone pillars to commemorate the deer's death. Yet, as Modiano observes, without real mourning Walter's killing of the hart becomes "profane," a "murder," in the words of the poem.[32] David Perkins reads the hunter's destruction of the stag as an egregious human act of "solipsistic egoism," similar to the Ancient Mariner's own "egoistic self-assertion" and memorialized not just by those three pillars but, appropriately, by the adjacent, grandiose pleasure house that Walter builds as an expression of his selfish desire.[33]

The deer's death is thereupon lamented by an inspirited, surveillant nature: "This beast not unobserv'd by Nature fell," the poet states, "[h]is death was mourn'd by sympathy divine" (163–64). The hart's loss thereby has two "lesson[s]" to teach: that humans must "Never . . . blend our pleasure or our pride / With sorrow of the meanest thing that feels" (179–80) and that the "Being" of nature "[m]aintains a deep and reverential care" for the "creatures whom he loves" (167–68, 177–80). Just as in Coleridge's sea ballad, animal death in "Hart-leap Well" leads human beings to recognize the holiness of sentient life—in Blake's words, that "All that lives is holy." Such loss reveals, moreover, the interdependence and intertwining of human and natural observances of death, and, more importantly, the dependence of human community upon such beloved and mourned, such *properly* mourned, animal dead.

In *Home At Grasmere* it is at this textual-topographical site of Hart-leap Well that the siblings, still transfixed in their "awful trance," receive the quasi-religious "intimation of the milder day / Which is to come, the fairer world than this" (B.243, 238–39). Perkins cites the standard commentary on this reference to a "milder day" as referring to "a future time when . . . 'all mankind' (l. 256) will share the 'blessedness' (254) that the poet and his sister now know in Grasmere."[34] He disputes this reading for its assumption of an overly sympathetic view of humanity, in a poem whose depicted humans are, after all, prone to murderous hunting.[35] One answer, to Perkins and to the poem's critical tradition, is that the siblings' "intimation" is primarily one just of their own blessings. They merely "trust" (255) that such commemoration will be extended, that their "love and knowledge" will have the power to bring "blessedness . . . hereafter" (254–55) to others of humankind. Much the same promissory social scheme is found in "Nutting," also from the second volume of *Lyrical Ballads,* as well as in the first volume's famous sea ballad. Johnston reads this same intertextual passage in much the terms Perkins disputes, as describing "a millennial moment of newly established right relations between Man and Nature with the Wordsworths' advent in Grasmere," but he connects this millennial change to the brother and sister's arrival.[36] I partly agree with Johnston but would argue that the causality of events suggests something slightly different in the poem. It is not the new pair's advent that makes possible "right relations" but instead those relations, more wrong than right (as a mourning and amending of wrong-doing), that makes the arriving couple's advent qua inclusion possible in the wintry vale. At least, it is those relations with the dead that promise (to promise) them a future dwelling and broader community in Grasmere.

For that auspicious intimation, with all its implicit social significance, comes in answer to the approaching couple's insecure perception of the vale's suspicious, almost hostile, queries. As the speaker relates, that inclement December day

> The naked trees,
> The icy brooks, as on we passed, appeared
> To question us. "Whence come ye? To what end?"
> They seemed to say. "What would ye?" said the shower,
> "Wild Wanderers, wither through my dark domain?"
> The Sunbeam said, "Be happy."
>
> (229–34)

Their existential "end" and potential happiness are promised not by the landscape, so exuberantly described and praised in the opening to *Home at Grasmere* (and in these lines, by comparison, described in far less inviting terms), but by their shared observance of past suffering and death. By their rites of commemoration, represented as tantamount to their sacred election, the arriving brother and sister are raised up,

> dejected as we were
> Among the records of that doleful place
> By sorrow for the hunted beast who there
> Had yielded up his breath. . . .
>
> (240–43)

In their "trance" the pair beholds a "Vision of humanity and of God / The Mourner, God the Sufferer" (244–45), of God the Paschal Lamb, really. Wordsworth's phrasing re-emphasizes the passage's intertextual linkage to sacrifice and to the quasi-eucharistic fellowship that memorial observances of loss make possible. Such communion was also augured, and emblematized, contrary to Walter's intentions, by those pillars of commemoration, starkly reminiscent of the three crosses of the Crucifixion. Now, God is a mourner.

In their "sadness" at the haunting retrospect of a being "suffer[ing] wrongfully," the pair finds an important "promise": that the "love" and "knowledge" produced by their sacralizing, quasi-Christian observance of a profane murder might "secure" them a "portion" of nature's benevolence (246–55). One marks in this passage as close a harmonizing of the schemes and powers of Nature and the Dead as can be found in Wordsworth. Much like the Greek goddess Artemis, the divine nature manifested at Hart-leap Well participates in, rewards, and ultimately demands the proper mourning of its animal dead. Such nature is positioned on the same side as human mourning—a problematical alliance, at best, as it turns out. Mourning's shared situation is both typical and oddly atypical of classical and neoclassical elegy, in which divinized nature participates in, or is invoked to participate in, the commemoration of human or animal death (see Chapter One). Ironically, for a poet who has so struggled with the conflicting interests of human mourning and natural restoration, in this episode it is human beings who, the narrative reveals, threaten the promise of mournful social cohesion. As the reader soon sees, the poem's drama turns upon the dead-oriented breach which that observance has itself opened: a breach between human cultures and mores, wherein nature, too, becomes troublingly implicated.

On one level, *Home at Grasmere*'s preamble simply affirms its speaker's hope that in a world where nature signifies the death of a hart the lives and deaths of humans will receive at least a similar accounting. He and Emma will be looked after in Grasmere's vale. On another level, the passage endows these newcomers with legitimacy, with rights to dwell in a land already occupied by others, like new Israelites entering Palestine. But the passage implies more: that death and memorialization provide, however problematically, the basis for dwelling in this locale—first the (local) violation, then the blessed recompense of sorrow to make sacred *(sacrificio)* the profaned. Here, as in contemporary works by Wordsworth, the sense of belonging to a place, and the concomitant sense of truly belonging to another person, of "twain" made "pair" (248–49), is grounded in mourning a prior loss. Community in Grasmere thus is neither independent, let alone whole, nor necessarily even all that "happy in itself," as Wordsworth fervently espouses. It is, as becomes clearer in subsequent lines, dependent upon death and commemoration for its social blessings of dwelling and social cohesion.

The importance of mourning the dead to the siblings' claim to a dwelling in the valley helps explain the poet's strange recollection, in the narrative's opening spot of time, of having once stopped, many years before, upon Loughrigg Terrace,

> And with a sudden influx overcome
> At sight of this seclusion, I forgot
> My haste—for hasty had my footsteps been,
> As boyish my pursuits—[and sighing said],
> "What happy fortune were it here to live!
> And if I thought of dying, if a thought
> Of mortal separation could come in
> With paradise before me, *here to die*."
>
>   (5–12; emphasis added)

In his consideration of death and society in *Home at Grasmere*, Ulmer observes that although this surmise's "pairing of paradise and death can appear . . . unexceptional" in the poem, its "intrusion" of death is nonetheless remarkable for ostensibly being so "oddly unmotivated."[37] Why think of death, of all things, in imagining the sweet prospect of dwelling in Grasmere's vale? One is reminded of Hartman's aforementioned observation about *The Prelude*'s "supervening" intrusions. Hartman associates such intruding death with the dark workings of the imagination, but there of course is another reason for such curious invasions of mortality and grief: that dwelling, and the communities in which that dwelling is to be situated, must be founded upon loss and repeated acts of mourning. "Build thy house" upon the grave.

Such a reading of the purpose of the dead and of mourning in *Home at Grasmere*'s "society of death"[38] is supported, and significantly complicated, by one of the poem's most well-known scenes, concerning the surmised death of a pair of local swans beloved by the siblings. In exuberantly describing the "mighty multitude" of Grasmere's flocks of wild ducks and swans, whose flight "is a harmony and dance / Magnificent" (290–92), the poet again allows a thought of grief to intrude upon his perception of the scene. I quote this important passage at length:

> But two are missing—two, a lonely pair
> Of milk-white Swans. Ah, why are they not here?
> These above all, ah, why are they not here
> To share in this day's pleasure? From afar
> They came, like Emma and myself, to live
> Together here in peace and solitude,
> Choosing this Valley, they who had the choice
> Of the whole world. . . . We knew them well—I guess
> That the whole Valley knew them—but to us
> They were more dear than may be well believed . . .
> They strangers, and we strangers; they a pair,
> And we a solitary pair like them.
> They should not have departed; many days
> I've looked for them in vain, nor on the wing
> Have seen them, nor in that small open space
> Of blue unfrozen water, where they lodged
> And lived so long in quiet, side by side.
> Companions, brethren, consecrated friends,
> Shall we behold them yet another year
> Surviving, they for us and we for them,
> And neither pair be broken? Nay, perchance
> It is too late already for such hope;

> The Shepherd may have seized the deadly tube
> And parted them . . . or haply both are gone,
> One death, and that were mercy given to both.
>
> (322–57)

Several readers discern in these lines a turning point or crisis for the poet and his narrative of desired dwelling. Modiano, for example, argues that the episode "profoundly unbalances the poem, undermining Wordsworth's endeavors to devote to Grasmere an 'Ode to Joy.'"[39] She interprets the swans' presumed loss in terms of its "active involvement in the [poem's] elaboration of a non-violent framework of exchange, that of the gift, which secures momentary relief from violence," although she also declares that these swans nonetheless "must die to secure his [William's] and Dorothy's survival" in the vale.[40] Before her, Bruce Clarke similarly asserted the local birds' mysterious disappearance to be owed to their symbolic displacement by the new, human pair of arrivals.[41] Drawing upon conjectures about the poem's compositional progress in 1800 and 1806, Johnston discerns in this supplanting or sacrifice of the avian pair a genuine crisis for the poet and his narrative: that at "the very height of his 'O altitudo!' Wordsworth looks down, sees death, poverty, and evil, and plunges to ground, not to resume the poem for over five years."[42] Whether or not this textual juncture represents quite the compositional disjuncture Johnston postulates, it does understandably present a problem for the poem's human pair of would-be dwellers. The very rights (and rites) they have vouchsafed for themselves appear now to alienate them from the people in whose midst they would live.

Having identified himself and his sister with the two swans—"They strangers, and we strangers; they a pair, / And we a solitary pair like them"— Wordsworth's speaker balks at his insinuation of some local resident's culpability in their murder, and by contiguity the culpability of Grasmere itself (for an act the community likely would regard merely as hunting, or at worst as poaching). And, once having entertained this rather reasonable explanation for the swans' disappearance, although it is by no means the only cause he or others might deduce,[43] the poet feels obliged to apologize to his new neighbors. He would not believe them capable of such deeds: of having transgressed, in effect, against the very basis for dwelling and community, at least for that of the approaching siblings themselves. The poet recoils, proclaiming that, were he simply to believe his eyes and beckon to the guiding, "presiding Spirit" of the landscape before him (364), he would surely be convinced that

> They who are dwellers in this holy place
> Must needs themselves be hallowed. They require

No benediction from the Stranger's lips,
For they are blessed already.

(366–69)

According to Johnston, in so determining the inhabitants of Grasmere *already* to be "hallowed," whatever their transgressions, Wordsworth provides a "curious apology" for his disconcerting surmise, one that "implies that all apologies are unnecessary because morally irrelevant."[44] Having suspected one or more of Grasmere's dalesmen of murder, the speaker compensates by focusing upon the encompassing landscape as so "holy"—presided over by a local "Spirit" of Nature—that its human inhabitants could neither be guilty nor stand in need of forgiveness. "They are blessed already," he proclaims, "hallowed" by the very natural world they appeared to have wronged. Nature, presumably the same nature that had both mourned the hart and blessed the two mournful siblings, is now asserted to be staunchly on the locals' side. Suspecting one or more of his future neighbors of egregious inhospitality to the avian pair, the speaker attempts in these lines to provide an alibi or vouchsafing measure for his and Grasmere's inherent worthiness and mutual suitability.

Although the brother's innocent extension of his social scheme from human beings to animals may hallow the latter, along with himself and his sister as mourners of the dead, in the case of the swans' disappearance it must also raise problems for dwelling here among the vale's human inhabitants. The paradigm of mournful community runs afoul (pardon the pun) of the socioeconomic and moral practices of the locale. Lamented animal death thereby becomes the principal source of the pair's social troubles because it implicates Grasmere's human beings, the couple's new neighbors, as killers rather than mourners—analogous to having the drowned man be pulled from Esthwaite Water with a knife in his back. Hence, as I've said, the brother does all he can to assuage or cancel this guilt, envisioning Grasmere's *sui generis* moral authority as pardoning those "dwellers in this holy place." By so doing, however, Wordsworth displaces a sympathizing, socially vouchsafing Nature from the side of mourning—of animals and the siblings—to the side of Grasmere's inhabitants and their traditional practices, including their killing of swans and, one should think, even the likes of the hart. The promissory basis for the couple's inclusion in the vale now serves doubly to alienate them: from the dalesmen of the locale and, in order to amend in some way those locals' putative act of violation, from nature itself, at least so long as the arriving pair would claim kinship with those animals whose mortal loss they have already insistently and sacredly mourned.

In succeeding lines (circa 1806, by Johnston's estimation), the speaker presents, as a form of communal offering, elegies and tributes for Grasmere's oft-grieving dalesmen and daleswomen, one of whom "died of his own grief"

(531), as well as tales of human-animal cooperation in the vale. He does so both to re-envision this place as the holy dell his and Emma's inaugural vision had seemed to secure and to make the aforementioned amends to those wronged by his prior imputations of guilt. He thereby attempts not only to harmonize for himself the vale's human-animal relations, casting them in a more favorable light (as in the exemplum of an ass bearing a cripple on its back), but also to insinuate himself among those of the dale, as one able, albeit retrospectively, to eulogize the Grasmerean dead. Quite the ruse. The poet thereby gains, and by this logic of eulogistic-epitaphic discourse really shows himself *already* to have gained, the right to dwell in the shadow of the grave in Grasmere. "No, we are not alone," he assures his sister, "we do not stand, / My Emma, here misplaced and desolate, / Loving what no one cares for but ourselves" (646–48). "Look where we will," he desperately proclaims, "some human heart has been / Before us with its offering. . . . / Joy spreads and sorrow spreads" (659–60, 664). Look where they will, they mourn the dead: at Hart-leap Well, at the lakeside where the swans are missed, even in these belated, palliative eulogies to Grasmere's dalesmen. Eulogy and elegy become the twin discourses of the couple's self-inclusion, and mourning ("sorrow"), the currency of their Grasmere community; hence those too-frequent intrusions of death and mourning. Yet, because of the strains and outright breaches it masks, this atoning eulogistic ruse produces at best an uneasy détente between the siblings and the living and deceased of the vale. For the poet's mourning and other gestures are, at bottom, a turning to and from the dead—to and from animal dead like the hart and the swans and to and from those living and dead human beings implicated in their deaths—and ultimately to and from Grasmere and its presiding "Spirit." Which nature, and which dead, will underwrite the poet's reception and his future dwelling? What dwelling will receive him?

Finding these elegiac and other sacralizing gestures to be ineffective, Wordsworth's poet retreats from the promise of inclusion in the human portion of Grasmere "entire," reasserting his and Emma's prior founding connection to the locale's migrating flocks of birds (now minus two). And he does so in markedly social terms:

> Whether in large communities ye dwell
> From year to year, not shunning man's abode,
> A settled residence, or be from far,
> Wild creatures, and of many houses, that come
> The gift of winds, and whom the winds again
> Take from us at your pleasure—yet shall ye
> Not want for this . . . an underplace
> In my affections.
>
> (758–66)

Secured by the bonds these "affections" for the birds produce—birds whose disappearance is explained (away) as a result of nature's and their own "plea-sure"—brother and sister can again hope, in accordance with their sacraliz-ing logic of dwelling, to establish a "true community . . . / Of many into one incorporate" (819–20). But that community is now to be set apart from false or less true collectivities. It will be "*divided* from the world / As if it were a cave, a multitude / Human and brute, possessors undisturbed / Of this recess . . . their glorious dwelling-place" (824–28; emphasis added). In mov-ing to Grasmere, Wordsworth certainly felt himself to be withdrawing in some manner from society, from London and its falsifying politics, especially. Yet, given the textual site of this proclamation, one cannot but see this "divided" community to be one set apart from some or all of Grasmere's human population, as well, since the "brute . . . possessors" here embraced would there have no lasting assurance of living "undisturbed." Grasmere is no Pantisocracy, the American utopia Coleridge and Southey had envisioned years before as a safe haven for humans and animals alike. In *Home at Gras-mere*, such community is in this sense only "one" and "incorporate" in its cave-like separation, as a form of hermitage.

Bypassing the impasse presented by his imputations of human-animal guilt, this newly envisioned micro-community will be predicated upon the ini-tial ground of mourning:

> And if this
> Were not, we have enough within ourselves,
> Enough to fill the present day with joy
> And overspread the future years with hope—
> Our beautiful and quiet home, enriched
> Already with a Stranger whom we love
> Deeply, a Stranger of our Father's house,
> A never-resting Pilgrim of the Sea. . . .
>
>   (859–66)

The poet returns to the idealized, delimited community conferred by his mourning rites at Hart-leap Well and by the lakeside. For he and Emma had thereby gained sufficient mourning-based "joy" to promise them that "milder day" and "fairer world"—sufficient joy even to "overspread the future years with hope." In these later lines, the added "Stranger" can be identified with the Wordsworths' mariner brother, John, another orphan from their "Father's house." Hence, so this detail implies, he is himself already a fellow mourner of the dead (i.e., of their dead father) and of lost dwelling (of their family home). In this respect he is "one" in common with them as one in similar standing and social need. He is likewise a fellow "Stranger" entering this landscape where mourning promises but also complicates inclusion and dwelling. Wordsworth's text in these and other ways restricts the intimated promise to those very few able, like the brother and sister, to share mourning, in fact leaving the commemorating of Grasmere's human and animal dead to these three *pilgrims.* The latter term indeed suggests their home to be a sacred community within and apart from a larger, profane society with which it exists in an uneasy tension, as a "cave" or hilltop refuge in a wide social wilderness. The founding is in this respect not far afield of that Nazarene fraternity of loss envisioned above Tintern Abbey years before.

For all his problems in envisioning the vale as a "unity" of humans and animals *and* as a dead-centered community founded upon animal death, Wordsworth appears to have deemed this textual complication to be so necessary as to warrant its retention, in 1800 and in 1806.[45] For in fact the troubling contents provided, for good or ill, in 1800 and even in 1806 after John's death, the foundation for the kind of community Wordsworth still instinctively envisioned. As an interloper approaching the vale, his poem's speaker gains symbolic elbow room for himself (and in some measure for his author), finding sources of consolation for his anxiety in thoughts of death accompanied by rites of mourning—even at the risk of "wrong[ing]" the dale to which he would belong. But such is the poet's Orphean proclivity in envisioning his and others' bonds of community: to think of and feel a blessed grief, entailing an act of autobenediction predicated upon and ensured by mourning.

Wordsworth's inclination to envision community as produced by mourning leads him into this quagmire of competing values and natures in Grasmere. One wonders that, in 1806, with the five-book *Prelude* behind him, the poet did not enlist the potential means of social connection to Grasmere's inhabitants which that work's opening book proffered.[46] Then, he had depicted himself as an Actaeon, a hunter turned hunted for having offended the goddess associated not just with hunting but with birth and with young animals.[47] Why not now proclaim *himself* guilty, say, of feeling "joy" at that retrospect of animal death at Hart-leap Well (as he and Dorothy indeed had felt) or of having himself wrongfully killed animals, as his autobiographical recounting of egg stealing, bird-springe thieving, and other childish escapades attests in *The Prelude*? The answer is uncertain. As one who, on account of such transgressions, had on occasion been pursued by "huge and mighty forms, that do not live / Like living men," he may have hesitated to revisit or further heap upon himself such guilt and the debts of mourning it imposed, especially after John's tragic loss. Ambivalence attends most of Wordsworth's recollections of the dead and his depictions of human beings' indebtedness to those dead, more so after 1804. Or perhaps the wrong that others committed in killing the swans was too great to allow any bridge-building of communion and atonement in shared human guilt. In *Home at Grasmere,* that path to a broader community of mourning, and of shared human guilt, is bypassed or blocked by intent, instinct, or chance.

Such conflict over mourning, guilt, and recompense, and the division it seemed inclined to interpose, may have contributed to Wordsworth's increasing tendency, in the years after the watershed of 1804, to turn further from the dead and from grief. The next, last chapter will have more to say about this later turn. Suffice it for now to point out that, in the likely circa-1806 closing lines of *Home at Grasmere*, Wordsworth's (re)conceptualization of a "true community" divided from the world and its mournful troubles—its sad music of animals and humanity—encapsulates his increasing desire to remove and protect himself from mourning while at the same time still relying upon its social powers. He withdraws into an insular familial community still conferred by grief, a community now secluded like a cave. One may also argue that what the narrative depicts and mythologizes is the establishment and vouchsafing of the very community Wordsworth had so long desired: an insulated, "significant group" of family and friends,[48] set apart from the profane world around it, like a hermitage in a social wilderness, yet with looser, in part mournful, ties to others around it. Both of these conclusions may be true. One thing, however, seems fairly certain. In the poet's later work the motif of such rural retirement (as retreat) becomes a dominant one, as does that of the quelling of grief.

The advancing wish to restrain mourning is precisely the topic of Wordsworth's later, unpublished narrative of mortal loss in the vale of Grasmere, *The Tuft of Primroses* (1808), some of whose lines he incorporates in the death-oriented but grief-quelling *Excursion* of 1814. The thirteen-book *Prelude*, written in part as a tribute to John, also reflects its grieving author's attempts to withdraw from the pains and trials of mourning, topographically manifested in the Wordsworths' change of residence in Grasmere from Town End to Rydal Mount, further from the graves of their recently deceased children (*MY* 2: 75–76). As the poet proclaims and in part laments in "Elegiac Stanzas," following the loss of John, death had imposed "a new controul."

7

"A New Controul" in
Poems in Two Volumes and *The Excursion*

> Bound to establish new communities. . . .
> —*The Excursion,* Book Ninth

Although the paradigm of dead-oriented community persists in Wordsworth's poetry until at least *The Excursion* (1814), it is less conspicuous in his output after 1804. The social model's diminution is noticeable in the thirteen-book *Prelude* (1805) and in *Poems, in Two Volumes* (1807). More importantly, one finds a shift in the *quality* of these later representations of mourning. Grief now tends to be delimited, mollified, or outright quelled, and to be eased less by fellowship or even nature-prompted consolation than by religious promises of the afterlife: a "faith that looks *through* death." Previous pages named the grand *Recluse* project as one culprit in Wordsworth's turn from the scheme of mournful community. But in these years, in addition to the poet's focus upon nature, it is especially faith, and the stability of Christian tradition and institutions, that operates in lieu of or against the communitarian powers of mourning, offering instead the promise of hope, permanence, and quiescence. The poet's mythic exemplar arguably now becomes less the heroic melancholic Orpheus than the cautionary tragic heroine Laodamia, killed by her own unceasing grief.

The Introduction and the previous chapter each stated that the poet's de facto formation of a physical community at Grasmere likely contributed, if not to his turn from the Dead, then at least to his decreased need for the troubled social articulations that model provided. Surrounded by a "significant group" of family, friends, neighbors, and admirers,[1] a close-knit community he arguably had sought in one form or another since his mother's death, Wordsworth at last could afford to explore a different poetics and sociology, suited to his locale. Similarly, in *Adventures* the long-desired cottage of *Salisbury Plain* and *An Evening Walk* had disappeared, perhaps in part because the author and his sister had at last realized that goal at Windy Brow.[2] And how had this Grasmere community been forged? As *Home at Grasmere* depicts matters, its author had desperately desired inclusion in the vale, but his mourning rites had themselves proved an obstacle (at least a textual obstacle) rather than an asset in his quest to win a community within Grasmere. Owed to the complications interjected by mourning, at poem's end he and his long-standing, long-implicit sociology appeared very nearly in crisis. In the aftermath, Grasmere Church may have provided some of what had then been missing: a bridge between Wordsworth's "pilgrim" micro-community of grief and the locale's broader community. The church's small congregation of dalesmen and women were gathered on a shared, to him familiar, site of defined and delimited rites of mourning (those of Communion), but with a good deal less dependence upon the doubts, pains, and instabilities of personal grief. Wordsworth in effect began to move from the churchyard to the church, viewing the graves of Grasmere's dead, and soon of his own dead, from the security of the church's sacred walls. It is less surprising, then, that a number of his succeeding works should treat his belief or earnest struggle to believe.[3] Wordsworth retreats as from storms that threaten the calm seas envisioned in *Essays upon Epitaphs,* whose troubled image of mortality resurfaces in the "Elegiac Stanzas" he composes for his brother.

Thomas McFarland reads John Wordsworth's death in 1805 off Portland Bill as the crisis that definitively cast the poet "back upon his final defense: stoicism," associated with the defensively "egotistical sublime."[4] Yet there were crises prior to this, arguably dating from at least "Tintern Abbey" (1798) in terms of any sort of crisis of imagination or nature and from at least "The world is too much with us" (1802–4) concerning a lamented personal deficit of religious faith, hope, or consolation. But John's untimely death was nevertheless pivotal, for it seems to have compelled his grieving brother to seek out and accept more specifically Christian sources of solace, as well as to adopt a more stoic defensive stance toward the mutable world. Hence, Richard Onorato finds signs in "Ode to Duty" (1805) of Wordsworth's turn "more towards God" as well as toward the "greater autonomy of the Christian soul."[5] The 1850 *Prelude*'s sentimental eulogy for Coleridge similarly, revealingly praises the deceased for having "relaxed" in the poet's "self-haunting spirit" the "overweening" hold of the "mystery . . . / Of Life and death," mainly by teaching him to lean "on the stay / Of Providence" (*14P* 14.282–87, 297–98). As Gordon Thomas says of these lines, "whatever or whoever was the cause of this improvement in outlook, and one suspects that both Dorothy and Mary are likelier sources . . . the fact that there was a change in Wordsworth is clear."[6] That the change involved the poet's view of life and especially of death also seems clear. Indeed, his romance *The White Doe of Rylstone* (1807–8) repre-sented, Wordsworth told Coleridge, "a human being, a Woman, who is intended to be honoured and loved for what she *endures,* and the manner in which she endures it; accomplishing a conquest over her own sorrows (which is the true subject of the Poem)" (*MY* 1: 222; original emphasis). The poet's shift from "Semi-atheist" to (semi-)Christian promised him, as Christian faith promised the *White Doe*'s exemplar, Emily Norton, the consolatory means for such a hoped-for "conquest" of loss and grief.

A few years later, with the almost unbearable loss in 1812 of his children Catherine and Thomas, Wordsworth's desire to quell grief became still more acute. He writes that he and his family now felt obliged, as a result, to "quit this House [at Town End] for Rydale Mount; we have too many distressful Memorials here. . . . I hope we shall be something less sad when we get away from the heavyness of this Dwelling in which we have been so pitiably smit-ten by the hand of providence" (*MY* 2: 75). The elegy "Surprized by joy— impatient as the Wind," written for Catherine, narrates the speaker's anguish over but a moment's forgetfulness of his "most grievous loss," a loss "That neither present time, nor years unborn / Could to my sight . . . restore" (*ShP,* ll. 9, 13–14). In lines originally written for *The Excursion,* a similarly bereaved mother finds in her soul "perpetually a Shadow" (*ShP,* p. 115, l. 36). "O teach me," she prays to God, "calm submission to thy will" (51). Only such religious "submission," owed to faith in immortality and to the suppression of sorrow-ful feeling, seems capable of ending grief. Hence, Wordsworth's epitaph for Thomas, "Six months to six years added, He remain'd," likewise asks the Lord to "teach us calmly to resign / What we possess'd and now is wholly thine" (5–6). Resignation is no worldly (or nature-related) matter. As the poet's later, quite telling "Malham Cove" (1818) proclaims, "Foundations must be laid / In Heav'n," not "mid the wreck of IS and WAS" (10–11). Yet, for all Wordsworth's desired or professed resignation and religious calm, the paradigm of the Dead is a looming, lingering presence in his later works, suf-fering sea changes, to be sure, but reaching an end only gradually, and arguably only completely with its author's death in 1850, well into the Vic-torian era.

I. FAITH AND RECLUSION IN *POEMS, IN TWO VOLUMES*

> Such sights, or worse, as are before me here.—
> Not without hope we suffer and we mourn.
>
> —"Elegiac Stanzas"

Poems in Two Volumes evinces both Wordsworth's reiteration of mournful community and his turn from the dead toward sources of consolation—before and, especially, after the time of his brother John's death, which haunts the volumes' later works. "The Sailor's Mother" (1800), a narrative of ceaseless mourning, and the ballad-influenced "The Affliction of Margaret ———— of ————" (1804) demonstrate the psychological and social consequences of not seeing the possibility of what the latter text describes as "intercourse / Betwixt the living and the dead" (*PTV,* ll. 59–60). These two poems thereby suggest the extent to which, as in the *Essays upon Epitaphs,* social "intercourse" between the living and dead is still very much a cohesive, triadic force for Wordsworth. But it is one which mourners like Margaret appear to be constitutionally incapable of embracing due to its inherent pain. "The Affliction of Margaret" thus attests both to mournful community's workings in 1804 and, it would seem, to the poet's growing sense that, as in "The Thorn" and *Home at Grasmere,* such communities have their limits and costs.

As readers have discerned, Wordsworth's near devotion to the sonnet form in these years suggests his desire to find means of restraint and closure, structures able to contain and exclude.[7] The sonnets from *Poems* similarly narrate their speakers' need to believe in something capable of containing faith and hope and excluding or at least delimiting grief and suffering. "The world is too much with us," composed before John's death, professes its speaker's desperate need for a "creed" to revitalize his "out of tune" perception of and connection to external nature (10, 8). "Great God!" he exclaims, "I'd rather be / A Pagan suckled in a creed outworn" than to stand before the sea feeling "forlorn" (9–12). Better, he believes, to be possessed of a mythology that inspirits the natural world: to "Have sight of Proteus coming from the sea" (13). Wordsworth's incorporation of the Platonic doctrine of metempsychosis in the Immortality Ode will similarly narrate this search for a "creed" to console dejection in the face of mortal change. The nature-god Proteus is of course not just immortal but also mutable and immutable, a god able to change and yet remain the same. The poem's poet needs an inspiriting belief, pagan or Christian, to sustain himself against nature's mutability as well as against his own mortality, to look through death to an unchanging reality.

Poems' succeeding, more overtly Christian sonnet, "It is a beauteous Evening, calm and free," provides such an immutable vision. Wordsworth's newly baptized daughter, Caroline, is reminded, "Thou liest in Abraham's bosom all the year; / And worshipp'st at the Temple's inner shrine, / God being with thee when we know it not" (12–14). She is encouraged to take comfort in the promise of divine presence and of now and forever dwelling with the Lord. Surely, if God is always with us in life we then can trust in finding the comfort of "Abraham's bosom" in death. The poem's displacement

of that comforting bosom from the next world to this one suggests its narrator's own need: for consolation in life against the impending shadows of death.
This sonnet may thus be read as one answer to the grief-related woes
lamented in "The world is too much with us." The semi-pagan "Ode," later
retitled "Ode: Intimations of Immortality from Recollections of Early Childhood," can be read as another.

Written in much the same vein as "The world," the Immortality Ode
more explicitly seeks a "faith that looks through death" (188). Mortality is
again associated with the poet's loss of nature's inspirited "glory" and with the
waning of his imaginative powers:

> —But there's a Tree, of many one,
> A single Field which I have look'd upon,
> Both of them speak of something that is gone:
> The Pansy at my feet
> Doth the same tale repeat:
> Whither is fled the visionary gleam?
> Where is it now, the glory and the dream?
>
> (51–57)

It was with these well-known lines' lament of lost imaginative power, and
really of loss itself, that Wordsworth apparently left the fragmentary text in
March 1802 (as John Worthen points out, one cannot be sure what those original lines precisely looked like[8]). Not until after reading Coleridge's dispiriting
response to this work in progress, in a verse letter addressed to Sara Hutchinson and thereafter published as "Dejection: An Ode," did Wordsworth apparently resume composition, now two years later, to correct its troubling melancholy.[9] Like Coleridge's poem, his *mortality* ode of 1802 had been vexed by
grief: "To me alone there came a thought of grief: / A timely utterance gave
that thought relief" (22–23). The "grief" was never specified; in 1802 as in
1804 it of course could not have been grief for John.[10] The speaker's crisis in
fact appears not so different from that lamented in "Tintern Abbey" several
years before. A nostalgic poet of nature faces a less immediate, less inspired
and inspiring landscape, along with his personal feelings of diminished poetical power. Yet this time the would-be nature poet responds not by turning to
another to structure a mournful community but by trying to transform this
seeming funeral of epistemological disjunction into a natural cycle of growth,
decline, and rebirth—what amounts to a protean world of survivable mutability. This pagan transformation suggests that the speaker's deeper problem is
less that of waning imaginative power than of mortal loss and its ensuing
pangs of grief, for it is death itself that is chiefly changed by his new (or,
rather, old) religious vantage.

Wordsworth's importation of the Platonic doctrine of metempsychosis naturalizes loss and offers hope of spiritual rebirth, raising a bulwark of mythology qua faith to fend off personal loss: "Our birth is but a sleep and a forgetting . . . trailing clouds of glory do we come / From God, who is our home: / Heaven lies about us in our infancy" (58, 64–66). Life becomes a falling into death, a gradual, cyclical, inevitable decline from past "clouds of glory." Death in turn becomes (or at least entails) a return to "our home" in Heaven. Grief thus can be assuaged:

> Though nothing can bring back the hour
> Of splendour in the grass, of glory in the flower;
>> We will grieve not, rather find
>> Strength in what remains behind,
>> In the primal sympathy
>> Which having been must ever be,
>> In the soothing thoughts that spring
>> Out of human suffering,
>> In the faith that looks through death. . . .
>
>> (180–88)

"We will grieve not," the poet declares. He, and potentially others, will withstand grief with the aid of this "faith that looks through death" to intimations of the soul's inherent immortality, re-envisioning even "suffering" as but a moment in life's natural diurnal course away from and then back to presence. Such faith produces no fellowship of mourning per se (the speaker is isolated, the "we" being perhaps of the royal variety). But it does arguably lay the religious ground for a vast communion of earthly loss and spiritual gain, wherein all human beings stand together (and stand and wait) in the same cycle of life and death.

The Ode therefore gives thanks, not for childhood's "[d]elight and liberty,"

> But for those obstinate questionings
> Of sense and outward things,
> Fallings from us, vanishings;
> Blank misgivings of a Creature
> Moving about in worlds not realiz'd,
> High instincts, before which our mortal Nature
> Did tremble like a guilty Thing surpriz'd:
>> But for those first affections,
>> Those shadowy recollections,
>>> Which, be they what they may,

> Are yet the fountain light of all our day,
> Are yet a master light of all our seeing. . . .

(139, 144–155)

The Introduction briefly considered these lines' allusion to *Hamlet*'s opening scene on Elsinore's battlements. Horatio reports how the ghost of Hamlet's dead father appeared and then, upon the coming of daylight, fled away "like a guilty thing / Upon a fearful summons" (I.i.148–49). The Ode describes human mortality's similar "trembl[ings] like a guilty Thing surpriz'd," but it is the self's, not the other's (in *Hamlet* the dead King's), guilt that is registered. On one level, the poem describes how in our early development we are startled by higher intimations of immortality. According to Wordsworth, children especially have access to these intimations; so he recalled from his own childhood feelings about death (*FN* 61).[11] But the allusion to *Hamlet* bears a good deal more baggage than this.

In *Hamlet* it is arguably not the departing ghost of the former King that really is "guilty," despite his afterlife in Purgatorial fires, but instead his murderous, as yet unpunished brother, Claudius, or even Prince Hamlet himself. The epithet is ironically transferred from one figure to the other, and asserts a similar logic in the Ode, where it serves to implicate the poet's oedipal guilt. According to William Ulmer, "it is as though the Ode were obligated to a transvaluative logic demanding the death of the father."[12] Although no longer himself a child, the speaker shares in the promise that redounds from what is, indeed, a transfer of immortality to childhood and of "the darkness of the grave" (l. 117) to adult life. This transfer underwrites a vision of children's "delighted contact with 'that immortal sea,'" from which the poem's adult speaker is necessarily "stationed 'inland far.'"[13] But any transfer of immortality appears to be complicated by this representation of childhood as seaside play, insomuch as the sea's "mighty waters" also potentially endanger those children "sport[ing] upon the shore" (169–70)—an image reminiscent of the unwitting mortal youths of Gray's Eton Ode as well as of Wordsworth's own Boy of Winander and Drowned Man of Esthwaite. Indeed, that sea is, Ulmer states, much the same as that which claimed the life of Lycidas in Milton's elegy, and so suggests all the more these children's "exposure to death."[14] Children may be born "trailing clouds of glory," but the poet seems unable to forget that they also die, as doomed parts of a natural as well as spiritual cycle. The narrative stumbles upon its quelled "thought of grief," led by "an eye" that has "kept watch o'er man's mortality" (200–1) very much indeed. In the end, the Ode uncannily gestures toward a community of "human heart[s]" all subject to death (203). But it is a community whose basis in loss the poem has sought at least on one level to deny or exclude from its "inland" reclusion (165), far, it hopes, from sea change.

After his brother's death in February 1805, Wordsworth's letters show, according to Geoffrey Hartman, the poet "turning toward the idea of another world," although in "Elegiac Stanzas" the consolation he seeks is "purely human" rather than divine (*WP* 287). In his elegy titled "To the Daisy," the grieving brother touchingly describes how John "[s]ix weeks beneath the moving Sea . . . lay in slumber quietly" (ll. 36–37). The poem closes with traditional motifs of a placid nature whose ocean makes a "mournful murmur for *his* sake" and whose flower shall "sleep and wake / Upon his senseless Grave" (54–56). If we trust Wordsworth's representations of his experience, for him the effects of John's death were far less tranquil or assuring. He encountered a reality of loss that left him, as he laments in another, untitled elegy, trembling at death's finality and finding "relief" only in "God's unbounded love" (p. 611, ll. 3–4) as well as in the comparatively "mild release" from "woe" provided by that "peaceful" flower John had so loved (74, 77, 79). An epitaphic shrine to his brother would thus proclaim to the passersby that he or she not foolishly "brood . . . / On any earthly hope, however pure!" (98, 100).

Wordsworth's most poignant and well-known poem to John, "Elegiac Stanzas, Suggested by a Picture of Peele Castle, in a Storm, *painted* by Sir George Beaumont," stands as one of his greatest elegies. In its emphasis upon mourning and in its related hailing of the painter, the poem might be classed with communitarian works like "Tintern Abbey" and *The Ruined Cottage*. But its struggle with grief is different from these past texts. More stoic and resistant, its stanzas are concerned less with the bonds such griefs can form than with the "power" grief has brought to an end, a "power . . . which nothing can restore" (35). As mentioned, McFarland sees John's death as having been for William a "betrayal by Nature," which forced the poet to retreat to his "final defense."[15] Hartman rightly asks how the "power" of Nature's presence can have been lost when for the poet it was never really there in the first place (*WP* 284). After all, one might add, "The world is too much with us" had already lamented lost power. Just what had been lost since then? Hartman rejects nature as the prime candidate, asserting that what Wordsworth had lost was his "capacity for generous error and noble illusion, which made life correspond to the heart's desire" (285). Of course, one can argue that this problem, too, was already lamented in the sonnet. Marjorie Levinson, in her own reading of "Elegiac Stanzas," contends that the lost power is that of "the Real . . . to impress itself as such on the mind of the poet, a mind which, by its ceaseless digestion of the universe of things, has finally implicated itself."[16] One might name that *real* and its occasioning incident death.

"Elegiac Stanzas" suggests that Wordsworth's "distress" at death, specifically at his brother John's loss at sea, has left him grasping for consolation, seeking to salve his feeling of loss, of what Esther Schor describes as a "perpetually present loss."[17] As the elegist laments,

> So once it would have been,—'tis so no more;
> I have submitted to a new controul:
> A power is gone, which nothing can restore;
> A deep distress hath humaniz'd my Soul. . . .
> The feeling of my loss will ne'er be old;
> This, which I know, I speak with mind serene.
>
> (33–36, 39–40)

For Levinson, "Elegiac Stanzas" here "marks the end of the line" insomuch as its "arrested dialectic" consummates the logic of "Tintern Abbey," "Michael," and the Ode.[18] Indeed, the text represents something of an end *and* a beginning in Wordsworth. At this point, the freshness of grief seems consistent with the mourning of Wordsworthian communities past, as, arguably, does the humanizing effect of "deep distress." Add the poet's new-won appreciation for Beaumont's storm-tossed painting of a foundering ship, and the poem would appear to depict a community of friends bonded by their shared feelings of loss. As in "A slumber did my spirit seal," death has awakened the elegist to the disquieting reality of human mortality. So it would seem.

The poet describes his prior displeasure with Beaumont's painting, whose depicted castle he then naively would have situated

> Amid a world how different from this!
> Beside a sea that could not cease to smile;
> On tranquil land, beneath a sky of bliss. . . .
> A Picture had it been of lasting ease,
> Elysian quiet, without toil or strife;
> No motion but the moving tide, a breeze,
> Or merely silent Nature's breathing life.
>
> (18–28)

Then, the poet had entertained the "fond delusion" that even "the mighty Deep" was "the gentlest of all gentle Things" (29, 11–12). That "deep" subtly returns as the poet's lamented "*deep* distress," suffused or littered with the dead. In that "mighty Deep" John Wordsworth lay, much like the dead in Clarence's visionary dream, recalled in the second of the *Essays upon Epitaphs* (*PrW* 2: 64). As the poem's insight into nature's false gentleness implies, it was an "Elysian quiet" subject to storm, a gentle nature belying its real, death-dealing force as well as the mutability described in *Richard III* and, more famously, in *The Tempest*. Death lurks beneath the calm surface the elegist would have painted in accordance with his misperception of nature. John's death irrevocably proves nature to be by no means "the gentlest of all gentle things," as the ghastly corpse drawn from Esthwaite Water might also have proved had the child not innocently painted over its bloated skin with the colors of "Grecian art and purest poesy." Imagination itself might then be read as what has been lost, at least an innocent (naïve) love or valuing of its coloring (over) of nature. But John's death seems for the poet to be a loss that has fundamentally changed loss itself, as the deepest of all deeps, social or otherwise. "A faith, a trust that could not be betray'd" *is* betrayed (32). That betrayal leads the poet to revise his belief in a beneficent nature and, more importantly, to reconsider his own capacity to endure grief, that former source of "power" that now, much as in the case of afflicted Margaret, has become too much to bear or even to share.

Chastened and "humaniz'd" by mortal loss and grief, Wordsworth's speaker envies rather than disdains Beaumont's depiction of the storm-tossed castle, set in bold contrast to the sinking (and oddly unmanned) vessel— implicitly Captain Wordsworth's Earl of Abergavenny—forever listing on the shoals.[19] And his admiration for that painting attests to his withdrawal from mourning:

> And this huge Castle, standing here sublime,
> I love to see the look with which it braves,
> Cased in the unfeeling armour of old time,
> The light'ning, the fierce wind, and trampling waves.
>
> (49–52)

Readers discover the poet's deeper desire: to brave mutability by becoming protectively encased like a knight in "*unfeeling* armour." Peele Castle indeed now is attractive to the poet as an image of withdrawal, of what Keats perhaps misread as Wordsworth's centrifugal egotism. In fact the speaker desires centripetal withdrawal into himself, away from the mutable world.[20] The castle's envied armor suggests a desire *not* to feel that which "is to be borne" (58), with hope serving as a shield against grief rather than as a bier to bear it, as in *The Vale of Esthwaite*. The speaker's "serene" control is, as Levinson perceived, "an armored look."[21] Having come face to face with mortal loss and with the inevitability of more painful deaths to come—with "frequent sights of what is to be borne!"—the speaker reaches after "hope" against mourning. And in this regard his author's renewed relationship to the English Church served, like armor or stone, as a defense not against sin or personal annihilation as much as against grief itself. It is the power to bear grief, to linger upon its shadowy absences and demands and to impart one's own mourning to others, that now is pronounced to be "gone." The elegist steels himself to grief, and hence, like Prince Hamlet, defers or quells his indebtedness, prodigally, "like a guilty Thing," to the ghostly dead.

By the time the Wordsworth household quit Town End, the poet had almost certainly developed a more stoic stance and had come to believe or need to believe more strongly in an afterlife. Wordsworth's post-1804 poems seek (and often fail) to reproduce textually what the family had effected topographically: a movement away from the dead and from the grief they impart. Hence "Laodamia" (1814) describes a woman tragically unable or unwilling to moderate her grief for her deceased husband, the first Greek to fall at Troy. She dies from her grief, lying "on the palace-floor[,] a lifeless corse" (*ShP,* 1. 121). In her trenchant, extensive reading of this text, Judith Page observes that the poem is "not an elegy like 'Lycidas' . . . but a poem that dramatizes the failure to accept death and to come to terms with grief"—in other words, "to accept the consolation of the spiritual realm."[22] "Ah, judge her gently who so deeply loved!" (122), the sympathetic speaker urges. But the poem nonetheless views her death as a failure, one of faith as well as of grief, however attractive or pathetic the cause. The speaker of the revised text of 1845, last of a long line of revisions, concludes that Laodamia died "as for a wilful crime" (p. 152), almost as a suicide. Although more sympathetic, even the 1814 text depicts her grief as excessive, selfish, and doomed, resistant even to the pleadings of the dead themselves, and leaving no promise of redemption. Throughout its revisions the elegy may well be read as a psychomachia of its author's divided feelings about grief and faith, wavering between Orphic refusal and the pious, grief-conquering religious submission and renunciation exemplified in the *White Doe of Rylstone.* Indeed, that "Laodamia" treats a recalcitrant, melancholy form of grief suggests the extent to which its author struggles in these years, amid his family's overwhelming deaths, to deal with mortal loss and to embrace a faith that looks through death. But the valence has shifted. Laodamia appears an unreconstructed Orphean, in need of solace and a religious promise she narrow-mindedly and, ultimately, wrongly refuses.

Poems, in Two Volumes reveals Wordsworth's turn not exactly from mourning, of which there is still plenty to be found, but from its interminability and its burdens, and hence also from its need to be shared. In this withdrawal from the perpetuity and pain of grief the Actaeon poet flees from the dead. Given his recent, painful personal losses, who would blame him? Retreat becomes the frequent figure of the works composed after 1804, with the hermitage serving as the emblem of a desire for protection from the cares of the mortal world, especially from those of incessant mourning and disquieting remembrance. What thereafter becomes of the scheme of mournful community is revealed in the excursive second of the three intended parts of *The Recluse.*

II. "The Churchyard among the Mountains": Quelling Mourning in *The Excursion* of 1814

> Four dear supporters of one senseless weight,
> From which they do not shrink, and under which
> They faint not, but advance towards the open grave. . . .
>
> —from Book Third

Against Francis Jeffrey's famous retort, "This will never do!" and a long succeeding line of dismissals and charges of mediocrity, David Simpson persuasively argues that *The Excursion* "must be central to any coherent understanding of Wordsworth."[23] So also, then, must be its "one major, confessed narrative intention: to educate the [character of the] Solitary out of what is said to be a self-consuming melancholy and into a state of active acceptance or peace of mind."[24] It is with this narrative mission and with the churchyard eulogies imparted to achieve it that this final chapter is concerned.

Kenneth Johnston contends that readers of Wordsworth's poem are in the presence of "buried foundations" difficult to perceive "because they are so much larger than we had imagined."[25] Those foundations are principally the foundation stones of a rural thanatopolis of the living and the dead. As Hartman, too, perceived, the poem's eulogies, of which there are many, give nature the "aspect of a large graveyard" (*WP* 299). Likewise, in her rhetorical reading of *The Excursion,* Alison Hickey sees the poem's landscape as one "harbor[ing] countless gravelike spots, some . . . cryptic, some more explicitly connected with the dead and their stories."[26] Schor's more mourning-oriented reading similarly discerns the dead's looming, still fundamental significance (akin, she argues, "to a Burkean embrace of the dead"),[27] as does Sally Bushell's *Re-Reading "The Excursion,"* which in fact finds in the poem a union of "the living with the dead."[28] Like these readings, my analysis uncovers a text connected to the dead, and a narrative built upon the foundations of buried community—a social scheme dependent upon eulogies of grief and consolation. The poem's excursion returns, hesitantly, to the uncanny terrain of the *Vale,* with the dead and grief for the dead still ambivalently sought. The paradigm of mournful community underlies much of the poem's dramatic action, such as it is, in what can justly be read as a *Ruined Cottage* redux writ large, a text expanding upon that elegiac narrative's dialogism and excursive movement. But that poem's social model is altered by its successor's express desire to quell grief, serving both the author's desire for consolation and *The Recluse*'s founding aim to conquer despondency and pessimism. This is not to say that *The Excursion* does not achieve a communitarian vision or promise of some sort, as a muted but intriguing extension of *The Ruined Cottage,* whose revised text occupies the opus's Book First.

Itself almost a prolegomenon to *The Excursion,* Wordsworth's unpublished fragment *The Tuft of Primroses* (1808) was originally composed for *The Recluse* but subsequently rejected. Like the above elegiac works from *Poems,* this text of some six hundred lines is a meditation upon loss, one that provides a helpful frame for considering the more broadly ranging *Excursion,* in which some of the poem's lines in fact were incorporated. *The Tuft of Primroses* opens with the poet and family's unhappy return to Grasmere. The Wordsworths had spent the winter and spring of 1807 in Coleorton, and, as Dorothy recounted to a friend, upon returning learned of "many persons . . . dead," including their friends and neighbors "old Mr. Sympson, his son the parson, young George Dawson, the finest young Man in the vale" (*MY* 1: 158). In response to these losses, the poem's narrative focuses upon the enduring prospect and retrospect of a local primrose flower, "reviv'd, / And beautiful as ever, like a Queen" (*TP,* ll. 7–8), blooming alone in "splendour unimpaired" (14). The grieving speaker addresses the everlasting primrose:

> Alas how much,
> Since I beheld and loved Thee first, how much
> Is gone, though thou be left; I would not speak
> Of best Friends dead, or other deep heart loss
> Bewail'd with weeping, but by River sides
> And in broad fields how many gentle loves,
> How many mute memorials pass'd away.
>
> (70–76)

The poet's stoic resistance to grief even in the act of elegizing is evident in his refusal to do much more than mention "best Friends dead, or other deep heart loss." Among the number of dead mourned must still be counted John Wordsworth, whom the poet here resists naming, along with others, that he might avoid repeating past grieving and "weeping."

Also among the mournful catalogue of "deep . . . loss[es]" are some recently felled, beloved trees, particularly a "lofty band of Firs that overtopp'd / Their antient Neighbour, the old Steeple Tower" (79–80). Those firs are especially to be missed for the gifts that have departed with them: the manner in which the trees often

> mingl[ed] their solemn strain
> Of music with the one determined voice
> From the slow funeral bell . . . and cast
> Their dancing shadows on the flowery turf,
> While through the Churchyard tripp'd the bridal train
> In festive Ribbands deck'd; and those same trees,

> By moonlight, in their stillness and repose,
> Deepen'd the silence of a hundred graves.
>
> (82–84, 89–93)

The trees are thus chiefly memorialized for having been almost a second order of gravestone or epitaph, deepening the graves' meditative silence. Prior to being cut down, the trees had helped maintain and expand that silence, quieting and covering over the dead's now too-visible graves.

Subsequent lines clarify the poet's more subtle reason for lamentation:

> Now stands the Steeple naked and forlorn,
> And from the spot of sacred ground, the home
> To which all change conducts the thought, looks round
> Upon the changes of this peaceful Vale. . . .
> The hoary steeple now beholds that roof
> Laid open to the glare of common day,
> And marks five graves beneath his feet . . .
> The Inmates of that Cottage are at rest.
>
> (126–29, 142–44, 148)

Those dwellers were the Sympsons, sparely elegized in subsequent lines later revised for Book Seventh of *The Excursion,* in which better-known context they shall be examined (see below). Particularly interesting in this passage is the manner in which "forlorn" Grasmere Church's steeple marks at its feet the five graves now lamentably left "open to the glare of common day." Much as for the Wordsworth household viewing the graves of Catherine and Thomas, the grave plots become too visible, conveying the "common" daylight of mortality lamented in the Ode. Wordsworth's poet's response is to seek protection in an enclosed sanctuary that provides "Continual and firm peace, from outrage safe / And all annoyance, till the sovereign comes" (261–62).

The poem textually retreats to the medieval hagiography of St. Basil, founder of Eastern Monasticism, and his friend Gregory Nazianzen (resembling Wordsworth and Coleridge, as Basil's sister, Macrina, resembles Dorothy). In this context what matters is less the ecclesiastical history upon which the text draws than the tale's monastic setting.[29] The narrator perceives, like many elegists before him, that if nature possesses a "voice that pleads, beseeches, and implores," it is nevertheless one that pleads "[i]n vain" (274–75). He sees, too, and laments that "the deafness of the world is here" in Grasmere and that "all too many of the haunts / Of Fancy's choicest pastime, and the best / And Dearest resting places of the heart / Vanish beneath an unrelenting doom" (275–79). In lines later put into the mouth of the Solitary in Book Third of *The Excursion,*[30] the poet poses a rhetorical but nonetheless important question:

> What impulse drove the Hermit to his Cell
> And what detain'd him there his whole life long
> Fast anchored in the desart? Not alone
> Dread of the persecuting sword, remorse,
> Love with despair, or grief in agony;
> Not always from intolerable pangs
> He fled; but in the height of pleasure sigh'd
> For independent happiness, craving peace,
> The central feeling of all happiness,
> Not as a refuge from distress or pain . . .
> But for its absolute self, a life of peace,
> Stability without regret or fear,
> That hath been, is, and shall be ever more.
>
> (280–93)

"Stability without regret or fear," protection from the mutability that prevents things from being "ever more," drives the hermit or anchorite to seek the cell's shielding power. His flight from death and from the agony of grief is "the master tie / Of the monastic brotherhood" (297–98).

In his brief reading of the *Tuft*, Johnston sees that initial change in the landscape (those lost firs) as one that in turn "exposes a new focal point for meditations upon change," the church itself.[31] As it will be in *The Excursion*, Grasmere Church is that new focus or "imaginative fulcrum," overseeing loss and providing protection against grief. The *Tuft*'s later lines about the Grande Chartreuse likewise demonstrate this desire for a "[h]umanly cloth'd," mythically or religiously "embodied" silence and its "perpetual calm" (538–41). Reclusion in a Christian or semi-Christian order, in an anchoring "brotherhood" secure amid life's turbulent seas, becomes the goal of a vexed self confronted with loss. To avoid, resist, or delimit mourning by discovering sources of consolation is *The Tuft of Primroses'* mission, as it is *The Excursion*'s. Both texts reflect their author's "determined refusal to mourn"[32] or at least to prolong mourning. From this vantage one may read many details in the *Tuft*— the felled trees, the tale of St. Basil—as tropes employed to avoid or defuse a grief too close or too great to be mourned.

Book Seventh, the second of *The Excursion*'s two books titled and set within "The Churchyard among the Mountains" (1809–12), significantly elaborates upon the *Tuft*'s elegy of the Sympsons.[33] Now it is not the Wordsworthian poet but instead a parson who eulogizes the neighbors, and for the edification of others rather than to impart his own grief. This instruction is specifically directed to "correct" the enduring "despondency" of the so-called Solitary, one of three typifying characters gathered as an audience before the Pastor in his Grasmere churchyard. Likely drawn from the narrator of Edward

Young's *Night Thoughts*,[34] the Solitary exemplifies the disillusioned, post-revolutionary idealist *The Recluse* was intended to heal: one of those who, in
Coleridge's words, had "thrown up all hopes of the amelioration of mankind"
and sunk "into an epicurean selfishness, disguising it under . . . contempt for
visionary *philosophes*" (*CLSTC* 1: 527). But the Revolution's failure is not the real
cause of this recluse's despondency. In keeping with Wordsworth's fundamental,
enduring orientation to the dead and with his longstanding, idiosyncratic sense
of what would really drive one to seek reclusion, the Solitary's biography reveals
his stubborn despondency to originate not in political disillusionment (per *The
Recluse*'s agenda) but in something considerably more mournful.

    Concluding his personal history's litany of disappointments, this recluse
compares his life, and all human life, to a stream. While at once appearing
calm, the stream's distant "murmur" or "roar" reveals

> Through what perplexing labyrinths, abrupt
> Precipitations, and untoward straits,
> The earth-born wanderer hath passed; and quickly,
> That respite o'er, like traverses and toils
> Must be again encountered.
>   (*Ex* 139–40; *PW* 5: 3.978, 982–86)[35]

The Solitary's self-elegy describes the mournful murmuring his more placid
exterior belies, and so suggests the underlying source of his quest for reclusion: his flight from the guilty pangs of suppressed grief. The history he narrates reveals his despondency to be a self-protective means of displacing
mourning, which is to say of mourning in the displaced form of disdain for
the state of the world. And so he murmurs without really mourning. His
desire to sustain this (screen of) despondency sets him quite apart from the
three other characters, the Pastor, the Poet, and the Wanderer (formerly the
pedlar of *The Ruined Cottage*). As the object of their shared attempts to effect
its "correction," his dejection occupies the buried center and foundation of
this elegiac text.

    Like the Wordsworthian speaker of *The Tuft of Primroses*, the Solitary
believes that the basis for humankind's age-old "yearning" for "the master tie
/ Of the monastic Brotherhood[,] upon Rock / Aerial," was and is a "longing
for confirmed tranquillity" (113; 3.392–94, 398), "Stability without regret or
fear; / That hath been, is, and shall be evermore!" (386–87). Much as in "Elegiac Stanzas," such desirable rock-like "stability" is desired principally for its
power to guard against mutability and human mortality: "Security from shock
of accident, / Release from fear" (112; 363–64). "Mutability," the Solitary
mournfully proclaims, "is Nature's bane" (116; 458). That desire and fear originate in the death of his wife and, before her, in the loss of their two children.

In this latter detail his story of course echoed Wordsworth's own recent, painful loss in 1812 of his children Catherine and Thomas, and so connects the poet and this more-than alter ego, whose biography resembles his author's in other details. Johnston argues that Wordsworth in fact "goes out of his way to invest himself in the Solitary's character, most bravely by th[is] late mention of the death of [the] children."[36] He indeed invests him with grief.[37]

The Recluse describes mourning his daughter, the first of his children to die, as an Orphic "longing to pursue" her into the shadowy, inaccessible underworld of the grave, where no "living Man" may enter (644). Although the experience would seem to have possessed precisely the required power to bind them together as each other's "remaining stay" (648), that is not what happened. After their son, too, was borne into that other world, the mother's now doubled grief took the form of steely Christian acceptance. "Calm as a frozen Lake when ruthless Winds / Blow fiercely," she protected herself against death with a bulwark of "thankfulness of heart / In Heaven's determinations, ever just" (125; 650–51, 657–58). Standing upon an "eminence" of faith in the justness of all God's judgments, she occupied an emotional citadel her grieving husband was "unable to attain" (659–60). Hence, he laments, "[i]mmense" became the "space that severed us!" (660–61). A perceptual space opened between heaven and earth, eternity and death, faith and the pains of grief. Yet, despite or because of the staid appearance of this "Partner of [his] loss," she soon fell from her eminence of imposed faith

> Into a gulph obscure of silent grief,
> And keen heart-anguish—of itself ashamed,
> Yet obstinately cherishing itself:
> And, so consumed, She melted from my arms;
> And left me, on this earth, disconsolate.
>
> (125–26; 669, 675–79)

Almost dead before her death, like Eurydice she melts into the underworld, leaving her husband inconsolably grieving her loss. Her "silent grief," unspoken and unshared, "consumed" her from within, sparking in her a destructive, fueling feeling of shame at its strength and at her weakness of belief. Each partner tragically became solitary and despondent—despondent because solitary—diseased by a mourning-work that was not shared, exchanged, and thereby eased.

The Solitary's present, typifying yearning for reclusion from attachment is owed not just to these painful feelings of mortal loss but, as in *The Vale of Esthwaite*'s originary dilemma, to grief over his mourning's premature cessation, to his mourning of mourning. "[I] suffer now, not seldom," he laments in recalling his wife's death, "from the thought / That I remember, and can weep no more" (117; 486–87). His ensuing flight from grief generated his turn first to philosophical abstraction, and to the promise of brotherhood and renovation heralded by the Revolution, and then to disappointed reclusion and the (hopeless) wish for a monastic life protected from mutability, loss, and grief. This recluse's idealized "pure Archetype[s] of human greatness" (951) and his envisioned utopian communities are relished to cover over or lend him strength to withstand that old, problematical grief: "to observe, and not to feel; / And, therefore, not to act" (135; 892–93). The resulting aporia between faith-imbued consolation on the one hand and unrelenting grief on the other of course likely reflects the author's own troubles of these years. Faith did not come easily to that would-be believer, either,[38] while grief had become for him, and for his wife especially, nearly intolerable.

It is because of the Solitary's underlying, troubled mourning that he and the three other men have gathered. Indeed, based upon his biography, the three of them have rightly diagnosed his disease; they perceive that his personal struggle over loss, rather than recent political or other disappointments, has produced and now sustains his despondency. Hence, it is appropriately in a churchyard that the Recluse listens to the Pastor in the company of the Poet and Wanderer, contemplating eulogies that describe mourners' experiences of loss. The poem "descend[s]" into the "silent vaults" of the grave (231; 5.668),[39] a core consisting, according to Gill, "not of indigestible metaphysical discourse as is popularly supposed, but of stories."[40] Those stories are recited by the Pastor in the hopes of "correcting" the Solitary's dejection. The Vicar's eulogizing of his parishioners' lives and deaths in turn shifts the poem's focus from the (causal) sufferings of the Solitary, as well as from those of Margaret of the ruined cottage, "to death and a plan of salvation."[41] Although not doctrinally Christian at every turn, the patient endurance of the most virtuous of the eulogized parishioners is credited to their faith, including their faith in the afterlife. The Pastor intends to show, through these selected eulogies, the extent to which, as the Wanderer concludes, "[w]e see . . . as we feel" (226; 5.558). But his stories also demonstrate that we feel as we see. Faith and fortitude buttress individuals against the onslaught of grief, to which they are otherwise painfully exposed. This initial, encapsulating example makes clear this one point: that in April, should you approach the churchyard's graves from the south side rather than from the north, "*Then* will a vernal prospect greet your eye, / All fresh and beautiful, and green and bright, / Hopeful and cheerful:—vanished is the snow" (226; 5.545–48; or, in the 1850 edition, "vanished is the pall / That overspread and chilled the sacred turf"). Even though, as Johnston states, the Parson is arguing for the complementarity of these dual vantages of the grave, the thrust of his Grasmere eulogies demonstrates that what is most necessary for human beings (fated to mourn) is to discern and thereafter to sustain this "hopeful" perspective of death.

Set apart as a group, the Sympson family plots are a conspicuous spot in the precinct of the Pastor's churchyard, prompting the Poet's inquiry, "Whence comes it . . . that yonder we behold / Five graves, and only five, that lie apart, / Unsociable company and sad . . . ?" (311; 7.34–36). The Pastor directs his interlocutor's gaze to a distant "outlet of the vale" and therein to a stand of trees, hiding a parsonage. There, he says, dwelt the "Patriarch of the Vale" (243)—historically identifiable, here as in the *Tuft*, with the Reverend Sympson[42]—to whose house death

> Had never come, through space of forty years;
> Sparing both old and young in that Abode.
> Suddenly then they disappeared:—not twice
> Had summer scorched the fields,—not twice had fallen,
> On those high Peaks, the first autumnal snow,—
> Before the greedy visiting was closed
> And the long-privileged House left empty—swept
> As by a plague. . . .
>
> (321; 245–52)

Except for the patriarch, all of the family were "swept" away by death in the space of two years. As in the similar lines from *Tuft of Primroses* (150–56), despite its acknowledgment of death's horrific power the eulogy resists viewing these events as cause to mourn. Like the Parson's example of the snow-covered graves, despite this sweeping loss all in fact "was gentle death, / One after one, with intervals of peace. / —A happy consummation! an accord / Sweet, perfect,—to be wished for!" (7.253–56). At the same time, the aged sire's survival of his wife, children, and grandchild troubles the eulogy's example of "gentle death," lending it, the Pastor fears, a sound resembling "harshness" (258). He laments, in much the same words as the *Tuft*'s narrator,

> "All gone, all vanished! he deprived and bare,
> "How will he face the remnant of his life?
> "What will become of him?" we said, and mused
> In sad conjectures, "Shall we meet him now
> "Haunting with rod and line the craggy brooks?
> "Or shall we overhear him, as we pass,
> "Striving to entertain the lonely hours
> "With music?"
>
> (322; 263–70)

Sympson's life is mourned as but remains. "Heaven was gracious," however, the eulogizing Pastor intercedes, for but "a little while" was this lone survivor obliged to endure "his inward hoard / Of unsunned griefs, too many and too keen" (278–81). Soon he, too, passed away, released from the "keen" pangs of grief, "overcome by unexpected sleep, / In one blest moment," as if a "shadow" had been "thrown / Softly and lightly from a passing cloud" (323; 282–84). The family "once more / Were gathered to each other" (290–92). The Pastor here envisions death not just as a relief but, more importantly, also as a reunion of the deceased.

Subsequent eulogies, such as that for the young Margaret Greene, similarly exemplify resistance to grief through Christian consolation. "[P]rayer and thought," the Pastor assures, convey even "to worst distress," to the depths of grief, "[d]ue resignation" (341; 688–89). One of the most moving of these churchyard eulogies, the story of Ellen, describes a *traviata* who likewise endured after having been seduced and abandoned. Left "to bewail a sternly-broken vow, / Alone, within her widowed Mother's house" (288; 6.853–54), Ellen bore a bastard child. Her straightened circumstances obliged her to leave the baby in her mother's care and become wet nurse to another child, whose parents cruelly forbid Ellen to visit her daughter. Her baby died, and thereafter this "rueful Magdalene" was frequently seen weeping beside the grave, mourning the child's death and "Her own transgression; Penitent sincere / As ever raised to Heaven a streaming eye" (294–95; 987, 990–91). Returned to her mother's house, she continued to suffer in her grief (as another guilty mourner) but nevertheless "stilled" all "words of pity" from others "with a prompt reproof" (297; 1044–45). To them she proclaimed her Christian faith that

> "He who afflicts me knows what I can bear;
> "And, when I fail, and can endure no more,
> "Will mercifully take me to himself."
> So, through the cloud of death, her Spirit passed
> Into that pure and unknown world of love,
> Where injury cannot come:—and here is laid
> The mortal Body by her Infant's side.
>
> (1046–52)

Like many of the other eulogies for the men and women of the Parson's parish, Ellen's story is one of mortal loss and patient endurance through faith. As faith in God softens her grief over her dead child, so the Pastor's faith eases his eulogistic mourning of Ellen. Her certain journey into heaven's "pure and unknown world of love, / Where injury cannot come," rights all wrongs and provides a peace not ever attained in life. There is still a tragedy to be recorded, of course, one of betrayal, uncompassionate actions, and suffering. But mourning for Ellen's loss is lessened or quelled by faith. Similarly, even notoriously, in the circa-1845, drastic revision of Book First, Wordsworth, responding in part to nagging criticisms of *The Excursion*'s heterodoxy but also following Ellen's own lead, depicts Margaret of the ruined cottage as one

> Who, in her worst distress, had ofttimes felt
> The unbounded might of prayer; and learned, with soul
> Fixed on the Cross, that consolation springs,
> From sources deeper far than deepest pain,
> For the meek Sufferer.

> (*PW* 5: 1.935–39)

Since Margaret grieves less and dies with the hope of salvation, so, it would seem, her latter-day mourners should grieve less, too. More than with his doctrine of the One Life, the Wanderer seems to negate the very basis for grief and hence also for the text's community of mourning. Wordsworth's effort to "controul" the self's exposure to grief was, in this respect, lifelong, as was his new reliance upon faith and prayer as the chief means of finding and sustaining consolation.

As the Wanderer observes at the end of the second of the churchyard books, in eulogizing these dead the Pastor has shown the value of "Tending to patience when Affliction strikes; / To hope and love; to confident repose / In God; and reverence for the dust of Man" (357; 7.1152–54). Removing any remaining doubt as to his own status as a preacher (one of three gathered here, the Solitary being himself a former parson), the Wanderer had previously asserted that, "[f]or the calamities of mortal life" there is but "[o]ne adequate support":

> an assured belief
> That the procession of our fate, howe'er
> Sad or disturbed, is ordered by a Being
> Of infinite benevolence and power,
> Whose everlasting purposes embrace
> All accidents, converting them to Good.
> —The darts of anguish *fix* not where the seat
> Of suffering hath been thoroughly fortified
> By acquiescence in the Will Supreme
> For Time and for Eternity; by faith,
> Faith absolute in God, including hope,
> And the defence that lies in boundless love
> Of his perfections. . . .

> (142; 4.10–24)

"Support," "defence," "fortified"—these words signify the desire of such faith: protection from grief for the "happy few" whose belief "quell[s]" doubt and enfranchises them from their lives' "mortal chains" (151; 230, 233–34). For Nicola Trott, the poem's eulogistic visions indeed all "figure an overriding wish to subdue mortality," with the "experience of death" being "most literally at the centre of the poem in th[es]e Books given to the Pastor and churchyard."[43]

That Grasmere churchyard is the center of a community of "the living and the dead," like those idealized in the three contemporary *Essays upon Epitaphs,* the first of which Wordsworth appended to *The Excursion.* It is this focus or reliance upon death that led Hartman to lament the poem's decline "into a massive communion with the dead," one of "noble raptures spoken above their graves" (*WP* 296). For him, the Wanderer's and Pastor's eulogies suggested that only the creative—I would say the *religious*—mind could answer the "more comprehensive question of how a man can face death or mutability and remain uninjured" (299). Such reconciliation with mortality is the aim of the Pastor's discourse, as it is, at least in part, of *The Excursion.* As Johnston states, the Vicar "must insist that there are no Christian tragedies, strictly speaking, only positive or negative illustrations of faith."[44] That is his function as the representative of the Church, protecting man, David Haney argues, "from the 'deserts infinite,' in which his affections would otherwise be swallowed."[45] Rather than it being the dead that organize community, by the end of these later books of *The Excursion,* it increasingly becomes community, emblematized less by the churchyard than by the Parsonage, that organizes and controls the relationship of these living and dead. The Pastor is, Lorna Clymer holds, "the sanctioned spokesperson who moderates how the living and the dead communicate with one another."[46]

This community becomes, in a manner not fully evinced even in *Poems* or the *Essays,* an institutional product, a result of "the establishment and observance of social customs . . . based in an awareness of immortality in the midst of life."[47] How to feel but not grieve? The answer is resistance owed to faith, a faith that would, if accepted by the Solitary, quell not just his grief but the core of the poem's social structure, which takes its start, after all, from troubled mourning for the dead. That the Solitary remains unpersuaded, and hence despondent, thus certainly prolongs not just the excursion but also its temporary community of mourner and nonmourners. It may be for this reason that the poem tends, as Bushell finds, to undermine its own assertions and progress, "undercutting itself, and questioning its own poetic authority."[48] Grief is cast within a dialogical framework, inherited from *The Ruined Cottage,* in which correction is steadfastly resisted and not infrequently undermined. At the same time, grief is no longer *common,* which is to say it is no longer shared. However much mourning may structure the poem's excursion, it does so despite the concerted efforts of the Solitary's three companions. In this sense, their excursion has traveled far indeed from the mournful terrain of *The Ruined Cottage* and of Book First itself (1814), where grief erupted and was then exchanged, shared, and sustained. The work of mourning is now more in line with what Freud will hold to be mourning's principal aim: the *end* of mourning. The poem thereby seeks, and in fact is predicated upon seeking, to end the raison d'être of its own dialogism, the prior, mournful *durance* by which the excursive quest was "bound to establish" community, over and over.

The characters' closing, symbolic excursion away from the churchyard to the Parsonage, and from that displacing center into Grasmere's surrounding landscape, implies that dialogical indeterminacy by no means keeps matters, nor draws the parameters of community, squarely in the churchyard. As Laura Dabundo states, *The Excursion* here "begins to look beyond the individual toward the community and to reflect upon personal responsibility toward one's community—one's duty and obligation socially—and to reflect upon what effect duty might have upon individual identity."[49] It is a change in direction discernible as well in the renunciatory "Ode to Duty." The Pastor's eulogies are in this sense, Dabundo argues, religious ballads "that *surpass* the individual self for the sake of [a] cross-grave community" able to "withstand . . . the inevitable, irresistible slipping from one of the nurturing, bonding 'significant' others in the horrid retreat toward solitude, toward life-in-death, toward death." The Wanderer, Pastor, and Poet "seek to devise a *new kind* of community" built upon "the grave of the old."[50] The Parson's eulogies repeatedly raise the problem of how to grieve when mourning haunts the solitary self, for correction threatens to renew or convey despondency. Simple reclusion, however fortified, is not enough. The Pastor's and others' corrections of grief thus are attempts not to promote monastic withdrawal or even stoic resignation so much as to invoke and produce a kind of self-cancelling.

Wordsworth had previously wrestled with the problem of individuality, notably in *Adventures on Salisbury Plain,* in which the dead spoke *through* the living and subjectivity was a form of subjection to specters. In the churchyard books of *The Excursion,* the grieving solitary self is to be similarly subsumed or transcended, not by the dead but by cultural tradition and institutionalism: by the consecrated ground of the churchyard mediated by the Parsonage. The perceptual chasm between grief and consolation, or between acknowledgment of suffering and its transcendence, is to be bridged by an envisioned corporate subject whose sole duty is to endure (to "stand and wait," in Milton's parlance), to see the self as part of a larger whole in which all griefs are reconciled and all wrongs are righted, if not in this world then in the next. The poem's trajectory is toward that formation of selfhood associated with the Victorian period: a self socially constituted and determined, set in contrast to the subjectivity of idealized Romantic individualism. Recall that a decade previous the Ode decried such social determination as decline, even as death.

Matters appear considerably changed by 1814 and thereafter. Hence, for Nancy Easterlin, Wordsworth's *Ecclesiastical Sonnets* (1822) reveal the author's "recognition that stable belief rests not simply on self-renunciation, but on the renunciation of individualism per se."[51] The latter was the predominant if qualified (because haunted and intersubjective) formation of selfhood required for Wordsworth's earlier communities of "the living and the dead," where private, tenacious grief, shared but never surrendered, instituted the drive toward being together. *The Excursion*'s eulogies signify the surrender of this form of self to tradition. As the Solitary perceives, the way not to grieve is not to *be*, or at least to be otherwise than as an isolated self whose basis for relationship is founded upon persisting, immanent grief.

Wordsworth later recalled that for *The Excursion*'s promised but never composed sequel his one "wish" had been that the Solitary should, with the Wanderer, have later witnessed in the mountains or fields of Scotland "some religious ceremony . . . which might have dissolved his heart into tenderness, and so done more towards restoring the Christian faith . . . than all that the 'Wanderer' and 'Pastor' by their several effusions and addresses had been enabled to effect. . . . But alas!" (*FN* 91). If it is to be trusted, Wordsworth's recollection reasserts the importance of faith to the Solitary's restoration and of the dissolution of the self's resistance to correction. But it also suggests the difficulty—the tentativeness and uncertainty—with which he viewed this task, even from his later, more traditionalist and Christian perspective.[52]

At the lakeside site of *The Excursion*'s conclusion, the group, now including the Pastor's wife and children, is described as "a broken Company" (407; 9.435). The adjective seems fitting (more than its author may have guessed), potentially recalling Dorothy's reference to the unbreakable "chain" that bound together the orphaned Wordsworth siblings, the "broken pane" and unshared grief of "Incipient Madness," and the "broken" pitcher of Ecclesiastes, alluded to in *An Evening Walk* and in *The Ruined Cottage*'s lament for the "broken" "bond of brotherhood." Against mourning the dead *The Excursion*'s broken conclusion sets a corporate subject instituted not just by the Church but also by empire and nation—by the dissemination of a supervening British subject. And yet even this project, which so anticipates the century's later character, is lampooned by the poem's decidedly broken progress at this point. The "Company" rows out to a small island, implicitly if unintentionally mimicking the Wanderer's previously espoused imperialist vision of modern Britons embarking over seas to new lands, "[b]ound to establish new communities" (404; 379).[53] For this company seems, on the surface of its own social seas, "bound to establish" little or nothing. At the same time, a key strength of the poem is precisely this inconclusive end. For here the company floats, suspended above the waters of the lake, not so far in space or time, or even in sociology, from that other company sounding the depths of Esthwaite Water for the unburied dead.

In this later, "broken" company's suspension looms the force that perpetuates this excursion and the micro-community excursively bent on its undoing. In this light, one is not so far from the détente that structured community in *The Ruined Cottage,* and hence not so far either from *The Excursion's* own haunted textual beginnings. *The Excursion* arrestingly depicts, and in its inconclusive end arguably preserves, one of Wordsworth's final communities of mourning, a community dependent upon troubled grief and its discursive and excursive, albeit now also increasingly renunciatory, supplementations. Wordsworth hardly endeavored to eliminate grief and mourning from his poem or to stage its dramatic dialogues far from the dead. He uncannily returned once more to the old churchyard ground of community. From this vantage the poet very nearly concludes *The Excursion* of 1814 where his poetic and sociological journey began.

But *The Excursion* does bear a more armored aspect, tempered to resist the recurrence and perpetual insistence of mortal grief, and so also designed to protect the self from the haunting power of a community of "the living and the dead." *The Excursion* is, in this sense, a culminating work. In the years that follow, Wordsworth writes much less of grief and death, excepting in his steely *Sonnets upon the Punishment of Death,* and much more on the State, the Church, and other less troubling topics and concerns. But that he does so may signal not the final transformation of his sociology or his personal victory over past death and grief. It may instead testify to his continuing, Orphean difficulty in representing community without again unburying the dead and their bonds of mourning.

NOTES

PREFACE

1. *New York Times,* 7 Sept. 1997, internatl. ed.: 1.

2. *Times* (London), 8 Sept. 1997: 8.

3. See Anthony Elliott's cultural study of *The Mourning of John Lennon* (Berkeley: University of California Press, 1999).

4. Stephen C. Behrendt, *Royal Mourning and Regency Culture: Elegies and Memorials of Princess Charlotte* (New York: St. Martin's Press, 1997), 213.

5. Esther Schor, *Bearing the Dead: The British Culture of Mourning from the Enlightenment to Victoria* (Princeton: Princeton University Press, 1994), 209.

6. Cf. Benedict Anderson's discussion of the relationship between newspaper print culture and British community, *Imagined Communities: Reflections on the Origin and Spread of Nationalism* (New York: Verso Press, 1991).

INTRODUCTION

1. A rejected revision of this episode, recorded in MS. W (DC MS. 38), more clearly credits the boy's report of the abandoned clothing as prompting the search for the swimmer: "Soon as I reached home / I to [our] little household of this sight / Made casual mention. The succeeding day . . ." (*13P* 2: 280).

2. My reading of the Drowned Man, here and in subsequent pages, is particularly informed by Peter J. Manning, "Reading Wordsworth's Revisions: Othello and the Drowned Man," *Studies in Romanticism* 22 (1983): 3–28, reprinted in *Reading Romantics: Texts and Contexts* (New York: Oxford University Press, 1990), 87–114; Susan J. Wolfson, "Revision as Form: Wordsworth's Drowned Man" (1984), in *Formal Charges: The Shaping of Poetry in British Romanticism* (Stanford: Stanford University Press, 1997), 100–132; Cynthia Chase, *Decomposing Figures: Rhetorical Readings in the Romantic Tradition* (Baltimore: Johns Hopkins University Press, 1986), 13–31; Andrzej Warminski, "Facing Language: Wordsworth's First Poetic Spirits," *Romantic*

Revolutions, ed. Kenneth R. Johnston et al. (Bloomington: Indiana University Press, 1990), 26–49; and David P. Haney, *William Wordsworth and the Hermeneutics of Incarnation* (University Park: The Pennsylvania State University Press, 1993), 83–85.

3. In *Poetry as Epitaph: Representation and Poetic Language* (Baton Rouge: Louisiana State University Press, 1990), Karen Mills-Court queries this prevalence of death in *The Prelude*: "Why the many encounters with death . . . ?" she asks. "What precisely *is* revealed?" (180).

4. David Ferry, *The Limits of Mortality: An Essay on Wordsworth's Major Poems* (Middletown: Wesleyan University Press, 1959).

5. For psychologically and biographically oriented interpretations of death in Wordsworth, see especially F. W. Bateson, *Wordsworth: A Re-interpretation* (New York: Longmans, 1956); Geoffrey Hartman, *Wordsworth's Poetry* (*WP*); Duncan Wu, "Wordsworth's Poetry of Grief," *The Wordsworth Circle* 21 (1990): 114–17, and (published as this study goes to press) *Wordsworth: An Inner Life* (Oxford, UK and Malden, Mass.: Blackwell, 2002); and the Freudian readings of Thomas Weiskel's *The Romantic Sublime: Studies in the Structure and Psychology of Transcendence* (Baltimore: Johns Hopkins University Press, 1976, rpt. 1986), David Ellis's *Wordsworth, Freud, and the Spots of Time: Interpretation in "The Prelude"* (Cambridge: Cambridge University Press, 1985), and Alan Richardson's "Wordsworth at the Crossroads: 'Spots of Time' in the 'Two-Part Prelude,'" *The Wordsworth Circle* 19 (1998): 15–20.

6. There are numerous considerations of death and genre in Wordsworth, as well as of the poet's treatment of death and language and of the connection between mourning and culture. In the first category, see Joshua Scodel, *The English Epitaph: Commemoration and Conflict from Jonson to Wordsworth* (Ithaca: Cornell University Press, 1991); Abbie Findlay Potts, *The Elegiac Mode: Poetic Form in Wordsworth and Other Elegists* (Ithaca: Cornell University Press, 1967); John W. Draper, *The Funeral Elegy and the Rise of English Romanticism* (New York: Phaeton Press, 1967); Peter Sacks, *The English Elegy: Studies in the Genre from Spenser to Yeats* (Baltimore: Johns Hopkins University Press, 1985); and Paul H. Fry, *The Poet's Calling in the English Ode* (New Haven: Yale University Press, 1980). Of those studies on death and language in Wordsworth not already cited, I would single out, for their influence on my work here, Frances Ferguson, *Language as Counter-Spirit* (New Haven: Yale University Press, 1977); Paul de Man, "The Rhetoric of Temporality," in *Blindness and Insight: Essays in the Rhetoric of Contemporary Criticism* (Minneapolis: University of Minnesota Press, rev. 1983), 187–228; and "Autobiography as De-Facement," in *The Rhetoric of Romanticism* (New York: Columbia University Press, 1984), 67–92; and J. Hillis Miller, *The Linguistic Moment: From Wordsworth to Stevens* (Princeton: Princeton University Press, 1985), 59–113. On the connection between Wordsworthian mourning and British culture, see especially Guinn Batten's *The Orphaned Imagination: Melancholy and Commodity Culture in English Romanticism* (Durham: Duke University Press, 1998) and Esther Schor's aforementioned *Bearing the Dead.*

7. Philippe Ariès, *The Hour of Our Death,* trans. Helen Weaver (New York: Vintage, 1982). See also Jacques Choron, *Death and Western Thought* (New York: Macmillan, 1963); Geoffrey Gorer, *Death, Grief, and Mourning* (Garden City: Doubleday

Books, 1965); Ernest Becker, *The Denial of Death* (New York: Free Press, 1973); and Garrett Stewart, *Death Sentences: Styles of Dying in British Fiction* (Cambridge: Harvard University Press, 1984).

8. Jean-Luc Nancy, *The Inoperative Community,* trans. Peter Connor et al. (Minneapolis: University of Minnesota Press, 1991). Nancy's argument responds to Maurice Blanchot's *The Unavowable Community,* trans. Pierre Joris (New York: Station Hill, 1988). See also Jacques Derrida's meditation on friendship and mourning, *Mémoirs: for Paul de Man,* trans. Cecile Lindsay, Jonathan Culler, et al. (New York: Columbia University Press, 1989).

9. Schor, *Bearing the Dead,* esp. 3–12, 117–25; William A. Ulmer, "The Society of Death in *Home at Grasmere," Philological Quarterly* 75 (1996): 67–83; Lorna Clymer, "Graved in Tropes: The Figural Logic of Epitaphs and Elegies in Blair, Gray, Cowper, and Wordsworth," *ELH* 62 (1995): 347–86; Michele Turner Sharp, "The Churchyard Among the Wordsworthian Mountains: Mapping the Common Ground of Death and the Reconfiguration of Romantic Community," *ELH* 62 (1995): 387–407; and my "Community and Mourning in William Wordsworth's *The Ruined Cottage,* 1797–1798," *Studies in Philology* 92 (1995): 329–45, revised and included in Chapter Four.

10. In terms of Romantic-era community per se, see especially Regina Hewitt, *The Possibilities of Society: Wordsworth, Coleridge, and the Sociological Viewpoint of English Romanticism* (Albany: State University of New York Press, 1997). See also Kenneth Eisold, *Loneliness and Communion: A Study of Wordsworth's Thought and Experience,* Salzburg Studies in English Literature: *Romantic Reassessment* 13 (Salzburg: University of Salzburg Press, 1973); Thomas McFarland, *Romanticism and the Forms of Ruin: Wordsworth, Coleridge, and the Modalities of Fragmentation* (Princeton: Princeton University Press, 1981); John Rieder, *Wordsworth's Counterrevolutionary Turn: Community, Virtue, and Vision in the 1790s* (Newark: University of Delaware Press, 1997); and Nader Saiedi, *The Birth of Social Theory: Social Thought in the Enlightenment and Romanticism* (Lanham: University Press of America, 1993).

11. McFarland, 138. Orville Dewey reported Wordsworth to have stated that he gave "twelve hours' thought to the conditions and prospects of society, for one to poetry" (cited Kenneth R. Johnston, *Wordsworth and "The Recluse"* [New Haven: Yale University Press, 1984], 100–1).

12. This detail first appears in MS. A of *The Prelude,* ca. 1805 (*13P* 2: 625). Wordsworth then incorporates it in the "C-stage" version of the poem (1818–20). The "anxious crowd" is retained, sans friends and neighbors, in the fourteen-book *Prelude* (*14P* 5.446). Other MS. A revisions refer to this "crowd" as a "Company assembled on the spot," and add that some people stood "[i]n anxious expectation on the shore" while others searched (*13P* 2: 625), the overall implication being that "company" is inclusive.

13. In *Romantic Voices: Identity and Ideology in British Poetry, 1789–1850* (Athens: University of Georgia Press, 1991), Paul Michael Privateer argues that Orpheus is "the archetype of the poet as *liberator* and *creator*" and that his sacrificial death is "a source of human communion" (117). Privateer focuses on the Orpheus of Ovid's *Metamor-*

phoses, and so finds in his readings of Wordsworth a rather different mythic figure than that depicted in Wordsworth's translation of the Orpheus passages from Virgil's *Georgics,* which Privateer does not consider.

14. Sharp, "The Churchyard Among the Wordsworthian Mountains," 391–92.

15. McFarland, 171.

16. I borrow the term "communitarian" (<Fr. *communautaire*) from Nancy, who enlists it as an alternative to the more familiar, religiously charged, immanence-riddled adjective "communal."

17. Thomas Paine, *The Rights of Man,* introd. Eric Foner, notes by Henry Collins (New York: Penguin, 1984), 163.

18. Eisold, *Loneliness and Communion,* 158.

19. My thinking here is informed by a number of discussions of Romantic social formation and its relation to the topoi of feeling, landscape, and region: James Averill, *Wordsworth and the Poetry of Human Suffering* (*PHS*); Colin Campbell, *The Romantic Ethic and the Spirit of Consumerism* (see n70, below); Jerome McGann, *The Poetics of Sensibility: A Revolution in Literary Style* (Oxford: Clarendon Press, 1996); Victoria Myers, "Sentiment and the Pantisocratic Community: Coleridge's Letters to Southey," *The Wordsworth Circle* 29 (1998): 75–79; Elinor Shaffer, "Myths of Community in the *Lyrical Ballads* 1798–1998: The Commonwealth and the Constitution," in *Samuel Taylor Coleridge and the Sciences of Life,* ed. Nicholas Roe (New York: Oxford University Press, 2001), 25–46; Toby R. Benis, *Romanticism on the Road: The Marginal Gains of Wordsworth's Homeless* (New York: St. Martin's Press, 2000); Jonathan Bate, *Romantic Ecology: Wordsworth and the Environmental Tradition* (London: Routledge, 1991); Tim Fulford, *Landscape, Liberty and Authority: Poetry, Criticism and Politics from Thomson to Wordsworth* (Cambridge: Cambridge University Press, 1996); and Raymond Williams, *The Country and the City* (New York: Oxford University Press, 1973), esp. 62–133.

20. That Wordsworth situates these communities in rural, largely pre-industrial landscapes is hardly surprising. He was raised in them and was, during the time of most of his early and later writings, living in them. They were, moreover, places he wished to preserve.

21. As will become clear in the chapters that follow, my understanding of mourning is indebted to Freud's essay "Mourning and Melancholia" (*SE* 14: 243–58) and to Walter Benjamin's "Allegory and Trauerspiel," from *The Origin of German Tragic Drama,* trans. John Osborne (New York: New Left Books, 1977), 159–235. It also owes much to Nicolas Abraham, "Notes on the Phantom: A Complement to Freud's Metapsychology," trans. Nicholas Rand, in *The Trial(s) of Psychoanalysis,* ed. Françoise Meltzer (Chicago: University of Chicago Press, 1987), 75–80; Nicolas Abraham and Maria Torok, "Introjection-Incorporation: *Mourning* or *Melancholia,*" trans. Nicholas Rand, in *Psychoanalysis in France,* ed. Serge Lebovici and Daniel Widlöcher (New York: International Universities Press, 1980), 3–16; Derrida, *Fors,* trans. Barbara Johnson, *Georgia Review* 31 (1977): 64–116; and Joel Fineman, "The Structure of Allegorical Desire," in *Allegory and Representation,* ed. Stephen J. Greenblatt (Baltimore: Johns Hopkins University Press, 1981), 26–60.

22. Derrida, *Mémoirs,* 38.

23. Paine, *Common Sense* 1; cited Godwin, *Enquiry Concerning Political Justice,* ed. K. Codell Carter (London: Oxford University Press, 1971), 69.

24. Ferdinand Tönnies, *Community and Society* (1887), trans. Charles P. Loomis (New York: Harper and Row, 1963), 33. See also Eisold, 160–62; and Hewitt, 61–66.

25. Nancy, 9, 11; original emphasis.

26. Cf. Nancy, xxxvii; Alan Bewell, *Wordswoth and the Enlightenment* (*WE*) 188, 195–96; and Alan Liu, *Wordsworth: The Sense of History* (Stanford: Stanford University Press, 1989), 38–42.

27. Nancy, xxxviii.

28. Marc Redfield, "Imagi-Nation: The Imagined Community and the Aesthetics of Mourning," *Diacritics* 29 (1999): 58–83; 59. Following upon the work of Benedict Anderson, Redfield argues that the nationally memorialized missing or unidentified corpse "marks . . . the absoluteness of an irrecuperable loss" and hence also "the resistance of anonymity to abstraction or formalization." Yet the nation is nonetheless consolidated by this corpse it cannot really bury or mourn, for the latter's memorialization translates singular loss "into the general loss suffered by the nation," restoring the anonymity of subjectivity (68–69). Redfield reads both imagination and nation as "fictions possessed of great referential force and chronic referential instability—fictions of an impossible, ineradicable mourning" (60). On this topic of nationalism, in addition to the studies cited below, see David Aram Kaiser's *Romanticism, Aesthetics, and Nationalism* (Cambridge: Cambridge University Press, 1999). My thinking in this paragraph is particularly indebted to Redfield's analysis, as it is to the work of Nancy.

29. Ian Buruma and Avishai Margalit, "Occidentalism," *New York Review* 49 (Jan. 17, 2002): 4–7; 6.

30. Nancy, 12, 14.

31. Nancy, 27. This social formation, Nancy avers, is "not a limited community as opposed to an infinite or absolute community, but a community *of* finitude, because finitude 'is' communitarian, and because finitude alone is communitarian."

32. Lakeland village society retained, according to Wordsworth, "till within the last sixty years" much of its medieval, feudalistic character, with here and there signs of beneficial republicanism (*GL* 59, 67).

33. Edmund Burke, *Reflections on the Revolution in France,* ed. Conor Cruise O'Brien (New York: Penguin, 1984), 119; cf. 117–20. In *The Rise of English Nationalism: A Cultural History, 1740–1830* (New York: St. Martin's Press, 1987) Gerald Newman unsettles the common argument about Wordsworth's indebtedness to Burke, arguing that Burke had "continually borrowed his . . . ideas from the English radical writings of the pre-1789 period" (228). For appraisals of Burke's influence on Wordsworth's views about society, see Schor, 76–88, 151–95; and James Chandler, *Wordsworth's Second Nature: A Study of the Poetry and Politics* (Chicago: University of Chicago Press, 1984), 36–43. Future assessments of Wordsworth's early debt to Burke

would benefit from a closer reading of the juvenilia, particularly *The Vale of Esthwaite,* composed before Burke's *Reflections*—and before the Revolution itself.

34. Adam Smith, *The Theory of Moral Sentiments,* ed. Dugald Stewart (London: Henry G. Bohn, 1853), 9. Cf. Schor, 5, 77. For Schor, Smith's use of economic metaphors implies that this "tribute" "paid" the dead, *in perpetuum,* is not freely given but is rather an "'indebted' consideration for the moral value with which the dead endow the living." Smith's metaphors do suggest an economy of mourning—a "diffusion of sympathy from the grave outward" (Schor, 5)—but to my mind they do not necessarily suggest mourning per se to be socially constitutive.

35. See, for example, Emma Rothschild, *Economic Sentiments: Adam Smith, Condorcet, and the Enlightenment* (Cambridge: Harvard University Press, 2001).

36. Johnston, "The Romantic Idea-Elegy: The Nature of Politics and the Politics of Nature," *South Central Review* 9 (1992): 24–43; 30–31.

37. Joshua Scodel argues that Wordsworth's successors valued him "not as the defender of a traditional 'community of the living and the dead' but as the individual, lyric interpreter of the relationship between the living and the dead, the past and the present" (*The English Epitaph,* 404).

38. Michael H. Friedman's Freudian *The Making of a Tory Humanist: William Wordsworth and the Idea of Community* (New York: Columbia University Press, 1979) provides one of the few extended analyses of the effects on Wordsworth of his mother's death (128–30).

39. On John Wordsworth's death and especially on his activities as Lowther's "political business agent," see Johnston, *HW* 93–94, 22–23.

40. Wu, "Wordsworth's Poetry of Grief," 115.

41. Wu, 115. See also Jonathan Wordsworth, "Two Dark Interpreters: Wordsworth and De Quincey," *The Age of William Wordsworth: Critical Essays on the Romantic Tradition,* ed. Kenneth R. Johnston and Gene W. Ruoff (New Brunswick: Rutgers University Press, 1987), 214–38, esp. 222–23.

42. In *Wordsworth's Anti-Climax* (Cambridge: Harvard University Press, 1935), Willard Sperry long ago speculated that Wordsworth's "orphaned childhood, [and] the homeless lot of his early years . . . may have planted in his mind the germ of the idea of human desolateness" (96). More recently, Scodel argues that Wordsworth sought in his writings "to recapture, for both himself and his readers, the traditional bond between the living and the dead" (386).

43. Salman Rushdie, "My Unfunny Valentine," *New Yorker,* 15 Feb. 1999: 29.

44. Stephen Greenblatt, gen. ed., *The Norton Shakespeare* (New York: Norton, 1997), 46. Greenblatt refers of course to another bard, not to Wordsworth.

45. George Wilbur Meyer, *Wordsworth's Formative Years* (Ann Arbor: University of Michigan Press, 1943), 9. See also Johnston, *HW* 94, 105.

46. See the thirteen-book *Prelude* 5.223–25, 247–48.

47. R. W. Harris, *Romanticism and the Social Order, 1780–1830* (New York: Barnes and Noble, 1969), 9.

48. Harris, 126.

49. See Arthur O. Lovejoy, *The Great Chain of Being: A Study of the History of an Idea* (Cambridge: Harvard University Press, 1936, 1964), 144–314.

50. Harris, 9–10.

51. Newman, 50.

52. My thinking here is influenced by Robert Darnton's essay "A Euro State of Mind," *New York Review* 49 (Feb. 28, 2002): 30–32; 31.

53. A. D. Harvey, *English Poetry in a Changing Society, 1780–1825* (New York: St. Martin's Press, 1980), 39.

54. A. S. Byatt, *Unruly Times: Wordsworth and Coleridge in Their Time* (London: Hogarth Press, 1989), 134.

55. Anderson, *Imagined Communities: Reflections on the Origin and Spread of Nationalism,* 11, 36. Among Coleridge's early assessments of Wordsworth was that, in addition to being "the best poet of the age," he was "a Republican & at least a *Semi-*atheist" (STC to John Thelwall, 13 May 1796 [*CLSTC* 1: 215–16]).

56. Greenblatt, *Hamlet in Purgatory* (Princeton: Princeton University Press, 2001), 256.

57. Greenblatt, 19, 102.

58. C. John Sommerville, *The Secularization of Early Modern England: From Religious Culture to Religious Faith* (New York: Oxford University Press, 1992), 26; cf. 25.

59. McFarland, *Romantic Cruxes: The English Essayists and the Spirit of the Age* (Oxford: Clarendon Press, 1987), 20.

60. McFarland, *Romanticism and the Forms of Ruin,* 189.

61. Concerning George III's "unhappy malady," see the *New Annual Register* (1788): 251.

62. Richard J. Onorato's *The Character of the Poet: Wordsworth in "The Prelude"* (Princeton: Princeton University Press, 1971) provides a Freudian reading of the creative neurosis and drive for "insistent utterance" produced in Wordsworth by the traumas of his mother's and father's deaths (65; cf. 60–66).

63. Leslie Brisman, *Milton's Poetry of Choice and its Romantic Heirs* (Ithaca: Cornell University Press, 1973), 264. Cf. Lionel Morton, "Books and Drowned Men: Unconscious Mourning in Book V of *The Prelude,*" *English Studies in Canada* 8 (1982): 23–37; 24.

64. Johnson's *Dictionary* (1755) (London: *Times,* 1983) defines the words "ghastly" and "ghostly" as synonyms—as apparently did Wordsworth, who in his later revisions of the episode of the discharged soldier substituted the latter term for the former (*14P* 4.434). For Wordsworth's literary predecessors and contemporaries the term "ghastly" similarly conveyed associations of ghosts, carnage, terror, and death.

65. In *Wordsworth's Revisionary Aesthetics* (Cambridge: Cambridge University Press, 1988), Theresa Kelley states that the drowned man's "return to the surface of a lake literalizes a more troubling return of sublime figures to the surface of the speaker's discourse," as one half of an antithesis "of the sublime and the beautiful" (93). See Jonathan Wordsworth's editorial notes, *NCP* 6. According to Wu, by 1790 Wordsworth had read Burke's *A Philosophical Enquiry into the Origin of the Sublime and Beautiful* (*WR* 21), although he could also have learned the gist of Burke's ideas from Akenside's *Pleasures of Imagination* or from William Gilpin's essays on the picturesque.

66. Hoxie Neal Fairchild argues that Wordsworth "derived his most characteristic philosophical and religious ideas largely, though of course not entirely, from poetry . . . of the eighteenth century" (*Religious Trends in English Poetry*, 6 vols. [New York: Columbia University Press, 1939–], 3: 185).

67. Christopher Wordsworth, *Memoirs of William Wordsworth*, 2 vols. (London: Edward Moxon, 1851), 1: 34.

68. See T. W. Thompson, *Wordsworth's Hawkshead*, ed. Robert Woof (London: Oxford University Press, 1970), 344.

69. Schor, 69.

70. Averill finds in the poem evidence of its author's prior reading of "a literature fascinated by emotional response" (*PHS* 34), revealing not only his understanding of the genre's conventions and moral platitudes but also his interest in "the psychology of tragic response" (37). Cf. Colin Campbell's *The Romantic Ethic and the Spirit of Consumerism* (Oxford: Blackwell Press, 1987), which sees the Calvinist concern for "displaying sadness, melancholy and self-pity" as having been transformed into a secular cult of feeling, "linked to an expressed sympathy for the plight of all the wretched and miserable," believed to be beneficial for the soul (135).

71. John Locke, *An Essay Concerning Human Understanding*, ed. Alexander Campbell Fraser (Oxford: Clarendon Press, 1959), 532. Wu lists the 1690 rather than 1701 edition of Locke's *Essay* as the one Wordsworth read in the spring or summer of 1787 (*WR* 88). That Wordsworth might have had access to the fourth edition, in the library at Hawkshead or in the home library of a friend or teacher, is certainly possible.

72. Locke, 532. I owe this citation to Haverkamp (see below).

73. Anselm Haverkamp, *Leaves of Mourning: Holderlin's Late Work—With an Essay on Keats and Melancholy*, trans. Vernon Chadwick (Albany: State University of New York Press, 1996), 106.

74. Martin Greenberg, *The Hamlet Vocation of Coleridge and Wordsworth* (Iowa City: University of Iowa Press, 1986), 168; original emphasis.

75. *Prose Works of William Wordsworth*, ed. Grosart (London, 1876), 3: 460; cited Greenberg, 147. For Coleridge, Hamlet emblematized "the prevalence of the abstracting and generalizing habit over the practical," a form of self-division with which he himself identified (*Table Talk, CWSTC* 14, in 2 vols., ed. Carl Woodring, I.76, 77n. 22; also cited Greenberg, 3).

76. Morton, "Books and Drowned Men," 36.

77. References to Shakespeare's plays refer to the previously cited *Norton Shakespeare*.

78. Greenblatt, *Hamlet in Purgatory*, 256.

79. Ariès, *The Hour of Our Death*, 609.

80. Scodel, 313.

81. *The History of Little Goody Two-Shoes; Otherwise called, Mrs. Margery Two-Shoes* (1765; London: John Newberry, 1881), 140; cited Scodel, 345.

82. Scodel, 345.

83. Schor, 20.

84. Schor cites Linda Colley's observation that the British economy was more dependent upon credit than was its neighbors, and that such an economic system requires "confidence that interest payments will be made at the correct level and at the correct time, and confidence that debts will ultimately be repaid" (*Britons: Forging the Nation 1707–1837* [New Haven: Yale University Press, 1992], 66–67. Cf. *The Critical Review* 62 (1786): 43.

85. Schor, 20.

86. John Milton, *Complete Poems and Major Prose*, ed. Merritt Y. Hughes (Indianapolis: Odyssey Press, 1957), 4.52; hereafter cited in text by book and line number. One finds a similar instance of the pains of eternal gratitude qua debt at the end of Fielding's *Joseph Andrews*.

87. Schor, 134; original emphasis.

88. Batten, *The Orphaned Imagination*, 19; original emphasis.

89. Derrida, *Mémoirs*, 29. In "By Force of Mourning," Derrida observes that "whoever . . . works at the work of mourning learns the impossible . . . that mourning is interminable." Mourners work at mourning "as both their object and their resource" (trans. Pascale-Anne Brault and Michael Nass, *Critical Inquiry* 22 [1996]: 171–92; 172).

90. Cf. Shelley's Plato-inspired essay "On Life." For Shelley it is not mourning that institutes a social bond but one's sense of lacking "the ideal prototype of every excellent or lovely thing that we are capable of conceiving as belonging to the nature of man" (*Shelley's Poetry and Prose*, ed. Donald H. Reiman and Sharon B. Powers [New York: Norton, 1977], 474). Regarding the Victorian era's "triumphant" end of the search for community, particularly as a nationalist project, see Newman, 227–28.

91. Onorato, 411.

CHAPTER ONE

1. Judith Butler, *Subjects of Desire: Hegelian Reflections in Twentieth Century France* (New York: Columbia University Press, 1987), 186.

2. In the remarks that follow I draw upon the information and arguments provided by Carol Landon and Jared Curtis's Cornell edition of Wordsworth's *Early Poems and Fragments, 1785–1797*. Rather than go into extensive detail about the manuscripts, their dating, and other editorial matters, I refer the reader to the appropriate pages of the volume. Unless stated otherwise, citations from Wordsworth's juvenilia refer to the reading text and line numbers of the Cornell edition, cited in text as *EPF,* excepting references to the reading text of *The Vale of Esthwaite,* cited as *VE.* References to the Cornell texts' photographic reproductions of the manuscripts refer to page numbers of the volume. On occasion I refer also to the previous standard edition of the early poems and juvenilia: the first volume of *The Poetical Works of William Wordsworth (PW),* edited by Ernest de Selincourt and Helen Darbishire.

3. Duncan Wu, "Wordsworth's Poetry of Grief," 114.

4. Thomas Percy, ed., *Reliques of Ancient English Poetry* (London: J. Dodsley, 1765), 3 vols., 3: 273–78. These two roughly contemporary eighteenth-century ballads are in turn based upon the minstrel song "Fair Margaret and Sweet William."

5. T. W. Thompson, *Wordsworth's Hawkshead,* 65–69. In *The Hidden Wordsworth* Kenneth Johnston provides a detailed history of Mary Rigge and of her and her son's connection to the Tysons (*HW* 101–2).

6. Percy, ll. 65–66.

7. "The Bride's Burial," Percy, pp. 19–24; "A Lamentable Ballad of the Lady's Fall," *Ancient Songs and Ballads from the Reign of King Henry the Second to the Revolution,* ed. Joseph Ritson (1790), 3rd ed., rev. W. Carew Hazlitt (London: Reeves and Turner, 1877), 244–48.

8. Bruce Graver, "Wordsworth's Georgic Beginnings," *Texas Studies in Literature and Language* 33 (1991): 137–59; 146–47.

9. Wu, "Wordsworth and Helvellyn's Womb," *Essays in Criticism* 43 (1994): 6–23; 8.

10. My citation departs from the Cornell edition reading text at line 28 ("And thrice a dismal shriek"), interpolated from the editors' transcription of the manuscript (*EPF* 641; cf. 213), and so differs from Cornell's enumeration in its reading text (my line 29 is its 28). Wordsworth jotted the line on the next page of MS. 5, where it was "left undeleted" (*EPF* 640). The revised word "dismal" is entered above the original term "horrid."

11. For the Latin text of *Georgics* IV I have consulted the Loeb Classical Library's edition of Virgil's *Eclogues, Georgics, Aeneid, Minor Poems,* ed. and trans. H. Rushton Fairclough, 2 vols. (Cambridge: Harvard University Press, 1916, rev. 1935, 1986), vol. 1; hereafter cited in text by book and line number. Wordsworth utilized Martyn's edition of the *Georgics* but also likely consulted Dryden's verse translation (see Wu, "Wordsworth and Helvellyn's Womb," 9). Graver notes that Wordsworth's text is also probably indebted to Joseph Warton's translation of the *Georgics* (1752), "especially for its rhymes" (158n. 26).

12. Graver, 151.

13. It is worth noting that in Virgil as in Dryden the phrase "swimming eyes" (*"natantia lumina"*) refers not to Orpheus but to Eurydice. Wordsworth transferred the metaphor from mourned to mourner (before his backward glance, Orpheus's senses are "swimming" [21]) and so to the mythical antitype of the elegiac poet. Wordsworth no doubt also recalled his use of the phrase in the *Vale* and in his "Sonnet, on seeing Miss Helen Maria Williams weep at a Tale of Distress." The description of the bird's "sighs" also seems to be Wordsworth's innovation.

14. Wu, "Navigated by Magic: Wordsworth's Cambridge Sonnets," *Review of English Studies* New Series 46 (1995): 352–65; 358, 361.

15. Wu, "Wordsworth and Helvellyn's Womb," 12.

16. Freud, *Letters,* trans. Tania Stern and James Stern, ed. Ernst Freud (New York: Basic Books, 1960), 386. Cf. Freud, "Mourning and Melancholia," *SE* 14: 243–58; and Peter Sacks, *The English Elegy,* 6, 72. In Wordsworth's text the refusal of substitution must be read to some extent as a refusal to be duped.

17. Kathleen Woodward, "Freud and Barthes: Theorizing Mourning, Sustaining Grief," *Discourse: Berkeley Journal for Theoretical Studies in Media and Culture* 13 (1990–91): 93–110; 95.

18. In *Poems* of 1815, Wordsworth published an "Extract" of *Vale* lines 354–65 (*PW* 1, ll. 498–513), titled "Extract from the conclusion of a Poem, Composed upon leaving School."

19. F. W. Bateson was among the first to treat the *Vale* seriously as a poem, discerning in its supernatural scenes a strange "nightmare quality" that seemed "not literary at all" (*Wordsworth: A Re-interpretation,* 49). This reading may have contributed to the psychological interest the poem has attracted. More typical of past critics' assessments of the *Vale* are Florence Marsh's *Wordsworth's Imagery* (London: Archon, 1963), which dismisses the poem as "too immature to warrant a very detailed examination" but acknowledges that the opening lines' details "occur again and again in Wordsworth" (29), and Thomas Weiskel's *Romantic Sublime,* which disparages the poem as mere "gothic claptrap" but intriguingly discerns in its motifs a mysterious "quest for the source of poetic power" (193).

20. John Turner, *Wordsworth's Play and Politics: A Study of Wordsworth's Poetry, 1787–1800* (New York: St. Martin's Press, 1986), 89. See also Wu's "Wordsworth's Poetry of Grief" and his more textually oriented "Wordsworth and Helvellyn's Womb."

21. The lines are found in *PW* 1, ll. 231–39 and *EPF* Extract XVI, 22–30. One line is also recorded in the *Vale* of MS. 3 (*VE,* l. 160).

22. Landon and Curtis's editorial policy prevents them from including these twenty-eight lines (now a portion of Extract XVI) from MS. 5 in their MS. 3–only reading text, although the episode may have been among the missing MS. 3 pages and a few of its lines are jotted in MS. 3 (AP II). The editors relegate the lines to the penultimate section of their reconstruction of *Various Extracts.* From Extract XVI, the MS. 3 *Vale,* and *Various Extracts* from MSS. 2 and 5, Landon and Curtis in fact propose that

"a third, ideal text might be produced," although "such editorial compilations are not the purpose of [the Cornell] edition" (414).

23. Johnston speculates that the opening lines, "[   ]s avaunt! with tenfold pleasure / I ga[ze] the landskip's varied treasure," show the poem's speaker at the outset to be "ward[ing] off the various specters that try to kill him," the lacuna likely having contained a phrase like "Ye shades of night" or "Ye thoughts of death" (*HW* 107).

24. De Selincourt read Wordsworth's handwriting to say "shew'd," whereas Landon and Curtis rightly or wrongly decode the scrawl as "view'd." Either reading makes sense, but the specter's *showing* rather than the poet's *viewing* the coffer arguably makes more dramatic sense and fits better with the surviving text and its context. Here and in following quotations from the *Vale* the punctuation in brackets is my own, informed in places by de Selincourt's editorial decisions. Italicized words in brackets are Wordsworth's additions or revisions and are from the Cornell edition's transcriptions or manuscript reproductions.

25. This particular denotation of *coffer* ("coffer" and "coffin" are both derived from the Latin *cophinus*) is found in Chaucer, Shakespeare, and, importantly, in Southey's *Madoc* (1805) ("and coffer'd them [the ashes of the dead] apart"). The latter citation suggests that an association between coffers and coffins persisted in the poetic diction of Wordsworth's day. Wordsworth's source may be *Pericles*'s "coffer," which likewise denotes a coffin (*Norton* 14.43; III.iii.43 in other editions). He appears to have read Shakespeare's play no later than 1787, given that the *Vale* likely alludes to it with the phrase "heavy load" (*WR* 124). My citations of *coffer* derive from the *Oxford English Dictionary* but also benefit from definitions listed in Johnson's *Dictionary* (1755) and Dyche-Pardon's *New General English Dictionary* (1740) (New York: Olms, 1972).

26. In a poem so much about poets, "song," and production it seems reasonable to describe the *penseroso* speaker as himself a poet.

27. My use of the term "affect" is indebted to Freud's descriptions. See especially "The Affect in Dreams," in *The Interpretation of Dreams, SE* 2: 460–87; cf. 10: 196–98, 20: 90–94, 130–51.

28. Jonathan Wordsworth, "Two Dark Interpreters: Wordsworth and De Quincey," 223.

29. Adam Smith, *Theory of Moral Sentiments,* 9. Cf. Esther Schor, *Bearing the Dead,* 5, 77.

30. The text Wordsworth most likely would have read circa 1787 would have been that published in William Mason's *The Poems of Mr. Gray, to which are prefixed Memoirs of his Life and Writings* (York: 1775). See *WR* 70–71.

31. As noted in the Introduction, Wordsworth may have drawn upon Gray's elegiac poem to such an extent that the ephebe later called up his precursor for censure. Cf. Harold Bloom, *The Anxiety of Influence: A Theory of Poetry* (London and New York: Oxford University Press, 1973), esp. 5–16; and *Poetry and Repression* (New Haven: Yale University Press, 1976), 1–27.

32. Peter J. Manning, "Wordsworth and Gray's Sonnet on the Death of West," *Studies in English Literature 1500–1900* 22 (1982): 505–18, reprinted in *Reading Romantics,* 53–67; 55–57.

33. Bateson observed that a "sense of guilt can . . . be detected because of the gap between what William did not feel and what he knew he ought to have felt" (50). Wu pursues this connection at some length, discovering in young Wordsworth's incomplete "grieving" both a source and "a particular technique" for the poet's "later work" ("Wordsworth's Poetry of Grief," 115, 117). Richard E. Matlak's *The Poetry of Relationship: The Wordsworths and Coleridge, 1797–1800* (New York: St. Martin's Press, 1997) reads the poet's grief as fundamentally oedipal (11–17, esp. 14–15).

34. Cf. Paul de Man's oft-quoted reference, with regard to autobiography, to a "linguistic predicament" in which "death" figures as a "displaced name" (*Rhetoric of Romanticism,* 81). My discussion of mourning also echoes his description of autobiography as "privative."

35. De Man, "The Rhetoric of Temporality," in *Blindness and Insight,* 207.

36. Jacques Derrida, *Mémoires: for Paul de Man,* 29.

37. Derrida, "By Force of Mourning," 172; original emphasis.

38. I draw here upon Walter Benjamin's idea of *"soviel Todverfallenheit"* ("so much falling into death"), from *The Origin of German Tragic Drama,* 166 (cf. 167, 174–85). The German text and translation quoted above are from Herman Rapaport's *Milton and the Postmodern* (Lincoln: University of Nebraska Press, 1983), 23–24.

39. The last line's final "s" is interpolated from de Selincourt's edition. I too read the described spirit as doing both the *guiding* and the *riding.*

40. Jonathan Wordsworth, 224.

41. Cf. Wu, "Wordsworth and Helvellyn's Womb," 8–9.

42. Jonathan Wordsworth, 223.

43. Dorothy Wordsworth, *The Journals of Dorothy Wordsworth,* ed. Helen Darbishire (London: Oxford University Press, 1958), 152.

44. See *Paradise Lost,* 1.678–90, undoubtedly the backdrop for this small tableau. The spiritual struggle between earthly "mammon" and God is set out in Matthew 6:24.

45. As previously noted, the phrase "linguistic predicament" is de Man's. The term "prison-house" draws upon Wordsworth's Immortality Ode, inspired by *Hamlet.* It has since been employed in Fredric Jameson's *The Prison House of Language: A Critical Account of Structuralism and Russian Formalism* (Ithaca: Cornell University Press, 1972).

CHAPTER TWO

1. As noted in Chapter One, my understanding of the chronology of these and other early works is indebted to Carol Landon and Jared Curtis's notes and commentary in their Cornell edition of the juvenilia.

2. Before their inclusion in Cornell's *Early Poems and Fragments,* two of these sonnets were printed in the first volume of Ernest de Selincourt's edition of *Poetical Works* (*PW*). Three of the four sonnets, including the two not in *PW,* later appeared in Duncan Wu's "Navigated by Magic: Wordsworth's Cambridge Sonnets," *Review of English Studies* 46 (1995): 352–65, edited from the Wordsworth Trust manuscripts.

3. Paul Fry's *The Poet's Calling in the English Ode* provides a brief but trenchant reading of "Remembrance of Collins" (136). Edwin Stein's *Wordsworth's Art of Allusion* (University Park: The Pennsylvania State University Press, 1988) helpfully examines the poem's "intensive experiment with tradition" (39; see 20–41).

4. As elsewhere, I follow the Cornell edition's reading text. But in this case, for the sake of readability, I interpolate (in brackets) the helpful punctuation of Wu's previous edition of the poem included in his above-cited essay.

5. *The Works of William Collins,* ed. Richard Wendorf and Charles Ryskamp (Oxford: Clarendon Press, 1979), ll. 15–16.

6. Wu, 357–58.

7. Cited Wu, 359. Cf. *WR* 117 for Wu's dating of Wordsworth's reading of *Pleasures.*

8. Landon and Curtis designate the fragment an affinitive piece (IV) of *The Vale of Esthwaite,* which it may or may not echo. The passage is also reproduced, in a truncated form, in *PrW* 1: 9. The text likely dates from early 1788, but its precise chronology is unclear (*EPF* 546).

9. John Milton, *Complete Poems and Major Prose,* l. 120.

10. Wu, "Navigated by Magic," 355.

11. De Selincourt contends that although in 1836 Wordsworth dated the poem to 1786, "nothing of it can be so early, except, perhaps, a phrase or two, and the underlying idea of remonstrance at the 'officious touch' of friends" (*PW* 1: 318). Landon and Curtis concur, as does Wu, who conjectures the poem could date from 1789.

12. The quotation follows Cornell's reading text but interpolates some punctuation, at lines 8, 11, and 12, and, in two lines where the Racedown Manuscript (MS. 11) has lacunae, text supplied from the revised *Morning Post* version (ll. 10–11). The bracketed word "sensitive," in line 13, is de Selincourt's surmise (*PW* 1: 3).

13. Wu, 362.

14. Wordsworth dated the poem "1789," ascribing it to that time when he "first became an author" (*PW* 1: 32). The major part of its composition appears to have occurred during summer vacation of 1789 (*WL* 42–44). In his editorial introduction to *An Evening Walk,* James Averill argues that the poem continued to be revised until the end of 1792 (*EW* 8).

15. Jonathan Wordsworth, ed., "Introduction" to *An Evening Walk, 1793* by William Wordsworth (Oxford: Woodstock Books, 1989). John Williams's *Wordsworth: Romantic Poetry and Revolution Politics* (Manchester: Manchester University Press, 1989) also usefully details *An Evening Walk*'s literary sources (19–35), as does Averill,

EW 6–7 and *PHS* 62–65; de Selincourt, *PW* 1: 320–24; and Stephen Gill, *WL* 41–42. Ashton Nichols's "Towards 'Spots of Time': Visionary Dreariness in 'An Evening Walk'" (*The Wordsworth Circle* 4 [1983]: 233–37) considers the poem's debt to John Dyer's "The Country Walk." Geoffrey Hartman grants Virgil's *Georgics* precedence for the poem's plan (*WP* 93). Wordsworth recalled that the plan had not "been confined to a particular walk or an individual place" and that the poem's depicted countryside was "idealized rather than described in any one of its local aspects" (*PW* 1: 318–19).

16. See Alan Liu, "The Politics of the Picturesque: *An Evening Walk*," in *Wordsworth: The Sense of History*, 61–137; and Nicola Trott, "Wordsworth and the Picturesque: A Strong Infection of the Age," *The Wordsworth Circle* 18 (1987): 114–21.

17. Toby R. Benis, *Romanticism on the Road*, 24.

18. Averill concurs about the poem's faults, stating that its young author "seems less interested in keeping his eye on the object than on other poems" (*EW* 6; cf. *PHS* 61–68). So do Thomas McFarland, in *Romanticism and the Forms of Ruin* (252), and Kenneth Johnston, who finds the poem to be "nearly unreadable to twentieth-century tastes," although it is also "a creditable piece of description and meditation in the mode of Sensibility" (*HW* 151).

19. See, for example, Dorothy Wordsworth's letter to her brother Richard, 28 May 1794 (*EY* 121). Wordsworth's (wisely) unpublished defense of the Revolution, his *Letter to the Bishop of Llandaff* (1793), would treat events considerably more directly and passionately.

20. I am indebted to Gill for much of the biographical and historical information that follows.

21. In "'The Faded Pain': Memory and Experience in Wordsworth's *An Evening Walk*" (*The Wordsworth Circle* 17 [1986]: 164–68), Anthony Dangerfield reads this landscape as "the very medium of memory" (164).

22. See Wordsworth's note to *EW*, l. 187.

23. See *EPF* 659–60; and *WR* 83–84, 144.

24. Mary Jacobus, *Tradition and Experiment in Wordsworth's "Lyrical Ballads" (1798)* (Oxford: Clarendon Press, 1976), 136–37; see also 137–39; and Williams, 29–31.

25. Benis, 25.

26. Liu, 119.

27. Liu, 125.

28. Liu, 135.

29. All citations from The Bible are from the King James Authorized Version.

30. Williams, 32–33.

31. Benis, 26.

32. John O. Hayden, "The Dating of the '1794' Version of Wordsworth's *An Evening Walk*," *Studies in Bibliography* 42 (1989): 265–71; 267. In accepting Hayden's

revised dating (based in fact upon his first-hand perusal of MS. 9) I follow Robert M. Ryan's lead in *The Romantic Reformation: Religious Politics in English Literature, 1789–1824* (Cambridge: Cambridge University Press, 1997), 91. In Chapter Four, I revisit Hayden's redating of MS. 9.

33. In *The Making of Wordsworth's Poetry, 1785–1798* (Cambridge: Harvard University Press, 1973), Paul Sheats likewise sees most of the 1794 revisions as elaborating the poem's "moral and emotional significance" (102).

34. Because the Cornell edition's line numbering on the facing transcription pages of MS. 10 refers only to the lines of the "1794" reading text edited from MS. 9, for the sake of clarity I cite quotations from MS. 10 by page number. I provide added punctuation, minimally, in brackets.

35. Thomas Gray, "Ode on a Distant Prospect of Eton College," *The Complete Poems of Thomas Gray,* ed. H. W. Starr and J. R. Henrickson (Oxford: Clarendon Press, 1966), l. 101.

36. The quoted lines are intralinear additions written in Wordsworth's hand on the second page of the notebook. I presume the revisions to have occurred at or around the same time as the other notebook revisions, namely in the spring of 1794.

37. The description of the female vagrant is largely omitted from these notebook revisions. The disputed MS. 9 lines contain few changes to the episode other than two interpolations, one of which substitutes the description of lightning illuminating the dead vagrant and her children with that of the startled gaze of a local swain (based upon the earlier version's "whistling swain"). The swain becomes a fellow eyewitness and potentially a fellow mourner.

38. Eric Birdsall, "Nature and Society in *Descriptive Sketches,*" *Modern Philology* 84 (1986): 39–52; 50.

39. Birdsall, 51–52.

CHAPTER THREE

1. William Paley, *Reasons for Contentment; Addressed to the Labouring Part of the British Public* (London: R. Faulder, 1793), 3. I am indebted for this quotation to John Rieder's "Civic Virtue and Social Class at the Scene of Execution: Wordsworth's Salisbury Plain Poems," *Studies in Romanticism* 30 (1991): 325–43; 334; revised and reprinted in Rieder's *Wordsworth's Counterrevolutionary Turn,* 91–107; 99.

2. Regina Hewitt, *The Possibilities of Society: Wordsworth, Coleridge, and the Sociological Viewpoint of English Romanticism,* 56. Cf. John Williams, *Wordsworth: Romantic Poetry and Revolution Politics,* 6–9, 84–104.

3. See Mark L. Reed, *Wordsworth: The Chronology of the Early Years, 1770–1799* (Cambridge: Harvard University Press, 1967), 147.

4. As Lucy Newlyn points out, in *The Prelude* Wordsworth views *Salisbury Plain* both as "the origin of his greatness," akin to a spot of time from a "pre-Coleridgean

past," and as the poem of all his poems, up to 1804–5, "to represent his claim to great-ness" (*Coleridge, Wordsworth, and the Language of Allusion* [Oxford: Clarendon Press, 1986], 183–84).

5. Paul Sheats, *The Making of Wordsworth's Poetry,* 84.

6. All citations from *Salisbury Plain* (*SP*) and *Adventures on Salisbury Plain* (*ASP*) refer to Stephen Gill's Cornell edition of the Salisbury Plain poems (*SPP*).

7. Mary Jacobus, *Tradition and Experiment in Wordsworth's "Lyrical Ballads" (1798),* 148. Nicholas Roe appears to support Jacobus's contention, arguing that "'Salisbury Plain' is poetry, not a polemical pamphlet" (*Wordsworth and Coleridge: The Radical Years* [Oxford: Oxford University Press, 1988], 127).

8. In contradistinction to Hartman, Gill argues that the poem's "attack on the oppression of the poor is the center from which all of [its] questioning radiates" (*SPP* 5). See also Kenneth Johnston's nuanced, more political assessment in *The Hidden Wordsworth* (*HW*), 345–50.

9. See K. D. M. Snell, *Annals of the Labouring Poor: Social Change and Agrarian England, 1660–1900* (Cambridge: Cambridge University Press, 1985), 62–65, 108, 110. For the conditions and numbers of England's poor in the 1790s, see Gertrude Himmelfarb, *The Idea of Poverty: England in the Early Industrial Age* (New York: Knopf, 1984), 70 ff.; and E. A. Wrigley and R. S. Schofield, *The Population History of England, 1541–1871: A Reconstruction* (Cambridge: Harvard University Press, 1981).

10. Toby R. Benis, *Romanticism on the Road,* 59.

11. David Collings, *Wordsworthian Errancies: The Poetics of Cultural Dismemberment* (Baltimore: Johns Hopkins University Press, 1994), 18.

12. Michael Friedman, *The Making of a Tory Humanist,* 137.

13. Karen Swann, "Public Transport: Adventuring on Wordsworth's Salisbury Plain," *ELH* 55 (1988): 811–34; 819.

14. Swann, 819–20.

15. Swann, 819. In fairness to Swann, although her essay does make reference to *Salisbury Plain,* her main argument focuses upon the much less Spenserian, considerably more gothic, revision of the poem as *Adventures on Salisbury Plain.*

16. There were, for example, a number of "gothic romances" written during the Revival. In the conclusion of his monograph "On the Origin of Romantic Fiction in Europe," prefixed to *The History of English Poetry* (London, 1781), Thomas Warton even speculated about a gothic link in romance's migration from Arabia into a Europe prepared by "Gothic scalds, who perhaps originally derived their ideas from the same fruitful region of invention." Here "gothic," in contrast to "romance," refers more to a time or place than to a genre.

17. Ian Duncan, *Modern Romance and Transformations of the Novel: The Gothic, Scott, Dickens* (Cambridge: Cambridge University Press, 1992), 21–23.

18. See Jon Klancher, "Godwin and the Republican Romance: Genre, Politics, and Contingency in Cultural History," *Modern Language Quarterly* 56 (1995): 145–65; 148.

19. Wordsworth does address the "insurmountable" difficulties attendant upon using the Spenserian stanza in English, but he does so only in 1829, in a letter to Catherine Grace Godwin written thirty-six years after composing *Salisbury Plain* (*LY* 2: 58).

20. See Stuart Curran, *Poetic Form and British Romanticism* (New York: Oxford University Press, 1986), 131.

21. James Thomson, Preface to *The Castle of Indolence*, in *The Poetical Works of James Thomson, James Beattie, Gilbert West, and John Bampfylde* (London: Routledge, Warne, Routledge, 1863), 141.

22. Arthur Johnston argues that Spenserian romance was "the inevitable choice" for allegories like Thomson's ("Poetry and Criticism After 1740," in *Dryden to Johnson*, vol. 4 of *The New History of Literature*, 4 vols., ed. Roger H. Lonsdale [New York: Peter Bedrick, 1987], 321).

23. See Sir Walter Scott, *Essays on Chivalry, Romance, and the Drama* (1834; Freeport: Books for Libraries, 1972), 135.

24. F. W. Bateson, *Wordsworth: A Re-interpretation*, 110.

25. In *Bearing the Dead*, Esther Schor likewise discerns the "Spenserian rhetoric of the [poem's] epilogue" and other parts (104). In *Salisbury Plain* antiquated terms like "unwares" and "thrill'd" pointedly allude to *The Faerie Queene*, while the wanderings of one of the poem's two principal figures, the female vagrant, recall Una's own travels through "deserts wyde" in search of a "dwelling place" (I.iii.10). Quotations and line numbers from *The Faerie Queene* refer to A. C. Hamilton's edition (New York: Longmans, 1977).

26. Mircea Eliade, *Cosmos and History*, trans. W. R. Trask (New York: Harper, rpt. 1959), 18.

27. See Arthur Johnston, 313–49, esp. 325. Thomson's romance hero, Sir Industry, struggles "to civilize" "a barbarous world" (II.xiv.5). Southey's *Thalaba* similarly draws upon the Spenserian topoi of quest, transformation, and reward. Scott described the standard conclusion of romance thus: in reward for his enduring of various "distresses and dangers," romance "assigns to the champion a fair realm, an abundant succession, and a train of happy years" (*Essays*, 142).

28. Horace Walpole, letter to W. Cole, 9 March 1768; cited in Gillian Beer's *The Romance* (London: Methuen, 1970), 56.

29. According to David Duff's *Romance and Revolution: Shelley and the Politics of Genre* (Cambridge: Cambridge University Press, 1994), romance's resuscitation was owed in part to antiquarians' shared project to revive alternative "English" social-political models and literary schemes (10–11).

30. Cited Duff, 12.

31. I am here indebted to Duff's detailing of the Jacobin and anti-Jacobin uses of the "magical narratives of romance" in the 1790s (13). Cf. Edmund Burke, *Reflections on the Revolution in France*, 130, 138, *passim*; Thomas Paine, *The Rights of Man*, 62–74. See also Duncan, 24–27.

32. Himmelfarb, *The Idea of Poverty*, 5, 18.

33. See Mary Wollstonecraft, *A Vindication of the Rights of Men* (Amherst, N.Y.: Prometheus Book, 1996), 88–94; and George Dyer, *The Complaints of the Poor People of England*, 2nd ed. (London, 1793), 55–58.

34. Wordsworth's witnessing of poverty and hardship in London (*13P* 7.610–23) and in the southwest so impressed him that fifty years later he could still well recall having sought in *Salisbury Plain* to show "the afflictions and calamities to which the poor are subject" (cited *SPP* 216).

35. See Patricia A. Parker, *Inescapable Romance: Studies in the Poetics of a Mode* (Princeton: Princeton University Press, 1979). Even in the Revival's early years such romance promise was accompanied by a haunting "sense that no real return was possible" (161).

36. Klancher, 160.

37. Schor, 32.

38. Cf. Marlon Ross, "Breaking the Period: Romanticism, Historical Representation, and the Prospect of Genre," *ANQ* 6 (1993): 121–31; Jonathan Culler, *Structuralist Poetics: Structuralism, Linguistics, and the Study of Literature* (Ithaca: Cornell University Press, 1975), 113–30; Umberto Eco, *The Role of the Reader: Explorations in the Semiotics of Texts* (London: Hutchinson, 1981), and "Over-interpreting Texts," *Interpretation and Overinterpretation*, ed. Stefan Collini (Cambridge: Cambridge University Press, 1992), 45–66; Newlyn, *"Paradise Lost" and the Romantic Reader* (Oxford: Clarendon Press, 1993), 10–13; and Ellie Ragland-Sullivan, "The Magnetism between Reader and Text: Prolegomena to a Lacanian Poetics," *Poetics* 13 (1984): 381–406.

39. For example, Una, whose grieving heart is described as "plunged in sea of sorrowes deepe" (*The Faerie Queene* I.vii.39; cf. I.vi.1, I.xii.1). The metaphor of life as being "at sea" is well fitted to uprootedness and homelessness and was also, as William Gilpin noted in *Observations of the Western Parts of England* (London: 1798; 2nd ed. 1808), well suited to Salisbury Plain itself (83). See Anne Janowitz, *England's Ruins: Poetic Purpose and the National Landscape* (Cambridge: Basil Blackwell, 1990), 104.

40. Rieder, *Wordsworth's Counterrevolutionary Turn*, 92.

41. Alan Liu, *Wordsworth: The Sense of History*, 183. See also James Chandler, *Wordsworth's Second Nature*, 130–31.

42. Collings, 24.

43. Sheats, 91. James Averill argues that the traveler's "acute" feeling of homelessness is revealed by the way his surroundings reflect back his own alienated situation (*PHS* 76).

44. For Wordsworth's classical sources on Druidism, see Liu, 192–97, and Sheats, 85–93.

45. Swann, 813.

46. Collings, 39.

47. Collings, 40.

48. In Wordsworth's day a spital was also called a "lazaret," "lazaretto," or "lazar-house" (<It. *lazaretto*) after the biblical leper Lazarus. "Lazaret" owes more to St. Luke's tale of the beggar-leper (16:20–31) than to St. John's account of the dead brother of Mary and Martha (11:1–44), but the latter tale also subtly underlies this "dead house" and its entombed corpse. As evidence of this intertextual connection, one may point to the fact that the female vagrant is, like St. John's Lazarus, bound with rags she "unbind[s]." In the King James translation Lazarus's "grave-clothes" are similarly "loose[ned]" after his resurrection.

49. Cf. Swann, 815. The etymology of *allegory* (<Gk. *allos,* "other" and *agoreuein*) itself suggests a "speaking otherwise in the marketplace or assembly."

50. Richard Elridge argues that in *Salisbury Plain* people recover social attachments "to specific others and places" by "reflecting these attachments in conversation" ("Self-Understanding and Community in Wordsworth's Poetry," *Philosophy and Literature* 10 [1986]: 273–94; 281).

51. Cathy Caruth, *Unclaimed Experience: Trauma, Narrative, and History* (Baltimore: Johns Hopkins University Press, 1996), 8–9.

52. Walter Benjamin, "Theses on the Philosophy of History," *Illuminations,* ed. Hannah Arendt, trans. Harry Zohn (New York: Schocken Books, 1969), 253–64; 254, 263.

53. Jacques Derrida, *Specters of Marx: The State of the Debt, the Work of Mourning, and the New International,* trans. Peggy Kamuf (New York: Routledge, 1994), xviii.

54. Janowitz, *England's Ruins,* 106.

55. Benis, 65–67.

56. Ross, 129. Such a community is of course not just discovered but constructed. As Klancher argues, in *The Making of English Reading Audiences, 1790–1832* (Madison: University of Wisconsin Press, 1987), "readers are *made,* created as a public through a network of circulatory channels" and by the author's own directing of readers' reading habits (33). For Wordsworth (ca. 1800) "language allows the writer to transform the [reader's] . . . reading habit," reforming (and hence in part manipulating) the modern "mind made dull and torpid" (37).

57. See Hans Robert Jauss, "Literary History as a Challenge to Literary Theory," *New Directions in Literary History,* ed. Ralph Cohen (London: Routledge, 1974), 13–41, with regard to a writer's means of anticipating his or her readers' "horizon of literary expectations" (18). Cf. Robert Scholes, *Textual Power: Literary Theory and the Teaching of English* (New Haven: Yale University Press, 1985), esp. 48; and Wolfgang Iser, *The Act of Reading: A Theory of Aesthetic Response* (London: Routledge and Kegan Paul, 1978), esp. 140.

58. Curran, *Poetic Form,* 10–11.

59. Janowitz, 96.

60. Bateson, 110–11.

61. See Steven Knapp, *Personification and the Sublime: Milton to Coleridge* (Cambridge: Harvard University Press, 1985), 108–20. Knapp finds a similar lack of "fit" between the Spenserian leech-gatherer and the contemporary aims of "Resolution and Independence."

62. John Turner, *Wordsworth's Play and Politics,* 48. Cf. Wordsworth's pronouncement, in a 1794 letter to William Mathews: "I recoil from the bare idea of a revolution" (*EY* 124).

63. Parker, 160. Parker refers not to Wordsworth but to Thomson, although given her argument she might well read Wordsworth's use of romance as a similarly "dangerous evasion" (160).

64. Michael Wiley, *Romantic Geography: Wordsworth and Anglo-European Spaces* (New York: St. Martin's Press, 1998), 32. Cf. Janowitz, 104.

65. Rieder, 13, 229; cf. 96–101.

66. A writer for *The Critical Review* summarized the general view of the poor laws, circa 1786, thus: "instead of answering the charitable purpose of their institution, they are a source of great public evil, oppressive to the industrious part of the nation, and pernicious to the morals of the indigent" (Review of *A Dissertation on the Poor Laws* by "a Well-wisher to Mankind," *The Critical Review* 61 [1786]: 44–49; 44).

67. Klancher contends that late eighteenth-century periodical writing was often predicated upon the "underlying faith" that "readers might exchange roles with writers" (*The Making of English Reading Audiences,* 22)—which also seems to be the aim and modus operandi of *Salisbury Plain.*

68. Duncan, 2.

69. Cf. Swann, 831.

70. In *Wordsworth's "Prelude": A Study of its Literary Form* (Ithaca: Cornell University Press, 1953) Abbie Findlay Potts finds *The Prelude* to be "an ethical romance, the ordeal of an eighteenth-century knight of poesy . . . conceived in the temper of Spenser's Red Cross Knight" (26).

71. I adhere to the chronology worked out by Gill with some help from Mark Reed. Although it is impossible for us to know for certain the precise make-up of the manuscript poem of 1795 and to what extent it was revised in its copying as MS. 2 in 1799, the evidence nevertheless credibly suggests that, while "the 1795 is now lost to us . . . it has survived[, if not in every detail,] . . . in the poem in MS. 2, *Adventures on Salisbury Plain*" (*SPP* 12).

72. Sheats, 116.

73. Sheats describes *Adventures* as "bitterly objective social realism" (109). Turner sees the poem as generically an "imitation of the popular criminal biography, most familiarly known perhaps in the collection of *The Newgate Calendar*" used by Godwin to write *Caleb Williams*—a literature concerned with "crime, remorse and repentance" (52).

74. Benis, 80. Benis helpfully details the political and social history of these years (80–90).

75. Jacobus, 153.

76. Arnold Schmidt, "Wordsworth's Politics and the Salisbury Plain Poems," *The Wordsworth Circle* 27 (1996), 166–68. Interestingly, at Hawkshead Wordsworth had been acquainted with Fletcher Christian, of Bounty fame (1789), in whose defense he wrote in 1796 (*B* 228).

77. Sheats, 108–9.

78. Jacobus, 153.

79. Collings, 35.

80. Collings, 35–36.

81. See Gary Harrison, *Wordsworth's Vagrant Muse: Poetry, Poverty and Power* (Detroit: Wayne State University Press, 1994), 94–99.

82. Collings, 36.

83. Enid Welsford, *Salisbury Plain: A Study in the Development of Wordsworth's Mind and Art* (Oxford: Blackwell Press, 1966), 23.

84. Sheats argues that the cottage "summarized hope in nearly every poem Wordsworth had written"—a hope for the reconciliation of man and nature as well as of man and man (91, 118).

85. Nicolas Abraham and Maria Torok, "Introjection-Incorporation: Mourning or Melancholia," 8.

86. Fry, *The Poet's Calling in the English Ode*, 145.

87. Schor, 109–10.

88. As Benis points out, these were disciplinary effects of the Murder Act of 1752 (81). On gibbeting and burial, see also Theresa Kelley, *Wordsworth's Revisionary Aesthetics*, 70. My use of the term *interpellation* draws upon Louis Althusser's analysis of subjectivity in "Ideology and Ideological State Apparatuses (Notes Towards an Investigation)," in *Lenin and Philosophy and Other Essays*, trans. Ben Brewster (New York: Monthly Review Press, 1971), 127–86.

89. Rieder, 102.

90. Derrida, *Specters of Marx*, xviii.

91. Swann, 813.

92. Kelley, 68.

93. Abraham, "Notes on the Phantom: A Complement to Freud's Metapsychology," 77; cited Swann, 827.

94. Derrida, *Fors*, 70, 78. On the "affect," see Freud, "The Affect in Dreams," in *The Interpretation of Dreams, SE* 2: 460–87; and *Inhibitions, Symptoms and Anxiety*, 20: 90–94, 130–51.

CHAPTER FOUR

1. The verse, from Robert Burns's "Epistle to J. L.*****k," is rather bungled by Wordsworth (*RC* 42), who probably drew from memory. The epigraph was excised by the time he revised *The Ruined Cottage* and recorded it in MS. D. Subsequent pages discuss the lines' significance.

2. In a note to these lines in the two-part *Prelude* of 1799, Jonathan Wordsworth or another of the Norton editors helpfully connects this intrusion of "hopes o'erthrown" to Coleridge's letter of September 1799, asking that Wordsworth "write a poem, in blank verse, addressed to those, who, in consequence of the complete failure of the French Revolution, have thrown up all hopes of the amelioration of mankind, and are sinking into an almost epicurean selfishness, disguising the same under the soft titles of domestic attachment and contempt for visionary *philosophes*. It would do great good, and might form a part of 'The Recluse'" (*CLSTC* 1: 527; cf. *NCP* 26 n9).

3. H. W. Piper, *The Active Universe* (London: Athlone Press, 1962), 71–75; cited *EW* 15.

4. Since Geoffrey Hartman's influential psychological reading of *The Ruined Cottage*, in *Wordsworth's Poetry* (*WP* 135–40), readers of the poem have tended to concentrate less on authorial psychology or biography than on issues concerning suffering and alienation. See Jonathan Wordsworth's landmark reading of the MS. D text, *The Music of Humanity: A Critical Study of Wordsworth's "Ruined Cottage"* (New York: Harper, 1969). See also Karen Swann's equally illuminating study, "Suffering and Sensation in *The Ruined Cottage*," *PMLA* 106 (1993): 83–95; and Kenneth R. Johnston's *Wordsworth and "The Recluse,"* which provides compelling analysis of the poem both on its own merits and as a part of *The Recluse* (see 19–27, 43–52). In marked contrast to my reading of community in *The Ruined Cottage*, Susan J. Wolfson's "Individual in Community: Dorothy Wordsworth in Conversation with William" argues that the pedlar and traveler are "isolated from community" because they have displaced sorrow "into something else in order for wisdom to be achieved" (*Romanticism and Feminism*, ed. Anne K. Mellor [Bloomington: Indiana University Press, 1988], 139–66; 159–60). Especially illuminating of the poem's pantheist doctrine and its complications is William A. Ulmer's "Wordsworth, the One Life, and *The Ruined Cottage*," *Studies in Philology* 93 (1996): 304–31, revised and reprinted as "Vain Belief: Wordsworth and the One Life," chapter two of *The Christian Wordsworth, 1798–1805* (Albany: State University of New York Press, 2001), 35–71. Among the poem's new-historicist readings, that proffered in David Simpson's *Wordsworth's Historical Imagination: The Poetry of Displacement* (New York: Methuen, 1987) is particularly helpful for its focus on the poem's interest in internecine tensions owed to "poverty, urbanization and the changes in patterns of labour and leisure" (192). See also James Chandler, *Wordsworth's Second Nature*, esp. 137–38; Marjorie Levinson, *The Romantic Fragment Poem* (Chapel Hill: University of North Carolina Press, 1986), 221–30; Jerome McGann, *The Romantic Ideology: A Critical Investigation* (Chicago: University of Chicago Press, 1983), 82–86; and Alan Liu, *Wordsworth: The Sense of History*, 311–56.

5. Jonathan Wordsworth, *Music of Humanity*, 7.

6. Peter J. Manning, *Reading Romantics*, 11.

7. Swann, "Suffering and Sensation," 87.

8. See J. Wordsworth, 7.

9. J. Wordsworth, 6.

10. Manning, 13. As pointed out in Chapter Two, Wordsworth enlisted this "bowl" metaphor in *Descriptive Sketches*, where he declared his love for Switzerland would last "'till Life has broke her golden bowl" (l. 741). In *An Evening Walk* his allusion was more direct: "For hope's deserted well why wistful look? / Chok'd is the pathway, and the pitcher broke."

11. John Turner, *Wordsworth's Play and Politics*, 93.

12. John Locke, *An Essay Concerning Human Understanding*, 532. As noted previously, Duncan Wu lists the 1690 rather than 1701 edition of the *Essay* as the one Wordsworth appears to have read in the spring or summer of 1787 (*WR* 88). Yet that Wordsworth had access to the later, fourth edition is certainly within the realm of possibility.

13. John Rieder, *Wordsworth's Counterrevolutionary Turn*, 125.

14. Paul Sheats, *The Making of Wordsworth's Poetry*, 141.

15. Turner, 92; emphasis added.

16. For Swann, the poem paints a "worst case scenario" of a "passion for representations" gone wrong, owed to (maternal) loss played out in an addictive *fort-da* of "phantasmatic signs" (87).

17. We know Wordsworth and Coleridge had met by September of 1795, when they conversed at Bristol, Coleridge's talents appearing to Wordsworth even then to be "very great" (*EY* 153).

18. J. Wordsworth, 9–16.

19. Rieder, 150. Jonathan Wordsworth postulates that a 120–line poem was read to Coleridge and was then expanded to some 370 lines (14–15). MS. A roughly contains lines 152–243 (91 lines total) of the MS. B *Ruined Cottage* "in almost their final shape" (7). John Alban Finch posits a longer early-1797 text of 174 lines ("*The Ruined Cottage* Restored: Three Stages of Composition," *Bicentenary Studies in Memory of John Alban Finch*, ed. Jonathan Wordsworth [Ithaca: Cornell University Press, 1970], 29–49). Although he casts doubt on the accuracy of Finch's calculations, Rieder nonetheless holds that the case for a June poem "of approximately two hundred lines remains strong." Johnston determines that of the "1300 lines" reported to have been completed by March 1798—including an early version of "The Old Cumberland Beggar," 170 lines about a discharged soldier (added to the 1805 *Prelude*), and a fragment later titled "A Night-Piece"—the story of Margaret occupied the bulk of the writing (5–8; cf. 19–27).

20. Jonathan Wordsworth argues for the preferability of MS. D (23), while Manning (11) and Turner (90) argue the contrary. Cornell editor James Butler notes that,

although Jonathan Wordsworth has "forcefully argue[d]" for the superiority of MS. D as "the best balanced and most coherent surviving version," since F. W. Bateson and F. R. Leavis critics have taken the side of MS. B in the textual debate, arguing both for its priority (Bateson) and its complexity (Leavis) (*RC* xii). Cf. Neil Hertz, "Wordsworth and the Tears of Adam," *Studies in Romanticism* 7 (1967): 15–33; 15; Reeve Parker, "'Finer Distance': The Narrative Art of Wordsworth's 'The Wanderer,'" *ELH* 39 (1972): 87–111; 88; and Jonathan Barron and Kenneth R. Johnston, "'A Power to Virtue Friendly': The Pedlar's Guilt in Wordsworth's 'Ruined Cottage,'" *Romantic Revisions,* ed. Robert Brinkley and Keith Hanley (New York: Cambridge University Press, 1992), 64–86.

21. Subsequent citations and line numbers from the manuscripts of *The Ruined Cottage*—MSS. A, B, and D—refer to the reading texts of the Cornell edition. Citations from the MS. B addenda are from the apparatus criticus, pp. 256–281, and refer to page rather than line numbers. Added punctuation appears in brackets.

22. Stephen Gill, "Wordsworth's Poems: The Question of the Text," *Review of English Studies* 34 (1983): 190.

23. Butler points to the poem's debt to social texts like Frederick Morton Eden's *State of the Poor* and to works like Goethe's *Der Wanderer* and (following the lead of Jonathan Wordsworth) Southey's *Joan of Arc,* the latter of which depicts a "poor, trembling, wretched woman['s] . . . tortured vigil at her cottage door as she awaits news of her soldier husband" (*RC* 5–6). In *Coleridge, Wordsworth, and the Language of Allusion,* Lucy Newlyn likewise argues that the "source" for the June *Ruined Cottage* was a passage in *Joan of Arc,* which Coleridge "had printed in *The Watchman* the previous year" (9). Stuart Curran finds a further source for the poem's central framing dialogue in the pastoral elegies of Theocritus and Virgil (*Poetic Form and British Romanticism,* 120–21). Other important details may be traced to Goldsmith's *Deserted Village,* Crabbe's anti-pastoral *The Village,* Cowper's *The Task,* and Fawcett's *Art of War.*

24. Cited in Willard Sperry, *Wordsworth's Anti-Climax* (Cambridge: Harvard University Press, 1935), 117.

25. Enid Welsford, *Salisbury Plain,* 68.

26. J. Wordsworth, 151. Regarding the transformation of Calvinist-Protestant concern for pathetic "display" into the secular cult of Sensibility, evident in such works as Mackenzie's *Man of Feeling* (and in Wordsworth), see Colin Campbell, *The Romantic Ethic and the Spirit of Consumerism,* 135–41, 177–82.

27. Helen Darbishire argues that the manuscript evidence "clearly shows that in the first version of the tale the Pedlar was a person unknown to the traveler, casually met on the road near the cottage, and not, as he became later, his old friend" (*PW* 5: 378). In his edition of *The Ruined Cottage, The Brothers, Michael* (Cambridge: Cambridge University Press, 1985), Jonathan Wordsworth attributes this intertextual transformation in the narrator and pedlar's relationship to Wordsworth's pragmatic decision to make the two men friends in order to increase our confidence in the pedlar "as a spokesman" for his own nature philosophy (29).

28. Joshua Scodel, *The English Epitaph,* 316. As in his later writing of epitaphs, Wordsworth's goal in this deeply elegiac text principally remains that of representing

the "conversion of the . . . 'stranger' into a 'friend'" (396). Compare Wordsworth's statement, in the first of the *Essays upon Epitaphs,* that, through the epitaph's mediations, "the stranger is introduced through its mediation to the company of a friend: it [the epitaph] is concerning all, and for all" (*PrW* 2: 59). The term *comrade* may be a better modern translation of this type of *friend* and *friendship,* which is triadic and dialogical, with a commonality of interest that makes the bonds produced add up to more than we today might mean by the term "friend." That said, the word "comrade" carries its own heavy, post-Romantic baggage.

29. See Evan Radcliffe, "Saving Ideals: Revolution and Benevolence in *The Prelude,*" *JEGP* 93 (1994): 534–59.

30. As Radcliffe states, Burke argued that true feeling for another was based not upon such abstractions as Price espoused but upon close, often familial, ties. James Mackintosh lectured on the priority only of "particular affections" (536–38).

31. Rieder detects in the pedlar's elegizing of Margaret (notably in his repeated assertions that "She is dead") an almost ritualistic repetition of "an earlier, more defiant stage of mourning" (169).

32. Turner likewise sees Margaret's condition to be owed to failed mourning and melancholia but attributes the latter to her "repression of [her] violent feeling[s]" at being abandoned (90).

33. J. Wordsworth, *The Ruined Cottage,* 7.

34. Citations from the Bible are those of the King James Authorized Version. I have also consulted the text and notes of *The New Oxford Annotated Bible,* RSV, ed. Herbert G. May and Bruce M. Metzger (New York: Oxford University Press, 1977).

35. See Jacques Lacan, "Direction of Treatment and Principles of Its Power," *Ecrits: A Selection,* trans. Alan Sheridan (New York: Norton, 1977), 263. Cf. Freud, *Letters,* 386; Sacks, *The English Elegy,* 6–10, 22–24; and Joel Fineman, "The Structure of Allegorical Desire," 42–47.

36. Swann, 94.

37. In *Women Writers and Poetic Identity: Dorothy Wordsworth, Emily Brontë, and Emily Dickinson* (Princeton: Princeton University Press, 1980), Margaret Homans provides a different vantage: "the Wanderer and the speaker see and learn what it is not permitted Margaret to see and learn. . . . The woman's death is lamented but made inevitable by the character of Wordsworth's project" (25). See also Anne K. Mellor, *Romanticism & Gender* (New York: Routledge, 1993), 19–20. I do not find "the buried presence of a maternal or feminine figure" to be the sine qua non of the poet's communitarianism, as Homans does. *The Vale of Esthwaite,* "Remembrance of Collins," "Michael," and the Matthew elegies attest, at the very least, to the poetic and social powers of buried paternal and masculine figures as well.

38. In "Knowing the Dead . . . : The Pete Laver Lecture 1986" (*The Wordsworth Circle* 18 [1987]: 87–98), John Kerrigan argues that even "bare stones . . . are *semai,* signs" (88). He also reminds us that the word for stone in ancient Greek is *herma,* the root of *Hermes,* god of "doorways, paths, exchange, writing, seacliffs, shores and the underworld," and psychopomp of the threshold of life and death.

39. MS. B has a lacuna in which the words "The calm" neatly fit. I interpolate them from the corresponding, otherwise identical, line 198 of MS. D.

40. Ulmer, "Wordsworth, the One Life, and *The Ruined Cottage*," 308.

41. These lines and subsequent lines from *Religious Musings* are cited from *Poetical Works I*, ed. J. C. C. Mays, *CWSTC* 16: 1, pt. 1.

42. Coleridge's formulation of pantheist doctrine was likely prompted by his reading of Joseph Priestley and of Ralph Cudworth's implicitly pantheistic *True Intellectual System of the Universe* (*WL* 106). His pantheism also drew upon Spinoza's argument for God's immanence, Berkeley's notion of the *anima mundi* ("You remember, I am a Berkleian," Coleridge noted), and upon the neoKantian idealism of Friedrich Schelling and of Salomon Maimon, whose *Versuch über die Transzendentalphilosophie* had been published in 1790. See Thomas McFarland, *Romanticism and the Forms of Ruin*, 615; J. Wordsworth, "The Two-Part Prelude of 1799" (1970), in *NCP* 567–85; 574; and Mary Jacobus, *Tradition and Experiment*, 63–68. See also John Gutteridge, "Scenery and Ecstasy: Three of Coleridge's Blank Verse Poems," *New Approaches to Coleridge: Biographical and Critical Essays*, ed. Donald Sultana (New York: Vision and Barnes & Noble, 1981), 151–71; 165; and Lewis Patton's and Peter Mann's introduction to *Lectures 1795 on Politics and Religion, CWSTC* 1: lxvi.

43. Jonathan Wordsworth describes Coleridge's fright at pantheism's radical albeit "logical enough" extension to a totalizing monism in which human and God are one (*NCP* 574–75). In *Coleridge and the Pantheist Tradition* (Oxford: Clarendon Press, 1969), McFarland argues that pantheism "exerted the strongest possible repulsion and the most extreme attraction upon Coleridge . . . throughout his career" (190). The poet's longstanding hope was to achieve "a systematic reconciliation of the 'I am' and the 'it is'" (191), of the transcendent and the immanent. See also Ulmer, *The Christian Wordsworth*, 65–66.

44. Coleridge, *Sibylline Leaves: A Collection of Poems* (1817), xi, *Errata* (to "Eolian Harp").

45. Cf. J. Wordsworth, "Wordsworth's Borderers" (1969), in *English Romantic Poets: Modern Essays in Criticism*, ed. M. H. Abrams, 2nd ed. (New York: Oxford University Press, 1975), 170–87, esp. 176.

46. Ulmer, "Wordsworth, the One Life, and *The Ruined Cottage*," 308.

47. Johnston, "The Romantic Idea-Elegy," 30. Cf. *CLSTC* 1: 527, quoted above, n. 2.

48. See J. Wordsworth, "On Man, on Nature, and on Human Life," *Review of English Studies* 31 (1980): 2–29, esp. 2–3; McFarland, "Wordsworth on Man, on Nature, and on Human Life," *Studies in Romanticism* 21 (1982): 601–18, esp. 608; and Johnston, *Wordsworth and "The Recluse*," esp. 18.

49. Robert M. Ryan, *The Romantic Reformation: Religious Politics in English Literature, 1789–1824*, 91. See John O. Hayden, "The Dating of the '1794' Version of Wordsworth's *An Evening Walk*," esp. 267.

50. See Jacobus, 175.

51. Esther Schor, *Bearing the Dead*, 123.

52. Sheats, 179. Cf. Newlyn, *Coleridge, Wordsworth, and the Language of Allusion*, 52; and especially Richard E. Matlak, *The Poetry of Relationship: The Wordsworths and Coleridge, 1797–1800*, 88–98.

53. Chandler, *Wordsworth's Second Nature*, 125. Johnston's *Hidden Wordsworth* details the similarities between the *Ancyent Marinere* and *The Ruined Cottage*: each is "a narrative of intense suffering, told by an old and uneducated man to a young man, evidently better educated and of higher class, the effect of which is to fundamentally shatter the young man's immediate preoccupations, and which seems likely to change his life forever after" (*HW* 554). Newlyn argues that Wordsworth's allusion to Coleridge's narrative (concerning the narrator's having become "a better and a wiser man") reveals *The Ruined Cottage* to be "adopting its didactic framework almost whole-sale" (52).

54. Schor, 117.

55. J. Wordsworth, *The Music of Humanity*, 93.

56. Manning, 24. Cf. Turner, 103; and Swann, 92.

57. Cf. Wolfson, *The Questioning Presence: Wordsworth, Keats, and the Interrogative Mode in Romantic Poetry* (Ithaca: Cornell University Press, 1986), 108; and Ulmer, *The Christian Wordsworth*, 70–71.

58. Schor, 123.

59. J. Wordsworth, 93.

60. Barron and Johnston, 83.

61. In "Relations of Scarcity: Ecology and Eschatology in *The Ruined Cottage*" (*Studies in Romanticism* 39 [2000]: 347–64), Peter Larkin reads this mourning not as uncompletable but rather as *"scarcely completed,"* what amounts to "a completed incom-pletion promising a return to life on behalf of the non-totality of life" (360–61).

62. Schor interprets these lines differently but finds in them a sense that "'mourn-ful thoughts may discover a life that signifies ministering, comfort, and—most impor-tant—continuity" (121). In *Romanticism and the Gothic: Genre, Reception, and Canon Formation* (Cambridge: Cambridge University Press, 2000), Michael Gamer holds that "Wordsworth's formulation requires a reader capable of something other than an over-literal act of sympathy to read its [the tale's] 'forms' worthily" (112).

63. Barron and Johnston, 79.

64. As mentioned in the Introduction, my use of the term "messianic" is chiefly owed to Walter Benjamin's discussion of low or "weak" messianism, in "Theses on the Philosophy of History," 253–64. Cf. *The Prelude*'s spot of time: an "efficacious spirit" of the past, "lurk[ing]" (*13P* 11.269) in the present "with distinct preeminence" (*2P* 1.289).

65. Schor, 12.

66. George Wilbur Meyer, *Wordsworth's Formative Years*, 236.

67. I borrow the term from Meyer's description of the pedlar's "sedative digressions" (227).

68. Ulmer, 59–60.

69. Edward E. Bostetter, *The Romantic Ventriloquists* (Seattle: University of Washington Press, 1963), 65. Sheats may state the problem best: "the pedlar's reverent naturalism does not permit a full and generous response to Margaret's plight, or, more broadly, to the plight of man" (178).

70. See Ulmer, 62–66.

71. Sheats, 179.

72. Sheats, 179.

73. Ulmer, "Wordsworth, the One Life, and *The Ruined Cottage*," 323–24.

74. Regina Hewitt, *The Possibilities of Society*, 106.

75. Hewitt, 73.

76. Matlak, 88.

77. De Quincey argued that in her "gadding about," Margaret was guilty of child-neglect; that the pedlar, in failing to supply details of her husband's whereabouts, was guilty of suppressing evidence; and that Wordsworth, in neglecting to mention available sources of relief, "vitiates and nullifies the very basis of the story" (*The Collected Writings of Thomas De Quincey*, ed. David Masson, 14 vols. [Edinburgh: Adam & Charles Black, 1889–90], 6: 306. See also Jonathan Bate, *Romantic Ecology: Wordsworth and the Environmental Tradition*, 12–15, 34–35; Johnston, "The Romantic Idea-Elegy," 33–34; and, especially, Barron and Johnston, "'A Power to Virtue Friendly,'" 64–86.

78. Johnston, "The Romantic Idea-Elegy," 33.

79. Johnston, 28, 32. McGann argues that in *The Ruined Cottage* sympathy and love replace the righteous indignation of the Salisbury Plain poems, quieting those poems' "sense of outrage" and quelling their "overflow of angry judgment upon those . . . accountable for helping to maintain the social conditions which generated a surplus of social evil" (*The Romantic Ideology*, 83–85). Chandler disparages the poem for its failure to hold "human institutions" accountable for Margaret's and others' deplorable conditions (*Wordsworth's Second Nature*, 137).

CHAPTER FIVE

1. Kenneth R. Johnston, *Wordsworth and "The Recluse*," 62. Butler and Green provide an illuminating history of Wordsworth and Coleridge's collaboration on *Lyrical Ballads*.

2. The 1800 text of the Preface proclaims *Lyrical Ballads* to treat, first and foremost, "the great and universal passions, the most general and interesting of their occu-

pations," and, only finally, after detailing these "moral" aspects, "the entire world of nature" (*LB* 754, 742).

3. Francis Jeffrey, from his review of Southey's *Thalaba* in the first number of the *Edinburgh Review* (October 1802); cited Peter J. Manning, "Troubling the Borders: *Lyrical Ballads* 1798 and 1998," *The Wordsworth Circle* 30 (1999): 22–27; 24; emphasis added.

4. John Rieder, *Wordsworth's Counterrevolutionary Turn*, 71; emphasis added.

5. Similar appraisals of death and the dead in "We are Seven" are provided by Alan Bewell, *WE* 195; Thomas McFarland, *Wordsworth and the Forms of Ruin*, 171; and Karen Sánchez-Eppler, "Decomposing: Wordsworth's Poetry of Epitaph and English Burial Reform," *Nineteenth-Century Literature* 42 (1988): 415–31.

6. Gary Harrison, *Wordsworth's Vagrant Muse*, 103.

7. Concerning the poem's rather problematical representation of the One Life, see William A. Ulmer, *The Christian Wordsworth*, 40–54. In addition to Ulmer's and those studies of "Tintern Abbey" cited below, I would like to express my general indebtedness to the following readings: Harold Bloom, *The Visionary Company: A Reading of English Romantic Poetry* (Ithaca: Cornell University Press, 1961, rev. 1971), 131–40; Geoffrey Hartman, *WP* 26–30, 176; Richard Onorato, *The Character of the Poet*, 29–87; and Albert O. Wlecke, *Wordsworth and the Sublime* (Berkeley: University of California Press, 1973), *passim*.

8. See Laura Quinney, "'Tintern Abbey,' Sensibility, and the Self-Disenchanted Self," *ELH* 64 (1997): 131–56; 142.

9. Rieder, 186.

10. David Bromwich, *Disowned by Memory: Wordsworth's Poetry of the 1790s* (Chicago: University of Chicago Press, 1998), 88.

11. Mary Jacobus, *Tradition and Experiment*, 125.

12. For the sake mainly of convenience, I follow most other readers in abbreviating the poem's title to "Tintern Abbey," despite the fact that doing so arguably elevates the abbey from its remoter location "a few miles" below.

13. James A. W. Heffernan, "Wordsworth's 'Leveling' Muse in 1798," in *1798: The Year of the "Lyrical Ballads,"* ed. Richard Cronin (New York: St. Martin's Press, 1998), 231–53; 238. See also J. R. Watson's aptly titled "A Note on the Date in the Title of 'Tintern Abbey,'" *The Wordsworth Circle* 10 (1979): 6–14.

14. Evan Radcliffe, "Saving Ideals: Revolution and Benevolence in *The Prelude*," 539. In *Goodness Beyond Virtue: Jacobins During the French Revolution* (Cambridge: Harvard University Press, 1998), Patrice Higgonnet states that at the first-anniversary celebration "the Revolution's universalist goals seemed self-evidently practical and true[;] millions appeared to be Jacobinically inclined" (14). The Terror left British republicans little choice but to recant, to retrench, and, at best, to reformulate. For many that meant asserting that universal fraternity and sympathy had been a dangerous fantasy (Radcliffe, 534).

15. In *William Wordsworth: Intensity and Achievement* (Oxford: Clarendon Press, 1992) McFarland reasonably queries whether July 13 really substitutes for July 14. "To what extent does a near miss qualify for parapractic use?" he asks. "And is nine years as good as ten?" (4). As a date the 14th would pack more punch, to be sure, as would a ten- rather than nine-year anniversary, had Wordsworth forestalled writing the poem or at least not completed it before Bastille Day (cf. *HW* 591). But then the date of the 14th would miss the mark of recalling the betrayal of Marat, betrayal being one of the poem's main murmuring concerns.

16. Johnston points out that the date of Marat's assassination, July 13, 1793, "had been headlined by Southey for the same reason in a poem in the *Morning Post* which Wordsworth saw on the morning after his return to Bristol [from Tintern Abbey]: 'July Thirteenth. Charlotte Corde Executed for Putting Marat to Death'"—the latter's death being cause to celebrate for the anti-Jacobin Southey: "Timely good in Heav'n, / CORDE, O martyr'd Maid" (*HW* 601).

17. Marjorie Levinson's reading of historical displacement and omission in "Tintern Abbey," in *Wordsworth's Great Period Poems* (Cambridge: Cambridge University Press, 1986), 14–87, is arguably the most influential new-historicist analysis of this oft-considered work, informing Jerome McGann's analysis in *The Romantic Ideology* (see 85–88) as well as numerous subsequent interpretations. See John Barrell, *Poetry, Language, and Politics* (Manchester: Manchester University Press, 1989), 137–67; Alan Liu, *Wordsworth: The Sense of History*, 215–18; and Johnston, "The Politics of 'Tintern Abbey,'" in *Romantic Poetry: Recent Revisionary Criticism*, ed. Karl Kroeber and Gene W. Ruoff (New Brunswick: Rutgers University Press, 1993), 124–38; cf. *The Hidden Wordsworth*, 588–98. Levinson's and others' interpretations of the poem's ideological maneuvers have also inspired their share of metacritical responses. See Helen Vendler, "*Tintern Abbey*: Two Assaults," *The Bucknell Review* 36 (1992): 173–90; McFarland, "The Clamour of Absence: Reading and Misreading in Wordsworthian Criticism," in *William Wordsworth: Intensity and Achievement*, 1–33; Quinney, "'Tintern Abbey,' Sensibility, and the Self-Disenchanted Self," 150–52; Meyer H. Abrams, "On Political Readings of *Lyrical Ballads*," in *Romantic Revolutions: Criticism and Theory*, ed. Kenneth R. Johnston et al. (Bloomington: Indiana University Press, 1990), 320–49; Fred V. Randel, "The Betrayals of 'Tintern Abbey,'" *Studies in Romanticism* 32 (1993): 379–97; and William Richey, "The Politicized Landscape of 'Tintern Abbey,'" *Studies in Philology* 95 (1998): 197–219, esp. 197–201. In "Troubling the Borders: *Lyrical Ballads* 1798 and 1998," Manning provides a further level of metacritical analysis, focused upon Vendler's and Abrams's problematical framing of "Tintern Abbey" both as a lyric and as a discrete text set apart from the varied contexts of the first edition of *Lyrical Ballads*.

18. My thinking here is informed by Abrams, "Structure and Style in the Greater Romantic Lyric," *Romanticism and Consciousness: Essays in Criticism*, ed. Harold Bloom (New York: Norton, 1970), 201–29; Vendler, "*Tintern Abbey*: Two Assaults," 175, 183–84; Anne Janowitz, *Lyric and Labour in the Romantic Tradition* (Cambridge: Cambridge University Press, 1998), 18–20; Sarah M. Zimmerman, *Romanticism, Lyricism, and History* (Albany: State University of New York Press, 1999), esp. 94–108; Paul H. Fry, *The Poet's Calling in the English Ode*, esp. 179; and Heidi Thomson, "'We Are Two':

The Address to Dorothy in 'Tintern Abbey,'" *Studies in Romanticism* 40 (2001): 531–46. Wordsworth noted that he had "not ventured to call this Poem an Ode; but [that] it was written with the hope that in the transitions, and the impassioned music of the versification would be found the principal requisites of composition" (*LB* 357). "Tintern Abbey" is perhaps best approached as a text of no single genre: neither wholly lyric, ode, pastoral, elegy, or locodescriptive poem.

19. Vendler, 175.

20. Janowitz, 18.

21. David Chandler, "Vagrancy Smoked Out: Wordsworth 'betwixt Severn and Wye,'" *Romanticism on the Net* 11 (1998): 6 pars.; par. 4, 5/20/2000, *http://www.users. ox.ac.uk/~scat0385/hermit.html*.

22. Bromwich, 82.

23. Richey, "The Politicized Landscape of 'Tintern Abbey,'" 198.

24. As Randel puts it, had Wordsworth wanted to suppress the associations prompted by the Abbey, "he would not have put it into the title at all" (383), for the ruins and date in the poem's title together "made contact with shared frames of reference" (391).

25. C. John Sommerville, *The Secularization of Early Modern England: From Religious Culture to Religious Faith* (New York: Oxford University Press, 1992), 24. Sommerville estimates that before the Act of Dissolution of 1536 possibly "one sixth of all the land" in England may have been endowed to monasteries (19–20).

26. Excepting the latter claim, I draw upon Sommerville's helpful discussion, 24–25.

27. Sommerville, 25–26. For a detailed analysis of Whig cartography in the years after the Act of Dissolution, see Richard Helgerson, "The Land Speaks: Cartography, Choreography, and Subversion in Renaissance England," *Representations* 16 (1986): 51–85.

28. Levinson, 35.

29. Sommerville, 26. The succeeding quotation from Webster is also provided by Sommerville, along with an intriguing reference to the "bare ruined choirs, where late the sweet birds sang" of Shakespeare's contemporary Sonnet 73.

30. Robert M. Maniquis, in "Holy Savagery and Wild Justice: English Romanticism and the Terror" (*Studies in Romanticism* 28 [1989]: 365–95), observes that in Wordsworth most any ruined church or abbey is marked by nostalgia "for the kind of sacramental, and hence communal, order it represents" (381).

31. Levinson, 25.

32. Levinson, 26. I find in the poem less elusion of than outright allusion to social and political history, particularly in the case of the poem's conspicuous siting.

33. Sommerville, 29.

34. Cardinal Francis Aidan Gasquet, *Henry VIII and the English Monasteries*, 2 vols. (London: John Hodges, 1889), 2: 495; cited Levinson, 28.

35. Levinson, 35.

36. Heffernan, 242.

37. Stephen Greenblatt, *Hamlet in Purgatory,* 144, 18. For all its problems and abuses, the doctrine of Purgatory brilliantly "engage[d] with intimate, private feelings" (102).

38. Heffernan, 244.

39. I agree with the gist of Elizabeth A. Fay's assessment, in *Becoming Wordsworthian* (Amherst: The University of Massachusetts Press, 1995), that "though 'Tintern Abbey' reveals Dorothy's presence only at its conclusion, we can see the effects of that presence throughout the poem as William's utterances are directed toward her, the attentive auditor of his meditation" (151). Heffernan likewise finds in the speaker's anticipation of her loss evidence that his voice has "already been inflected by hers— even before he mentions her presence" (244). Richard E. Matlak's *The Poetry of Relationship* (119–37) provides a similar appraisal as well as an accounting of some of what Wordsworth and family had undergone in those five long years.

40. Cf. Vendler, 186.

41. Alan Grob, "William and Dorothy: A Case Study in the Hermeneutics of Disparagement," *ELH* 65 (1998): 187–221; 217. Richey reads matters differently, with the poet's address "willfully flouting," in its sororial repetitions, "the wisdom of the philosopher [Godwin] he had formerly revered" (210). It is certainly true that the speaker in no way *rejects* his familial connection to his sister. But she is hailed as a "friend" first, with all the egalitarian, liberating force that noun then evoked. Vendler argues that in addressing his sister as a *friend* the speaker indeed proffers the "nascent equality of women to men," based upon the fundamental "indistinguishability of female from male psychic life rather than on political or biological grounds" (179).

42. Radcliffe, "Revolutionary Writing, Moral Philosophy, and Universal Benevolence in the Eighteenth Century," *Journal of the History of Ideas* (1993): 221–40; 231.

43. Grob, 213. The speaker of the fragment "For let the impediment be what it may" (ca. late 1798 to early 1799) views familial "affections" as "false" at "their very core" insomuch as they can never "assume / The appearance of a voluntary act" (*LB,* ll. 8–11). Pelagianism similarly insisted upon universal charity as a paramount virtue. Cf. Fielding's *Joseph Andrews.*

44. I am grateful to Ezra Spilke for identifying this echo of Numbers.

45. David Simpson, *Wordsworth's Historical Imagination,* 110. On a similar note, in *Revision and Authority in Wordsworth: The Interpretation of a Career* (Philadelphia: University of Pennsylvania Press, 1989), William H. Galperin argues that in this curious scene "what seems an intensely private moment . . . [is] a very public one" (84).

46. Richey, 215.

47. Mona Ozouf, *Festivals and the French Revolution,* trans. Alan Sheridan (Cambridge: Harvard University Press, 1988), 280–81 .

48. Simpson, 112–13.

49. This term is also employed in Toby R. Benis's *Romanticism on the Road*, 127.

50. James Soderholm, "Dorothy Wordsworth's Return to Tintern Abbey," *New Literary History* 26 (1995): 309–22; 309. Cf. Johnston's similar assessment that "where one stands now on 'Tintern Abbey' makes a big difference in Romantic scholarship" (*HW* 591). Heidi Thomson situates most critics at "two critical poles," one disparaging the poet's "selfish exclusion of anything else," including Dorothy, "that might impede his [Wordsworth's] privileged vision into 'the life of things'" (see below), the other, more "affirmative" group, peopled by earlier critics and by more recent readers, interprets the poem as the pronouncement "of a wise speaker who has heard and incorporated the 'still, sad music of humanity'" ("We Are Two," 531).

51. Judith W. Page, *Wordsworth and the Cultivation of Women* (Berkeley: University of California Press, 1994), 45. See Margaret Homans, *Women Writers and Poetic Identity*, 26–27; Anne K. Mellor, *Romanticism & Gender*, 19; Levinson, 38, 47; Susan J. Wolfson, *The Questioning Presence*, 67–69; Simpson, 110–11; Barrell, *Poetry, Language, and Politics*, esp. 160–66; and Randel, 392–93. Vendler takes particular issue with Barrell's reading of Dorothy's depiction (180–88). See also the above-cited essays by Soderholm and Grob.

52. Thomson, 533. See also Janowitz's *Lyric and Labour*, 20; and Vendler, 184.

53. Thomson, 541–42. Thomson argues that the poet's sister is "not only a sounding board or a repository; instead she is part of a lasting community which constitutes the 'we are two' (as in 'we are seven') against 'evil tongues'" and other hostile, alienating forces (544). See also John Turner, *Wordsworth's Play and Politics*, 163; Richey, 215–16; and Benis, 137.

54. Hartman, *The Unremarkable Wordsworth*, 40.

55. Levinson, 23.

56. Stephen Maxfield Parrish, *The Art of the "Lyrical Ballads"* (Cambridge: Harvard University Press, 1973), 162; cited *LB* 26.

57. As Mark Jones states in *The "Lucy Poems": A Case Study in Literary Knowledge* (Toronto: University of Toronto Press, 1995), this grouping together of the five Lucy lyrics is principally "an invention of Victorian criticism," having not been "explicitly proposed" until 1871, by Margaret Oliphant, and not presented in print until Matthew Arnold's selection of Wordsworth's poetry, in 1879 (7). Jones's study provides further discussion of the poems' critical tradition; see esp. 147–87. Regarding the grouping's textual inclusions and exclusions, see 6–26, esp. 6–13. Brian G. Caraher's *Wordsworth's "Slumber" and the Problematics of Reading* (University Park: The Pennsylvania University Press, 1991) considers additional candidates for inclusion in the Lucy group as well as Wordsworth's own quasi-groupings of Lucy lyrics (16n. 1, 41–42, 121). In "The 'Lucy' Poems: Poems of Mourning" (*The Wordsworth Circle* 30 [1999]: 28–36), Pamela Woof contemplates Wordsworth's 1815 decision to divide the group between poems of the imagination and of the affections (28).

58. For a recent example, see G. Kim Blank, *Wordsworth and Feeling: The Poetry of an Adult Child* (London: Associated University Presses, 1995), 149–50.

59. Woof, "The 'Lucy' Poems," 30.

60. On the problem of reading "A slumber" as a Lucy poem, see Jones, 8–11, 26, 67–75, 236.

61. Paul de Man, "The Rhetoric of Temporality," in *Blindness and Insight,* 223.

62. See Jones 46, 72.

63. Alan Liu reads Lucy as, in the old sense of the term, a "'natural' child." Lucy becomes the poster child and "body of Lakeland bastardy" (*Wordsworth: The Sense of History,* 308). For contrast, see Virginia Ireys's "The Death of the Muse: Wordsworth's Lucy as Pastoral Heroine," *Papers on Language and Literature* 24 (1988): 384–403, which situates the Lucy poems in the tradition of Greco-Roman and English pastoral.

64. See also Ulmer, *The Christian Wordsworth,* 99–100. Contrary readings—that Lucy's ubiquitous rolling is tantamount to the "motion" and "spirit" of the One Life proclaimed in "Tintern Abbey"—can be found in John Beer, *Wordsworth in Time* (London: Oxford University Press, 1979), 83–84; and F. W. Bateson, *English Poetry: A Critical Introduction* (London: Longmans, 1950, 2nd ed. 1966), 33.

65. David P. Haney reads the poem as becoming "in the space between the two stanzas . . . a treatise on the unthinkability of death," one that seeks to hide the "acknowledgment of death by hiding it in a mythical structure of repetition" (*Wordsworth and the Hermeneutics of Incarnation,* 96–97).

66. David Ferry, *The Limits of Mortality,* 76. By contrast, see Jones, 73.

67. Not until his final publication of "A slumber" in *Poetical Works* of 1849–50 does the then circa-Victorian Wordsworth change the exclamation mark to a less impassioned, more humble period (*PW* 2: 216). It is this authorized text that many past and present anthologies reprint. But until the middle of the nineteenth century the author had retained that mark in all editions of *Lyrical Ballads* as well as in the 1815 edition of his poetry (*Poems 1815* [Oxford: Woodstock Books, 1989], 315). Regarding this difference and other differences in punctuation among different editions, see Caraher, *Wordsworth's "Slumber,"* 18n. 6.

68. Marlon B. Ross, "Naturalizing Gender: Woman's Place in Wordsworth's Ideological Landscapes," *ELH* 53 (1986): 398.

69. "'An Epitaph,' says Weever[,] 'is a superscription (either in verse or prose) or an astrict pithie Diagram, writ, carved, or engraven, upon the tomb, grave, or sepulchre of the defunct, briefly declaring . . . the name, the age, the deserts, the dignities, the state, *the praises both of body and minde,* the good and bad fortunes in the life and the manner and time of the death of the person therein interred'" (*PrW* 2: 88–89; original emphasis). Wordsworth cites this "just" definition in the third of the *Essays upon Epitaphs,* adding that a "perfect epitaph" also ought to impart to the reader what the deceased "had in common with the species" (89), including, of course, his or her mortality.

70. I am thinking here of one parody identical to "She dwelt" but for the last word, with "me" changed to "her." That basic idea is implicit in Hartley Coleridge's well-known parody, "He lived amidst th' untrodden ways" and arguably also in F. B.

Doveton's "Emancipation" ("She dwelt within unyielding stays"). These and other parodies of the Lucy poems are collected together in Walter Hamilton's anthology, *Parody of the Works of English and American Authors* (London: Reeves and Turner, 1888), 5: 94–95, and are considered by Jones, 97–98, 112–19.

71. Mary R. Webb, "The Lucy Poems," *The Charles Lamb Bulletin* 92 (1995): 178–92.

72. See Irene H. Chayes, "Little Girls Lost: Problems of a Romantic Archetype," *Blake: A Collection of Critical Essays,* ed. Northrop Frye (Englewood Cliffs: Prentice-Hall, 1966), 76; cited Ireys, 391.

73. In his Fenwick note to "Lucy Gray," Wordsworth described the girl's death as having been based, according to Dorothy's report, upon an actual "little girl, who not far from Halifax in Yorkshire was bewildered in a snow-storm." Her body had been "found in the canal" (*LB* 385).

74. For discussions of the poem's ballad, biblical, and other sources, see Bewell, *WE* 204; Averill, *PHS* 187–88, 195; and Jacobus, 211.

75. In *Specters of Marx,* Jacques Derrida similarly argues that mourning "consists always in attempting to ontologize remains, to make them present, in the first place by identifying the bodily remains and by localizing the dead" (9).

76. See de Man, "The Rhetoric of Temporality," in *Blindness and Insight,* 223–26, helpfully analyzed (as in part being "parodic of standard critical procedures") by Jones, 203–212. See also Frances Ferguson, "The Lucy Poems: Wordsworth's Quest for a Poetic Object," *ELH* 40 (1973): 432–48, reprinted in *William Wordsworth: Language as Counter-Spirit,* 173–94; J. Hillis Miller, "On Edge: The Crossways of Contemporary Criticism" (1979, postscript 1984), in *Theory Now And Then* (Durham: Duke University Press, 1991), 171–200; "Narrative," in *Critical Terms for Literary Study,* ed. Frank Lentricchia and Thomas McLaughlin (Chicago: University of Chicago Press, 1990), 66–79, esp. 76–79; and Hartman, *Easy Pieces* (New York: Columbia University Press, 1985), 145–54.

77. The names Lucy and Emma were by no means uncommon for lost, dead, or dying women in literature. As Butler and Green note, "literary uses of the name Lucy to refer to a dead lover abound in the eighteenth century"—for example, in Collins, Rogers, Lyttleton, and Moore (*LB* 383). Ireys points out how familiar the name and the poems' situations and tropes were to English readers—those familiar, for example, with "Written on a Spot Commanding a Distant Prospect," from *Gentleman's Magazine* (July 1795), in which "a poet mourns the death of his Lucy, whom he will never see again" (Ireys, 393). Lucy's and Emma's literary ubiquity is also evidenced in J. Coombe's narrative *The Peasant of Auburn, or the Emigrant, a Poem,* excerpted in *The Critical Review* 56 (1783): 149–50. Coleridge surmised the identity of the Lucy of "Strange fits of passion" to be Dorothy (*LB* 383), whom Wordsworth in turn of course frequently dubs "Emma," as in *Lyrical Ballads'* Lucy-like "'Tis said, that some have died for love," the commemorative naming-of-places poem "It was an April morning: fresh and clear," and in *Home at Grasmere.*

78. Cf. Kenneth Eisold, *Loneliness and Communion,* 129.

79. In "Wordsworth, Inscriptions, and Romantic Nature Poetry" (*Beyond Formalism: Literary Essays, 1958–70* [New Haven: Yale University Press, 1970], 206–30), Hartman argues that the poem represents a "sense of continuity between the noble dead and the noble living" (227).

80. David Collings, *Wordsworthian Errancies,* 158; cf. 173.

81. Collings, 173; cf. 177.

82. Wordsworth based the poem upon his conflation of the tragedy of Jerome Bowman of Ennerdale, who, near Scalehow Force, died from a broken leg, and that of an unnamed son who (according to Coleridge's notebook) had sleepwalked off the top of Proud Knot (*LB,* p. 380).

83. Jonathan Wordsworth, *The Ruined Cottage, The Brothers, Michael,* 48.

84. Cf. Tilottama Rajan's discussion of the hermeneutic problem that "there never really is any communication between the priest and Leonard" (*The Supplement of Reading: Figures of Understanding in Romantic Theory and Practice* [Ithaca: Cornell University Press, 1990], 163).

85. Turner, *Wordsworth's Play and Politics,* 209.

86. In *Romantic Geography,* Michael Wiley conjectures that Leonard's reintegration into Ennerdale fails because his previous actions as a mariner have precluded it. Galperin provides a quite different reading of Leonard's actions; see *Revision and Authority,* 125–32.

87. Wolfson, *The Questioning Presence,* 84.

88. Bromwich, 109.

89. Michele Turner Sharp, "The Churchyard Among the Wordsworthian Mountains," 394. Readers interested in Wordsworth's *Essays'* treatment of epitaph as representation will wish to consult Sharp's perceptive "Re-membering the Real, Dis(re)membering the Dead: Wordsworth's 'Essays upon Epitaphs,'" *Studies in Romanticism* 34 (1995): 273–92. See also Dewey W. Hall, "Signs of the Dead: Epitaphs, Inscriptions, and the Discourse of the Self," *ELH* 68 (2001): 655–77, esp. 658–62. "What remains implicit in Wordsworth's epitaphic discourse," Hall similarly argues, "is the rather compelling power of the dead to attract the living" (661).

90. Cf. John Kerrigan's "Knowing the Dead . . . ," and its previously mentioned reading of even "bare stones" as "*semai,* signs" (88).

91. Regina Hewitt, *The Possibilities of Society,* 76.

92. Hewitt, 77.

93. Bromwich, 158.

94. Hewitt, 78.

95. Wolfson, 89.

96. Tracy Ware, "Historicism Along and Against the Grain: The Case of Wordsworth's 'Michael,'" *Nineteenth-Century Literature* 3 (1994): 360–74; 370.

97. See Jones, "Double Economics: Ambivalence in Wordsworth's Pastoral," *PMLA* 108 (1993): 1098–1113; 1107. Jones's reading of "Michael" as "parodic" is one of the poem's most insightful interpretations.

98. Stuart Peterfreund, "Wordsworth on Covenants: 'Heart Conditions,' Primogeniture, Remains, and the Ties that Bind in 'Michael' and Elsewhere," *Criticism: A Quarterly for Literature and the Arts* 40 (1998): 191–215; 213n. 20. As a masculine form of Lucy, the name *Luke* becomes not just "doubly" named (as Jones argues) but triply named and valued.

99. Wiley, 61.

100. Cf. Bromwich, 159. See also Levinson, 60.

101. Wolfson, 89.

102. Wolfson, 89.

103. Deanne Westbrook, "Wordsworth's Prodigal Son: 'Michael' as Parable and as Metaparable," *The Wordsworth Circle* 28 (1997): 109–19; 118.

104. Bruce Graver, "Wordsworth's Georgic Pastoral: *Otium* and *Labor* in 'Michael,'" *European Romantic Review* 1 (1991): 119–34; 129.

105. Graver, 131. Westbrook similarly concludes that "Michael" really "proposes neither social cause nor social cure for the situation of the old shepherd; for whatever the turnings of plot, Michael is not driven from his land, but dies on it and is buried on it" (118).

106. Graver, 131.

107. Westbrook, 118.

108. Levinson, 76. Cf. Annabel Patterson, *Pastoral and Ideology: Virgil to Valéry* (Berkeley: University of California Press, 1987), esp. 267–69; Susan Eilenberg, "Wordsworth's 'Michael': The Poetry of Property," *Essays in Literature* 15 (1988): 13–25; and Simpson, 140–49. Jones argues that to "charge Wordsworth's pastoral with occluding or mystifying history or reality is to presume that his pastoral might and ought to be true, a rather odd demand to make of poetry that proclaims itself pastoral" (1099).

109. For Levinson, the allusion to the sacrifice of Isaac serves to displace its historical referents, the "external mimetic objects" of "the Northern statement, rural depopulation, public policy," in favor of the covenant of poetic vocation and audience (69). Cf. Ware, 361–64; Eilenberg, 20–21; and Jones's correction of Levinson, 1102–3, cf. 1106–8.

110. Collings, *Wordsworthian Errancies*, 176.

111. Eilenberg, 23.

112. Jones, 1109.

113. Eilenberg, 22.

114. Cf. Reeve Parker, "Finishing Off 'Michael': Poetic and Critical Enclosures," *Diacritics* 17 (1987): 53–64.

115. Collings, 178.

116. I am drawing upon the relationship between parasite and host outlined by Miller's "Critic as Host," reprinted in *Theory Now and Then,* 143–70.

CHAPTER SIX

1. There are at least two mythic explanations for Actaeon's crime: that he boasted of his hunting prowess or that he discovered Artemis (Diana) in her bath. Wordsworth most likely had read Ovid's *Metamorphoses'* version of the latter account. Either way, the metaphor alludes to Actaeon's punishment by the goddess of hunting and chastity: he is transformed into one of his prey and pursued and killed by his own hounds.

2. Kenneth R. Johnston, *Wordsworth and "The Recluse,"* 107.

3. Johnston, 107–8.

4. William A. Ulmer, *The Christian Wordsworth,* 144. Cf. M. H. Abrams, *Natural Supernaturalism: Tradition and Revolution in Romantic Literature* (New York: Norton, 1971), esp. 107–22. As Ulmer points out, Mark Reed offers a dissenting editorial voice, conversely arguing that it was the five-book poem's own "foes' theme," rather than the looming *Recluse,* that caused the scheme to unravel in MS. W (Ulmer, 142–48). Cf. Reed, "The Five-Book *Prelude* of Early Spring 1804," *JEGP* 76 (1977): 1–25.

5. For those readers more familiar with the expanded 1805 *Prelude,* this prior version's first three books are nearly identical to those of the thirteen-book text. They include the preamble, the spots of time of Books One and Two, Book Three's recounting of Wordsworth's life at Cambridge and fall from Nature, and Book Four's lines of his restorative return to Hawkshead, including his meeting with the discharged soldier. The thirteen-book text splits that fourth book between Books Fourth and Fifth, adding to the former a eulogy to Ann Tyson and to the latter the Dream of the Arab, tributes to poetic precursors, and a eulogy for Wordsworth's mother.

6. Duncan Wu has reconstructed the five-book poem from the surviving "penultimate" drafts in MSS. W and WW, from the slightly later MS. M (a letter to Coleridge that includes fair copy of the poem's first three books, one week after the scheme had been abandoned), and a few other related manuscripts. Assuming those first two drafts to be penultimate and the text of MS. M to be *close* to that of the first three books, I side with Wu on the credibility of the five-book poem's reconstruction, despite the fact that, as Ulmer notes, some of the surviving drafts indeed are "extremely rough" (141). For Wu's rationale, see *5P* 13–22. See also Johnston, 107–8.

7. Hartman locates the cause for this "supervening thought of death" in the vogue of epitaph.

8. Cynthia Chase, *Decomposing Figures,* 16–17. Cf. J. Hillis Miller, *The Linguistic Moment,* 75–77.

9. David P. Haney, *William Wordsworth and the Hermeneutics of Incarnation,* 82.

10. Michele Turner Sharp, "The Churchyard Among the Wordsworthian Mountains," 390. Sharp is here drawing upon Wordsworth's own wording.

11. Nancy Easterlin's *Wordsworth and the Question of "Romantic Religion"* (Lewisburg: Bucknell University Press, 1996) provides a different reading, interpreting the church's forgetfulness not as "revealing indifference" but as attesting "to wisdom and love" (104).

12. Haney, 82–83.

13. Thomas Pfau, *Wordsworth's Profession: Form, Class, and the Logic of Early Romantic Cultural Production* (Stanford: Stanford University Press, 1997), 337. Pfau's analysis of the Drowned Man episode's problematic or "crisis" of cultural mediation is intriguing (333–37). I refer the reader to the Introduction's list of other readings that have especially influenced my interpretation of this spot of time.

14. Sharp, 391–92.

15. Chase argues that in the context of Book 5 the 1805 *Prelude*'s polemic about education—"do away with the schoolmasters!—gets transformed . . . into an incident that literally does away with one" (31), the drowned man often being equated with the schoolmaster James Jackson, who drowned in the lake in June 1779 (*5P* 127n. 104; cf. *NCP* 176n. 4). I rather like Gordon K. Thomas's own reading: "the schoolboy's first lesson at Hawkshead came from a schoolmaster, but not in the classroom." See "'Orphans Then': Death in the *Two-Part Prelude*," *The Charles Lamb Bulletin* 96 (1996): 157–73; 159.

16. Chase, 19.

17. Haney, 118.

18. Johnston, 71.

19. John Kerrigan, "Knowing the Dead," 88. Thomas Weiskel similarly reads the scene as drawing an equation between writing and death—or rather "the intimation of death" (*Romantic Sublime,* 178). Toby R. Benis's *Romanticism on the Road* finds the murderer's name to become "less his than the appropriated property of a community" (217).

20. British lore frequently associated the hawthorn with death, although not of course as commonly as it did the yew, favored tree of churchyards. Cf. Vaughan Cornish, D.SC., *The Churchyard Yew & Immortality,* introd. Archbishop of York (London: F. Muller, 1946).

21. Averill argues that it is the "emotional mixture of [oedipal] guilt and sorrow [that] attaches 'far other feelings' to the archetypes" associated with the event (*PHS* 249). William H. Galperin's *Revision and Authority in Wordsworth* provides a markedly different view of the poet's struggle with tradition in this spot (186–87).

22. Alan Richardson, "Wordsworth at the Crossroads," 18. Cf. Weiskel, 174–75, 181–85.

23. Johnston, 70.

24. Richardson, 18.

25. Lionel Morton, "Books and Drowned Men," 33–34.

26. Johnston, 84.

27. As with "Tintern Abbey," this poem invites readers to identify speaker and sister as William and Dorothy, which is reasonable—up to a point. But, although the poem originated in its author's experience, one should be mindful of the fact that it was written as the first part of a generalized philosophical poem and that the speaker's sister is addressed not as Dorothy but as (the generic, even elegiac) "Emma." Why name her thus, as was Wordsworth's custom, if not to distinguish her from her flesh-and-blood counterpart?

28. Johnston, 83.

29. Johnston, 82; original emphasis. In *The Hidden Wordsworth*, Johnston provides a more detailed history of the Wordsworths' arrival in Grasmere (*HW* 686–708).

30. Cf. Johnston, *Wordsworth and "The Recluse,"* 85.

31. My essay "'Sweet Influences': Human/Animal Difference and Social Cohesion in Wordsworth and Coleridge, 1794–1806" (*Romanticism & Ecology*, ed. James McKusick, *Romantic Circles Praxis Series* [2001]: 31 pars. *http://www.rc.umd.edu/praxis/ecology/fosso/fosso.html*) offers a similar but more animal-oriented reading of the Hart-leap Well episode (see pars. 21–27).

32. Raimonda Modiano, "Blood Sacrifice, Gift Economy, and the Edenic World: Wordsworth's 'Home at Grasmere,'" *Studies in Romanticism* 32 (1993): 481–521; 499.

33. David Perkins, "Wordsworth and the Polemic against Hunting: Hart-Leap Well," *Nineteenth-Century Literature* 58 (1998): 421–45; 439. Cf. Tilottama Rajan's *Supplement of Reading*, 150.

34. Perkins, 443.

35. Perkins, 444–45.

36. Johnston, 85.

37. Ulmer, "The Society of Death in *Home at Grasmere*," 68.

38. Ulmer, 68. See also Tim Fulford, "Fields of Liberty? The Politics of Wordsworth's Grasmere," *European Romantic Review* 9 (1998): 59–86; and Anthony John Harding, "Forgetfulness and the Poetic Self in 'Home at Grasmere,'" *The Wordsworth Circle* 22 (1991): 109–18.

39. Modiano, 512. Modiano refers to a remark made by Johnston (see Johnston, 86).

40. Modiano, 512, 483.

41. Bruce Clarke, "Wordsworth's Departed Swans: Sublimation and Sublimity in *Home at Grasmere*," *Studies in Romanticism* 19 (1980): 355–74; 370–71.

42. Johnston, 89.

43. Readers have too readily assumed, Ulmer argues, that the swans have been killed, missing the fact that the text leaves the pair's fate "uncertain," a matter of con-

jecture, of "pure surmise" (70). Arguably, their fate's indeterminacy makes their presumed loss all the more enduring.

44. Johnston, 91. Although my argument tracks a different course, these and following pages are indebted to Johnston's reading of crisis in the poem.

45. Cornell's editor Beth Darlington deduces that a number of the poem's passages "express events and feelings of March and April, 1800" (*HG* 8), but she does not assert, as Johnston does, how much composition occurred before 1806, when the MS. B text was recorded. See her introduction to the Cornell edition; Jonathan Wordsworth's "On Man, on Nature, and on Human Life," 17–29; and Johnston, 85–91, especially his plea to treat "the five hundred-odd lines of 'Home at Grasmere' written in 1800 as a unit" (86).

46. One might read biographical matters in reverse: first Grasmere's rejection of the newcomers and then the surmised, almost criminal, basis for reclusion. But this scenario would seem to exaggerate events, the Wordsworths having initially been happy at Town End.

47. My ideas here were inspired in part by the collection of hunting-oriented paintings, tapestries, and sculptures displayed in the Château de Chambord, in the Loire Valley.

48. As noted in the Introduction, this particular coinage is Thomas McFarland's.

CHAPTER SEVEN

1. Thomas McFarland, *Romanticism and the Forms of Ruin*, 148.

2. Cf. Paul Sheats, *The Making of Wordsworth's Poetry*, 116.

3. Robert M. Ryan argues that "Wordsworth's decision to 'rejoin' the Church of England . . . was closer to a pledge of allegiance than to a confession of faith. . . . As late as 1805 he still seems to have been struggling toward a confident assurance of an afterlife. In the spiritual crisis that followed the death of . . . John in that year, Christian doctrine gave him a comfort that his own religious instincts could not provide" (*The Romantic Reformation*, 98).

4. McFarland, 162. Some critics attribute these changes in orientation to Wordsworth's "loss of confidence in social man" (*PW* 5: 117) or to his growing conservatism, including his improved relationship with the staunchly Tory and notorious Earl of Lonsdale. See, for example, John Williams, *Wordsworth: Romantic Poetry and Revolution Politics*, 179–80. In *Unruly Times*, A. S. Byatt lays the blame for the poet's change in outlook not upon alterations in habitation or in politics but precisely upon his egotism. Increasingly, in *The Prelude* and thereafter, the poet's focus is on "the cultivation of his own powers" rather than on others and other themes (44–45).

5. Richard Onorato, *The Character of the Poet*, 393.

6. Gordon K. Thomas, "'Orphans Then': Death in the *Two-Part Prelude*," 164.

7. See Nancy Easterlin, *Wordsworth and the Question of "Romantic Religion,"* 118–19.

8. John Worthen, *The Gang: Coleridge, the Hutchinsons & the Wordsworths in 1802* (New Haven: Yale University Press, 2001), 138.

9. See Gene Ruoff, *Wordsworth and Coleridge: The Making of the Major Lyrics, 1802–1804* (New Brunswick: Rutgers University Press, 1989), esp. 237 ff.; and Wordsworth, *FN* 61. Worthen's *The Gang* provides a compelling reassessment of the two poets' circa-1800–04 intertextual conversations, particularly concerning the two great odes, each having been a longstanding work in progress. See especially 136–54.

10. For Marjorie Levinson that "grief" is owed to "the failure of the French Revolution," (mis)represented "as exclusively the poet's loss, and as a strictly emotional, epistemological loss" (*Wordsworth's Great Period Poems*, 83). Worthen speculates that the circa-1802 fragment may have been begun as early as October 1800 (139).

11. In the Fenwick notes, Wordsworth famously pronounced that as a child he had been all but unable "to admit the notion of death as a state applicable to my own being" (*FN* 61).

12. William A. Ulmer, *The Christian Wordsworth*, 127.

13. Ulmer, 128.

14. Ulmer, 130.

15. McFarland, 162.

16. Levinson, 102.

17. Esther Schor, *Bearing the Dead*, 137.

18. Levinson, 102.

19. See Richard Matlak, "Captain John Wordsworth's Death at Sea," *The Wordsworth Circle* 31 (2000): 127–33. Matlak points to the discrepancy between Beaumont's representation of the sinking vessel and that of the actual event, a discrepancy that "transforms accident and human frailty," including John's culpability, "into destiny" (132). "Peele Castle" functions as a means of historical denial. Yet, despite prior magazine engravings, no one in 1806 would likely have associated the depiction with the shipwreck of the Abergavenny—"except the poet" (127).

20. Freud's *Beyond the Pleasure Principle* provides an intriguingly similar scheme of withdrawal and self-protection as a kind of scabbing (*SE* 18: 26–28).

21. Levinson, 103.

22. Judith W. Page, *Wordsworth and the Cultivation of Women*, 91.

23. David Simpson, *Wordsworth's Historical Imagination*, 185.

24. Simpson, 200.

25. Kenneth R. Johnston, *Wordsworth and "The Recluse,"* 288–89.

26. Alison Hickey, *Impure Conceits: Rhetoric and Ideology in Wordsworth's "Excursion"* (Stanford: Stanford University Press, 1997), 31.

27. Schor, 154; see also 151–95.

28. Sally Bushell, *Re-Reading "The Excursion": Narrative, Response and the Wordsworthian Dramatic Voice*, in The Nineteenth Century Series, gen. eds. Vincent Newey and Joanne Shattock (Aldershot, England, and Burlington, Vt.: Ashgate, 2002), 208. Bushell's study has appeared too recently for me to give it all the consideration it deserves. Largely integrated into *Re-Reading*, Bushell's "Exempla in *The Excursion*: The Purpose of the Pastor's Epitaphic Tales" (*The Charles Lamb Bulletin* 105 [1999]: 16–27) discerns in the poem a "union of the living and the dead" (26).

29. The Cornell edition's introduction discusses the hagiographic history of St. Basil in some detail, along with considering where Wordsworth likely read of it. See especially *TP* 20–24.

30. Cf. *Ex* 3.374–410. In terms of the *Tuft*'s revision and incorporation in *The Excursion*, see *PW* 5: 153 and *TP* 47.

31. Johnston, 246.

32. Johnston, 246.

33. My understanding of the chronology of *The Excursion*'s composition is informed by Helen Darbishire's notes to the 1850 edition, printed in the fifth volume of *Poetical Works* (*PW* 5: 376–475), and by Hickey's discussion in *Impure Conceits* (3, 183n. 12), derived from Darbishire's commentary and from Mark L. Reed's *Wordsworth: The Chronology of the Middle Years, 1800–1815* (Cambridge: Harvard University Press, 1975), 22–25, 659–85.

34. This similarity is pinpointed by Lorna Clymer, in "Graved in Tropes," 377. See also Bushell, *Re-Reading*, 96. The character of the Solitary may also be drawn from that of the misanthropic Jacques, from *As You Like It*, and from the prior bilious figures of the old comedy.

35. Unless stated otherwise, all citations from *The Excursion* refer to the text and pagination of the Woodstock Books facsimile of the 1814 edition (Oxford: Woodstock Books, 1991). Given the 1814 text's lack of line numbers, I also include the numbering of the 1850 edition in *Poetical Works*.

36. Johnston, 271. See also Mary Webb, "Industrialization and the Moral Law in Books VIII and IX of *The Excursion*," *The Charles Lamb Bulletin* 81 (1993): 5–25; 24.

37. For Hartman, the Solitary may represent "a dangerous part of the poet's mind," belying aspects fearful and fundamental (*WP* 307). See also Ryan, 107.

38. See Ryan, 114.

39. Hartman describes the poem's structural trope as being that of *katabasis* (*WP* 321).

40. Stephen Gill, *William Wordsworth and the Victorians* (Oxford: Clarendon Press, 1998), 124.

41. Johnston, 286. Johnston holds that the scheme imparted by the Pastor is "only nominally Christian," despite the fact that many of those he eulogizes clearly "led lives based on Christian assumptions." Like some readers of the poem, I find a more Chris-

tian scheme. "Are you a Xtian?" Lamb inquired, "or is it the Pedlar & the Priest who are?" (cited Ryan, 104). Ryan reads *The Excursion* as a more heterodox work, due to Wordsworth's "effort to be true to the entirety of his experience, to the radical humanism and the natural religion he had espoused earlier in his life as well as the Christian faith he had more recently embraced" (101).

42. For Wordsworth's later recollections concerning the Sympsons, and for other details about the family, see *FN* 87–88.

43. Nicola Trott, "*The Excursion*: Types and Symbols of Eternity," *The Charles Lamb Bulletin* 79 (1992): 239–52; 246.

44. Johnston, 302.

45. David P. Haney, *William Wordsworth and the Hermeneutics of Incarnation*, 178.

46. Clymer, 379.

47. Clymer, 379.

48. Bushell, 13; cf. 73.

49. Laura Dabundo, "The Extrospective Vision: *The Excursion* as Transitional in Wordsworth's Poetry and Age," *The Wordsworth Circle* 19 (1988): 8–14; 9. The eulogized are, Dabundo observes, "individuals buried in consecrated . . . land," men and women who "were born, lived, and then died in the bosom of community deep within the network of village life" (11–12).

50. Dabundo, 12; emphasis added.

51. Easterlin, 127.

52. According to Bushell, this envisioned sequel's "unambiguous 'conversion' and restoration of the Solitary" makes the poem's "reluctance . . . to commit itself to full Christianity still more apparent" (96). She surmises Wordsworth's intention to have been to produce an inconclusive text, one whose "moral teaching" would not be "limited to the moment of utterance" or to a single vantage (102). Cf. Dewey W. Hall's contention that *The Excursion* becomes like "a sermon to be heard and lived out in the lives of its parishioners" ("Signs of the Dead," 664). By contrast, for William Howard the "pervading doubt" of the conclusion spells failure, revealing "the difficulty of the task undertaken in the first place and the impotence of rhetoric as a means of persuasion." See "Narrative Irony in *The Excursion*," *Studies in Romanticism* 44 (1985): 511–30; 528.

53. William H. Galperin's *Revision and Authority in Wordsworth* finds the poem to displace certain key social or political problems by representing them as *symptoms* of disease (29–63). See also Simpson, 184–216.

SELECTED BIBLIOGRAPHY

Abraham, Nicolas. "Notes on the Phantom: A Complement to Freud's Metapsychology." *The Trial(s) of Psychoanalysis*. Ed. Francoise Meltzer. Chicago: University of Chicago Press, 1987, 75–80.

Abraham, Nicolas, and Maria Torok. "Introjection-Incorporation: Mourning or Melancholia." *Psychoanalysis in France*. Ed. Serge Lebovici and Daniel Widlöcher. New York: International Universities Press, 1980, 3–16.

Abrams, Meyer H. *Natural Supernaturalism: Tradition and Revolution in Romantic Literature*. New York: Norton, 1971.

———. "On Political Readings of *Lyrical Ballads*." *Romantic Revolutions: Criticism and Theory*. Ed. Kenneth R. Johnston et al. Bloomington: Indiana University Press, 1990, 320–49.

———. "Structure and Style in the Greater Romantic Lyric." *Romanticism and Consciousness: Essays in Criticism*. Ed. Harold Bloom. New York: Norton, 1970, 201–229.

Akenside, Mark. *The Pleasures of Imagination. The New Oxford Book of Eighteenth-Century Verse*. Ed. Roger Lonsdale. Oxford: Oxford University Press, 1984, 392–97.

Althusser, Louis. "Ideology and Ideological State Apparatuses (Notes Towards an Investigation)." *Lenin and Philosophy and Other Essays*. Trans. Ben Brewster. New York: Monthly Review Press, 1971, 127–86.

Anderson, Benedict. *Imagined Communities: Reflections on the Origin and Spread of Nationalism*. New York: Verso, 1983, rev. 1991.

Ariès, Philippe. *The Hour of Our Death*. Trans. Helen Weaver. New York: Knopf, 1981.

Averill, James. H. *Wordsworth and the Poetry of Human Suffering*. Ithaca: Cornell University Press, 1980.

Barrell, John. *Poetry, Language, and Politics*. Manchester: Manchester University Press, 1989.

Barron, Jonathan, and Kenneth R. Johnston. "'A Power to Virtue Friendly': The Pedlar's Guilt in Wordsworth's 'Ruined Cottage.'" *Romantic Revisions*. Ed. Robert Brinkley and Keith Hanley. New York: Cambridge University Press, 1992, 64–86.

Bate, Jonathan. *Romantic Ecology: Wordsworth and the Environmental Tradition.* London: Routledge, 1991.

Bateson, F. W. *English Poetry: A Critical Introduction.* London: Longmans, 1950; 2nd ed., 1966.

———. *Wordsworth: A Re-interpretation.* New York: Longmans, 1956.

Batten, Guinn. *The Orphaned Imagination: Melancholy and Commodity Culture in English Romanticism.* Durham: Duke University Press, 1998.

Becker, Ernest. *The Denial of Death.* New York: Free Press, 1973.

Beer, John. *Wordsworth in Time.* London: Oxford University Press, 1979.

Behrendt, Stephen C. *Royal Mourning and Regency Culture: Elegies and Memorials of Princess Charlotte.* New York: St. Martin's Press, 1997.

Benis, Toby R. *Romanticism on the Road: The Marginal Gains of Wordsworth's Homeless.* New York: St. Martin's Press, 2000.

Benjamin, Walter. *Illuminations.* Ed. Hannah Arendt. Trans. Harry Zohn. New York: Schocken, 1969.

———. *The Origin of German Tragic Drama.* Trans. John Osborne. New York: New Left Books, 1977.

Bewell, Alan. *Wordsworth and the Enlightenment: Nature, Man, and Society in the Experimental Poetry.* New Haven: Yale University Press, 1987.

Birdsall, Eric. "Nature and Society in *Descriptive Sketches.*" *Modern Philology* 84 (1986): 39–52.

Blanchot, Maurice. *The Unavowable Community.* Trans. Pierre Joris. New York: Station Hill, 1988.

Blank, G. Kim. *Wordsworth and Feeling: The Poetry of an Adult Child.* London: Associated University Presses, 1995.

Bloom, Harold. *The Anxiety of Influence: A Theory of Poetry.* New York: Oxford University Press, 1973.

———. *Poetry and Repression.* New Haven: Yale University Press, 1976.

———. *The Visionary Company: A Reading of English Romantic Poetry.* Ithaca: Cornell University Press, 1961, rev. 1971.

Bostetter, Edward E. *The Romantic Ventriloquists.* Seattle: University of Washington Press, 1963.

Brisman, Leslie. *Milton's Poetry of Choice and Its Romantic Heirs.* Ithaca: Cornell University Press, 1973.

Bromwich, David. *Disowned by Memory: Wordsworth's Poetry of the 1790s.* Chicago: University of Chicago Press, 1998.

Burke, Edmund. *Reflections on the Revolution in France.* Ed. Conor Cruise O'Brien. New York: Penguin, 1984.

Buruma, Ian, and Avishai Margalit. "Occidentalism." *New York Review* 49 (January 17, 2002): 4–7.

Bushell, Sally. "Exempla in *The Excursion*: The Purpose of the Pastor's Epitaphic Tales." *The Charles Lamb Bulletin* 105 (1999): 16–27.

———. *Re-Reading "The Excursion": Narrative, Response and the Wordsworthian Dramatic Voice*. The Nineteenth Century Series. Gen. eds. Vincent Newey and Joanne Shattock. Aldershot, England and Burlington, Vt.: Ashgate, 2002.

Butler, Judith. *Subjects of Desire: Hegelian Reflections in Twentieth Century France*. New York: Columbia University Press, 1987.

Byatt, A. S. *Unruly Times: Wordsworth and Coleridge in Their Time*. London: Hogarth Press, 1989.

Campbell, Colin. *The Romantic Ethic and the Spirit of Consumerism*. Oxford: Blackwell, 1987.

Caraher, Brian G. *Wordsworth's "Slumber" and the Problematics of Reading*. University Park: The Pennsylvania State University Press, 1988.

Caruth, Cathy. *Unclaimed Experience: Trauma, Narrative, and History*. Baltimore: Johns Hopkins University Press, 1996.

Chandler, David. "Vagrancy Smoked Out: Wordsworth 'betwixt Severn and Wye.'" *Romanticism on the Net* 11 (1998): 6 pars. 5/20/2000. *http://users.ox.ac.uk/~scat0385/hermit.html*.

Chandler, James. *Wordsworth's Second Nature: A Study of the Poetry and Politics*. Chicago: University of Chicago Press, 1984.

Chase, Cynthia. *Decomposing Figures: Rhetorical Readings in the Romantic Tradition*. Baltimore: Johns Hopkins University Press, 1986.

Chayes, Irene H. "Little Girls Lost: Problems of a Romantic Archetype." *Blake: A Collection of Critical Essays*. Ed. Northrop Frye. Englewood Cliffs: Prentice, 1966.

Choron, Jacques. *Death and Western Thought*. New York: Macmillan, 1963.

Clarke, Bruce. "Wordsworth's Departed Swans: Sublimation and Sublimity in *Home at Grasmere*." *Studies in Romanticism* 19 (1980): 355–74.

Clymer, Lorna. "Graved in Tropes: The Figural Logic of Epitaphs and Elegies in Blair, Gray, Cowper, and Wordsworth." *ELH* 62 (1995): 347–86.

Coleridge, Samuel Taylor. *The Collected Letters of Samuel Taylor Coleridge*. Ed. Earl Leslie Griggs. 6 vols. Oxford: Oxford University Press, 1956.

———. *The Collected Works of Samuel Taylor Coleridge*. Gen. ed. Kathleen Coburn. 16 vols. Bollingen Series 75. Princeton: Princeton University Press, 1971–2001.

———. *The Poems of Samuel Taylor Coleridge*. Ed. Derwent and Sarah Coleridge. London: Edward Moxon, 1852.

Colley, Linda. *Britons: Forging the Nation 1707–1837*. New Haven: Yale University Press, 1992.

Collings, David. *Wordsworthian Errancies: The Poetics of Cultural Dismemberment.* Baltimore: Johns Hopkins University Press, 1994.

Collins, William. *The Works of William Collins.* Ed. Richard Wendorf and Charles Ryskamp. Oxford: Clarendon Press, 1979.

Coombe, J. *The Peasant of Auburn, or the Emigrant, a Poem. The Critical Review* 56 (1783): 149–50.

Cornish, Vaughan, D.SC. *The Churchyard Yew & Immortality.* Introd. Archbishop of York. London: F. Muller, 1946.

Culler, Jonathan. *Structuralist Poetics: Structuralism, Linguistics, and the Study of Literature.* Ithaca: Cornell University Press, 1975.

Curran, Stuart. *Poetic Form and British Romanticism.* New York: Oxford University Press, 1986.

Dabundo, Laura. "The Extrospective Vision: *The Excursion* as Transitional in Wordsworth's Poetry and Age." *The Wordsworth Circle* 19 (1988): 8–14.

Darnton, Robert. "A Euro State of Mind." *New York Review* 49 (February 28, 2002): 30–32.

De Man, Paul. *Blindness and Insight: Essays in the Rhetoric of Contemporary Criticism.* Minneapolis: University of Minnesota Press, 1971, rev. 1983.

———. *The Rhetoric of Romanticism.* New York: Columbia University Press, 1984.

De Quincey, Thomas. *The Collected Writings of Thomas De Quincey.* Ed. David Masson. 14 vols. Edinburgh: Adams & Charles Black, 1889–90.

Derrida, Jacques. "By Force of Mourning." Trans. Pascale-Anne Brault and Michael Nass. *Critical Inquiry* 22 (1996): 171–92.

———. *Fors.* Trans. Barbara Johnson. *Georgia Review* 31 (1977): 64–116.

———. *Mèmoires: for Paul de Man.* Trans. Cecile Lindsay, Jonathan Culler, et al. New York: Columbia University Press, 1989.

———. *Specters of Marx: The State of the Debt, the Work of Mourning, and the New International.* Trans. Peggy Kamuf. New York: Routledge, 1994.

Draper, John W. *The Funeral Elegy and the Rise of English Romanticism.* New York: Phaeton Press, 1967.

Duff, David. *Romance and Revolution: Shelley and the Politics of Genre.* Cambridge: Cambridge University Press, 1994.

Duncan, Ian. *Modern Romance and Transformations of the Novel: The Gothic, Scott, Dickens.* Cambridge: Cambridge University Press, 1992.

Dyche, Thomas and William Pardon. *A New General English Dictionary (1740).* New York: Verlag, 1972.

Dyer, George. *The Complaints of the Poor People of England.* 2nd ed. London: J. Ridgway and H. D. Symonds, 1793.

Easterlin, Nancy. *Wordsworth and the Question of "Romantic Religion."* Lewisburg: Bucknell University Press, 1996.

Eco, Umberto. *Interpretation and Overinterpretation.* Ed. Stefan Collini. Cambridge: Cambridge University Press, 1992.

———. *The Role of the Reader: Explorations in the Semiotics of Texts.* London: Hutchinson, 1981.

Eilenberg, Susan. "Wordsworth's 'Michael': The Poetry of Property." *Essays in Literature* 15 (1988): 13–25.

Eisold, Kenneth. *Loneliness and Communion: A Study of Wordsworth's Thought and Experience.* Vol. 13 of *Romantic Reassessment.* Ed. Dr. James Hogg. Salzburg, Austria: University of Salzburg Press, 1973.

Eliade, Mircea. *Cosmos and History.* Trans. W. R. Trask. New York: Harper, rpt. 1959.

Elliot, Anthony. *The Mourning of John Lennon.* Berkeley: University of California Press, 1999.

Ellis, David. *Wordsworth, Freud and the Spots of Time.* London: Cambridge University Press, 1985.

Elridge, Richard. "Self-Understanding and Community in Wordsworth's Poetry." *Philosophy and Literature* 10 (1986): 273–94.

Fairchild, Hoxie Neal. *Religious Trends in English Poetry.* 6 vols. New York: Columbia University Press, 1939.

Fay, Elizabeth A. *Becoming Wordsworthian.* Amherst: The University of Massachusetts Press, 1995.

Ferguson, Frances. *William Wordsworth: Language as Counter-Spirit.* New Haven: Yale University Press, 1971.

Ferry, David. *The Limits of Mortality: An Essay on Wordsworth's Major Poems.* Middletown: Wesleyan University Press, 1959.

Finch, John Alban. "*The Ruined Cottage* Restored: Three Stages of Composition." *Bicentenary Studies in Memory of John Alban Finch.* Ed. Jonathan Wordsworth. Ithaca: Cornell University Press, 1970, 29–49.

Fineman, Joel. "The Structure of Allegorical Desire." *Allegory and Representation.* Ed. Stephen J. Greenblatt. Baltimore: Johns Hopkins University Press, 1981, 26–60.

Fink, Z. S. *The Early Wordsworthian Milieu.* Oxford: Oxford University Press, 1958.

Freud, Sigmund. *Letters.* Trans. Tania Stern and James Stern. Ed. Ernst Freud. New York: Basic Books, 1960.

———. *The Standard Edition of the Complete Psychological Works of Sigmund Freud.* Ed. and trans. James Strachey et al. 24 vols. London: Hogarth, 1953–74.

Friedman, Michael H. *The Making of a Tory Humanist: William Wordsworth and the Idea of Community.* New York: Columbia University Press, 1979.

Fry, Paul H. *The Poet's Calling in the English Ode.* New Haven: Yale University Press, 1980.

Fulford, Tim. "Fields of Liberty? The Politics of Wordsworth's Grasmere." *European Romantic Review* 9 (1998): 59–86.

———. *Landscape, Liberty and Authority: Poetry, Criticism and Politics from Thomson to Wordsworth*. Cambridge: Cambridge University Press, 1996.

Galperin, William H. *Revision and Authority in Wordsworth: The Interpretation of a Career*. Philadelphia: University of Pennsylvania Press, 1989.

Gamer, Michael. *Romanticism and the Gothic: Genre, Reception, and Canon Formation*. Cambridge: Cambridge University Press, 2000.

Gill, Stephen. "'Adventures on Salisbury Plain' and Wordsworth's Poetry of Protest 1795–97." *Studies in Romanticism* 11 (1972): 48–65.

———. *William Wordsworth: A Life*. New York: Oxford University Press, 1989.

———. *Wordsworth and the Victorians*. Oxford: Clarendon Press, 1998.

———. "Wordsworth's Poems: The Question of the Text." *Review of English Studies* 34 (1983): 190.

Godwin, William. *Enquiry Concerning Political Justice*. Ed. K. Codell Carter. London: Oxford University Press, 1971.

Gorer, Geoffrey. *Death, Grief, and Mourning*. Garden City: Doubleday, 1965.

Graver, Bruce E. "Wordsworth's Georgic Pastoral: Otium and Labor in 'Michael.'" *European Romantic Review* 1 (1991): 119–34.

Gray, Thomas. *The Complete Poems of Thomas Gray*. Ed. H. W. Starr and J. R. Hendrickson. Oxford: Clarendon Press, 1966, 37–43.

Greenberg, Martin. *The Hamlet Vocation of Coleridge and Wordsworth*. Iowa City: University of Iowa Press, 1986.

Greenblatt, Stephen. *Hamlet in Purgatory*. Princeton: Princeton University Press, 2001.

———. Gen. ed. *The Norton Shakespeare*. New York: Norton, 1997.

Grob, Alan. "William and Dorothy: A Case Study in the Hermeneutics of Disparagement." *ELH* 65 (1998): 187–221.

Gutteridge, John. "Scenery and Ecstasy: Three of Coleridge's Blank Verse Poems." *New Approaches to Coleridge: Biographical and Critical Essays*. Ed. Donald Sultana. New York: Visions and Barnes & Noble, 1981, 151–71.

Hall, Dewey W. "Signs of the Dead: Epitaphs, Inscriptions, and the Discourse of the Self." *ELH* 68 (2001): 655–77.

Hamilton, Walter. *Parody of the Works of English and American Authors*. London: Reeves and Turner, 1888.

Haney, David P. *William Wordsworth and the Hermeneutics of Incarnation*. University Park: The Pennsylvania State University Press, 1993.

Harding, Anthony John. "Forgetfulness and the Poetic Self in 'Home at Grasmere.'" *The Wordsworth Circle* 22 (1991): 109–18.

Harris, R. W. *Romanticism and the Social Order, 1780–1830*. New York: Barnes & Noble, 1969.

Harrison, Gary. *Wordsworth's Vagrant Muse: Poetry, Poverty and Power*. Detroit: Wayne State University Press, 1994.

Hartman, Geoffrey H. *Beyond Formalism: Literary Essays, 1958–1970*. New Haven: Yale University Press, 1970.

———. *Easy Pieces*. New York: Columbia University Press, 1985.

———. *The Unremarkable Wordsworth*. Minneapolis: University of Minnesota Press, 1987.

———. *Wordsworth's Poetry, 1787–1814*. Cambridge: Harvard University Press, 1964, rpt. 1987.

Harvey, A. D. *English Poetry in a Changing Society, 1780–1825*. New York: St. Martin's Press, 1980.

Haverkamp, Anselm. *Leaves of Mourning: Holderlin's Late Work—With an Essay on Keats and Melancholy*. Trans. Vernon Chadwick. Albany: State University of New York Press, 1996.

Hayden, John O. "The Dating of the '1794' Version of Wordsworth's *An Evening Walk*." *Studies in Bibliography* 42 (1989): 265–71.

Heffernan, James A. W. "Wordsworth's 'Leveling' Muse in 1798." *1798: The Year of the "Lyrical Ballads."* Ed. Richard Cronin. New York: St. Martin's Press, 1998, 231–53.

Helgerson, Richard. "The Land Speaks: Cartography, Choreography, and Subversion in Renaissance England." *Representations* 16 (1986): 51–85.

Hertz, Neil H. "Wordsworth and the Tears of Adam." *Studies in Romanticism* 7 (1967): 15–33.

Hewitt, Regina. *The Possibilities of Society: Wordsworth, Coleridge, and the Sociological Viewpoint of English Romanticism*. Albany: State University of New York Press, 1997.

Hickey, Alison. *Impure Conceits: Rhetoric and Ideology in Wordsworth's 'Excursion.'* Stanford: Stanford University Press, 1997.

Higgonnet, Patrice. *Goodness Beyond Virtue: Jacobins During the French Revolution*. Cambridge: Harvard University Press, 1998.

Himmelfarb, Gertrude. *The Idea of Poverty: England in the Early Industrial Age*. New York: Knopf, 1984.

Homans, Margaret. *Women Writers and Poetic Identity: Dorothy Wordsworth, Emily Brontë, and Emily Dickinson*. Princeton: Princeton University Press, 1980.

Howard, William. "Narrative Irony in *The Excursion*." *Studies in Romanticism* 44 (1985): 511–13.

Ireys, Virginia. "The Death of the Muse: Wordsworth's Lucy as Pastoral Heroine." *Papers on Language and Literature* 24 (1988): 384–403.

Iser, Wolfgang. *The Act of Reading: A Theory of Aesthetic Response*. London: Routledge and Kegan Paul, 1978.

Jacobus, Mary. *Tradition and Experiment in Wordsworth's "Lyrical Ballads" (1798)*. Oxford: Clarendon Press, 1976.

Jameson, Fredric. *The Prison House of Language: A Critical Account of Structuralism and Russian Formalism*. Ithaca: Cornell University Press, 1972.

Janowitz, Anne. *England's Ruins: Poetic Purpose and the National Landscape*. Cambridge: Basil Blackwell, 1990.

———. *Lyric and Labour in the Romantic Tradition*. Cambridge: Cambridge University Press, 1998.

Jauss, Hans Robert. "Literary History as a Challenge to Literary Theory." *New Directions in Literary History*. Ed. Ralph Cohen. London: Routledge, 1974, 13–41.

Johnson, Samuel. *A Dictionary of the English Language (1755)*. London: Times, 1983.

Johnston, Arthur. "Poetry and Criticism After 1740." *Dryden to Johnson*. Vol. 4 of *The New History of Literature*. 4 vols. Ed. Roger H. Lonsdale. New York: Peter Bedrick, 1987, 321.

Johnston, Kenneth R. *The Hidden Wordsworth: Poet, Lover, Rebel, Spy*. New York: Norton, 1998.

———. "The Politics of 'Tintern Abbey.'" *Romantic Poetry: Recent Revisionary Criticism*. Ed. Karl Kroeber and Gene W. Ruoff. New Brunswick: Rutgers University Press, 1993, 124–38.

———. "The Romantic Idea-Elegy: The Nature of Politics and the Politics of Nature." *South Central Review: The Journal of the South Central Modern Language Association* 9 (1992): 24–43.

———. *Wordsworth and "The Recluse."* New Haven: Yale University Press, 1984.

Johnston, Kenneth R., and Jonathan Barron. "'A Power to Virtue Friendly': The Pedlar's Guilt in Wordsworth's 'Ruined Cottage.'" *Romantic Revisions*. Ed. Robert Brinkley and Keith Hanley. New York: Cambridge University Press, 1992, 64–86.

Jones, Mark. "Double Economics: Ambivalence in Wordsworth's Pastoral." *PMLA* 108 (1993): 1098–1113.

———. *The "Lucy Poems": A Case Study in Literary Knowledge*. Toronto: University of Toronto Press, 1995.

Kaiser, David Aram. *Romanticism, Aesthetics, and Nationalism*. Cambridge: Cambridge University Press, 1999.

Kelley, Theresa M. *Wordsworth's Revisionary Aesthetics*. Cambridge: Cambridge University Press, 1988.

Kerrigan, John. "Knowing the Dead . . . : The Pete Laver Lecture 1986." *The Wordsworth Circle* 18 (1987): 87–98.

Klancher, Jon. "Godwin and the Republican Romance: Genre, Politics, and Contingency in Cultural History." *Modern Language Quarterly* 56 (1995): 145–65.

———. *The Making of English Reading Audiences, 1790–1832.* Madison: University of Wisconsin Press, 1987.

Knapp, Steven. *Personification and the Sublime: Milton to Coleridge.* Cambridge: Harvard University Press, 1985.

Lacan, Jacques. *Ecrits: A Selection.* Trans. Alan Sheridan. New York: Norton, 1977.

Larkin, Peter. "Relations of Scarcity: Ecology and Eschatology in *The Ruined Cottage*." *Studies in Romanticism* 39 (2000): 347–64.

Leavis, F. R. *Revaluations: Tradition and Revolution in English Poetry.* London: Oxford University Press, 1936.

Levinson, Marjorie. *The Romantic Fragment Poem: A Critique of a Form.* Chapel Hill: University of North Carolina Press, 1986.

———. *Wordsworth's Great Period Poems: Four Essays.* Cambridge: Cambridge University Press, 1986.

Liu, Alan. *Wordsworth: The Sense of History.* Stanford: Stanford University Press, 1989.

Locke, John. *An Essay Concerning Human Understanding.* Ed. Alexander Campbell Fraser. Oxford: Clarendon Press, 1959.

Lovejoy, Arthur O. *The Great Chain of Being: A Study of the History of an Idea.* Cambridge: Harvard University Press, 1936, 1964.

Maniquis, Robert M. "Holy Savagery and Wild Justice: English Romanticism and the Terror." *Studies in Romanticism* 28 (1989): 365–95.

Manning, Peter J. *Reading Romantics: Texts and Contexts.* New York: Oxford University Press, 1990.

———. "Troubling the Borders: *Lyrical Ballads* 1798 and 1998." *The Wordsworth Circle* 30 (1999): 22–27.

Marsh, Florence. *Wordsworth's Imagery.* Hamden, London: Archon, 1963.

Matlak, Richard E. "Captain John Wordsworth's Death at Sea." *The Wordsworth Circle* 31 (2000): 127–33.

———. *The Poetry of Relationship: The Wordsworths and Coleridge, 1797–1800.* New York: St. Martin's Press, 1997.

May, Herbert G., and Bruce M. Metzger, eds. *The New Oxford Annotated Bible* RSV. New York: Oxford University Press, 1977.

McFarland, Thomas. *Coleridge and the Pantheist Tradition.* Oxford: Clarendon Press, 1969.

———. *Romantic Cruxes: The English Essayists and the Spirit of the Age.* Oxford: Clarendon Press, 1987.

———. *Romanticism and the Forms of Ruin.* Princeton: Princeton University Press, 1981.

———. *William Wordsworth: Intensity and Achievement.* Oxford: Clarendon Press, 1992.

———. "Wordsworth on Man, on Nature, and on Human Life." *Studies in Romanticism* 21 (1982): 601–18.

McGann, Jerome J. *The Poetics of Sensibility: A Revolution in Literary Style*. Oxford: Clarendon Press, 1996.

———. *The Romantic Ideology: A Critical Investigation*. Chicago: University of Chicago Press, 1983.

Mellor, Anne K. *Romanticism & Gender*. New York: Routledge, 1993.

Meyer, George Wilbur. *Wordsworth's Formative Years*. Ann Arbor: University of Michigan Press, 1943.

Miller, J. Hillis. *The Linguistic Moment: From Wordsworth to Stevens*. Princeton: Princeton University Press, 1985.

———. "Narrative." *Critical Terms for Literary Study*. Ed. Frank Lentricchia and Thomas McLaughlin. Chicago: University of Chicago Press, 1990, 66–79.

———. "The Still Heart: Poetic Form in Wordsworth." *New Literary History* 2 (1971): 297–310.

———. *Theory Now and Then*. Durham: Duke University Press, 1991.

Mills-Courts, Karen. *Poetry as Epitaph: Representation and Poetic Language*. Baton Rouge: Louisiana State University Press, 1990.

Milton, John. *Complete Poems and Major Prose*. Ed. Merritt Y. Hughes. Indianapolis: Odyssey Press, 1957.

Modiano, Raimonda. "Blood Sacrifice, Gift Economy, and the Edenic World: Wordsworth's *Home at Grasmere*." *Studies in Romanticism* 32 (1993): 481–521.

Moorman, Mary. *William Wordsworth: A Biography*. Vol. 1, *The Early Years, 1770–1803*. Oxford: Clarendon Press, 1957, rpt. 1967.

Morton, Lionel. "Books and Drowned Men: Unconscious Mourning in Book V of *The Prelude*." *English Studies in Canada* 8 (1982): 23–37.

Myers, Victoria. "Sentiment and the Pantisocratic Community: Coleridge's Letters to Southey." *The Wordsworth Circle* 29 (1998): 75–79.

Nancy, Jean-Luc. *The Inoperative Community*. Trans. Peter Connor et al. Minneapolis: University of Minnesota Press, 1991.

Newlyn, Lucy. *Coleridge, Wordsworth, and the Language of Allusion*. Oxford: Clarendon Press, 1986.

———. *Paradise Lost and the Romantic Reader*. Oxford: Clarendon Press, 1993.

Newman, Gerald. *The Rise of English Nationalism: A Cultural History, 1740–1830*. New York: St. Martin's Press, 1987.

Onorato, Richard. *The Character of the Poet: Wordsworth in "The Prelude."* Princeton: Princeton University Press, 1971.

Ozouf, Mona. *Festivals and the French Revolution*. Trans. Alan Sheridan. Cambridge: Harvard University Press, 1988.

Page, Judith W. *Wordsworth and the Cultivation of Women*. Berkeley: University of California Press, 1994.

Paine, Thomas. *The Rights of Man*. Introd. Eric Foner. Ed. Henry Collins. New York: Penguin, 1984.

Paley, William. *Reasons for Contentment: Addressed to the Labouring Part of the British Public*. London: R. Faulder, 1793.

Parker, Patricia. *Inescapable Romance: Studies in the Poetics of a Mode*. Princeton: Princeton University Press, 1979.

Parker, Reeve. "'Finer Distance': The Narrative Art of Wordsworth's 'The Wanderer.'" *ELH* 39 (1972): 87–111.

———. "Finishing Off 'Michael': Poetic and Critical Enclosures." *Diacritics* 17 (1987): 53–64.

Parrish, Stephen Maxfield. *The Art of the "Lyrical Ballads."* Cambridge: Harvard University Press, 1973.

Patterson, Annabel. *Pastoral and Ideology: Virgil to Valéry*. Berkeley: University of California Press, 1987.

Pepper, Thomas W. "The Ideology of Wordsworth's 'Michael: A Pastoral Poem.'" *Criticism: A Quarterly for Literature and the Arts* 31 (1989): 367–82.

Percy, Thomas, ed. *Reliques of Ancient English Poetry*. 3 vols. London: J. Dodsley, 1765.

Perkins, David. "Wordsworth and the Polemic Against Hunting: Hart-Leap Well." *Nineteenth-Century Literature* 58 (1998): 421–45.

Peterfreund, Stuart. "Wordsworth on Covenants: 'Heart Conditions,' Primogeniture, Remains, and the Ties that Bind in 'Michael' and Elsewhere." *Criticism: A Quarterly for Literature and the Arts* 40 (1998): 191–215.

Pfau, Thomas. *Wordsworth's Profession: Form, Class, and the Logic of Early Romantic Cultural Production*. Stanford: Stanford University Press, 1997.

Pinion, F. B. *A Wordsworth Chronology*. London: Macmillan, 1988.

Piper, H. W. *The Active Universe*. London: Athlone Press, 1962.

Potts, Abbie Findlay. *The Elegiac Mode: Poetic Form in Wordsworth and Other Elegists*. Ithaca: Cornell University Press, 1967.

———. *Wordsworth's Prelude: A Study of Its Literary Form*. Ithaca: Cornell University Press, 1953.

Privateer, Paul Michael. *Romantic Voices: Identity and Ideology in British Poetry, 1789–1850*. Athens: University of Georgia Press, 1991.

Quinney, Laura. "'Tintern Abbey,' Sensibility, and the Self-Disenchanted Self." *ELH* 64 (1997): 131–56.

Radcliffe, Evan. "Revolutionary Writing, Moral Philosophy, and Universal Benevolence in the Eighteenth Century." *Journal of the History of Ideas* (1993): 221–40.

———. "Saving Ideals: Revolution and Benevolence in *The Prelude*." *JEGP* 93 (1994): 534–59.

Ragland-Sullivan, Ellie. "The Magnetism Between Reader and Text: Prolegomena to a Lacanian Poetics." *Poetics* 13 (1984): 381–406.

Rajan, Tilottama. *The Supplement of Reading: Figures of Understanding in Romantic Theory and Practice*. Ithaca: Cornell University Press, 1990.

Randel, Fred V. "The Betrayals of 'Tintern Abbey.'" *Studies in Romanticism* 32 (1993): 379–97.

Rapaport, Herman. *Milton and the Postmodern*. Lincoln: University of Nebraska Press, 1983.

Redfield, Marc. "Imagi-Nation: The Imagined Community and the Aesthetics of Mourning." *Diacritics* 29 (1999): 58–83.

Reed, Mark L. "The Five-Book *Prelude* of Early Spring 1804." *JEGP* 76 (1977): 1–25.

———. *Wordsworth: The Chronology of the Early Years, 1770–1799*. Cambridge: Harvard University Press, 1967.

———. *Wordsworth: The Chronology of the Middle Years, 1800–1815*. Cambridge: Harvard University Press, 1975.

Richardson, Alan. "Wordsworth at the Crossroads: 'Spots of Time' in the 'Two-Part Prelude.'" *The Wordsworth Circle* 19 (1998): 15–20.

Richey, William. "The Politicized Landscape of 'Tintern Abbey.'" *Studies in Philology* 95 (1998): 197–219.

Rieder, John. "Civic Virtue and Social Class at the Scene of Execution: Wordsworth's Salisbury Plain Poems." *Studies in Romanticism* 30 (1991): 325–44.

———. *Wordsworth's Counterrevolutionary Turn: Community, Virtue, and Vision in the 1790s*. Newark: University of Delaware Press, 1997.

Ritson, Joseph, ed. *Ancient Songs and Ballads from the Reign of King Henry the Second to the Revolution* (1790). 3rd ed. Revised by W. Carew Hazlitt. London: Reeves and Turner, 1877.

Roe, Nicholas. *Wordsworth and Coleridge: The Radical Years*. Oxford: Oxford University Press, 1988.

Ross, Marlon B. "Breaking the Period: Romanticism, Historical Representation, and the Prospect of Genre." *ANQ* 6 (1993): 121–31

———. "Naturalizing Gender: Woman's Place in Wordsworth's Ideological Landscapes." *ELH* 53 (1986): 391–410.

Rothschild, Emma. *Economic Sentiments: Adam Smith, Condorcet, and the Enlightenment*. Cambridge: Harvard University Press, 2001.

Ruoff, Gene W. *Wordsworth and Coleridge: The Making of the Major Lyrics, 1802–1804*. New Brunswick: Rutgers University Press, 1989.

Rushdie, Salman. "My Unfunny Valentine." *New Yorker*. 15 Feb. 1999: 29.

Ryan, Robert M. *The Romantic Reformation: Religious Politics in English Literature, 1789–1824.* Cambridge: Cambridge University Press, 1997.

Sacks, Peter. *The English Elegy: Studies in the Genre from Spenser to Yeats.* Baltimore: Johns Hopkins University Press, 1985.

Saiedi, Nader. *The Birth of Social Theory: Social Thought in the Enlightenment and Romanticism.* Lanham: University Press of America, 1993.

Sánchez-Eppler, Karen. "Decomposing: Wordsworth's Poetry of Epitaph and English Burial Reform." *Nineteenth-Century Literature* 42 (1988): 415–31.

Scholes, Robert. *Textual Power: Literary Theory and the Teaching of English.* New Haven: Yale University Press, 1985.

Schor, Esther. *Bearing the Dead: The British Culture of Mourning From the Enlightenment to Victoria.* Princeton: Princeton University Press, 1994.

Scodel, Joshua. *The English Epitaph: Commemoration and Conflict from Jonson to Wordsworth.* Ithaca: Cornell University Press, 1991.

Scott, Sir Walter. *Essays on Chivalry, Romance, and the Drama.* 1834. Freeport, N.Y.: Books for Libraries, 1972.

Shaffer, Elinor. "Myths of Community in the *Lyrical Ballads* 1798–1998: The Commonwealth and the Constitution." *Samuel Taylor Coleridge and the Sciences of Life.* Ed. Nicholas Roe. New York: Oxford University Press, 2001, 25–46.

Sharp, Michele Turner. "The Churchyard Among the Wordsworthian Mountains: Mapping the Common Ground of Death and the Reconfiguration of Romantic Community." *ELH* 62 (1995): 387–407.

———. "Re-membering the Real, Dis(re)membering the Dead: Wordsworth's 'Essays upon Epitaphs.'" *Studies in Romanticism* 34 (1995): 273–292.

Sheats, Paul D. *The Making of Wordsworth's Poetry, 1785–1798.* Cambridge: Harvard University Press, 1973.

Simpson, David. *Wordsworth's Historical Imagination: The Poetry of Displacement.* New York: Methuen, 1987.

Smith, Adam. *The Theory of Moral Sentiments.* Ed. Dugald Stewart. London: Henry G. Bohn, 1853.

Snell, K. D. M. *Annals of the Labouring Poor: Social Change and Agrarian England, 1660–1900.* Cambridge: Cambridge University Press, 1985.

Soderholm, James. "Dorothy Wordsworth's Return to Tintern Abbey." *New Literary History* 26 (1995): 309–22.

Sommerville, C. John. *The Secularization of Early Modern England: From Religious Culture to Religious Faith.* New York: Oxford University Press, 1992.

Spenser, Edmund. *The Faerie Queene.* Ed. A. C. Hamilton. New York: Longmans, 1977.

Sperry, Willard L. *Wordsworth's Anti-Climax.* Cambridge: Harvard University Press, 1935.

Stein, Edwin. *Wordsworth's Art of Allusion*. University Park: The Pennsylvania State University Press, 1988.

Stewart, Garrett. *Death Sentences: Styles of Dying in British Fiction*. Cambridge: Harvard University Press, 1984.

Swann, Karen. "Public Transport: Adventuring on Wordsworth's Salisbury Plain." *ELH* 55 (1988): 811–34.

———. "Suffering and Sensation in *The Ruined Cottage*." *PMLA* 106 (1993): 83–95.

Thomas, Gordon K. "'Orphans Then': Death in the *Two-Part Prelude*." *The Charles Lamb Bulletin* 96 (1996): 157–73.

Thompson, T. W. *Wordsworth's Hawkshead*. Ed. Robert Woof. London: Oxford University Press, 1970.

Thomson, Heidi. "'We Are Two': The Address to Dorothy in 'Tintern Abbey.'" *Studies in Romanticism* 40 (2001): 531–46.

Thomson, James. *The Poetical Works of James Thomson, James Beattie, Gilbert West, and John Bampfylde*. London: Routledge, Warne, Routledge, 1863.

Tönnies, Ferdinand. *Community and Society*. Trans. Charles P. Loomis. New York: Harper and Row, 1963.

Trott, Nicola. "*The Excursion*: Types and Symbols of Eternity." *The Charles Lamb Bulletin* 79 (1992): 239–52.

Turner, John. *Wordsworth's Play and Politics: A Study of Wordsworth's Poetry, 1787–1800*. New York: St. Martin's Press, 1986.

Ulmer, William A. *The Christian Wordsworth, 1798–1805*. Albany: State University of New York Press, 2001.

———. "The Society of Death in *Home at Grasmere*." *Philological Quarterly* 75 (1996): 67–83.

———. "Wordsworth, the One Life, and *The Ruined Cottage*." *Studies in Philology* 93 (1996): 304–31.

Vendler, Helen. "*Tintern Abbey*: Two Assaults." *The Bucknell Review* 36 (1992): 173–90.

Virgil (Publius Vergilius Maro). *Eclogues, Georgics, Aeneid, Minor Poems*. Trans. H. Rushton Fairclough. 2 vols. Harvard University Press, 1986.

Ware, Tracy. "Historicism Along and Against the Grain: The Case of Wordsworth's 'Michael.'" *Nineteenth-Century Literature* 3 (1994): 360–74.

Warminski, Andrzej. "Facing Language: Wordsworth's First Poetic Spirits." *Romantic Revolutions*. Ed. Kenneth R. Johnston et al. Bloomington: Indiana University Press, 1990, 26–49.

Warton, Thomas. "On the Origin of Romantic Fiction in Europe." Prefixed to *The History of English Poetry*. London, 1781.

Watson, J. R. "A Note on the Date in the Title of 'Tintern Abbey.'" *The Wordsworth Circle* 10 (1979): 6–14.

Webb, Mary R. "Industrialization and the Moral Law in Books VIII and IX of *The Excursion.*" *The Charles Lamb Bulletin* 81 (1993): 5–25.

———. "The Lucy Poems." *The Charles Lamb Bulletin* 92 (1995): 178–92.

Weiskel, Thomas. *The Romantic Sublime: Studies in the Structure and Psychology of Transcendence.* Baltimore: Johns Hopkins University Press, 1976.

Welsford, Enid. *Salisbury Plain: A Study in the Development of Wordsworth's Mind and Art.* Oxford: Blackwell, 1966.

Westbrook, Deanne. "Wordsworth's Prodigal Son: 'Michael' as Parable and as Metaparable." *The Wordsworth Circle* 28 (1997): 109–19.

Wiley, Michael. *Romantic Geography: Wordsworth and Anglo-European Spaces.* New York: St. Martin's Press, 1998.

Williams, John. *Wordsworth: Romantic Poetry and Revolution Politics.* Manchester: Manchester University Press, 1989.

Williams, Raymond. *The Country and the City.* New York: Oxford University Press, 1973.

Wlecke, Albert O. *Wordsworth and the Sublime.* Berkeley: University of California Press, 1973.

Wolfson, Susan J. *Formal Charges: The Shaping of Poetry in British Romanticism.* Stanford: Stanford University Press, 1997.

———. "Individual in Community: Dorothy Wordsworth in Conversation with William." *Romanticism and Feminism.* Ed. Anne K. Mellor. Bloomington: Indiana University Press, 1988, 139–66.

———. *The Questioning Presence: Wordsworth, Keats, and The Interrogative Mode in Romantic Poetry.* Ithaca: Cornell University Press, 1986.

Wollstonecraft, Mary. *A Vindication of the Rights of Men.* Amherst, N.Y.: Prometheus Books, 1996.

Woodward, Kathleen. "Freud and Barthes: Theorizing Mourning, Sustaining Grief." *Discourse: Berkeley Journal for Theoretical Studies in Media and Culture* 13 (1990–91): 93–110.

Woof, Pamela. "The 'Lucy' Poems: Poems of Mourning." *The Wordsworth Circle* 30 (1999): 28–36.

Wordsworth, Christopher. *Memoirs of William Wordsworth.* 2 vols. London: Edward Moxon, 1851.

Wordsworth, Dorothy. *The Journals of Dorothy Wordsworth.* Ed. Helen Darbishire. London: Oxford University Press, 1958.

Wordsworth, Jonathan. *The Music of Humanity: A Critical Study of Wordsworth's Ruined Cottage.* New York: Harper, 1969.

———. "On Man, on Nature, and on Human Life." *Review of English Studies* 31 (1986): 2–29.

————— . "Two Dark Interpreters: Wordsworth and De Quincey." *The Age of William Wordsworth*. Ed. Kenneth R. Johnston and Gene W. Ruoff. New Brunswick: Rutgers University Press, 1987, 214–38.

————— . "Wordsworth's Borderers." *English Romantic Poets: Modern Essays in Criticism*. Ed. M. H. Abrams. 2nd ed. New York: Oxford University Press, 1975.

Wordsworth, William. *The Borderers*. Ed. Robert Osborn. Ithaca: Cornell University Press, 1982.

————— . *Descriptive Sketches*. Ed. Eric Birdsall. Ithaca: Cornell University Press, 1984.

————— . *Early Poems and Fragments, 1785–1797*. Ed. Carol Landon and Jared Curtis. Ithaca: Cornell University Press, 1997.

————— . *An Evening Walk*. Ed. James H. Averill. Ithaca: Cornell University Press, 1984.

————— . *The Excursion 1814*. Introd. Jonathan Wordsworth. Oxford: Woodstock Books, 1991.

————— . *The Fenwick Notes of William Wordsworth*. Ed. Jared Curtis. London: Bristol Classics Press, 1993.

————— . *The Five-Book Prelude*. Ed. Duncan Wu. Oxford: Blackwell, 1997.

————— . *The Fourteen-Book "Prelude."* Ed. W. J. B. Owen. Ithaca: Cornell University Press, 1985.

————— . *Guide to the Lakes* (1835). Ed. Ernest de Selincourt. Oxford: Oxford University Press, 1977.

————— . *"Home At Grasmere": Part First, Book First, of "The Recluse."* Ed. Beth Darlington. Ithaca: Cornell University Press, 1977, corr. 1989.

————— . *The Letters of William and Dorothy Wordsworth: The Early Years, 1787–1805*. Ed. Ernest de Selincourt, rev. Chester L. Shaver. Oxford: Clarendon Press, 1967.

————— . *The Letters of William and Dorothy Wordsworth: The Later Years, 1821–1850*. Ed. Ernest de Selincourt, rev. Alan G. Hill. 4 vols. Oxford: Clarendon Press, 1978–88.

————— . *The Letters of William and Dorothy Wordsworth: The Middle Years, 1806–1820*. Ed. Ernest de Selincourt, rev. Mary Moorman and Alan G. Hill. 2 vols. Oxford: Clarendon Press, 1969–70.

————— . *"Lyrical Ballads," and Other Poems, 1797–1800*. Ed. James Butler and Karen Green. Ithaca: Cornell University Press, 1992.

————— . *Poems 1815*. Introd. Jonathan Wordsworth. Oxford: Woodstock Books, 1989.

————— . *"Poems, in Two Volumes," and Other Poems, 1800–1807*. Ed. Jared Curtis. Ithaca: Cornell University Press, 1983, corr. 1990.

————— . *The Poetical Works of William Wordsworth*. Ed. Ernest de Selincourt and Helen Darbishire. 5 vols. Oxford: Clarendon Press, 1940–49, rev. 1952–59.

————— . *The Prelude, 1798–1799*. Ed. Stephen Parrish. Ithaca: Cornell University Press, 1977.

———. *The Prelude: 1799, 1805, 1850.* Ed. Jonathan Wordsworth, M. H. Abrams, and Stephen Gill. New York: Norton, 1979.

———. *The Prose Works of William Wordsworth.* Ed. W. J. B. Owen and Jane W. Smyser. 3 vols. Oxford: Oxford University Press, 1974.

———. *"The Ruined Cottage" and "The Pedlar."* Ed. James Butler. Ithaca: Cornell University Press, 1977.

———. *The Ruined Cottage, The Brothers, Michael.* Ed. Jonathan Wordsworth. Cambridge: Cambridge University Press, 1985.

———. *The Salisbury Plain Poems of William Wordsworth.* Ed. Stephen Gill. Ithaca: Cornell University Press, 1975, corr. 1991.

———. *Shorter Poems, 1807–1820.* Ed. Carl H. Ketcham. Ithaca: Cornell University Press, 1989.

———. *The Thirteen-Book "Prelude."* Ed. Mark L. Reed. 2 vols. Ithaca: Cornell University Press, 1991.

———. *"The Tuft of Primroses," with Other Late Poems for "The Recluse."* Ed. Joseph F. Kishel. Ithaca: Cornell University Press, 1986.

Wordsworth, William, and Samuel Taylor Coleridge. *Lyrical Ballads (1798).* Ed. W. J. B. Owen. Oxford: Oxford University Press, 1969.

Worthen, John. *The Gang: Coleridge, the Hutchinsons & the Wordsworths in 1802.* New Haven: Yale University Press, 2001.

Wrigley, E. A., and R. S. Schofield. *The Population History of England, 1541–1871: A Reconstruction.* Cambridge: Harvard University Press, 1981.

Wu, Duncan. "Navigated By Magic: Wordsworth's Cambridge Sonnets." *Review of English Studies* 46 (1995): 352–65.

———. "Wordsworth and Helvellyn's Womb." *Essays in Criticism* 43 (1994): 6–23.

———. "Wordsworth's Poetry of Grief." *The Wordsworth Circle* 21 (1990): 114–117.

———. *Wordsworth's Reading, 1770–1799.* Cambridge: Cambridge University Press, 1993.

Zimmerman, Sarah M. *Romanticism, Lyricism, and History.* Albany: State University of New York Press, 1999.

INDEX

Abraham, Nicolas, 91, 94
Actaeon, myth of, 164–65, 169, 191, 203
Akenside, Mark, 17
Althusser, Louis, 240n. 88
American Revolution, 15–16, 54
American War of Independence, 16, 48, 54, 57–59, 68, 75–77, 87–90, 106, 108
Anderson, Benedict, 14, 219n. 6, 223n. 28
Ariès, Philippe, 3, 20
Arnold, Matthew, 2–3, 252n. 57
Averill, James H., 30, 54, 58, 62, 98, 115, 179, 226n. 70, 232n. 14, 233n. 18, 237n. 43

Barron, Jonathan, 118
Basil, Saint, 206–7
Bateson, F. W., 71, 83, 229n. 19, 231n. 33
Batten, Guinn, 22
Beattie, James, 14, 18, 54, 71
Beaumont, Sir George, 200–2
Behrendt, Stephen C., x–xi
Benis, Toby R., 54, 58, 61, 69, 83, 86, 92
Benjamin, Walter, 79, 231n. 38, 246n. 64
Bewell, Alan, 3, 5, 121, 128, 142, 144–45, 171, 254n. 74
Bible, 138, 161: Genesis, 123–24, 161; Numbers, 137–38; Psalms, 136; Ecclesiastes, 59–60, 100, 109, 206, 216; Matthew, 115; Luke, 138, 238n. 48; John, 238n. 48

Birdsall, Eric, 65–66
Blake, William, 124
Blanchot, Maurice, 221n. 8
Blank, G. Kim, 252n. 58
Bostetter, Edward, 120
Bowles, William Lisle, 48
Bowman, Thomas, 18, 28
Brisman, Leslie, 17
Bromwich, David, 131, 133, 158
Burke, Edmund, 8–9, 16, 18, 65, 72, 204, 244n. 30
Burns, Robert, 6, 54, 241n. 1
Buruma, Ian, 8
Bushell, Sally, 204, 214, 263n. 52
Butler, James, 105, 127, 141, 242n. 20
Byron, George Gordon, Lord, 22

Calvert, William, 68
Campbell, Colin, 226n. 70, 243n. 26
Caraher, Brian G., 252n. 57
Caruth, Cathy, 79
Catholicism, 15, 20, 133–35, 138
Catullus, Gaius Valerius, 18, 29
Chandler, David, 133
Chandler, James, 114, 249n. 79
Charlotte, Princess of Wales: mourning of, x–xi
Chase, Cynthia, 169, 175
Christian, Fletcher, 240n. 76
Christianity. *See* Bible; Catholicism; Cistercian order; Communion; Wordsworth, William: Anglican liturgy, Christian consolation